MANAGING SCHOOLS TOWARDS

HIGH PERFORMANCE

Linking school management theory

to the school effectiveness

knowledge base

EDITED BY
ADRIE J. VISSCHER,

FACULTY OF EDUCATIONAL SCIENCE AND TECHNOLOGY
UNIVERSITY OF TWENTE, THE NETHERLANDS

SWETS & ZEITLINGER
PUBLISHERS

| LISSE | ABINGDON | EXTON (PA) | TOKYO |

Library of Congress Cataloging-in-Publication Data

Managing schools towards high performance and linking school
 management theory to the school effectiveness knowledge base /
 edited by Adrie J. Visscher.
       p.   cm. -- (Contexts of learning)
    Includes bibliographical references and index.
    ISBN 9026515464
    1. School improvement programs. 2. School management and
 organization. 3. Educational productivity. 4. School improvement
 programs--Netherlands. 5. School management and organization-
 -Netherlands. 6. Educational productivity--Netherlands.
 I. Visscher, Adrie J., 1956- . II. Series
 LB2822.8.M37 1999
 371.2--dc21   99-13939

Cover design: Ivar Hamelink
Printed in The Netherlands by Krips, Meppel

ISBN 90 265 1546 4

• Introduction •

There are several reasons for writing this book on the organization and management of schools.

In the last decade conceptualization, research and theory development on the functioning and management of schools has progressed. This has made it necessary to refine the picture of how school organizations operate and the results produced by different strategies. A problem with many school organization books is that they are biased regarding the literature and school systems to which they refer (e.g. a European, British or American bias). There was a need for a book based on international scientific literature that represents current scientific knowledge regarding the organization and management of schools across the typical features of specific school systems.

However, this book has not only been written to present a comprehensive overview of the school organization and school management knowledge base. What makes it different from other books in the field is that it attempts to connect school management theory with school effectiveness theory. So far, theory development with respect to the functioning and management of school organizations has barely inspired school effectiveness research. The latter has focused particularly on instructional variables promoting school effectiveness (e.g. structured teaching, effective learning time, teacher attitudes and expectations). At the same time, school organization and school management research has hardly benefited from the findings of school effectiveness research. Moreover, in the former line of research, the way different school organizational arrangements influence the effectiveness of schools in terms of student achievement is seldom analyzed.

In our attempt to close the gap between both branches of theory development we have divided the book into three major themes:

I. An introduction to school organization and school management, and to research into school effectiveness.

II. A discussion of five important organization and management aspects of schools. These are: the structuring of the primary process (i.e. the teaching-learning process) at school level; coordination and control; teacher motivation and commitment; school leadership; and the alignment of the organization to its environment. Moreover, because of the importance of human resource development in schools an analysis is made of human resource development within corporations to find out what we can learn from this.

III. An analysis of the actual and desired integration of school organization and school management theory, on the one hand, and school effectiveness research and theory on the other.

The contents of each chapter are now treated in more detail.

The first chapter introduces the organizational aspects of educational institutions. Organization perspective and organizational theoretical concepts like the structure, processes and culture of school organizations, and organizational alignment to the environment are reviewed. Moreover, categories of school management problems are discussed as well as structural constraints on the administration of schools.

Chapter two focuses on the school effectiveness perspective and method of inquiry. Various perceptions on school effectiveness (e.g. economic and organizational theoretical views) are discussed, and a choice made for the economic perspective, i.e. effectiveness as the quality and quantity of the outputs of the primary production process (for instance, in schools the teaching-learning process). Alternative effectiveness criteria like adapting to the environment; staff cohesion, satisfaction and motivation are considered significant, however, as supportive conditions for productivity. In this type of research an attempt is made to ascribe school output differences to differences in school characteristics. In this chapter a broad outline of the underlying model of school effectiveness research and an integral school effectiveness model are presented. Finally, two major theoretical propositions for explaining the findings of empirical school effectiveness research based on the integral model are discussed: evaluation-centered rational control and public choice theory.

The second chapter also presents the central perspective for subsequent chapters (3-8). In these a comprehensive, up-to-date overview of the organization theoretical knowledge base about the subject(s) central to that chapter is presented, and the question addressed on what is known about each subject as a school effectiveness enhancing condition.

The third chapter applies general organizational theoretical concepts to the school context to clarify the nature of the operations technology (the expertise and skills applied for transforming school input into school output). An analysis is made of the degree to which the so-called long linked, the mediating and the intensive technology are applicable to schools as well as to what extent the operations technology of schools is uncertain, complex and leads to interdependence between school staff. Finally, the implications of the nature of schools' operations technology and the possibilities and desirability of organizational control are analyzed as a 'leg up' to the next chapter.

In chapter four coordination is seen as the organizational 'glue' that holds together all different organizational tasks, activities and elements, and directs them to the goals of the organization. Six coordination mechanisms are explained and translated to the school context, while their coordination potential in schools is discussed. The major part of the chapter is devoted to analyzing the explanatory power of three major theories on school organizational coordination: classic bureaucratic, loosely coupled systems (including institutional theory, and organized anarchy theory) and Mintzberg's professional bureaucracy theory. Empirical evidence for each theory is also reviewed.

It was human relations theory that pointed to the value of motivated and committed staff within organizations. This is also an extremely important precondition for the functioning of schools, especially motivation and commitment of those who work in the operating core of schools - the teachers. The fifth chapter therefore deals with this subject. Firstly, the features of the teaching job in terms of the skills and knowledge required, workload and teacher salaries in various countries are analyzed. There appears to be huge differences between countries on these points. Then, motivation and commitment as concepts are analyzed and various motivation and commitment theories presented. The demands on teachers which may influence teacher motivation and commitment are also described. Possibilities for improving teacher motivation and commitment are discussed and a plea made for a more professional school organization, providing teachers with good support, better working conditions and task differentiation to increase their mobility.

Chapter 6 moves to the school leader level, portraying the responsibilities of school leaders, distinguishing between managing and leading a school, and reviewing the features of those teachers who lead schools, and the relationship between their working situation and their leadership style. The chapter also analyzes whether leadership is something that is only represented by the activities of a school leader or that substitutes for leadership can also occur.

The seventh chapter focuses on the relationship between school organization and its environment. School environments have become dynamic and as such imply threats and opportunities. School environmental variation and the factors influencing school environmental uncertainty are identified, and strategies for aligning the school to its environment are presented.

Job related skills and the expertise of teachers, managers and other school employees have a strong impact on what school staff and schools achieve. Human resource development has received considerable attention in the corporate world. The experience gained there can serve as a valuable source of inspiration for how human resource development should be dealt with in schools. Chapter 8 describes the features of human resource development in corporate training departments from an organizational viewpoint and identifies what schools can learn from this.

The concluding chapter attempts to draw together the various aspects related to the theme of the book - the link between school management theory and school effectiveness research - by first summarizing the outcomes of the preceding chapters and then reflecting on the way school effectiveness is conceptualized and studied. Conclusions are then drawn regarding our insight into the school organizational factors influencing school effectiveness. Finally, the contents of the book are synthesized and a proposal made to further integrate research on school management and school effectiveness.

The contributors to this book work in the department of educational administration of the Faculty of Educational Science and Technology at the University of Twente in the Netherlands. The department is well known for its school effectiveness research program, which is aimed at determining school characteristics that positively contribute to school effectiveness in terms of student achievement as well as the models and theories that explain the operation of these conditions.

Although the target readers of this book include the international academic community in the field of school management and school effectiveness, university and higher education students, and decision makers at various levels within education systems, practitioners may also find the contents inspiring in their attempts to allow schools to become (more) satisfying work environments and (more) productive institutions, by adopting new ways of coordination, leadership, human resource developmental strategies and so on.

It is our hope that this book is a step forward for the integration and cross-fertilization of the school management and school effectiveness line of inquiry, and that it will lead to a better understanding of how schools function and how we can make them as effective as possible. As this is the first edition of this volume there will certainly be room for improvement. We would therefore like to invite all readers to offer any constructive feedback that will enable us to optimize the content of any future editions.

Adrie J. Visscher
Department of Educational Administration
Faculty of Educational Science and Technology
University of Twente, The Netherlands
e-mail: Visscher@edte.utwente.nl

• CONTENTS •

PART I

School Management and

School Effectiveness:

A Perspective

• CHAPTER 1 •

Introduction to Organizational
and Management Aspects of Schools

A.J. Visscher
University of Twente, The Netherlands

1.1 Introduction

The overall goal of this chapter is to provide the reader with some insight into the features of schools as organizations. The following topics are addressed: How is the organization called 'school' structured? Which major organizational activities take place in them? Does the organization of schools cause problems for those who have to run these institutions? What possibilities does the administrative context of schools offer for controlling them?

The chapter consists of five elements. It starts in section 1.2 with a description of the increased attention given to the organizational and management perspective on educational institutions. Subsequently, a conceptual framework for analyzing educational institutions from an organization's point of view is presented (section 1.3). This framework explains the meaning of the 'organization' concept and important features of (school) organizations: their structures, processes, cultures, and the relationship between an organization and its environment.

The third element (section 1.4) concerns a description of the organizational problems with which secondary schools must cope. In section 1.5 some structural constraints on the administration of schools are discussed which influence how and the degree to which schools can be administered and managed. Finally, the chapter is summarized in section 1.6.

1.2 The organization and management perspective in education

We are living in a juncture in which the management of organizations is considered increasingly important. From the media emerges a picture of fast and rational managers who, supported by modern tools like computer-assisted management information systems and planning instruments, operate efficiently and effectively. When they are confronted with an organizational problem its characteristics and causes are determined, possible problem solving strategies generated, and, after having analyzed their features, the best strategy is chosen and the problem is solved effectively.

A boom can be observed in management literature and in courses on the management of time, personnel, information, finance, and social matters.

Declining financial resources coupled with increasing competition between organizations have caused administrative rationalization to become a trend: an increase in the scale of organizations (mergers), closing down non-profitable branches, cutting jobs, and reducing resource consuming stocks. To rationalize institutions in these ways implies that extra attention must be paid to their organizational aspects.

In the field of education, attention for the organization and management of schools has grown considerably over the past fifteen years. It has for instance become commonplace to think and speak of the output (products) of educational institutions and of ways to improve their efficiency and effectiveness. In previous years, views which held schools to be organizations which receive some sort of input (students with specific background characteristics) that has to be transformed into a desired output (students trained and educated at a certain level) was taboo in the 'pedagogical province'. However, it has gradually become clear that schools do not only consist of a primary process in which teachers teach students. This process is surrounded by other organizational processes influencing what takes place within the classroom: e.g. setting (and adjusting) organizational goals; planning how to accomplish these goals; allocating financial, personnel and other resources to organizational actors; coordinating the various organizational activities; registering, and processing data; evaluating how teachers function and which policy measures may improve their functioning; and assessing the degree to which organizational goals are met. None of these activities is a goal in itself; they are carried out to fulfil the required conditions for the teaching-learning process. The more these preconditions are met, the greater the likelihood of achieving a high quality educational process. For instance, the greater the degree to which the organizational goals to be accomplished have been discussed and agreed upon, and if their realization has been planned better, the probability that staff will realize them is higher than if this had not been the case. Personnel evaluation and personnel management can help reduce the negative sides of school staff jobs and ensure that staff are offered more challenges. Sound financial management and information management promote the availability of financial resources for investments, and informed decision-making. Finally, a close coordination of the work of teachers by responsible management staff is meant to prevent teachers from striving toward different goals, and from operating inconsistently in other ways.

The management perspective on schools has resulted in the design and development of tools that can be helpful in trying to accomplish an administratively sound school organization: instruments for quality care, personnel management, financial planning, computer-assisted information systems, etcetera. These management tools have become valuable as the governments of many countries make their schools more autonomous, making school-based management important in areas where the government previously decided what was to be done.

In order to clarify the organizational and management features of educational institutions, a conceptual framework concerning the school organization is presented in the next section.

1.3 A conceptual framework regarding schools as organizations

1.3.1 Introduction

The school organization is characterized here by means of the following concepts from organization theory: organization, organizational structure, organizational processes, organizational culture and the relation between a school organization and its environment. This section is partly based on Scheerens and Van Vilsteren (1988) which has been adapted and extended by the author.

1.3.2 Some basic concepts

1.3.2.1 Organization

The 'organization' concept can be used in a number of ways. Sometimes it is used to point at a specific (type of) organization: 'The University of Twente is an organization', or 'schools are non-profit organizations'. Both are examples of using the *institutional* meaning of the organization concept.

The concept is used in an *instrumental* way if the structured, ordered character of an institution is pointed at in sentences like 'Corporation X has a centralized organization', or 'Schools have a flat organization'.

When 'organization' is used in the *functional* way the process of organizing (for instance organizational processes like planning and coordination) is crucial: 'The organization of that innovation takes a lot of energy'.

Kieser and Kubicek (1977) integrate the three different meanings of the term in the following definition "Organizations are social constructs durably directed towards a goal, having a formal structure, by means of which the activities of the members of the organization are directed to the organizational goal in a coordinated way" (p. 1).

1.3.2.2 Organizational structure

General characterization

According to Mintzberg (1979) "The structure of an organization can be defined simply as the sum total of the ways in which it divides its labor into distinct tasks and then achieves coordination among them" (p. 2). This definition shows the two central aspects of the structuring of organizations: on the one hand the *division* of tasks, units and competencies, and on the other hand *connecting* the divisions that have been made (coordination). Since one person or a few persons can not carry out all the work that has to be done within an organization, the division of labor is necessary. Coordination is used to put organizational staff carrying out different tasks under one supervisor (e.g. the activities of all teachers in one school division who teach different subjects are coordinated by the head of that division). However, building a supervision structure is only one way of structural coordination. Formalization -that is, developing formal rules for organizational behavior (e.g. procedures for handling truants or students who are late)- is an example of another coordination mechanism (see chapter 4 for a more detailed analysis of organizational coordination).

Organizational structures can be characterized with respect to the way in which organizational tasks have been divided, hierarchical supervision has been arranged, and organizational behavior has been formalized. For instance a well-known organization type, the bureaucracy, is characterized by a high degree of formalization, a clear hierarchy and a strong division of labor into relatively simple repeatable tasks.

The structure of organizations is discussed now by presenting Mintzberg's basic organizational parts, and by presenting some examples of different organizational structures.

Operating core and strategic apex

The *operating core* concerns that part of the organization where the work for which the organization has been founded is carried out. The central product(s)/service(s) of an organization is/are produced there by the operators. In other words, the primary process (the main organizational process, like producing cars in a car factory or teaching children in schools) is executed in the operating core. The structure of the operating core is determined by how tasks have been divided there and how employees have been allocated to tasks. In schools, the operating core is the domain of the teachers (including deans and counsellors who assist students if they face problems, have to choose subjects, curricular tracks, etcetera).

In education, the structure of the operating core is determined to a high degree by the way in which students and teachers are grouped (examples are the so-called year group system, and differentiation within classes). The degree of task differentiation between teachers also plays an important role (e.g. subject specific teachers in secondary education and year group teachers who teach a variety of subjects in primary education).

In addition to the division of tasks, the operating core also has mechanisms to connect elements: for instance subject departments for coordinating teachers who teach the same subjects and transition class heads who coordinate what is done in the transition grade.

Since organizational work is divided among staff who only look after their specific job, organizations need one or more persons at higher organizational levels who overlook the (part of the) organization they are responsible for.

The *strategic apex* of an organization is "... charged with ensuring that the organization serve its mission in an effective way, and also that it serve with the needs of those people who control or otherwise have the power over the organization (such as owners, government agencies, unions of the employees, pressure groups)" (Mintzberg, 1979, p. 25).

The apex has three duties:

1. direct supervision to ensure that the organization functions smoothly and in an integrated manner;
2. management of the organization's relationship with the environment (e.g. with influential people);
3. development of the organization's strategy.

Schools also have a managerial structure. First of all they have a school board which in many countries is legally responsible for what happens and what will happen in schools. However, in every day school practice principals and deputy heads are the most important elements of the strategic apex.

Small schools have one principal. However, when they grow, joint management is needed: a principal with one or more deputy-heads. Vertical managerial specialization goes even further when schools appoint middle managers (e.g. subject department coordinators, heads of grades or of school divisions) supervising and managing certain organizational parts.

The features of the managerial structure can change as a result of changes in administrative processes. When schools are, for instance, expected to develop school policy more intensively, this demands more from school management, and may result in the decision to let the school leader be an all around manager and to let deputy-heads operate more as educational leaders.

Three other basic parts of organizations

Mintzberg (1979) distinguishes between five basic organizational parts (see Figure 1.1).

The strategic apex and the operating core have already been discussed. The *middle line* connects the strategic top with the operating core by the chain of middle line managers with formal authority. Supervision of operators requires close contact between manager and operator, which implies that a manager can only supervise a limited number of subordinates. It is therefore impractical to supervise the operators from the strategic apex; managers are needed at one or more lower organizational levels. The middle-line manager collects information on the performance of the unit he is responsible for and passes aggregated information on to the management levels above him. He also manages the internal and external environment of his unit and is concerned with formulating his unit's strategy. In other words, the middle-line manager performs all managerial roles of the chief executive, but in the context of managing his own unit (Mintzberg, 1979, p. 29).

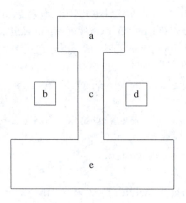

Legend: a: strategic apex
               b: technostructure
               c: middle line
               d: support staff
               e: operating core

Figure 1.1: *Mintzberg logo with five basic organizational parts*

The middle-line of schools is small. Heads of departments, and heads of grades or school divisions are examples of middle line managers in schools. Since most middle managers in schools also belong to the strategic apex, they are in a difficult position: they are responsible for the school as a whole, and are expected to defend the interests of the organizational unit they are leading.

The *technostructure* consists of analysts and other experts carrying out specialist analysis and design tasks (e.g. engineers who optimize production processes, personnel officers and planning experts). They design, plan and change the activities of those who work in the operating core. Some analysts try to adapt the organization to environmental change, others are concerned with standardizing organizational activities (e.g. work study analysts), outputs (e.g. long-range planners and budget controllers), skills (personnel analysts, including trainers and recruiters). Just like the middle line, the technostructure of schools is small which is related to the fact that teachers operate relatively autonomously. As a result, there are only limited possibilities for interference from staff other than teachers in the primary process, with the aim of influencing how the primary process is carried out. However, there are some examples of technostructural planning and formalizing work in schools. Sometimes a school committee prepares how a new subject will be taught, and the timetabler plans which lesson group will be taught, when, by which teacher, in which classroom and in which subject (he does, however, not plan the contents of education). Other ways of influencing what happens in the operating core from the technostructure are the recruitment of new staff and (re)training of teachers.

The *support staff* is not part of the operating core, yet it supports the activities there indirectly. In contrast with the technostructure the support staff is not concerned with analyzing, planning and standardizing. It performs all kinds of different functions: mail room, reception, cafeteria, pay roll, etcetera. In schools this organizational part is more elaborated than the administrative parts: the librarian, caretaker, gardener, food service staff, laboratory assistants, and clerical staff. None of them belongs to the operating core, however each provides indirect support to it.

In summary, we get a picture of schools as flat (little supervision and coordination of the work in the operating core) organizations with a small strategic apex and technostructure, a thin middle line, a relatively well developed support staff and an operating core as the largest part of the organization. Some members of the school organization work in several parts of the organization. This is especially true of staff with a management position (the deputy principals). They belong to the strategic apex and as such take part in strategic policy formulation. In the meantime, many of them teach classes for some part of the week, and fulfil tasks in the technostructure (e.g. composing classes, timetable construction). Moreover, they have to manage that part of the school they are responsible for. The combination of roles within one person makes double role problems probable. Actually, schools do not have employees who exclusively fulfil activities in the technostructure.

The school has so little planning and standardizing activities that most of this work is done by members of the organization, next to other activities.

Different types of organizational configurations

All organizations are not alike. Effective organizations achieve coherence among their component parts. According to Mintzberg (1979) the grouping of organizational elements should be consistent with the situation of the organization (e.g. its age, size, environmental conditions). Mintzberg distinguishes between five organizational *configurations*, that are distinct in the situations in which they are found and in their structures: the simple structure, the machine bureaucracy, the professional bureaucracy, the divisionalized form, and the adhocracy. Three of them are discussed briefly below.

In the *Simple structure* the key part of the organization is the strategic apex. Coordination is primarily achieved by means of direct supervision from the apex: the chief executive who gives orders. Little of its behavior is standardized or formalized. There is a minimum of staff and middle line. The simple structure is found in young, small organizations with a simple, non-regulating technical system (= instruments used for production). The power of top management is great.

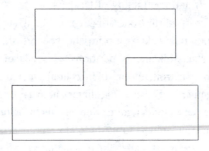

Figure 1.2: *The Simple Structure*

In the *Machine bureaucracy* the technostructure comprises the key part of the organization. Work is mainly coordinated by standardization of highly specialized routine work. This type of organization works as a regulated machine in which mass-production takes place. The organization consists of large production units.

The machine bureaucracy is old, large, its technical system ranges from not simple to fairly complex, however highly regulating. The organizational environment of this configuration is simple and stable. The staff in the operating core has very little influence on what is done in the operating and how it is carried out. Top-down, centralized decision-making is a feature of this organizational structure. Uncertainty is minimized as much as possible by, among other methods, having a large internal support staff that makes the organization more independent from external influences and that increases the probability that the machine will not stop.

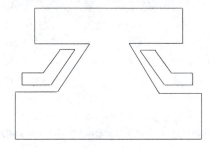

Figure 1.3: *The Machine Bureaucracy*

Although schools are quite different from typical machine bureaucracies like car producing factories or an enterprise like McDonalds, some features of the machine bureaucracy can be found in schools. For instance, schools often work according to standard procedures with respect to handling student absenteeism, student admission, financial matters, student promotion, etcetera. These standards have been developed by schools themselves or by the government. However, the standardized procedures do not concern the primary process (in the machine bureaucracy work is specialized and standardized) but in the processes around it.

Professional bureaucracies are coordinated primarily by the standardization of the skills of highly trained professionals in the operating core, who are backed up by considerable support staff. Neither its technostructure nor its middle line is very elaborate. The operating core concerns the key part of the organization. This configuration is found in complex yet stable environments. The work is complex and asks for professional operator control. However, since the skills of the professionals are more or less standardized during their long professional training, this organization is also bureaucratic.

The professional bureaucracy is the organization structure of organizations like schools, accounting firms, and hospitals. Because of the intensive training of the professional operators, a technostructure is hardly needed. The size of the operating unit can be very large and few first-line managers are needed because professionals are capable of working rather independently.

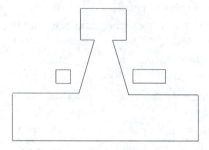

Figure 1.4: *The Professional Bureaucracy*

The linkages between the organizational parts are varied (there is no one best way they function together) and complex. Each of the five configurations is an abstract ideal, a simplification. Yet every organization experiences the pulls that underlie each of them: the pull to centralize by top management (simple structure), to formalize by the technostructure (machine bureaucracy), and to professionalize by the operators (professional bureaucracy). Where one pull dominates, the organization will tend to organize itself close to one of the configurations. However, one pull does not always dominate. Sometimes there is too much going on in an organization to describe it as one configuration or another. However, the configuration framework can still be of help in understanding how the organizational parts are organized and fit together, or refuse to (Mintzberg, p. 114). The configurations can serve as an effective tool in diagnosing the fit among component parts.

Five perspectives on organizations
Mintzberg states that the five basic parts are joined together by four different flows: the flow of *authority, material, information,* and *decision processes.* Each flow represents an organization theoretical school of thought.
The first flow concerns the organization as a system of *formal authority.* Everyone knows the organization charts (organigrams) representing the flow of formal power down through the hierarchy. They concern a clear but very partial description of how organizations function because much more happens informally in organizations than the organigram tells. However, it does give a lot of information on the division of labor (organizational positions and units) and on how formal authority is distributed among them.
The organization as a system of *regulated flows* concerns a second perspective on organizations in which they are seen as well-regulated and smoothly functioning networks. The

well regulated, systematically coordinated and controlled flows of material, information and decision processes within the organization are stressed in this view. Mintzberg (1979) discerns the operating work flow, the flow of control information and decision processes, and the flow of staff information.

The operating work flow concerns the flow of material and information through the operating core. In schools one may think of the flow of students (the 'material' to be processed) through the school when they are transformed from input into output. Next to the material, information on the material needed for the transformation process (e.g. information on student achievement and absenteeism) also flows through the school according to a regulated pattern of activities.

The flow of control information and decisions concerns:

1. *The feedback information on operating activities.* To use the information for control it must be clear who is allocated to make which control decisions. In schools one can think of information on student and teacher performance, to evaluate and control the primary process. However, since teachers operate rather autonomously they, to a strong degree, evaluate and control their work themselves. Nevertheless, school managers can collect performance data and control 'at a distance'.

2. *The commands and instructions that flow down.* This process starts at the strategic apex with global goals and instructions, and then gradually descends with instructions becoming more detailed. Since goals of educational organizations are often ambiguous and multiple (cf. McPherson et al. 1986), in combination with the strong teacher autonomy and the flat hierarchy, the downward flow of instructions and commands in these institutions is limited.

3. *Control decisions at each management level.* More specifically, this is the communication between line and staff (i.e. technostructure and support staff) with the purpose of line decision-making. The role of the technostructure is important in providing information to the line management, and in assisting managers in working out plans for lower organizational levels.

   Since line managers in schools often combine their technostructural work with teaching and management work, most of this communication is not necessary. In special cases (e.g. an ad hoc school committee elaborating standards) communicating the results of this activity usually will not create enormous problems.

   Communication between support staff (especially clerical staff) and line managers is rather important in schools. Clerks will have to provide managers with data on students, teachers, classes, subject, and so on.

In addition to the formal authority and the regulated flow view on organizations, Mintzberg discerns three other perspectives on organizations:

- The organization as a system of *informal communication*: which refers to the map of who actually communicates with whom. This view stresses the informal, that what has not been regulated formally (the sociogram instead of the organigram). In every organization non-official power centers exist next to the formal power channels.

- The organization as a system of *work constellations*: people in organizations cluster into peer groups (not always regulated according to the hierarchy or the five basic parts) to get the work done. All kinds of work constellations are possible, for instance:
  - in the operating core (for instance constellations of staff recruiting students, or of teachers cooperating in student counselling);
  - support staff, a middle line manager and technostructure staff in timetabling;
  - managerial and financial staff.

- The organization as a system of *ad hoc decision processes*: in contrast to when the flow of regulated decision processes was discussed, attention is now drawn to more flexible and ad hoc decision processes. Of importance is how decisions link together and which roles the various participants play in the different phases of decision processes. For instance, a teacher may have an idea to develop new options for students to specialize. This idea may flow to higher organizational levels, leading to the decision to elaborate it, and finally, to the decision to implement it.

1.3.2.3 Organizational processes

When the organizational structure was discussed in the previous section, the composition of the organization in terms of its elements and the more durable relations between units -that is, the way in which work and authority are distributed- was central, just as the ways in which liaisons between organizational parts are structurally made (e.g. by means of a managerial superstructure, by formalization, or the flow of material). Organizational processes are related with the *dynamics* of organizational functioning. Communication, decision-making and the production, or primary process, are some examples of organizational processes.

Discussing the need for a merger with another school in a staff meeting is an example of formal communication. Informal communication takes place, for instance, when university staff complain about their professor being absent too frequently. School management makes a decision when it decides to ask a management consultant to set up a new campaign for recruiting students. Teaching students how to make calculations using fractions is something that is done in the primary process.

Three types of school organizational processes are treated in more detail now: the primary process, control, and informal processes.

The primary process

The process of knowledge transmission and acquisition in teaching-learning situations comprises the primary process of schools, which is treated at length in chapter 3. Here this process is defined by means of concepts from systems theory. Within so-called open systems theory, an organization is not considered to be a closed total of elements, people and processes, but a configuration that intensely interacts with its environment. Sometimes the organization is depicted as a 'black box' with people and material as inputs being transformed into products or services (output). De Leeuw (1982) defines primary processes as follows: "those transformation processes that result in the production of the product or service that is characteristic for a specific organization" (p. 22). It must be stressed here that an organization can have more than one primary process: a university has for instance two core activities: research and the training of students.

An organization's operations technology can be described as the know-how and instruments used to transform organizational input into output. In the case of schools, this concerns the knowledge, skills and procedures for:
• analyzing the characteristics of the input of the transformation process (e.g. the entrance level of students);
• educating students in the required way (e.g. using the right instruction strategies);
• evaluating the degree of success of the transformation process by means of reliable and valid tests.

In chapter 3 is explained which operations technology features have consequences for the structure of an organization.

Control processes

The concept 'control' encompasses activities like leading, coordinating, regulating, evaluating an organization and organizational policy-making. Control can be defined as any form of influence from someone who controls on an object to be controlled. Control requires a goal. Since in the literature many different characterizations of control, coordination and policy-making activities exist, the so-called control paradigm from systems theory is used now to typify control processes.

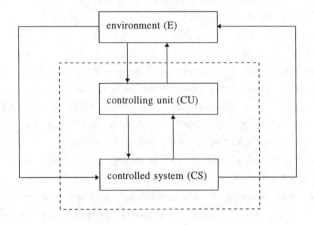

Figure 1.5: *The control paradigm*

The rectangle marked with a dashed line shows the borderline between the environment and the organization, the latter consisting of a control unit and a controlled system. Within the controlled system the primary transformation processes take place. The arrow from E to CS points at the input, the one from CS to E at the output of the primary process. The principal and his deputies form an example of a controlling school unit. Teachers who organize primary processes concern the controlled system. The arrow from E to CU shows that the control goals are also determined by the environment. For instance, the labor market asking the educational system to 'produce' a labor force qualified in a certain way. The arrow from CU to CS depicts the direct influence from the CU on the CS. An example from the world of education may be school management prescribing a new mathematics method for teachers. The arrow from CS to CU concerns the throughput of information required for control. School managers who can benefit from the advantages of computer-assisted attendance registration systems can, for instance, more effectively tackle the problem of absenteeism. That a school organization is not a passive receiver of environmental influences is shown by the arrow from CU to E. A school can try to influence the environment, for instance, by developing school marketing activities. In the control paradigm the following types of control are distinguished.

Routine control
In the case of routine control the structure of the CS, the goal and the environment are considered to be given. The most important goal is to keep the primary process of the

organization going. Examples from the educational context: looking after the availability and adequate application of teaching methods; apparatus and learning materials for planned instruction processes; a sound coordination of the work of teachers who teach the same subject in different grades; and making sure that student inflow is big enough. In other words, routine control has to do with the operations technology, organization and with the care that the environment delivers sufficient input. The administration of finance, material and staff (personnel management) can also be regarded as an element of routine control.

Adaptive control

This type of control permits the adaptation of, and interference in the structure of the CS. This may concern influencing the character of the production process (e.g. by introducing computer-assisted instruction), or in the structure of the CS (for instance introducing a two year transition period in secondary education), or by changing the structure of external relations (e.g. by tapping new funds).

Goal control

The CU can lower its goals, for instance when they proved not to be feasible in previous years. In those cases it may be a problem that the CS has its own goals, something very real in education (teachers often have and work on their own goals). In that case goal control should also be directed at unifying all goals that exist in a school. Choosing a long term goal, on an organizational strategy is another example of goal control.

Finally, another form of control should be mentioned: meta-adaptive control. Meta-adaptive control (controlling control) distinguishes a second CU which has a 'lower' CU as a CS. In this case the structure of a CU is changed by a meta-CU: the original CU may for instance be decentralized by an external consultancy bureau.

By means of these three types of control measures other concepts like 'management' and 'organization design' can be defined more precisely: management must be regarded as routine control, adaptive control and goal control. Organization design can be characterized as meta-adaptive control (the structure of the CS as well as the structure of the CU are objects of control).

The concept 'coordination' can also be described by means of the types of control discussed. Structural coordination concerns those control measures that are meant to change the structure in the CS and/or CU, thus adaptive control and meta-adaptive control. However, coordination procedures within a given organizational structure must be considered to be routine control. Examples of these coordination procedures are:

a. mutual adaptation: e.g. two employees who in mutual consultation adapt their work to each other;

b. direct supervision (a person higher in the hierarchy supervises the activities of someone at a lower hierarchical position);

c. standardization (e.g. prescribing in advance how the work should be done).

However, none of these coordination mechanisms plays a very important role in schools because teachers usually operate very autonomously. Chapter 4 addresses the issue of how schools coordinate their activities.

Informal processes

So far, organizational processes have been discussed in terms of the formal processes necessary to 'keep the organization going'. However, especially when the organization is approached from the position of its individual staff, there proves to be more. Communication takes place only partly via the official channels; informal communication is very important.

Informal processes are not dysfunctional -on the contrary- organizations probably could not function without informal communication between staff and without the extra motivation that may come from their own interpretations of the official organizational policy. In this respect schools do not differ from other types of organizations.

1.3.2.4 Organizational culture

When one visits a school for the first time one gets an impression of the nature, the characteristic, that is, of the culture of that school. The impression concerning a school's organizational culture is based on indicators like how (in)formally students approach teachers, how neat the school building is, which posters hang on the walls, what is 'not done', etcetera (Maslowski, 1997). That the culture of an organization is important is shown, for instance, in the fact that the merger of schools sometimes fails because their cultures do not match. Sometimes (Peters & Waterman, 1982), the culture of corporations is labelled as creative, risk taking, innovative as an explanation for organizational success. An organization's culture is then considered more important than its structure, market strategy or reward system.

Since the concepts 'school culture' and 'school climate' are often confused, the difference between the two is explained here. According to Maslowski (1997), the school climate reflects the degree to which school staff are satisfied with certain characteristics of their work environment (for example with the work pressure, safety at work, esteem from colleagues, the extent of participation in decision-making). Their appreciation of these school features is dependent on the actual school characteristics and on their values and norms (Figure 1.6).

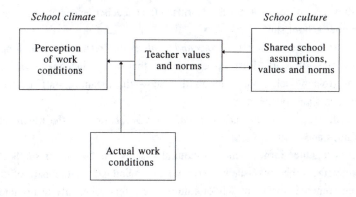

Figure 1.6: *The relationship between school climate and school culture*

Figure 1.6 shows that according to Maslowski (1997), organizational culture concerns a pattern of common assumptions, values and norms. While adapting their behavior to the behavior of other staff, the members of an organization develop a shared value and norm system that gives a meaning to their actions. The culture of an organization becomes self-evident, while organizational staff are not consciously aware of the assumptions, values and norms underlying their behavior. According to Schein (1985), staff behavior is less influenced by rules, job descriptions, procedures, budgeting, structures, or training than often assumed. Values and norms on how to cooperate with colleagues, students, leaders and the task to be carried out direct staff behavior much more drastically. In Schein's view "There is a real possibility that the only thing of real importance that leaders do is create and manage culture" (p. 2).

Van Hoewijk (1989) distinguishes between four cultural shells: the inner circle concerns the '*taken for granted assumptions*' (Schein, 1985) of organizational staff. These are unconscious opinions on what is fundamentally right: e.g. 'most important is the student', or 'student achievement is for the major part a matter of aptitude'. These opinions strongly determine the role staff ascribe to education and the essential features of their teaching activities.

The second shell concerns the *values and norms* of staff that show what they consider good, right and worthy to strive for. For instance, teachers can for instance value mutual cooperation very much, or appreciate full autonomy concerning their own work. Common values are shown in behavioral norms. Norms reflect teacher expectations concerning the behavior of other school staff.

The third shell concerns the *myths, heroes and symbols* that reflect the shared assumptions, values and norms of staff. Respectively things that have happened, valued personal characteristics (role models), and symbols that show the meaning staff ascribe to school functions, elements and processes.

The fourth shell consists of the *habits, rituals and procedures* in the organization which also show values and norms.

The four shells together form a school's cultural system: the two inner shells concern the latent invisible; the other two shells make up the manifest, visible part of the cultural system. When someone speaks of school culture one refers especially to the latent culture, the assumptions, values and behavioral norms in a school.

Culture implies the communality of assumptions, values and norms. They are shared by the majority of staff, although not every member of the organization will share all values and norms. However, even if teachers do not share specific assumptions, these will still influence their behavior, because they comply with the expectations of others, or offer resistance against these expectations. School culture can therefore be defined as the shared assumptions, values and norms of staff that influence their functioning.

In contrast with the structure of an organization, it is not easy to describe its culture. Handy (1976) distinguishes between four types of organizational culture. Each of them describing what really happens in a school, instead of what has been written down formally:

- The *Zeus or club culture:* one central charismatic functionary knows what is good and determines what happens. He recruits staff on the basis of recognition. Few rules, a self confident attitude and trust in the individual are characteristic for this culture. The manager makes all decisions autocratically, with the result that the teachers can devote all of their time to teaching activities.

- *The Athens or task culture*: in this culture, management's most important task is problem solving. The organization is task directed, result oriented, and professional. Units are rather autonomous and at the same time have a specific responsibility. The resulting integration of different task cultures may be a problem.

- *Dionysus or person culture*: the organization serves the individual here. Managers and employees are equal. Management is considered something unpleasant which has to be done. Its most important basis is a set of agreements between staff and managers. All staff try to realize their own personal desires.

- *Apollo or role culture*: an organization built according to the laws of logic: rules and procedures are clear and provide for stability and predictability. Important in this culture is which function a person or organizational organ has, not which person it concerns (in contrast with the person culture), or which (temporarily) tasks have to be carried out (like in the task culture).

In the view of Handy (1976) schools are pulled in all four cultural directions. There is always a tendency toward a role culture, especially if schools are big. The need for standardized teaching is increased by examination norms as well as the fact that students are taught by several teachers. The opposite pull concerns the fact that teachers teach their own subject behind closed doors (the person culture). The contrast between the person and the role culture may be solved by a task culture, although this asks for a change in the attitude of school managers (more autonomy for staff and divisions). Divisions become more autonomous, and differentiated. The fact that there is little time for the management of schools may lead to the choice to have all decisions made by an autocratic school leader and to let teachers teach (the club culture). One may also divide the work among fairly independent units. However, integration of these different task cultures requires some role culture characteristics. The orientation of teachers makes certain school cultures more probable than others. How do they see their work? Do they consider themselves independent professionals with their own clients? Do they feel themselves cooperators, or creators of products (the person, club, task culture respectively)?

Ernst Marx (1986) discerns school cultures from another perspective:
- The *liberal* school with a *heterogenous culture* in which the teacher operates very autonomously. The only shared value in this culture is that everybody is free to think what one wants to (within the boundaries of decent behavior). School managers create the conditions for autonomous behavior of the teaching staff. Shared goals and ideals are in contrast with this type of organization. There is very little consultation among staff and decisions are made at the top of the organization.
- The *ideal directed* school with a *homogenous* culture: staff work on the basis of a shared ideal concerning the role of the school and the way students should be treated. Within the framework of governmental rules, the school designs education in its original way. Teachers and managers strive for the same ideal which makes rules relatively unimportant. (Consensus) decisions are made in consultation with each other.
- The *innovative* school with a *multiple stream culture*: although the existence of several (sub)cultures is characteristic for this school, there is one shared orientation: 'let us make things better'.

21

Because of the subcultures, its structure is more complex than in the liberal or in the ideal directed school. Consultation within a subculture and negotiation between subcultures is directed at finding compromises. The more this leads to integrated visions, the more features of the homogeneous culture come into being. If a compromise is not translated into behavior, the stronger is the tendency toward a heterogeneous culture (each goes his own way). An innovative school can only function if the social values are shared: learn from mistakes, openness, negotiate fairly, willing to change, and compromises are part of the game.

The literature on (school) organizational culture shows that schools are, in some respects, similar with respect to their culture. However, they also differ. Cultures are dependent on factors like size, influence from the environment, the nature of the work in the operating core and the features of staff. An Apollo culture, for instance, is not probable in a small school just like an Athens culture is not likely to be found in an old school. A Zeus culture is more likely to be found in a school in crisis, and an Apollo culture in a school that is primarily led on the basis of detailed external rules.

Ernst Marx stresses that in some schools the culture is the most important control tool since the culture is comprehensive, refers to all school areas, and is shared by most staff. In other schools the culture may be strong but only encompass some general 'guidelines'. The cultural heterogeneity or homogeneity must match with the structure of the school organization and vice versa.

In case of fundamental changes in the organization, (e.g. changes in the type of instruction, decision-making procedures, student promotion criteria, teaching material) cultural aspects play a role. These changes require changes in the values and norms: what is considered important, what should be rewarded, and which solutions are acceptable. However, changing, the culture of an organization usually is not 'the' solution for any organizational problem. In most cases, a mix of approaches and problem solving strategies is required (including traditional ones like task descriptions, reward systems, budgeting, rules). An important effect of 'the cultural wave' is that critical attention for the culture of organizations has become one of the possible (partial) problem solving strategies. An interesting question that goes beyond the scope of this chapter is whether the culture of schools can be changed, and if so, how this can be done.

1.3.2.5 The relationship with the environment

The environment of a school organization concerns everything external to the school: e.g. its customers, competitors, geographical location, and the economic and political climate in which it must function.

The school environment can be characterized regarding the degree to which it is dynamic or stable. Stability does not mean that the environment does not change, just as dynamic is not synonymous with change. The two concepts refer to the degree to which environmental change can be predicted. The degree to which an organizational environment is stable is determined by governmental action, economic developments, the demands from clients, and initiatives from competitors. If the market of an organization asks for new products/services every year, competition is very intense, and the government changes its laws continuously, the environment of an organization is considered to be much more dynamic than when a monopolistic organization can provide the same group of customers with the same products/services in a country with a stable political situation.

The Dutch educational system had operated in a stable and predictable environment for a long time. However, in the nineteen fifties and sixties this began to change when education was regarded as a tool that could be used to reduce social inequality. Experiments were set up with new school types. Since the nineteen eighties new goals have been added to this equity perspective: improving educational quality, the efficiency of the educational system, decentralization of policy-making from governmental to school level, and the transition from education to work. In general, societal pressure on the educational system has increased and has made the school environment less stable. A development with a similar impact concerns the declining birth rate which produces employment problems in schools.

Despite these changes in the school environment there is still quite a lot of certainty for schools, for instance concerning the legal status of school staff. Moreover, schools do not work in an environment that is characterized by intense output-evaluation and fierce competition between schools. Evaluation of the performance of school staff is almost never followed by drastic sanctions.

The latitude of the organization with respect to external influences concerns another aspect of an organization's relationship with its environment. The leeway schools have in policy-making varies with the area of school policy-making (Liket, Van Marwijk-Kooij & Van Bruggen, 1985). For instance, the legal status of Dutch school staff is to a high degree determined at central governmental level, whereas formally, school boards are fairly autonomous concerning the contents and form of education in their school. However, the government also strives for more decentralization in the fields of finance, personnel and examination.

Next to these general national environmental conditions, the features of the local school environment also play a role. When schools have to invest more to obtain the essential inputs (especially students), a more intense contact with the direct local environment may be expected.

Schools are not only dependent on their environment; they can also actively exert influence on it, for instance by means of advertisement and other marketing activities (cf. chapter 7).

The demands regarding the output of educational institutions concerns another aspect of the school-environment relationship. Although the Dutch government influences what is taught in the higher grades of secondary education, external demands on schools are limited and an external instrument to check whether schools meet societal demands is missing. As a result, schools are free to a high degree in choosing their educational goals.

Organizational implications of environmental features

Schools are not used to coping with a turbulent environment. Nowadays, school managers do not only have to deal with purely clerical, representative and legal-status affairs. Political skills in negotiation processes, actively scanning important environmental segments, and other new skills (e.g. budgeting) also have become more important (this point concerns vocational schools in particular).

In many cases, teachers' involvement in school policy-making is required to make broadly based decisions. However, this demands a participative way of decision-making that is missing in most schools. Many schools are probably of a 'segmental' nature, consisting of two more or less segregated spheres: the teacher zone and the management zone (Hanson, 1981). Coordination and cooperation between these zones is limited. Organizational development is required in these schools if they want to operate successfully as a whole (and not only its managers) in an environment that calls for an active approach.

1.3.2.6 Organizational effectiveness

Boyd & Crowson (1981) in their well-known article on the characteristics of (the study of) educational administration observe a strong process-orientation in this discipline, and a limited concern with school outcomes and organizational effectiveness - especially in terms of student outcomes. This limited product-orientation is certainly related with:
- the difficulty of measuring certain goals of schooling;
- a lack of consensus on school goals and effectiveness criteria;
- the long causal chain from organizational conditions to school output;
- the complexity and non-linearity of relationships between factors.

Various authors (Scott, 1981; Quinn & Rohrbaugh, 1983; Quinn et al., 1996) suggest that the theoretical organizational perspectives followed in practice imply which organizational effectiveness criteria are important. Cameron & Whetten (in Boerman, 1998) state that since various effectiveness criteria are important, a single best organizational effectiveness criterion does not exist. Next to efficient production (rational goal model), a number of criteria are considered important for organizational effectiveness such as: responsiveness to changing political and environmental demands in order to acquire resources and grow (open systems theory); staff commitment; motivation and satisfaction (human relations theory); internal control and stability (internal process model). Although these criteria can be in conflict with each other from a conceptual point of view, that does not mean that in daily practice organizations cannot and should not pay attention to several effectiveness criteria and balance them off against each other. Which criterion receives most attention in a specific situation will probably depend on matters like the management perspective, the organizational situation, and the nature of the organizational environment.

Although many authors assume that various effectiveness criteria are worthy of use in evaluating an organization, some authors rank those criteria in order of importance.

In the next chapter, Scheerens will explain why he considers the productivity criterion most important, just as he sees the other criteria as preconditions for the productivity criterion. In the last chapter of this book, Bosker & Scheerens pay attention to the question of how fair it is to judge schools on the productivity criterion.

1.4 Some school organization and school management problems

In the previous section a framework with respect to the school as an organization has been presented. Now attention is paid to the organizational problems that are experienced in schools.

Van Dongen et al. (1989) studied the organization and management problems in Dutch secondary schools. About a hundred schools participated in their research project. Information was gathered among school management, teachers, and teachers with coordinating tasks. In sum 2895 problems were initially identified which were subsequently reduced to a limited number of problem clusters. One of the problem clusters 'internal school functioning' consists of five subcategories of organization and management problems: problems concerning the general organization of schools, school management, teachers, departments and committees, and the contents of education. Each of these subcategories is discussed now.

A. General school organization problems
Within this problem category the following major problems are mentioned:
- communication and consultation at school level: too little time for communication (among reasons as a result of the timetable), the enormous flood of circulares from the government, problems concerning participation in consultation and extra-curricular activities, and the fact that appointments are not kept;
- underdeveloped policy-making concerning personnel (no functionary takes care of this activity, no coaching of teachers), students (rules for students not clear and not used

enough), finance and administration (budgets are too small and not allocated clearly);
- logistic problems: a variety of problems connected with constructing the timetable (part-timers, the difficulty of planning consultation), and the fact that classes are too big and heterogenous.

The most serious problems (according to about 30% of the respondents these problems are fairly/very serious) concern the difficulties with respect to personnel-policy, checking whether rules and appointments are kept, and problems with respect to class size.

B. Problems with regard to school management
The following problem categories are mentioned here:
- communication and consultation of school management with others: school boards receive colored information from school managers, in the opinion of teachers their ideas/desires are taken into account too little by managers, and relations between managers and the municipality and support staff often are not very good;
- communication and consultation between school managers: some problems are connected with the personal characteristics of school managers (incompatible characters, limited human relations skills, passing the buck to someone else), others with the division of tasks (unequal, not clear);
- policy-development and the expertise of school managers: too little long term planning, educational vision and innovation, too little coaching of new teachers, an inadequate student selection policy, no clear financial policy, not capable of solving timetable problems;
- the workload is too high (often functionaries have management tasks in addition to teaching responsibilities).

School managers need to have expertise in many different areas (human relations skills, external relations, clerical work, personnel affairs, organizing skills). In the professional bureaucracy, a great deal of school management power is due to personal power. Teachers are relatively autonomous and therefore their cooperation depends on first being convinced of plans by school managers. A manager without persuasiveness cannot direct his team in the desired direction, conflicts are not solved, the school climate deteriorates, and the danger exists that teachers will withdraw themselves deeper into their autonomous kingdoms.

In many countries school boards are formally responsible for school policy-making, and school managers have to execute their policies. In those countries school management is formally only 'primus inter pares', the first among equals. However, school boards often do not develop school policy, but only supervise school management. School management, therefore, can not base its actions on a school board policy. Moreover, school management does not have the background (usually they are teachers), time (because of purely administrative activities) and authority (central government still decides on many matters) for policy-making. As a result, a shared long term vision on education and on the future of the school are often missing.

As a consequence, school policy has only been developed to a limited degree. Moreover, personnel policy is restricted to recruitment, selection and legal status affairs. Little attention is paid to labor conditions, in-service training, career counselling and performance evaluations. The limited attention for personnel matters may negatively influence the motivation and labor satisfaction of school staff.

Smets (1981) points to a time management problem of school managers; they are overburdened with activities (e.g. paperwork, meetings, contacts) and as a result are short term directed. Which activities a manager develops, according to Smets, depends on his/her task conception and/or personal interest. Satisfying everyday needs is also important: substituting for ill teachers, realizing timetable mutations, solving student problems and the like. Moreover, purely administrative work takes a lot of the management time (clerical work, finance and personnel affairs, etcetera).

C. Problems with regard to teachers

Teacher problems proved to be the largest problem area in this study (one in five of the problems mentioned proves to be a teacher problem):

- A high work burden and a low job satisfaction comprises one of the most serious problems (only 7% of the respondents reported that this did not, or hardly cause any problems). Causes are connected with the personal characteristics of the teacher (varying participation as a result of their age, private situation, low financial rewards, busy job), the uninterested student attitude, the heavy work load because of non-instructional activities, large classes, participation in innovations, and keeping demanding parents satisfied.

- Another category of problems is connected with teacher professionalism. The time required to keep expertise at par reduces teacher leisure and preparation time. Young colleagues tend to experience discipline problems.

- Moreover, teachers operate very autonomously. How they function is not evaluated, and they receive little in-service training. Agreements (e.g. concerning absence registration, the time at which lesson periods start and end) often are not clear and it is not checked whether they are adhered to or not. This in turn fails to encourage staff to honor their agreements. Their 'profession' is more important than the organization they work in. Participation of teachers in school affairs is therefore not self-evident, and collective policy-making at school par level is far from easy. Moreover, teachers participating in consultation organs do not experience much influence on the decisions made at the school.

- Communication between teachers and contacts with colleagues and school management are too limited. Schools often have an 'inner circle' of teachers who have already worked for a long time in a specific school and who are closely involved in school affairs, and an 'outer circle' of part-time relatively new teachers who only teach. Teacher subgroups are also based on criteria like age, educational vision, 'soft' versus 'hard' subjects. Teachers mainly communicate within groups (e.g. the group of new or old teachers, or those who teach in general education or vocational education), and do not have a say in the allocation of teaching periods to staff. Communication between teachers and students is often a problem because teachers have little information about the private situation of students.

  Communication is very important since it determines whether problems can be solved or not. In some of the schools involved in this study a certain conflict was very undermining for the school, however, its solution proved to be beyond reach because no channels existed to communicate the problem.

- The composition of teaching staff in the view of the respondents causes some problems: too few full-time female teachers, an ageing teaching staff and young teachers are the ones to be dismissed first.

  Many teachers do not have a full-time job. The large number of part-time teachers makes the management job with respect to organizing teacher meetings and constructing the timetable more difficult.

The ageing of teachers in 'shrinking schools' is considered a problem because older teachers in general are less energetic, motivated and experience the generation gap between teacher and student most acutely. The term teacher 'burn out' is used (Prick, 1983) to characterize the fact that older teachers feel burned out after many years of teaching, which results in high teacher absenteeism figures among other problems. The impact at school level may be that tasks are not carried out, lessons are cancelled, substitute teachers have to be found, and consultation and coordination within the school become a problem.

The tasks of teachers are many and varied: preparing lessons, teaching, non-instructional activities like coaching students, participating in meetings and organizing extra-curricular activities. As a result, many teachers experience a high work burden which produces intense physical and mental complaints, and high teacher absenteeism rates. The research results show that teachers on average work 10% more than the time they are paid for.

In the Netherlands the so-called committee Future of the Teaching Profession (Commissie Toekomst Leraarschap, 1993) observes a number of problems that have to be solved to make the teaching profession more attractive:

- the internal mobility (within a school to other jobs in that school) and external mobility (from the school to other organizations) of teachers are very limited, teachers feel trapped;
- job size and burden, absenteeism due to illness and incapacitation are high, whereas financial compensation is relatively low, and the status of the teaching profession is controversial;
- professional development of teachers is very limited; schools do not pay much attention to performance evaluation, and the development, coaching and in-service training of teachers.

The committee Future of the Teaching Profession (FTP) attributes these problems to the characteristics of the Dutch educational system and school organizations. The central government is not very active in developing personnel policy: career and staff development, reducing staff absenteeism, personnel counselling. The distance between the government and schools is too big for the government to take care of the interests of staff in individual schools. The detailed governmental regulations on the other hand have left very little room for developing personnel policy at school level.

Teachers are often described as employees with considerable professional autonomy. Behind the classroom door they make all relevant decisions and are fully responsible for what happens. Their decisions are often very intuitive. The safe classroom is important for the development of students and probably is cherished by the teaching staff who is not interested in the interference from other members of the organization. There is no call for super- and intervision. However, this freedom also makes teachers more isolated; they cannot share their responsibility much, and possibilities for mutual support and problem solving are limited. "The general isolation of teachers is a continuing source of strain and limits the range of professional response to educational challenges. Few, if any other, occupations place such faith in the organizational unit of the solitary professional. Nor is it well understood by people outside education how tiring teaching in front of a class actually is. A further general problem is that as long as teachers choose to follow their vocation and remain in the classroom, the actual nature of teaching changes little throughout the career, even if new materials, tasks and groups of students are added" (Neave, 1992).

In the opinion of the FTP, the solution for the problems mentioned lays in transforming schools into modern professional labor organizations. Schools need more room for policy-development leading to more flexible, efficient and varied staff input. Personnel policy should include teacher career development, a gradual development from junior teachers

29

(limited teaching load and intensive coaching) to senior teachers (full teaching task and more independence). Personnel policy in schools is still in its infancy. In most schools neither consultation with staff about their level of performance, nor a long term staff planning occur. Job differentiation and career development have progressed very little, although quite a lot of different tasks are fulfilled in schools.

Teachers and managers, according to the FTP, have to sustain the modern school. Instead of the national government school boards should become employers, who develop personnel policy and human resource management within framework-agreements. The latter is done by means of personnel selection and job allocation, reward structures, performance evaluation, training and development. Cooperation, support and consultation between teachers can be used to decrease teachers' task burden.

Teachers should also cooperate more. Instead of a model-teacher, more differentiation between teachers is needed in combination with more cooperation in solving teaching problems in a multi-disciplinary way. Such an approach demands an open school organiz-ation that is characterized by cooperation and shared responsibilities between staff. The latter enables the exchange of knowledge and mobility of staff, and prevents teachers from getting into too isolated and demanding a position.

In such a school the organization rests with all members of the staff and the employer is approachable concerning in-service training, salary, job changes, etcetera.

The modern professional school should be a self-regulating system of policy development and execution. This link between developing and execution of policy is crucial: positive and negative results of policy measures cannot be attributed to external factors. When the professional labor organization becomes reality, the policy making capacity of a school becomes very important. Increasing the policy area of schools by decreasing central governmental regulations necessitates that schools develop quality control instruments enabling schools to determine their results and to correct undesired effects.

D. Problems with regard to departments and committees

The existence of many departments in a school makes communication difficult, and as a result of unclear task descriptions and coordination, decisions concerning departments are made at (too) many different locations.

According to their members, school committees sometimes have too little authority and mutual conflicts arise due to the fact that the tasks of committees are often not clear-cut.

How departments function is dependent on teachers' willingness to bring their autonomy up for discussion, and on the degree of clarity in departmental decision-making. Making and carrying out decisions is not easy within departments; agreements are not adhered to and communication, consultation and coordination produce problems.

Readiness to participate in committees is endangered since the matters treated are often connected with the school as an organization, and not so much with the work of teachers within the classroom.

E. Problems with regard to the contents of education

The transfer from one type of education to another (e.g. from primary to secondary, or from one type of secondary education to another) and the transition from school to work prove to be difficult as a result of what has been taught and what students have learned.

Problems with the examination subjects chosen: certain subjects are considered to be underrepresented, possibilities for students to choose are too restricted, or too many subject combinations are allowed (which produce timetable problems) because of competition considerations.

Initiating, coordinating and evaluating educational innovations also causes problems. In many cases one is not very motivated to innovate and likes neither the uncertainty concerning the contents and organization of central government initiated innovations nor the fact that the resources to innovate are limited.

Innovation of the contents of education is also connected with certain organization and management problems. Consultation (structures) and decision-making are a prerequisite for realizing innovations. In the case of innovations, however, often no decisions are made concerning decision-making procedures which leads to consultation and decision-making problems (for instance the innovation goals and contents are not clear).

Innovations can also interfere with existing roles and positions within the school; they can, for instance, endanger the autonomy of teachers.

The internal organization of innovations like the tasks to be fulfilled, task differentiation, new school organs, committees and resources, also causes problems.

The more complicated an innovation, the more intense the innovation process and the more probable it is that problems concerning the organization of the innovation process should arise.

1.5 Structural constraints on the administration of schools

Those who manage schools do not live in a vacuum; the features of the context in which they operate influence what they can and can not do and achieve. A description is given here of six structural constraints Corwin & Borman (1988) distinguish, that limit the capacity of American school district administrators to control teachers and students in schools. Much of their message can be translated to the administrative and management contexts of other countries. In the case that schools are not part of school districts, the same problems may go for the relationship between a school board and a school. In the view of Corwin & Borman (1988), it is important to understand the social context that frames administrative choices and sets parameters of managerial power and authority. Their thesis is "... that because of the way power and authority are distributed within school districts, normative conflicts are systematically patterned into their structures." (p. 209). This causes a number of dilemmas which imply the need to make choices among socially structured alternatives.

1. *The dilemma of administrative control*

Although central school district administrators are legally responsible for the actions of schools, total administration is neither administratively nor technically feasible. Many school policies are determined by the actions of schools; only certain decisions are centralized. District administrators can never fully control the decentralized ones. As a result, administrators are held accountable for things they cannot always control.

The tensions between central administration at district level and schools are products of a complex balance of power. Central control is constrained by the need to delegate certain decisions, and because of the fact that subordinates can independently exert influence over spheres that are the official responsibilities of administrators. Top-down control can interfere with the ability of schools to solve local problems.

On the other hand, schools are constrained by the district policy, and often by the limited capacities of principals to protect the independence of their schools. The relationships between schools and central administration are products of negotiation. The hierarchy helps administrators protect the ability to control and it helps shield teachers from pressures exerted by their constituencies.

2. *The dilemma of teacher autonomy*

To acquire discretion in the classroom, teachers have relinquished some of their claims to exercise control over fundamental parameters of their work. They are subordinates but also members of powerful unions. Collective bargaining power has been gained at the expense of personal autonomy. This includes three subdilemmas:
• the dilemma of teacher discretion: the contradiction between the subordinate status of teachers and their discretion in classrooms;
• the dilemma of subordination: inconsistencies in their power as subordinates compared to their collective power as members of a teacher organization;
• the dilemma of collective power: the sacrifice teachers sometimes must incur in their personal discretion in order to achieve collective power.

These inconsistencies among their positions show that their features vary according to their position: in classrooms, in the school, or in the school district. According to Lortie

(1969), the central problem of school administrators is to achieve an optimal balance between control and autonomy. They give teachers a strong degree of autonomy in some spheres (instruction), however constrain them in others (especially in purely administrative matters).

The balance of power between teachers and local education agencies fluctuates tenuously. Administrators must share their authority with teachers who are not closely supervised, and who can exercise discretion over instructional matters in their classrooms. As a result of their discretion in this capacity, they can resist administrative initiatives, compete among themselves for status and resources, and circumvent certain types of administrative restraints. Teacher autonomy clearly limits administrative control.

Teachers can also exercise influence over some policy areas through collective bargaining. However, Corwin & Borman (1988) stress that teachers, despite their autonomy and collective power, remain subordinates subject to district policies, rules and procedures. Their autonomy is never absolute, but always subject to negotiation. As a group they have gained some of their autonomy at the price of more control over district policy than thus far achieved. Their collective power has been further weakened by role overload, preference for isolation, fragmentation into specialties and grade levels, interpersonal competition, and jurisdictional disputes.

3. The dilemma of occupational status

Compliance with administrative policies and procedures can interfere with professional norms. The most compliant teachers are not necessarily responsive to the circumstances of their students. Routine teacher work is not equally appropriate for all students. The goals of service are also jeopardized by pragmatism and the requirements of survival. Although professionals are a potential threat to administrative control, they seem to be endorsed by only a small but influential group of teachers. Professional norms seem to have accommodated to administrative constraints rather than posing a real challenge to administrative control.

4. The dilemma of career

Providing incentives for teachers is difficult. Lifelong teaching means no formal advancement after midcareer, and promotion always requires leaving the classroom. Informal professional recognition from peers is minimized by strong segmentation within the job. In the opinion of Corwin and Borman (1988), the way the labor market for teaching has been structured imposes serious impediments to administrative control. The truncated career ladders have drastically restricted the options for administrators to provide the incentives needed for recruiting and rewarding good teachers.

5. The dilemma of order

Arrangements necessary to maintain order in classrooms can subvert the goals of instruction. Student resistance and childhood values (student subcultures) are important sources of constraint on administrative control. According to Corwin & Borman, the limits imposed by student subcultures are at least as important as the power of teachers.

There is a fluid power balance between teachers and students. What children learn from one another apart from adults is an important part of their education. Moreover, teachers often negotiate with students, adapting teaching strategies and administrative and instructional policies to the condition of students and the demands of their various subcultures.

On the other hand, adults have relinquished control, and student conduct has been legislated by codes administered by districts. Adults face the problem that they have to adapt professional norms and administrative policies to student subcultures while trying to overcome student resistance and providing quality education.

The demands of maintaining order often dictate classroom teaching practices and some administrative policies as well. Often the requirement of order seems more important than the concern for how students learn. Possibly what students learn is determined more directly by the values of their own subcultures than by teacher and administrator behavior.

6. The dilemma of equity

For purposes of instruction, students are classified into different schools, programs, tracks, classrooms, and student groups. Some of the most profound administrative choices entail compromising ideologies favoring egalitarian treatment and individualized attention. The number of students in schools is one of the most fundamental constraints on administrative control. Schools are blamed when children fail. Each student classification must be treated differently, but tradeoffs are so complex that they certainly will produce some inequities.

The dilemma is that many learning theories and teaching practices are based on the individual learner, whereas schools are based on batch-processing technologies.

Many critics state that some students are disadvantaged by 'tracking' into ability groups. There are three related issues:

* *can teachers be fully sensitive to individual differences within classroom settings?*

   In comprehensive classrooms it is difficult to provide much individualized instruction. For practical reasons, students are allocated to tracks within schools and groups within classrooms. In creating groups, teachers do not seem to be concerned with adapting instruction to individual differences. Grouping seems more related to how abilities and other features are distributed in classrooms. Grouping involves complex tradeoffs between different kinds of instructional arrangements. It is difficult to determine which alternative type of grouping is more individualized.

- *to what extent is ability grouping based on ascriptive criteria (social skills, family background) instead of academic abilities?*

There is mix of both, but how relative is each? One view is that ascriptive criteria are dominant. A related theme is that even when students are initially assigned to groups on the basis of proven abilities, they become stereotyped in such a way that the chance of moving to other groups as their performance changes is limited. Corwin & Borman refer to research showing that teachers treat different groups differently. Students in low-ability groups suffer, whereas high-ability groups profit from grouping. In the long run grouping would serve to broaden the gap between academic performance levels.

- *does grouping on the basis of their past academic performance consign them to a social caste from which there is no escape?*

Some writers question whether stereotyping is as rigidly imposed as often pictured. Barr & Dreeben (1988) point to research findings indicating that teachers conscientiously grouped students, and matched material to ability levels. They assigned students on the basis of performance and moved them to other groups as performance improved. Grouping in itself is a neutral act according to the authors.

Some authors state that even if assignments are solely based on student ability, and transfer among groups as performance improves is ensured, the practice of ability grouping has detrimental latent side effects because students learn about their social identities in such groups. They identify themselves with members of segregated social crowds based on ability which in turn help to crystallize their classroom status.

There is a great deal of evidence that teachers tailor lessons to the level of a group's collective ability, especially in reading, science and social science. Teachers interact differently with students of different ability levels (e.g. more tolerance and understanding for high achievers).

The ability composition of the classroom influences the benefits students receive (the higher the level the greater the gains). The ability level of a given classroom is to a greater or lesser extent an important administrative decision.

To Corwin & Borman it appears that it is very difficult to provide individualized instruction within the present structure of schools. In most cases teaching involves the class as a whole, dominated by recitations from a segment of students. Grouping, a compromise between both extremes, entails other dilemmas related to finding ways to:

a. assign students to such groups and yet prevent individuals from becoming victims of a rigid stratification system on the basis of their prior achievement;

b. minimize adverse social and moral consequences associated with ability hierarchies.

Perhaps multidimensional classrooms provide an answer as they seem to minimize the ascriptive tendencies often associated with grouping and tracking.

Although the six dilemmas overlap, the first two are associated with the administrative context of work in schools, the next two with the structure of teaching, and the last two with classrooms as social systems and work settings. According to Corwin & Borman (1988) these three dimensions constitute the main parameters of work in schools. The dilemmas are not necessarily experienced uniformly from one school to another. Each dilemma is caused by instructural incompatibilities within school systems and its resolution requires extensive organizational reform.

1.6 Summary

In this chapter the reader has been introduced to several characteristics of the organization and management of schools. The increased attention for the management perspective in education has been portrayed and explained in section 1.2. Thereafter, a framework with respect to schools as organizations has been presented in section 1.3, by introducing and explaining concepts from organization theory: organization, organizational structure, organizational processes, organizational culture, and the organization-environment relationship.

Furthermore, categories of important school organization and school management problems of Dutch secondary schools as found in the study of Van Dongen et al. (1989) have been presented: general school organizational problems, problems regarding school management, teachers, school departments and committees, and the contents of education (section 1.4). Finally, in section 1.5 some six structural constraints have been described that limit the capacity of administrators to control staff and students.

The organizational features discussed so far at a general level will be treated in more depth in the following chapters.

• CHAPTER 2 •

Concepts and Theories of School Effectiveness[1]

J. Scheerens
University of Twente, The Netherlands

2.1 Introduction

School effectiveness is the degree to which schools achieve their goals. Basically the analysis of a school's - or any other type of organization's - effectiveness is an analysis of means and goals or, stated differently, an analysis of antecedent conditions and effectiveness criteria. Behind this rather simple structure of means/goals relationships there is considerable complexity, since several categories of goals (effectiveness criteria) and several types of antecedent conditions may be distinguished.

Different schools of thought in organizational science have emphasized different effectiveness criteria. These different perspectives on organizational effectiveness are discussed in section 2.2 of this chapter, where they are also compared to the economic view on organizational effectiveness. The predominant model in empirical school effectiveness research conforms to the economic view on organizational effectiveness, with productivity of the teaching and learning process as the effectiveness criterion.

Different strands of educational effectiveness research have emphasized different categories of antecedent conditions. Early educational sociologist's studies on educational (in)equality and economically oriented 'production function' research concentrated on simple resources and material inputs of schooling and of proxy indicators of school facilities such as, for instance, the number of books in the school library. Research on exceptionally effective schools concentrated on school organizational and school managerial characteristics at the school level, such as 'instructional leadership' and 'an achievement-oriented school climate'. Instructional effectiveness studies and research on

---

[1] Part of this chapter was published earlier in:
J. Scheerens (1992), *Effective Schooling. Research, Theory and Practice*, published by Cassell, London, as chapter 1;
J. Scheerens (1990), Process indicators of school functioning. In *School Effectiveness and School Improvement*, vol. 1; and in
J. Scheerens (1994), Conceptual Frameworks on School Effectiveness. In D. Reynolds et al., *Advances in School Effectiveness Research and Practice*. Oxford: Pergamon.

productive teaching has classroom level processes as its main focus, with variables such as 'time on task' and 'content-covered in basic subjects'.

In more recent approaches to school effectiveness research, these various approaches have become integrated. The main empirical research results are summarized in a three-level conceptual model, where conditions at school organizational level are seen as supporting or facilitating conditions at classroom level that are considered to enhance effectiveness (section 2.3 of this chapter).

In section 2.4 two major theoretical propositions are compared for their potential to explain the findings of empirical school effectiveness research: evaluation-centered rational control on the one hand and 'choice' on the other.

Section 2.5, finally touches briefly on the implications of empirically-grounded school effectiveness models for issues discussed in other chapters.

2.2 Perceptions on school effectiveness

What do we mean with the statement that a school is 'effective'? In an educational discussion, the term 'effective' is often associated with the quality of education. Some authors (Corcoran, 1985) give an even broader meaning of the word by speaking of the general 'goodness' of a school. Other concepts which are used (rightly or wrongly) as synonyms for effectiveness include efficiency, productivity and the survival power of an organization.

It is clear that a more precise definition is required. Moreover, we also run up against the problem that effectiveness is defined differently according to various disciplines. In this section, economic (2.2.1) and organization-theoretical (2.2.2) definitions will be considered.

2.2.1 Economic definitions of effectiveness

In economics concepts like effectiveness and efficiency are related to the production process of an organization. Put in a rather stylized form a production process can be summed up as a 'turnover' or transformation of 'inputs' to 'outputs'. *Inputs* of a school or school system include students with certain given characteristics and financial and material aids. *Outputs* include student attainment at the end of schooling. The transformation *process* or *throughput* within a school can be understood to be all the instruction methods, curriculum choices and organizational preconditions which make it possible for students to acquire knowledge. Longer term *outputs* are denoted with the term *'outcomes'* (see Table 2.1).

Table 2.1: *Analysis of factors on the education production process*

Inputs	Process	Outputs	Outcomes
e.g.	e.g.	e.g.	e.g.
funding	instruction methods	final primary school test scores	dispersal on the labor market

Effectiveness can now be described as the extent to which the desired output is achieved. *Efficiency* may then be defined as the maximum output against the lowest possible cost. In other words, efficiency is effectiveness with the additional requirement that it is achieved in the least expensive manner. (For variations on the meaning of efficiency reference is made to Boorsma & Nijzink, 1984, p. 17-21; Windham, 1988).

Naturally, it is vitally important for the economic analysis of efficiency and effectiveness to indicate whether the value of inputs and outputs can be expressed in terms of money. For determining efficiency, it is even necessary that input costs such as teaching materials and teachers' salaries are known. When the outputs can also be expressed in financial terms, efficiency determination is more like a cost-benefit analysis (Lockheed, 1988, p. 4). It has to be noted, however, that an extreme implementation of the above-mentioned economic characterization of school effectiveness runs up against many problems.

These already start with the question of how one should define the 'desired output' of a school. For instance, the "production" or returns of a secondary school can be measured by the number of students who get their diploma. The unit in which production is measured in this way is thus the 'final examination student'. Often, however, one will want to establish the units of production in a finer way and will want to look, for instance, at the grades achieved by students for various examination subjects. In addition, there are all types of choices to be made with regard to the scope of effectiveness measures. Should only performance in basic skills be studied? Should there also perhaps be a concern with higher cognitive processes? And should not social and/or affective returns on education be established? Other problems related to the economic analysis of schools is determining monetary value on inputs and processes and the prevailing lack of clarity how the production process operates (precisely what procedural and technical measures are necessary to achieve maximum output).

Relevant to the question on how useful one regards the characterizing of effectiveness in economical terms is the acceptableness of the school as a metaphor for a production unit.

2.2.2 Organization-theoretical views on effectiveness

Organizational theorists often maintain that the effectiveness of organizations cannot be described in a straightforward manner. Instead, a pluralistic attitude is taken with respect to the interpretation of the concept in question. Organizational theorists assume that the interpretation depends on the organization theory and the specific interests of the group posing the question of effectiveness (Cameron & Whetten, 1983; Faerman & Quinn, 1985). The main perceptions on organization which are used as background for a wide range of definitions on effectiveness will be briefly reviewed.

Economic rationality
The economic description of effectiveness mentioned earlier is seen by organizational experts as deriving from the idea that organizations function rationally: i.e., purposefully. Goals which can be operationalized as pursued outputs are the basis for choosing effect criteria (effect criteria are the variables by which effects are measured, i.e. study achievement, well-being of the students etc.). There is evidence of economic rationality whenever the goals are formulated in the sense of outputs of the primary production process of the school. In the entire functioning of a school other goals can also play a part, such as having a clear-cut policy with regard to increasing student intake. With regard to this type of objective, a school can also operate rationally; only this falls outside the specific interpretation given to economic rationality. Effectiveness as defined in terms of economic rationality can also be identified as the productivity of an organization. In education, the rational or goal-orientated model that can be used for both curriculum development and educational evaluation is mainly propagated via Tyler's model (Tyler, 1950). Of the remaining perceptions on organization, the economic rationality model is dismissed as being both simplistic and out of reach. Professionals in the teaching field know all too well how difficult it is to reach a consensus on goals and then to operationalize and quantify them. From the position that other values besides productivity are just as important for organizations to function, the rational model is regarded as simplistic.

The organic system model
According to the organic system model, organizations can be compared to biological systems which adapt to their environment. The main characteristic of this approach is that organizations openly interact with their surroundings. Thus, they need in no way be passive objects of environmental manipulation but can actively exert influence on the environment themselves. Nevertheless, this viewpoint is mainly preoccupied with an organization's 'survival' in a sometimes hostile environment. For this reason, organizations

must be flexible, namely to assure themselves of essential resources and other inputs. According to this viewpoint, therefore, flexibility and adaptability are the most important conditions for effectiveness in the sense of survival. A result of this could be that the effectiveness of a school is measured according to its yearly intake, which could partly be attributed to intensive canvassing or school-marketing.

No matter how remarkable this view on effectiveness may seem at first glance, it is nevertheless supported by an entirely different scientific sphere: microeconomics of the public sector. Niskanen (1971) demonstrated that public sector organizations are primary targeted at maximizing budgets and that there are insufficient external incentives for these organizations - schools included - to encourage effectiveness and efficiency. In this context I think it would be interesting to examine whether the canvassing activities of schools consists mainly of displaying acquired facilities (inputs) or of presenting output data such as previous years' examination results.

Finally, it is conceivable that the inclination towards the inputs of the organic system model coincides with a concern for satisfying outputs, particularly in those situations where the environment makes the availability of inputs dependent on the quantity and/or quality of achievements (output) realized earlier. This principle is presently applied in the so-called output financing of universities and vocational colleges in The Netherlands.

The human relations approach of organizations

If there is an inclination towards the environment in the open system perception of organizations, with the so-called human relations approach, the eye of the organization analyst is explicitly focused inward. This fairly classical school of organizational thought has partly remained intact even in more recent organizational characterization. In Mintzberg's concept of the professional bureaucracy, aspects of the human relations approach reoccur, namely in emphasizing the importance of the well-being and motivation of the individuals in an organization, the importance of consensus, and collegial relationships (Mintzberg, 1979). From this perception, the job satisfaction of workers and their involvement with the organization are likely criteria for measuring the most desired characteristics of the organization. The organizational theorists who share this view regard these criteria as effectiveness criteria.

The bureaucracy

The essential problem with regard to the administration and structure of organizations (in particular those such as schools that have many relatively autonomous sub-units), is how to create a harmonious whole. Appropriate social interaction and opportunities for personal and professional development - see the human relations approach - provide a means to reach this goal. A second means is provided by organizing, clearly defining and formalizing these social relations. The prototype of an organization in which positions and duties are formally organized is the 'bureaucracy'. It is well-known that bureaucratic organizations tend to produce more bureaucracy. The underlying motive behind this is to ensure the continuation, or better still, the growth of one's own department. This continuation can start operating as an effect criterion in itself.

The political model of organizations
Certain organizational theorists see organizations as political battlefields (Pfeffer & Salancik, 1978). Departments, individual workers and management staff use the official duties and goals in order to achieve their own hidden - or less hidden - agendas. Good contacts with powerful outside bodies are regarded as very important for the standing of their department or for their own standing. From a political-model perspective, the question of the effectiveness of the organization as a whole is difficult to answer. One is more interested in the extent to which internal groups succeed in complying with the demands of certain external interested parties. In the case of schools these bodies could be school-governing bodies, parents of students or the local business community. From studies carried out by Van der Krogt & Oosting (1988) it appeared that the external orientation of intermediate vocational secondary schools in The Netherlands is by no means highly developed.

It has already been mentioned that organizational concepts on effectiveness not only depend on theoretical answers to the question of how organizations "are pieced together", but also on the position of the factions posing the effectiveness question. On this point there are differences between these five views on organizational effectiveness. With regard to the economic rationality and the organic system model, the management of the organization is the main "actor" posing the effectiveness question. As far as the other models are concerned, department heads and individual workers are the actors that want to achieve certain effects.
In Table 2.2 the chief characteristics of the organization-theoretical perceptions on effectiveness are summarized.
The diversity of views on effectiveness which organizational theory makes leads to the question as to which position should be taken: Should we indeed operate from a position that there are several forms of effectiveness? Should a certain choice be made, or is it possible to develop from several views, one all-embracing concept on effectiveness?

2.2.3 A broad outline of the underlying model of school effectiveness research

School effectiveness research has various disciplinary backgrounds and has meanwhile acquired a certain life history of its own. Here only a broad outline of school effectiveness research is given.

In school-effectiveness research, school characteristics are linked to output data. The most widely employed output data are test results in basic skills such as language and arithmetic in elementary schools, and in the mother tongue, mathematics and foreign languages in secondary schools.

Table 2.2: *Organizational effectiveness models*

theoretical background	*effectiveness criterion*	*level at which the effectiveness question is asked*	*main areas of attention*
(business) economic rationality	productivity	organization	output and its determinants
organic system theory	adaptability	organization	acquiring essential inputs
human relations approach	involvement	individual members of the organization	motivation
bureaucratic theory	continuity	organization + individual	formal structure
political theory on how organizations work	responsiveness to external stakeholders	subgroups and individuals	independence power

The school characteristics chosen vary according to the different areas of educational effectiveness research. Sometimes the emphasis is on financial inputs and organizational characteristics such as a school's size, other times 'process' characteristics are studied such as school leadership, aspects of the curriculum and teaching methods.

Associating these latter characteristics and output data largely occurs by means of calculating correlations. Put simply, correlations are totals which indicate how far high or low scores of a group of schools or of students on one variable converge with similar high or low scores on another variable. Correlational relationships can be distinguished from associations between variables that can be established in experimental research. The main difference is that, strictly speaking, with correlations it is impossible to obtain unequivocal insight into the question as to whether the one variable can be seen as the cause of the other, even though a certain impression can be gained. Experimental research gives more certainty on this score. The fact that most school effectiveness research is correlational creates problems as far as interpreting results is concerned. While it is largely assumed that school characteristics are the causes, and levels of achievement the results (outputs), in some case the reverse is true. Several school effectiveness studies have established that in schools where teachers have high expectations of students, the level of achievement is higher. One interpretation here could be that students are motivated by the positive attitude of the teachers. Another interpretation, just as plausible, is that the teachers, on the basis of knowing the levels of achievement of their students have realistic expectations, whereby high expectations go hand-in-hand with high levels of achievement. In short, the high expectations characteristic can be both a cause and a result of high levels of achievement.

2.2.4 Position with regard to economic and organization-theoretical definitions of effectiveness

The above general outline of school effectiveness research will be compared to the economic and organization-theoretical definitions of effectiveness discussed in previous sections. Cameron & Whetten (1983) have developed a checklist to determine organization- effectiveness models. This will be applied to the general outline on school effectiveness research.

Question 1: *From whose perspective is effectiveness judged?*
This question draws attention to the practical implication of school effectiveness research, which is not always self-evident. In fact, this research can also be seen as an area of scientific research in which theory development is uppermost and practical application of results takes second place. Notwithstanding, most areas of school effectiveness research are narrowly linked to specific application. Political questions on education on unequal opportunity, developing compensatory education and encouraging school improvement programmes are probably more important sources of inspiration for school effectiveness research than pure scientific questions. According to Ralph & Fennessey (1983) school effectiveness research is dominated by the school improvement perspective and by educational support institutions. They mention the effective schools *movement* and by that imply that in adopting results of school effectiveness research there is a discernable 'ideology of reform'. According to them this ideological movement explains the important practical significance given to the results of school effectiveness research. They believe

that the impact of these fairly limited number of empirical school effectiveness studies does not justify this degree of practical influence.

It is still difficult to say which area of education service would make the most use of school effectiveness research. There are examples of its application both within local school guidance services and in-depth studies attached to national assessment programmes and evaluation studies for department of education initiatives.

A third category of potential users are the consumers of education, parents and students. Last but not least, schools could be inspired to use these results to improve their own practices.

Question 2: *Which area of activity within an organization determines effectiveness?*
In some of the models of organizational effectiveness looked at in the preceding section the emphasis was on the activities of the management to acquire, for instance, essential resources or on activities directed at increasing staff motivation. In school effectiveness research, the results of the primary production process - students' attainment levels - are mainly studied. In addition, one looks for 'predictors' or 'determinants' of these results (outputs). In effective schools research these determinants are defined as characteristics of the school. Sometimes these characteristics such as management, organization and curriculum can be defined purely at school level. There are also characteristics which are the sum total of education in the various classes: classroom characteristics aggregated to school characteristics.

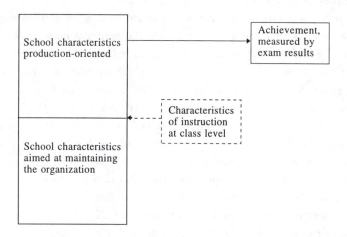

Figure 2.1: *The area of activity (reproduced in terms of effectiveness determinants and criteria) of school effectiveness research.*

The diagram in Figure 2.1 indicates the main area that school effectiveness research focuses on. The variables in the dotted box are seen as classroom characteristics aggregated to school level. The broken arrow indicates the aggregation of instruction characteristics, measured at class level, to school level.

Question 3: *At which level of the organization is effectiveness analyzed?*
This question has in fact been answered above. As a rule, school effectiveness is analyzed at school level. However, more can be said on this question on the grounds of research technicality. The output variable in school effectiveness research (e.g., the scores of final primary school year tests) are determined for each individual student. School characteristics are only defined on a school level. Thus the concern here is to relate variables defined at school level to those at student level. Especially when we are establishing these sort of links and wish to correct for background characteristics of students it has advantages to keep the information at the lowest aggregate level (the student) in the analysis. There are specific technical problems linked to relating data measured at different levels to one another but multi-level analysis techniques provide a solution.

Question 4: *How is effectiveness defined in terms of time?*
Subsidiary questions which play a role here are (a) the frequency with which effectiveness is determined and (b) the specific measurement moments in management and/or production processes by which effectiveness is gauged.
With regard to the first it is conceivable that there are instruments to keep a more or less permanent check on whether an organization functions well and produces sufficiently. At national level, monitoring by means of so-called educational indicators make such permanent quality control possible. At individual school level a school management information system fulfills this role (Visscher, 1992). With regard to the prototype of school effectiveness research, the effectiveness is determined once only.
Examples of research whereby the output of schools is determined at several points in time (longitudinal study) are rather scarce. Studies where this is the case are those of Brandsma and Knuver, 1988; Mortimore et al., 1988 and Rutter et al., 1979.
As far as the second question (b) concerning the point at which effectiveness is gauged, this occurs generally at the end of training. According to some critics of school effectiveness research it is unreasonable to call a school effective just because at the end of the last school year it appears that the average level of achievement is relatively high. Ralph & Fennessey (1983) state, for instance, that an effective school should be able to demonstrate relatively high levels of attainment every year. Moreover, they feel that schools only deserve the label 'effective' when they have performed well over several

46

years; in other words when school effectiveness appears as a stable factor.

Question 5: *What sort of data is used to form an opinion on effectiveness?*
Cameron & Whetten put forward objective data as opposed to subjective data. In effective schools research, objective data are mainly used to measure effect criteria, whereas in establishing determinants of effectiveness often subjective opinions from those directly involved can be decisive. In some studies use is made of expert assessments (thus essentially subjective data - Hoy & Ferguson, 1985, for example).

Question 6: *What standards or measures are used in order to make effectiveness judgments?*
Organizational effectiveness assessments can be made by comparing similar kinds of organizations (e.g., schools) to one another (cross-sectional comparative measurement), by assessing the same organization at various points in time (longitudinal comparative) or by comparing the output achieved to an absolute standard such as a prefixed target figure.

In school effectiveness research, the cross-sectional comparative measurement is used most. More specifically, comparisons between schools can be in the nature of a) placing 'extremely good' schools against 'extremely bad' schools, b) comparing a particular school with standard data which could be established per country or province, or c) comparing schools that have taken part in an improvement programme with schools that have not.
An important matter when using comparative measurements is to decide when differences between schools are to be considered as meaningful.

In summing up, it can be established that the underlying model for school effectiveness research compared to other models for organization effectiveness can be described as a multi-level, process-product model of learning achievement propelled by the quest for knowledge by school reformers and national policy makers in which as much use as possible is made of objective data, a short-term perspective is discernable and assessment standards are largely comparative.
The problem of defining school effectiveness could have been approached more directly simply by pointing out the obvious common ground it shares with the economic typification of effectiveness (within the broader perspective of efficiency and productivity) and with the related organizational model of economic rationality. However, a conscious choice has also been made for discussing alternative effectiveness views within the field of organization theory. This broader conceptual framework is regarded as necessary in order to reach a more considered determining of position. It is important to keep in mind that

various points of view exist in regard to effectiveness. Even when one rejects this plurality in the long run, as will be the case here, a confusion of ideas can be avoided by comparing the final choice of typification with alternative concepts.

More important, however, is that this excursion into the area of organizational theory demonstrates that organizations need more than a smooth running production process in order to function properly. Back-up functions, often identified as buffers, are necessary so that the primary production process can run undisturbed. Moreover, it is important to be aware that organizations can loose out with these back-up functions by acquiring (for instance) far too many resources than is strictly needed for an efficient production, or by allowing 'conviviality' to be an aim in itself to such an extreme extent that productive working hours suffer.

Means/goal ordering of criteria

The above formulation conveys that productivity, that is to say an effective output of the primary process, should be seen as the actual dimension of effectiveness. Alternative effectiveness criteria, such as adaptability towards the environment, job satisfaction, consensus and continuity guaranteed by a formalized structure, can be seen as 'means' or intermediary goals.

Figure 2.2 illustrates this means-goal-character of the various effectiveness perceptions.

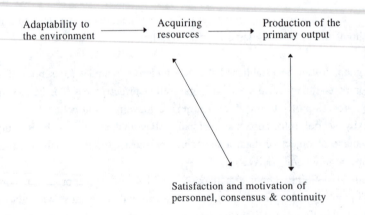

Figure 2.2: *Means-goal-relationships between effectiveness criteria*

The arrows pointing in both directions show that satisfaction, solidarity and the oneness of structures can be seen as both the cause *and* the effect of high productivity. It is not implausible that the staff of a productive organization is more satisfied than the personnel of one which is hardly productive.Putting this relationship pattern of Figure 2.2 within an educational context, one can see as an example of the criterium 'adaptability' specific measures, instruments and organizational forms to make the school curriculum more relevant to the needs of the labor market.

Another example is to have an organizational structure that can withstand drastic changes in the direct environment, such as externally imposed increases in scale (Gooren, 1989). As an example of acquiring vital resources one can think of machines that are needed for technical education and which can sometimes be obtained through contacts with the local industry. Examples of process-support criteria such as solidarity, motivation and continuity are: working on a shared vision of education within a teaching team, working with specialist departments and their accompanying consultative bodies and a certain amount of decision-making delegated from the school management to the teaching staff.

The criteria as competitive values

An integral "harmonious model" of alternative effectiveness criteria was discussed in the previous section. Earlier is was stated that the whole thing gets unstuck when the 'means' become goals in themselves. For further information on this phenomenon of 'goal displacement' see Etzioni, 1964, pp. 10-12. Particularly when one does not want to choose between effectiveness criteria and support conditions, one can also see the various alternative criteria in competition with one another. This viewpoint has been elaborated upon by Faerman & Quinn (1985). They emphasize the fact that organizations vary among one another to the degree that they focus on productivity, adaptability to the environment, continuity and solidarity. The first two categories of criteria express an external orientation, while the second two have an internal inclination. The more energy spent on one or two of these criteria, the less time can be automatically spent on the others. An interesting elaboration of this competing values framework is the assumption that the pattern of priorities among these criteria changes during the course of an organization's development. Young organizations would be largely externally orientated in order to obtain vital resources, while more established organizations would be more concerned with consensus and internal stability. Ultimately, more of a balance could exist, whereby productivity and acquiring input again receive slightly more emphasis than the internal support values.

The competing values perspective can be linked with the means-goal-perspective by assuming that the support conditions (see Table 2.1) could reach certain optimum values, whereby "too much" emphasis on consensus, for instance, would be literally counterproductive.

In this book, the term 'effectiveness' has been reserved for the quantity and quality of the outputs of the primary production process. Within this viewpoint, school effectiveness studies always employ output data (or possibly outcome, see Table 2.1) as criteria. Effectiveness research is of course not only concerned with measuring these outputs, but also strives to ascribe differences in outputs to certain school characteristics. Alternative effectiveness criteria such as adaptability, cohesions, etcetera are seen as conditions that are supportive of productivity. This choice does not imply in any way that these support conditions are insignificant. On the contrary, they are even seen as essential points for attention in order to better understand the effective functioning of schools. Additionally, when translating the results of school effectiveness research in terms of specific practical situations, one should take into account such accompanying organization conditions.

A final observation is that this type of research seldom goes into the question about the priority a school gives to increasing effectiveness in the sense of productivity when confronted with other competing value positions.

2.2.5 Summary and conclusions

The concept of effectiveness is clearly related to means-to-end relationships. When applied to educational phenomena, effectiveness then refers to the degree to which educational means or processes result in the attainment of educational goals. In the language of a simple input-process-output systems model of education, effectiveness could be referred to as the transition of inputs by means of processes into desired outputs and outcomes.

This abstract definition, however, does not resolve all debate on the delineation of the concept of educational effectiveness. Although it can easily be aligned with *economic* constructs like productivity (i.e. the delivery of outputs in a sufficient quantity and quality) and efficiency (sufficient productivity at the lowest possible cost), contributions from organization theory paint a more divergent picture of the construct. Productivity in the economic sense is judged as just one of several definitions of effectiveness, alternative criteria being the flexibility or adaptability of the organization to external circumstances, responsiveness to external stakeholders, involvement and satisfaction of personnel and continuity in the internal functioning of the organization.

Various positions with respect to these alternative effectiveness criteria are possible:
1. A pluralistic and relativistic attitude, where adherence to any one of the criteria is
   thought to be dependent on the actor's position regarding the organization or one's

organization-theoretical preference.

2. A "contingency" perspective, where the predominance of a particular effectiveness criterion is thought to be dependent on the stage in the life-history of organizations or other contingencies.

3. A view, (the one preferred by the author) according to which the available effectiveness criteria are ordered as means-to-end, and whereby productivity is seen as the ultimate effectiveness criterion. The dominant underlying model in school effectiveness research more or less coincides with this latter notion, although the idea to use 'alternative effectiveness criteria' as antecedent conditions to productivity is hardly represented in the available research literature. Questions as to the perspective of actors concerned with effectiveness issues, the scope and temporal context of these issues as well as the dominant methods in assessing achievement serve to make the underlying conception of the dominant model employed in school effectiveness research more explicit. It is concluded that this model can be described as a multi-level, process-product model of learning achievement, propelled by the quest for knowledge by school reformers and national policy-makers, in which as much use as possible is made of objective data, a short-term perspective is discernable and assessment standards are largely comparative.

This section has sought to convey a taste for the complexity of the effectiveness issue. Apart from the various perspectives from which effectiveness has been approached it should be emphasized that, so far, it has been treated in a formal, relatively 'empty' way. In actual practice substantive differences will occur as to which educational goals (cognitive or affective, academic versus more directly functional to every day practice etc.) are more important than others. There has been a strong emphasis on basic skills in traditional school subjects such as, reading, language skills and arithmetic. In the next part of this chapter the main empirical results of various strands of school effectiveness research are summarized in a three-level conceptual model.

2.3 Types of school effectiveness research; towards a comprehensive model

Generally speaking, school effectiveness research is aimed at discovering school characteristics that are positively associated with school output, usually measured as students' achievement. Various research traditions can be subsumed under this heading, including (in)equality of education (sociological), educational production functions (economical), school improvement and effective schools, and teacher- and instructional effectiveness (psychological). Apart from these, more theoretical and analytic contributions from organizational science and micro-economic theory of public-sector organizations can also be sources of inspiration in selecting process indicators (see Cameron & Whetten, 1983 and Niskanen, 1971, respectively).

In this section, the main findings of each of the four types of school effectiveness research will be briefly summarized and used to generate proposals for process indicators.

2.3.1 Research on (in)equality in education and school effects

The Coleman report (Coleman et al., 1966) on the Equal Educational Opportunity Survey should be seen as the impressive starting point for school effectiveness research. Although the major thrust of the Coleman survey was to investigate (in)equality in education, it also became quite famous for its supposed negative conclusions on the influence of school on educational achievement. Coleman et al. found that schools accounted for approximately 10% of the variance in student achievement, after statistical adjustments had been made for the influence of background characteristics of students. The significance of this finding for judging the importance of process indicators on school functioning is that all feasible process indicators one could think of would not account for more than ten percent of the variance in student achievement.

Other large-scale studies replicated Coleman's findings in their pessimistic conclusions on the importance of schooling as such and its possibilities to lower educational inequality (Hauser, Sewell & Alwin, 1976; Jencks et al., 1972, 1979; Thorndike, 1973). Specific school characteristics that were measured in these studies were mainly resources and material inputs (such as the age of the school building, per student expenditure and the number of books in the library) although some measurements of teacher attitudes and classroom management were used. The significance of this first generation of school effectiveness research for the issue of educational indicators can be summarized in three points:

a. School process variables account for relatively little variance in educational achievement. The educational significance of this will be given further consideration in a subsequent section.

b. Resources and "material" inputs are not very promising in explaining school output, though this would not necessarily imply that they should not be included in indicator systems, because in heterogeneous school systems in, for instance, developing countries, they might still be of great importance.

c. Student background characteristics such as socio-economic status or race should be used to adjust raw output measures in order to arrive at fair and valid performance indicators and to allow for an unbiased interpretation of the influence of process characteristics on the functioning of schools.

52

2.3.2 Research on educational production functions

The economic approach to school effectiveness is concerned with the question which inputs lead to more output, also considering the cost of the inputs. Stated in more abstract terms, knowledge about stable relationships between input and output variance is sought in order to specify a function that could express the effects more inputs would have on output. This school of effectiveness research is both known as input output analysis and as research on educational production functions. In fact this type of research is very similar to other types of educational effectiveness research in that the relationships between school characteristics and achievement is investigated, while adjusting for the background characteristics of students (such as level of intelligence and socio-economic status). The characteristic that sets this research tradition apart is the choice of a particular category of inputs that are readily expressed in monetary terms, such as teacher salary, teacher experience, teacher-student ratio, teacher qualifications, per student expenditure.

The results of this type of effectiveness research are rather disappointing. Research reviews like those of Averch (1974), Glasman & Biniaminov (1981), Hanushek (1979, 1986) and Mosteller & Moynihan (1972) agree about the inconsistency of research findings and the rather small effect of the input variables concerned. A research synthesis by Hanushek (1986, p. 1161) shows that only the variable 'teacher experience' shows some consistency, in that 30% of estimated coefficients appeared to be statistically significant. Hanushek's overall conclusion is that educational expenditure is not consistently related to achievement as of yet. He suggests that it would take greater variation in inputs to expect important effects. For instance, the variance in teacher salaries would be expected to increase and significant effects in student achievement might be revealed in most countries where teacher salaries are strictly regulated and rather uniform, if a system of "merit pay" were suddenly to be introduced. The larger significance of input characteristics in effectiveness studies conducted in Third World countries supports this point (see e.g. Windham, 1988).

Although this research tradition does not focus on 'process' measures - in this respect the production functions are rather primitive in that the whole area of educational technology remains a black box - some of the input variables could be considered for inclusion in indicator systems. Judging from Hanushek's research synthesis, teacher experience would be the most likely candidate. Yet, I think, particularly when one wishes to construct educational indicators for international comparison, it would be wise to include variables like per student expenditure and teacher/student ratio, since these might show significant variance between countries.

2.3.3 Effective schools research

After the Coleman report a second wave of school effectiveness research came into being. Its pioneer studies can be seen as a reaction against Coleman's negative conclusions. As titles like "Schools can make a difference" (Brookover et al., 1979) and "School matters" (Mortimore et al., 1988) show, refuting the message of the Coleman report has been, and still is, an important motive for this more recent research. The most important characteristic that distinguishes the effective schools research from earlier school effectiveness research is that the black box of what happens within schools is opened and school variables are revealed that include school organization, school culture and educational technology.

Studies within this new type of school effectiveness research vary from case studies of exceptionally effective schools (e.g. Lezotte et al., 1974; Weber, 1971), to evaluations of school improvement projects (e.g. Achilles & Lintz, 1986; MacCormack-Larkin, 1985; Miller et al., 1985) and to studies that combine relatively large sample survey research with in-depth case-studies (Brookover et al., 1979; Mortimore et al., 1988).

School characteristics that were found to be consistently associated with positive achievement were:

- a safe and orderly school climate
- high expectations of students and an achievement oriented school policy
- educational leadership (i.e. a school leader who is actively involved in developing and monitoring educational activities, and who is more than just an administrator)
- frequent evaluation of the students' progress
- clear objectives concerning basic skills
- continuity and consensus among teachers

It is quite obvious that these effective school characteristics would ideally require intensive data collection and high inference measurement. Some of them, however, can be operationalized in terms of relatively uncomplicated scales or questionnaire items. Some examples are:

Educational leadership
- the amount of time head-teachers spend on educational matters, as opposed to administrative and other tasks
- whether head-teachers discuss test results about students' progress with teachers
- the amount of instructional issues on the agenda of staff meetings

Achievement oriented policy
- the amount of overt statements in official school documents that express an achievement oriented emphasis in school policy

54

Orderly and safe climate
- statistics on absenteeism, lesson drop-out and delinquency as instances of the degree of order in the school
- ratings of school discipline by teachers and head-teachers

Clear objectives
- whether or not explicit school curricula, stating educational objectives and levels of achievement are available

High expectations
- estimates by teachers and/or head-teacher of the percentage of students that will complete their secondary schooling
- student estimates of their further educational career

Monitoring/evaluation of students' progress
- the frequency of the use of curriculum specific tests at each grade level
- the frequency of the use of standardized achievement tests
- whether or not the school uses a (computerized) system to monitor students' progress at all grade levels

Continuity and consensus among teachers
- the amount of changes in staff over a certain period
- the presence or absence of school-subject related working groups of teachers (secondary education)
- the degree of opportunity for communication and cooperation among staff

Some characteristics associated with school effectiveness could be assessed by unobtrusive observations by researchers or inspectors. For instance, the presence or absence of graffiti in and around the school and the noise level in school corridors.

2.3.4 Research on instructional effectiveness

It would be far beyond the scope of this article to attempt to give a comprehensive overview of the research literature on teacher effectiveness, effective classrooms, instructional effectiveness and the like. The distinguishing characteristic of this stream of educational research - compared to the various types of school effectiveness studies, described earlier - is the fact that process characteristics of education are studied at the teacher or classroom level. Therefore, when we consider variables at this level that have been found to be associated with achievement, we are really delving into the primary process of schooling.

Since a detailed overview of the relevant research literature is out of the question, the next best solution in the search for the most promising process variables is to use already existing research reviews. Fortunately, many excellent reviews are available (e.g. Brophy

& Good, 1986; Kyle, 1985). Moreover, a growing amount of quantitative syntheses of research on educational productivity has become available (Fraser et al., 1987; Kulik & Kulik, 1982; Walberg, 1984).

This literature review reveals a set of categories of variables that has repeatedly been shown to be positively associated with achievement. For a more detailed account of the selection of these variables see Scheerens, 1989b. These are:

Effective learning time or 'time on task'. Specific aspects of learning time are: the duration of the school day, school week and school year; whether or not students get homework assignments; the amount of the official duration of lessons actually spent on task-related work; absenteeism; drop-out of lessons; and the reallocation of the total amount of time available for instruction over school subjects. Issues of school discipline are also relevant here since disturbances reduce the amount of time that is effectively available for instruction.

Although interpreting the results of increased effective learning is straightforward, two points should be noted. First, it is obvious that extending the official school hours must at some point become contra-productive. Second, moderate increases in learning time have yielded only moderate effects on achievement (cf. Levin, 1988; Walberg, 1984).

Structured or 'direct' teaching. The general idea of structured or 'direct' teaching is the application of frequent interventions to support the learning process. Examples of these include stating educational objectives clearly, dividing the total subject matter that must be learned into relatively small units, providing a well-planned sequence of these units, providing many opportunities for students to do exercises, giving cues and hints, questioning frequently and testing in order to monitor progress, and giving feedback.

Mastery learning is a didactic approach in which most of these principles are represented. Although direct teaching has been demonstrated to be particularly effective in primary education and for the teaching of basic skills, it has also been shown to work in secondary education and in the teaching of higher order cognitive skills (though in a somewhat modified form - larger steps in subject matter presentation, more initiative for students; cf. Collins & Stevens (1982); Doyle (1985)). Adaptive instruction, i.e. adapting instruction to student characteristics, in matters like tempo and way of presentation, can be seen as a more individualized use of structured teaching.

Opportunity to learn or 'content covered'. The essence of 'opportunity to learn' is the correspondence between the subject matter that has been taught and the content of the tests that are used to measure achievement. As is to be expected, students do better when the subject matter is covered by test-items.

Teacher attitudes and expectations. As was shown in older literature on teacher research, the enthusiastic attitude of teachers is important. From more recent studies where effective teaching is compared to less effective teaching in inner-city schools, it seems important for teachers to remain optimistic about the capabilities of their students; nothing seems worse than a defeatist attitude. This attitudinal factor of teacher functioning directly corresponds to the high expectations variable known from school effectiveness literature.

Enhancing student motivation. According to Walberg's (1984) research synthesis, the variable most strongly related to achievement is reinforcement. This variable is closely related to structured teaching, where frequent monitoring of progress and feedback are important. It appears that praise, or positive feedback, work far better than punishment. (See Brophy & Good (1986) for a more detailed analysis.)

The alterable curriculum of the home. This category of variables - as it was named by Walberg (1984) - covers the ways in which the home situation of students can affect school performance. Positive instances of this category include parental interest in what children do at school, reading to children at home and moderate television viewing.

2.3.5 Towards a comprehensive model

As was apparent from the research review in the previous section, the various schools of educational effectiveness research each concentrate on different aspects and different organizational levels (school and classroom level). When an attempt is made to integrate the results of these different types of effectiveness research, a few 'ordering principles' are required.

First, the analytic systems model, recognizing context, input, process and output variables, serves quite well as a general frame of reference to determine the position of process-indicators.

Second, a multilevel framework is needed in order to do justice to the fact that process-indicators can be defined at the level of the school environment, the institutional level (i.e., the school level) and the classroom level. Furthermore, the student level must also be taken into account, since educational outputs - to which process-indicators should be 'anchored' - should preferably be measured at the lowest level of aggregation.

Third, we need some theoretical perspectives to view the interrelationships between variables at different levels. As such, we could use the basic principles of contingency theory, developed in the field of organizational theory and that of micro-economic theory on the functioning of public sector organizations.

Briefly stated these say the following:

- Contextual characteristics such as environmental and technological constraints determine, whether or not organizational structures or managerial processes will be effective. A specific class of these environmental characteristics are external incentives of organizational efficiency.
- Meso (school-organizational) conditions are to be seen as facilitating conditions of micro (classroom level) conditions.

These two points will be elaborated in the following sub-sections. Further details are given in Scheerens (1989a+b) and in Scheerens & Creemers (1989).

Contingency perspective
The general view of contingency theory is that it depends on contextual characteristics whether or not specific organizational structures or managerial processes will be effective (e.g. Mintzberg, 1979). At first glance contingency theory seems at odds with school effectiveness research, which is concerned with a set of school characteristics that is very robust in predicting effectiveness. On closer analysis of the research and literature on school effectiveness it becomes clear that claims regarding the generalization of effective predictors across contexts have only partly survived empirical tests (Firestone & Herriott, 1982a; Scheerens, Nanninga & Pelgrum, 1989; Teddlie et al., 1987). In fact, the inclusion of contextual variables, such as student-body composition, school type, or national educational context can be seen as a relatively new and very interesting development in school effectiveness research. Some studies even try to establish interactions between various contextual conditions and performance (e.g. Friedkin & Necochea, 1988, who investigated the interactional effect of school size and SES student-body composition on performance).

As school effectiveness research shows, schools differ in the degree to which achievement is emphasized in school policy and teacher expectations. Moreover, achievement orientation is generally found to be positively related to actual achievement. The organizational conceptualization that recognizes effectiveness criteria other than productivity and explains their relative influence in a particular setting by referring to contextual conditions help answer the question why some schools are more achievement oriented than others.

Another instance of contingency thinking relevant to school effectiveness is recognizing the importance of external *incentives* on achievement oriented school policy.

The political will of a school to achieve is perhaps the most essential condition for actual school effectiveness. When higher administrative bodies, consumers, or other stake-holders also emphasize achievement or even reward schools for high achievement and 'punish' others for low, this political will can even be seen as a malleable factor. In this respect a range of measures including output finance of schools, 'privatizing' schools, deregulation, voucher systems and publishing schools' performance in local newspapers is relevant. Micro-economic theories on the efficiency of public sector organizations (i.e. Breton & Wintrobe, 1982; Niskanen, 1971) explain how these mechanisms operate. For our purpose we can put all these external mechanisms to stimulate schools to be effective under the heading *achievement incentives in the local and the larger school environment*. At the local level we could look at the presence or absence of achievement standards for schools, clear objectives, evaluation systems and public records on school achievement. When comparing national educational systems one could measure the presence or absence of assessment projects, the degree to which the inspectorate employs output evaluation, the development of consumerism on education whether or not output finance is used, etc.

Meso-micro relationships
In the review of different types of educational effectiveness research, research which focused on process characteristics at the school level and instructional effectiveness research at the teacher or classroom level were discussed. Both research schools have yielded a list of the most promising process characteristics, i.e. school and instructional characteristics respectively. The relationship between these two categories is an important aspect of the envisaged integrated model of school effectiveness. The most straightforward way of seeing this meso (school level) - micro (classroom level) relationship is to assume that meso-level conditions facilitate micro-level conditions. This implies that instructional processes are seen as the most direct determinants of school learning and achievement, and that organizational and curricular conditions at school level are thought of as more indirect conditions of educational achievement.

When we examine the actual research outcomes on meso and micro conditions of educational achievement more closely, it is evident that some important variables are meaningful at both the school and teacher/classroom level:

- structured teaching at classroom level can be stimulated by means of explicit curricular policy at school level (e.g. by using school development plans);
- high expectations of student performance is essentially a variable defined at the teacher level, though its aggregate, an achievement oriented school policy, may be taken as a whole that is more than the sum of its parts;
- order in classrooms will be enhanced by an orderly atmosphere in other parts of the school building;
- the frequent monitoring of students' progress will usually take place at classroom level, though this evaluation may be a result of a school evaluation policy and will benefit from instruments at this level, such as computerized school evaluation or a management information system;

- the opportunity to learn can be defined at the classroom level, but can also be seen as being enhanced by a school curriculum that is closely linked to the educational objectives that determine the contents of achievement tests.

Apart from these factors that can be defined at both school and classroom level, we can discern a second class of conditions at school level that facilitate effective instruction at classroom level. Their successful operation is dependent on the organization's superstructure (e.g. management, coordination structures) protecting the core production process against disturbances and external uncertainties (Thompson, 1967). Instructional leadership, the degree of collaborative planning, collegial relationships and an active policy in recruiting students and acquiring resources are examples of the latter type of conditions that have received some support in research literature on school effectiveness.

Synthesis

The ingredients for an integrated model of school effectiveness are in place. To summarize we have:

- an analytic systems model recognizing context, input, process and output variables;
- a multi-level framework discerning student-, classroom-, school and environmental characteristics;
- perspectives to view the interrelationships between variables defined at different levels, most notably contingency theory and organizational conditions that facilitate the schools' primary process;
- substantive findings from different types of educational effectiveness research.

Figure 2.3 gives a schematic summary of the model.

One observation that should be made, when considering the variables in Figure 2.3 is that these variables differ in the degree to which they have been supported by empirical research. Generally speaking there is stronger empirical basis for the instructional characteristics at classroom level than for the contextual and school level characteristics.

Theoretical notions about the interrelationships of the various categories of variables provide an extra dimension that the model in Figure 2.1 distinguishes from a mere listing of the most promising variables. Although the empirical testing of this integral model and its theoretical assumptions is clearly beyond the scope of indicator development, its present tentative formulation might nevertheless be helpful in selecting those process variables that are most relevant in exploring the causes of achievement differences between schools.

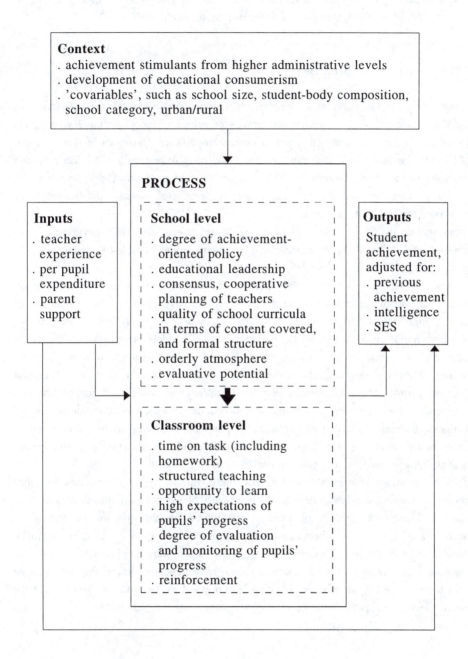

Figure 2.3: *Integrated model of school effectiveness*

In the next section two major theoretical propositions are compared for their potential to explain the findings of empirical school effectiveness research.

2.4 Theories on school effectiveness

Bearing in mind the multi-level structure of comprehensive educational effectiveness models, it is clear that there are different types of relevant theory. At the lowest levels theories on learning and instruction are of central importance. Examples of these are the well-known Carroll model and more recent constructivist perceptions on learning and instruction. At the level of school organization, several models of coordination, such as the so-called garbage-can model, the construct of loosely-coupled systems and the image of professional bureaucracy are relevant.

As far as the interface between schools as organizations and their environment are concerned public choice theory and contingency theory come into play (Scheerens, 1992, 1993).

All these models and theories offer some kind of explanation as to why certain instructional, organizational and administrative conditions appear to be conducive of relatively high educational achievement whilst others do not. Apart from these theories that offer hypothetical explanations on more static models about "what works in education", one should also discern more dynamic perceptions on how to improve schooling. Here the question about the levers of change in education are of central importance. Approaches like emphasizing the self-renewing capacity of schools through professionalization, expecting a technological revolution in education through the use of information technology, posing accountability requirements and emphasizing choice can be seen as modern instances of Bennis, Benne and Chin's (1969) distinction of normative re-educative, rational-analytic and power-coercive strategies respectively.

Referring for more extensive treatments of these various types of theories to other publications (Scheerens, 1992, 1993 and 1993a), just two conceptual frameworks will be discussed. These two schools of thought concentrate on the question of control in education and are seen as alternative and perhaps competing views on how to make schooling more effective. Although these two views are usually employed at the level of the school organization and the school and school-environment interface, they can also be shown to be geared to alternative views on learning and instruction. The labels used for these two basic conceptual frameworks are 'rational control' and 'choice'.

2.4.1 Evaluation-centered rational control

From the perspective of control theory the availability of an evaluation mechanism is a basic prerequisite for control (De Leeuw, 1974). The availability of an evaluation mechanism is also seen as the least demanding characterization of an organizational goal. Thus, organizational functioning is amenable to rational (i.e. goal-oriented) control, whenever the state of affairs at a given point in time can be assessed, for instance through appraisal by a committee of experts.

Conceptually, evaluation of goal-attainment is very close to the concept of effectiveness (i.e. successful goal-attainment) itself. Evaluation has a central place in most conceptual models and theories that bear upon educational effectiveness. Frequent assessment is one of the basic properties of direct teaching and instructional approaches aimed at mastery-learning. At the organizational level evaluation and monitoring are at the core of the concept of organizational learning (Morgan, 1986) and of the image of the learning organization (Senge, 1990).

In empirical school effectiveness research, assessment at classroom level and the use of records for school management have repeatedly been shown to be positively associated with achievement.

Rational control that depends on monitoring, evaluation and appraisal of organizational functioning can be seen as a 'modest' retroactive type of organizational decision-making that is closer to incrementalism than to synoptic planning. Rather than thinking of control and planning in terms of setting objectives and then using systematic or even scientific methods to select the most effective strategies or methods to attain the objectives, retroactive planning or evaluation-centered policy-making starts the other way around by assessing the current state of the system and then setting concrete targets in terms of improved performance.

The evaluation-feedback-reinforcement sequence allows for both cognitive (learning theory) and motivational (control theory) interpretations. It can thus be seen as a central explanatory mechanism of effective schooling: the better it functions the greater the likelihood of an effectively functioning educational organization. The cognitive interpretation can be associated with stimulating learning processes at both the classroom and organizational level, while the control-theoretical interpretation focuses on the possibility of holding educational organizations accountable and to suppressing goal-displacement. It should be noted that this type of evaluation-centered control allows for complete liberty as to the choice of methods and processes by schools.

Nevertheless evaluation-centered control of educational organizations does pose some problems. First, it may prove difficult in actual practice to reconcile the controlling and the cognitive aspect, that is the use of evaluations for accountability purposes as well as for purposes of self-improvement. Second, evaluations may give rise to certain types of undesired side-effects such as resistance from teachers, overt sabotage and political bias in the use of outcomes.

Third, evaluation-centered policy could lead to formalization, too much standardization and 'red tape' and thus frustrate rather than stimulate effectiveness-enhancing innovations. Fourth, evaluations may be blatantly reductionistic, technically unsound and lead to problems in the communicative aspects of interpreting and feeding back the results.

These difficulties and draw-backs do not, however, undermine the thesis that properly conducted evaluation-feedback-reinforcement cycles are central to the effective functioning of school organizations.

2.4.2 Choice

In many industrialized countries the distribution of authority across administrative levels is presently being reconsidered, resulting in formerly "decentralized" systems tending to become more centralized in certain areas (e.g. a national curriculum in the U.K.), while formerly 'centralized' systems delegate more authority to the school (e.g. France)-OECD, 1993. However, the general tendency of these shifts in the authority distributions is to make schools more autonomous. Sometimes it appears as if governments see decentralization as a panacea - expecting that more school autonomy will in some miraculous way enhance quality and educational effectiveness.

Although aspects of 'restructuring' such as increasing school autonomy, school-based management and strengthening the professional role of teachers appear to be part of a more market-oriented change in educational policy, strictly speaking they are not. The essence of choice as an alternative to the bureaucratic controls that result from the way representative democracy works is that a completely different, more 'local' type of democracy is called for in which most authority is vested directly in the schools, parents and students (Chubb and Moe, 1990, p. 218). In their 'proposal for reform' these authors draw a picture of an educational system where almost all higher level authority is eliminated and where there is a lot of liberty to found schools, a funding system that is largely dependent on the success of schools in free competition for students, freedom of choice of schools for parents and freedom for schools to have their own admission policies. According to this philosophy schools would be legally autonomous and free to govern themselves as they want (ibid p. 226). Chubb and Moe are emphatic in renouncing hybrid constructions in which some measures to strengthen choice are combined with modified forms of bureaucratic control (such as posing centralized accountability requirements to otherwise decentralized educational systems), because they fear that such measures will eventually paralyse the incentives to be client-centered and efficient, which are expected when operating in a free market situation. The theory behind the propagation of choice as an alternative control mechanism in education is the economic theory of political processes, more often labelled as 'public choice theory'. Part of this theory refers to the functioning of public sector *organizations*, such as government departments and schools.

In essence this part of the theory states that the incentive structure within public-sector organizations is such that the motives of managers and employees are likely to be distracted from efficient goal attainment and goal-displacement. This latter phenomenon can be depicted as a situation in which the means of the organization become an end in itself, which will then lead to higher budgets, more staff, more activities and more management than efficient production would require. Moreover, review and evaluation procedures by higher administrative levels are seen as inadequate controls, because of lack of time and expertise, because production functions are unknown or kept secret and because of opportunities for officials to successfully fend off critical evaluations. The remedy for all these ailments in the functioning of public-sector organizations, as Chubb and Moe (ibid) have stated, is to allow market forces to operate and make schools more like private enterprises. There are some intrinsic problems with the application of the choice-framework to education. In the first place, it is unrealistic to expect that educational goals (and their assessment) will ever be completely determined at a local level. More general societal demands and requirements that stem from a particular culture will have to be met by schools. Accepting this implies accepting that there will be some central regulations, such as minimal attainment targets and accountability requirements. Second, it is hard to imagine how the choice-framework can cope with the ideal of providing equal opportunities in education. In all probability better educated parents will be able to profit more from information needed to optimize choice of schools for their children than parents from lower social economic levels. Finally, public choice theory may draw too bleak a picture of the knowledge available on educational productivity and the technical developments in educational evaluation and assessment. To the degree that these are better, the application of evaluation-centered control as discussed in the previous section is more feasible than partisans of the choice-framework would have us believe. The theoretical position discussed in this chapter has some implications for educational effectiveness research. First, it draws attention to the comparative effectiveness of private and public schools, particularly as to hypothetical explanations of achievement differences (that have mostly favored private schools). Second, incentives and 'micro-economics' of central processes in education should receive emphasis in future effectiveness-oriented research. And third, as discussed in the previous section, attention is drawn to the functioning of evaluation and review processes in educational systems.

2.4.3 Contingency theory as an encompassing framework

As pointed out before, the two theoretical frameworks are not exhaustive in any consideration of the various theories that are relevant in providing an explanatory background of comprehensive educational effectiveness models. For instance, they do not directly bear upon questions about further professionalization of teachers and on the application of modern information technology in education.

Nevertheless, they can be seen as two basic control mechanisms that are behind two more encompassing theories on the functioning of educational systems. Rational control is in line with comprehensive educational effectiveness models as induced from various categories of empirical educational-effectiveness research. Choice can be seen as the central mechanism of a multi-level conceptual framework of restructuring. A comparison of these two multi-level frameworks is depicted in Figure 2.4 (from Scheerens, 1993a).

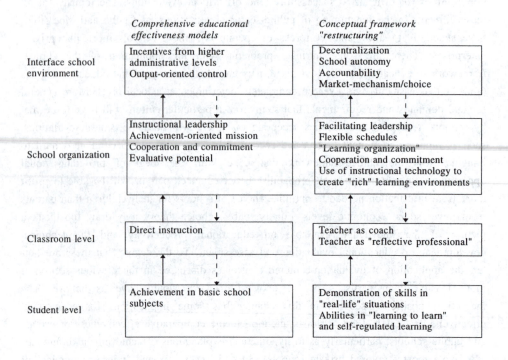

Figure 2.4: *Global comparison of comprehensive school effectiveness models and conceptual framework of restructuring*

The arrows in solid lines indicate the direction for design (bottom up). The arrows in dotted lines indicate the actual functioning of the system where higher level processes are seen as facilitative conditions for lower levels.

The basic dimension that distinguishes these two frameworks is the amount of structure provided from a higher level to a lower level. At the instructional level, direct teaching implies a lot of structure provided to the learner by the teacher and/or the teaching method, whereas constructivistic approaches emphasize discovery learning-types of instructional settings. At the level of the school organization, effectiveness research has generated the picture of an instructional leader actively involved in arranging instructional conditions at the lower (classroom) level, whereas restructuring speaks of a school-leader as a facilitator and of teacher-empowerment. The distinction between rational, output-oriented control on the one hand and choice on the other, discussed in the preceding sections, is met at the level of school governance.

In drawing matters to a close, the following questions need to be addressed:

- To what extent are the two conceptual frameworks of rational control and choice and the related frameworks of comprehensive school effectiveness and restructuring models irreconcilable?
- Would a contingency-plan be useful in which the needed amount of higher-level structuring should be seen as dependent on the 'situation'?
- How useful are these conceptions of 'comprehensive' models and 'encompassing' frameworks to the furthering of school effectiveness research?

It should be noted that the concept of evaluation-centered control is a modified version of the model of rational or synoptic planning in that it makes no requirements in terms of blue-prints, long term objectives and process-control. In this it is a sparse and 'lean' derivative of rational planning. Contrary to the position that Chubb and Moe (1990) have taken on this issue, a case can be made for a functional combination of evaluation-centered educational policy and for providing opportunities for choice. This would come down to the monitoring of certain output-indicators and attainment targets by administrative levels above the schools and for the rest leaving it up to the schools to choose their ways and means of reaching these targets. Moreover, attainment-targets and outcome indicators might be limited to the 'basics' of schooling. It could even be argued that without valid (i.e. value-added) output indicators, the informational basis needed by the consumers of education in order to make rational choices would be insufficient, so that 'choice' could not even be seen to function properly without a proper evaluation mechanism.

As to the second question, contingency theory would maintain that in certain situations or contexts higher- level structuring would be warranted and in others not. For instance, in the relatively stable situation of primary schools structuring in terms of fixed objectives, core curricula, didactic approaches and assessment would be expected to be more effective than in-service training schemes for adults within the context of companies operating in a dynamic environment. Likewise, higher-level structuring would be expected to meet with less resistance in educational systems that have a more centralistic tradition than these with more decentralized systems.

The problem with hypotheses that can be deducted from contingency-theory is that they tend to be rather general and provide lots of difficulties as far as empirical testing is concerned (although international comparisons and historical investigations offer interesting possibilities). This in facts leads to the third question about the usefulness of comprehensive models and encompassing conceptual frameworks for the furthering of educational effectiveness research and school improvement. To the extent that the search for central mechanisms that could explain the workings of educational effectiveness models has been successful, the results (the evaluation - feedback- reinforcement sequence, choice and the degree of structuring from a higher administrative level) could be used in selecting the key-variables for comparative (correlational or quasi-experimental) studies. Objects of such comparisons could be direct instruction vs. constructivist instructional practice, instructional leadership vs. facilitative leadership aimed at teacher-empowerment; and choice controlled vs. 'evaluation-controlled' school systems.

A less global use of contingency-thinking could be made if it is connected to the generalizibility claims of comprehensive educational-effectiveness models. In that case more specific hypotheses about the impact of the central variable 'degree of higher level control' could be raised, and depending on the context, the particular sub-group of students concerned and the type of educational outcomes. In that way the question of the validity of general vs. more partial educational-effectiveness models can be settled empirically.

2.5 Conclusion

In this chapter a lot of ideas about what makes schools effective have been presented.

These ideas provide a particular orientation to organizational phenomena that are discussed in other chapters. With respect to *coordination*, effective schools research has emphasized consensus on school goals, particularly a common orientation towards achievement in subject matter related educational objectives. Apart from agreement on this basic orientation, at a more practical level, alignment of curriculum planning across grades has been underlined. In this respect the message of school effectiveness departs from descriptions of the school as a 'loosely coupled' system, or even 'organized anarchy'. It is important to note, however, that implications from school effectiveness research do not merely state that there should be more coordination. There is also a substantive orientation as to what should be the contents of this coordination, namely achievement orientation and alignment of curricular offerings throughout the school. Effective schools research also offers some prescriptions with respect to the technology of the *primary process of teaching and learning*. Structured approaches, like mastery learning and 'direct instruction' have been shown to be most effective. In these structured approaches educational objectives are clearly stated and the learning process is closely guided and monitored by presenting subject matter in small steps and frequently assessing learning progress. In recent, more constructivist orientations to learning and instruction, there is a somewhat contrary orientation in emphasizing independent learning (see section 2.4). On closer analysis, differences may not be as absolute as they seem, and structuring can be seen to have a place in more constructivist oriented approaches too.

An aspect of the findings of instructional effectiveness research that remains unchallenged is the importance of good classroom management which optimizes 'time on task' and 'opportunity to learn' in the sense of a good correspondence between subject matter taught and subject matter tested.

School effectiveness research has been quite consistent in underlining the importance of 'instructional' or 'educational *leadership*'. This position with respect to leadership and school management implies that effective school leaders not just 'mind the shop' and take care of a smooth running of administrative and organizational matters. Instructional leadership means that the school leader is overtly concerned with the school curriculum, the learning and teaching in classrooms and the records on student achievement. This overt concern should not be seen as a head-teacher, but rather as a type of meta-control, which means that facilitative conditions are created and that outcomes are monitored.

With respect to *school environment connections,* school effectiveness research has been mostly concerned with contacts with parents. Parental involvement has repeatedly been shown as a relevant condition of effective schooling. Parent involvement can vary from parents being members of school boards and advisory committees, to parents being actively involved in classrooms. With one exception other external contacts have not received much attention in empirical school effectiveness research. The exception is the relationship with the school board. There is some evidence that achievement press from a higher administrative level, like the school board or the municipality, is conducive to school effectiveness.

Teacher *commitment* to an achievement-oriented educational philosophy is an important aspect of the type of school climate that school effectiveness research has pointed at.

In fact the empirical findings of school effectiveness research relate to *cultural* aspects like achievement orientation, commitment and high expectations on the one hand and *structural* aspects like frequent assessment and structured teaching on the other.

PART II

Aspects of School Organization
and Management

• CHAPTER 3 •

The Primary Process from an Organizational Point of View

A.J. Visscher

University of Twente, The Netherlands

3.1 Introduction

In this chapter the concept 'technology' is treated from the point of view of organizational theory, meaning that the so-called *operations technology* of organizations is discussed. In section 3.2 'primary process' and 'technology' are defined followed by a characterization of technology of schools according to three types of technology distinguished by Thompson (1967): the long linked, the mediating and the intensive technology. In section 3.3 the technology of educational institutions is portrayed further on the basis of three of its dimensions: uncertainty, interdependence and complexity. In section 3.4 empirical evidence is presented on the degree to which features of the primary process influence school effectiveness.

3.2 Two definitions

Before going further, we must first define two central terms: 'primary process' and 'technology'.

The primary organizational process concerns the major, central process within an organization. All other organizational processes and elements operate in support of this (primary) process of which the ultimate aim is to realize the organizational goals. These goals vary between organizations, for instance from maximizing car sales in the case of a car dealership, to developing a municipal policy within a municipality. In an educational organization, the primary process concerns the teaching-learning process within which students are trained and educated. All other organizational processes within the school, such as recruiting students, constructing timetables, registering student data and copying instructional material are carried out in support of the primary process.

In a school, the teaching-learning process is by far the largest organizational process with most school staff comprised of teachers who operate mainly within the primary process of the school. A relatively small part of a school's organizational staff does not operate in this 'operational core' (Mintzberg, 1979), but in organizational parts whose job it is to control (school management), support (e.g. the caretaker, cleaning service, school cafeteria staff), or prepare and optimize (for instance a school committee developing a curriculum) the primary process. In this respect schools differ from other types of organizations which exhibit different relationships between their organizational elements (in terms of their relative size and importance). In a company producing cars the operating core is smaller, whereas the number of staff supporting, preparing, optimizing and managing the primary process is much larger.

In the primary process a certain type of technology is used. It is stressed in this chapter that the meaning of the concept 'technology' from organizational theory is central. In other words, other meanings of the concept as in 'information technology' (the combination of hardware and software) and in a 'technological approach' (a specific way of operating, problem solving) are not under discussion here.

Although the term 'technology' is a central concept in organizational theory, it is interpreted in various ways. Mintzberg (1979) refers to Child who states "the term technology is employed in almost as many different senses as there are writers on the subject".

In organizational theory the term 'operations technology' is used for the know-how and skills of organizational staff, and the methods used by them to transform input into output (McPherson et al., 1986). Included in this concept are both techniques applied to analyze the relevant features of the raw material (the input of the organization), as well as techniques for designing the transformation process (input into output), and all kinds of arrangements made on the shop floor to realize the desired output.

After this abstract characterization of the technology concept, an illustration is called for. In a car factory the raw material entering the primary process consists of steel that is first analyzed on features relevant to the transformation process (e.g. its hardness and overall quality). Subsequently, the steel is manipulated by applying various techniques in such a way that the production process finally results in a car that rolls from the assembly belt. Since large numbers of the same output are produced, a standard production method can be followed for transforming input into output. The technology used in the factory is routine and predictable, and can therefore even be translated into machines and robots.

In a school the raw material consists of students who have been admitted. They are 'raw' because they are relatively untrained and uneducated with respect to the attainment targets of the school. The operations technology of schools consists of the knowledge, skills and techniques used to bring students to the level of the attainment targets of a specific school

type. In other words, it concerns the expertise, skills and techniques used to:
- determine student features (e.g. their educational level, background, interests and so on);
- choose the most suitable instructional contents for a specific group of students;
- search for the most desirable instructional strategy: e.g. the sequence with which subject matter components are taught, required grouping patterns, assignments etcetera.

Put more generally, the technology of schools concerns the expertise in the subject areas taught, as well as know-how with respect to the didactics of subject-matter and with regard to general pedagogical-didactical principles (e.g. how to deal with undesirable behavior).

3.2.1 Three technology types

Thompson (1967) distinguishes three principles for creating the technological core of an organization:
- 'the long linked technology': a long chain of activities that need to be carried out *after each other*. An operation must be completed before the next can start. The assembly line with its strict sequence of activities is the most obvious example of the long linked technology.
- 'the mediating technology': an organization brings various categories of otherwise independent elements together to enable each member to fulfil his needs (which would not have been fulfilled otherwise). A bank is an organization which is designed to bring together people with the complementary desires to borrow or lend money.
- 'the intensive technology': in this organization various operations have to be carried out in mutual adjustment. The selection, combination and sequence of activities is important and influenced by information about and from the object to be treated itself (feedback). For example, the therapy a patient receives has to be the result of a careful consideration, and moreover has to be adjusted as a consequence of the feedback a patient gives in response to the therapy.

To what degree do we recognize these three technology types in educational organizations? The *long linked technology* is for instance found in the sequence of grades in schools and in the sequence of subject matter elements within grades.
The *mediating technology* is also applicable to education in the sense that if one regards the educational system as a whole, education is a matter of searching for 'matching' instruction (in terms of educational levels, school types and subjects). In other words, those in need of a specific type of instruction are brought together with those who can

supply it.

In the case of *intensive technology*, the close cooperation between teachers, for example concerning teaching and student counselling are central. Instruction is not provided in one standard manner as is done in case of mediating technology. The teaching staff now cooperates intensively and pays a lot of attention to the specific characteristics of each individual student and to his/her feedback on a certain type of instruction. This type of technology is especially used in the transition grades of schools which are meant to determine which school type is best suited for which students, given their capacities, motivation and so on. In transition grades, student groups are heterogeneous; they have not been selected according to achievement level and interest. Some schools invest quite a lot of energy in this orientation and selection process. Teachers in these grades individualize their instructional activities and communicate with one another about the way in which students react to instructional strategies. Subsequently, they adapt their instructional activities on the basis of the feedback received.

Of these three technologies the mediating technology is probably the most dominant in schools: there is little interdependency between the teaching staff; on the basis of assumed similarities, students are sorted out into school types and classes in which each student group receives a standard treatment.

The intensive technology can also be important in education, namely when students are treated in accordance with their individual characteristics, and when instruction is modified as a result of student feedback. However, intensive communication and mutual adjustment between teachers are prerequisites for this type of technology, conditions that have not been met in many schools.

Although the long linked technology is clearly visible, it is least dominant in educational institutions since the continuity in the links of the chain are broken at some spots (for example as a result of the transfer between school types). Moreover, the required planning of activities among teaching staff is not always fulfilled. The planning of chains of didactical actions is to a strong degree imposed upon by the commercial instructional material used.

3.3 Three technology dimensions

The technology applied in the primary process of schools is characterized now by means of three generally accepted technology dimensions: uncertainty, interdependence and complexity (McPherson et al., 1986).

3.3.1 Uncertainty

There is a lot of uncertainty in schools. Because financial resources (especially jobs) vary every year as a result of fluctuations in student enrolment, (student numbers determine a school's budget) planning in the allocation of resources for a period greater than one school year could be considered unrealistic.

Another cause of uncertainty is that the organizational goals of educational institutions in many cases form no clear line of action for school staff. They are often formulated in abstract terms and therefore can be carried out in many ways. Moreover, individual goals of school staff differ frequently from the official organizational goals.

Since it is often vague what an educational organization strives for and how organizational activities can best be directed to the organizational goals, it is very difficult to evaluate the degree to which the targets of the organization have been achieved. Evaluation is also difficult because most student tests only determine the mastery of cognitive know-how and skills which usually only represent part of the school's goals. To what degree the other school goals are achieved remains unclear.

One can also question the objectivity of specific achievement tests (different teachers judge the same answers in different ways, and based on that arrive at different evaluations of the quality of the primary process). Finally, the number of variables influencing student achievement is so great (e.g. features of students, the school, the media, the peer group and the family) that it is difficult to determine which factor(s) has/have caused certain effects.

Huberman (1983) typifies achievement tests as 'substitute indices'. They are meant to indicate educational results, however the degree to which test scores are actually attributable to the instructional activities is unsure.

The described uncertainty in schools with respect to resources, organizational goals and the effects of organizational activity makes it difficult to determine and choose the preferable technology.

Huberman (1983) has carried out a situational analysis of the classroom. He typifies the work of teachers as being multidimensional; teachers have to carry out many different tasks such as presenting subject matter, reacting, organizing, asking questions, stimulating, and evaluating. Moreover, they have to pay attention to different matters simultaneously. One student asks a question, another raises his finger to react, a third has not returned from the toilet yet, and a group of other students needs attention because they misbehave.

Huberman states that the teaching situation will always remain uncertain and never be controlled perfectly. Not everything that happens in it can be understood and explained from a scientific viewpoint. In this respect Huberman refers to Lortie (1975) who observes that the mood a teacher is in influences his teaching behavior strongly. A well prepared lesson may not produce the desired results, whereas un unprepared lesson may prove to be very effective.

Teachers do not have an awful lot of time to reflect on what happens in their classrooms and on their own role. Their primary goal is to solve the short term problem of how to attract the attention of students and how to promote their efforts. To teach is to a large extent 'to improvise well', that is, to judge intuitively what should be done in a specific situation and use heuristics and tricks that have proven to work in the past.

Teachers take decisions before (on instructional content, activities and organization), during (react to what happens) and after instruction (evaluation). Riehl et al. (1992) conclude that two conditions of teacher work provide special constraints on their information handling:

a. they receive much fast-breaking news (Stinchcombe, 1990) on the social and cognitive student features from the students they have contact with, makes heavy demands on teachers' information processing capacity;

b. there is little time in which teachers do not spend time with students, during which the overwhelming body of information on students can be processed, and in which strategies for its use can be developed.

Despite the constraints on their information use teachers do use a lot of information about students. They react to the two aforementioned work conditions by using only the most salient information, and reducing their need for information processing. Greater salience of information means that information is:

- generated by themselves;
- vivid, emotionally compelling, concrete and close to their own experience (personalistic/qualitative instead of abstract/quantitative, and pertaining to social/behavioral as opposed to academic matters);
- presented in face to face interaction and continuously (no long or irregular intervals);
- confirming their own experience;
- considered necessary for their work;
- linked to immediate courses of action.

The reduction of the need for information processing is caused by the flood of data, in combination with the limited time for considering student needs and teaching objectives (an instructional decision is taken about every 2 minutes), and the limitations of the human information processing capacity.

This is done by relying on instructional routines that have proven to be successful in the past, basing actions on a simple model of reality, and interpreting and using information rapidly and selectively (Shavelson & Stern, 1981). In addition, certain techniques are used to simplify information collection and processing e.g. collecting information on a student sample as a point of reference for the whole student population. Students are evaluated quickly, and on the basis of incomplete information.

The perceived information quality is more important than its objective quality. Information is 'good' if it comes quickly, is immediately accessible, and serves as a starting point for actions. It must fit into how teachers work and into their frames of reference (acting intuitively and welcoming information that can be used to reduce uncertainty).

Pijl (1988) on the basis of his research concludes that teachers have a global impression of a student (group) on the basis of which they choose a standard instructional strategy from the tool kit of action plans they possess as a result of their professional training and previous teaching experience. A chosen strategy encompasses a whole range of decisions regarding 'what is done and how', implying that many decisions do not have to be taken anymore. Only very radical changes in their opinion on a student (group) may result in a switch to a different (standard) approach.

Teachers tend to have relatively stable judgements about the academic ability and/or needs of students. Assessments made at the start of a school year usually change very little thereafter (Morine-Dershimer, 1978).

Summarizing, teachers have to make many decisions in an uncertain context and are burdened with information with little time to process and reflect on it. They therefore reduce their need for information processing and use information selectively. Full rational behavior in terms of choosing the best mode of operation for achieving explicit goals, after having analyzed all relevant information is rare. Many actions are uninformed or based on inaccurate information. The perceived information quality is more decisive for its usage than its objective quality. There is a strong preference for up-to-date, quickly available, directly usable, informal, clear and action triggering information.

In general terms, technological uncertainty can be caused in organizations as a result of:
• variation in the input to be transformed;
• exceptions in the transformation process;
• variation in the output to be produced.

The greater the variability in the material (the input) to be transformed, as well as in the product (the output), the larger the number of exceptions in the transformation process and, the greater the uncertainty and less routine the technology will be.

On the basis of two variables, namely the degree of stability in the raw material to be transformed, and the extent to which the players know how to operate in case of exceptions, Perrow (1970) makes a distinction between four types of technology that in his view occur in different types of organizations, and that vary concerning their degree of uncertainty (see Table 3.1).

79

In cell A of Table 3.1 there are few exceptions in the raw material, but if exceptions do occur, the employee is on his own to find a solution. In this case, control of work processes is greatly in the hands of employees, for example a craftsman who makes furniture.

In cell B the situation is very uncertain. There is a lot of variation in the raw material to be transformed in this cell. Moreover, ready-made solutions for dealing with exceptions are missing. Organizational consultancy agencies and advertising agencies are some examples of enterprises operating in such situations: every order is different and requires a creative approach for solving it.

In the case of cell C routine work like mass production is central: there is little variation in the raw material, and in case of variation there is little uncertainty concerning what needs to be done. The output to be realized and the way in which output should be produced are primarily determined by staff other than the employee who carries out the work.

Table 3.1: *Types of technology according to Perrow (1970)*

how to handle exceptions	stability of raw material	few exceptions	many exceptions
unanalyzable search		A craft	B non-routine work
analyzable search		C routine work	D engineering

On the contrary, in variant D there exists a lot of variation in the raw material, but here it is known how exceptions should be dealt with. Surgeons and designers of computer-assisted information systems, for example, operate in such situations. Their 'raw material' is rarely completely identical, but it is nevertheless clear what should be done since the problem is a variation to a known situation and suitable techniques can be applied. In cell C the problems are also known problems just as are their solutions. In cells A and B, on the contrary, experience, personal insight and intuition of employees are crucial since they are confronted with exceptions the solution to which are unknown.

The question arises of course where schools should be located in Table 3.1. An unequivocal answer to this question is impossible since the vision that school staff have of their raw material is decisive in this context. In *people-changing organizations* the way in which the staff views the raw material (people) determines the extent of uncertainty that prevails within a specific organization. If the people entering such an organization who are to be transformed in a certain way are considered to be more or less similar, and if these people are treated in a standard way, then the -self created- certainty is relatively great. On the other hand, if every client is approached as being unique and needing a tailored 'treatment', then uncertainty is much greater.

This phenomenon can also be observed in the world of education. Think for instance of the difference between a school providing only one type of education and comprehensive schools. The former school type has been set up to cater to students who are considered suitable for one specific type of education as far as intellectual capacities and interests are concerned. Although a standard treatment of students is probably dominant in these schools (dependent of the educational philosophy of the teaching staff) not all schools of this type honor differences between students to the same degree. In other words, even in these schools staff may individualize instruction to a certain degree as a result of their view on variation in student features.

Comprehensive schools are more directed toward taking into account the differences between students. In contrast with schools providing one type of education for one type of student, comprehensive schools are composed of students with varying capacities, interests and backgrounds, with particular regard to their first grades, student groups are heterogenous and uncertainty is big: instable raw material and many exceptions in the transformation process. However, as clarity with respect to student capacities and student motivation grows, stability and certainty also increase.

In schools the educational philosophy of school staff also contributes to the extent of uncertainty in the teaching-learning process. The more a school wishes to take into account the differences between students, the more instruction has to be adjusted, and the greater uncertainty is.

A general conclusion must be that the way in which a school views its students determines in which cell that school should be placed. The way in which individual differences between students in terms of intelligence, previous training, socio-cultural background, motivation etcetera are viewed, and the degree to which a school wishes to honor these differences influences the magnitude of uncertainty in the primary process of schools.

With respect to technological uncertainty in schools the research of Rowan, Raudenbush, & Y.F. Cheong (1993) is very interesting. Rowan et al. studied the relevance of contingency theory for research on schools by investigating the extent of task routinization in schools, thereby focussing on the following questions:

- which instructional conditions make teaching nonroutine?;
- do organic management forms for coordinating and controlling instruction arise if teachers' work becomes nonroutine?;

- does organic management promote the job related learning of teachers and thereby enhance their effectiveness?

Rowan and colleagues, following Perrow (1967) and Thompson (1967) argue that two dimensions of task environments have important effects on the nature of work in organizations:

- the extent to which task environments contain *variability*; work is supposed to become less routine as workers confront inputs and task demands that (are perceived to) vary;
- *task knowledge*, for some tasks clear rules are available to cope with task variation and complexity, for more nonroutine tasks this certainty may not exist.

The study of Rowan et al. strongly confirms that the degree to which teachers perceive variation in students affects the extent to which teaching becomes a nonroutine task. It also shows that the task knowledge differs across academic disciplines (some subjects are more routine than others) and influences routinization. Disciplinary specialization goes together with different assumptions about the nature of teaching. The teaching of certain subjects is perceived as being more routine than the teaching of others. There is for example less diversity in topics, goals and approaches in teaching mathematics than in teaching social studies (even if one and the same teacher teaches the two subjects). In other words, there is more routine in the teaching of mathematics.

The foregoing implies that the extent to which teaching becomes a nonroutine task varies between schools and between subjects, or, put differently, between and within schools. It also means that the extent to which teacher work is uncertain varies! School organizations do not contain one but many different technologies. Compared with specific other organizations the technology of schools is complex, however this is a very strong generalization since it goes more for some subjects than for others.

The results of Rowan et al. support the assumption that technology differences between and within schools go together with management differences. Rowan et al. distinguish between mechanistic management (characterized by centralization, formalization, and directive leadership) and organic management (participative decision-making, teamwork, collaborative problem-solving, supportive leadership). Organic management is assumed to accomplish organizational effectiveness in uncertain, nonroutine environments since it enables employees to learn from each other, to work effectively in those environments. The research results of Rowan et al. did show that teachers who work in nonroutine task environments do experience more job-related learning, however this was not facilitated by organic management. Rowan et al. suggest that if there is no relationship between organic management and teachers' job-related learning, the function of organic school management may be that organic management increases:

- teacher motivation and commitment to the uncertain task of teaching;

- teachers' personal sense of efficacy, allowing them to enact a variety of instructional techniques in order to cope with student diversity.

Since task routinization is strongly related with school management patterns the study of how task routinization is related with teachers' beliefs, disciplinary specialization and instructional arrangements is important. The research on educational administration and the study of teaching can be connected in this way and answer questions of the following type. "Does organic management improve classroom teaching and school effectiveness, and if, how?" "Which organizational arrangements match with how subjects are taught?" Rowan et al. hold a plea for more contingency theory based research on the conditions under which different teachers work, how these conditions make classroom teaching more or less routine and which school organizational and management arrangements match best with specific primary process features.

Certain dimensions of school organizations and school management vary as well between as within schools! The task environments of different school organizational sub units varies and control over instruction varies across sub units within schools.

Schools that desire more certainty in the primary process can accomplish this by making their clients and work processes more predictable. This can be achieved by:

a. regarding variety in clientele immaterial to transformation process (treat all in the same way);

b. not allowing specific input (students), and/or selecting admitted students;

c. recruiting experienced, trained personnel mastering a repertory of modes of operation (= standard program) who discern patterns in variability which permits to respond in predetermined ways (some routinization), and who know how to operate under uncertain classroom situations.

Regarding option b:

A school can admit students and thereafter track them into categories or 'production lines' (school divisions) in which a category of students is approached in one standard way. Mintzberg (1979) typifies this method as 'pigeonholing': constructing 'boxes' (= production lines), a student is allocated to one of them and within this box the student receives the standard treatment which is characteristic for that box. This mode of operation offers the advantage that not every piece of raw material to be transformed has to be treated in an unique way, but at the same time one may question whether the differences between students receive enough attention. In many cases the previous training a student has received is the most important basis for his/her allocation to a 'pigeon hole'. Such factors as how a student learns, as well as his/her interests and needs play little or no role in this allocation process.

Regarding option c:

As a result of their training, all teaching staff have acquired subject matter know-how, and didactical skills which means that different teachers operate in a more or less standard way in their classrooms. This is another way of bringing some certainty into the complex work (unpredictable student behavior, subject matter complexity) of educational institutions.

The 'tried and true' (McPherson et al., 1986), 'this is how we do it, because we have good experiences with it' (which is not the same as 'the method that produces the best results') determines how teachers operate to a great extent which leads to a certain degree of stability.

Despite these arrangements there remains quite a lot of uncertainty in the work of teachers. This is especially true for instructional situations without a long tradition, like new school types in which the most suitable instructional methods are still being sought. If classroom innovations are carried out, uncertainty also increases. To be able to cope with these uncertainties, a teacher has to be a professional and possess considerable autonomy.

3.3.2 Interdependence

Interdependence between the work processes of organizational staff concerns the second dimension upon which the operations technology of organizations can be characterized. When the performance of one worker poses contingencies for the performance of the other interdependence exists between them (Weick, 1976). Thompson (1967) makes a distinction between three types of inter-dependence: pooled, sequential and reciprocal interdependence. *Pooled* interdependence concerns the sharing of common organizational resources, something that is done in every organization. Teachers for example share the financial resources of their school, its classrooms, audio-visual equipment services and so on. This type of dependence remains restricted to the resources shared and does not form a problem as long as these resources are not scarce.

Sequential interdependence means that a series of organizational activities are carried out with a strict sequence. Some activities have to be carried out before others can and after others have been carried out. In a mass-producing car enterprise, the parts of a car are first produced and subsequently assembled in a strict sequence. In this case employees are more interdependent than in the case of pooled interdependence since taking away one activity from the chain of activities disturbs the execution of all subsequently planned in activities. One activity determines the starting situation for subsequent activities, but not vice versa.

This type of interdependence can also be observed in education: a strict sequence of grades and subject matter elements; one may say that 'the product' is produced by means of a strict sequence of operations. However, the comparison with the assembly-line does not completely match with this situation. In education the degree of interdependence is less strong than in a real production line, where the success of an activity is to a high degree determined by the quality of the preceding step. In education the input for an instructional activity is in few cases completely standard (in other words, students entering an instructional activity in most cases differ with respect to features relevant for instruction). Since some students frequently do not fully master certain subject matter, supplementary and/or refresher activities are not unusual. However, in many cases it also does not cause insurmountable problems that (some of the) students miss specific knowledge labeled as 'required prior knowledge'. Although global attainment targets are strived for in educational institutions, there is no exactly described standard level that each student finally reaches. Students differ when they enter and when they leave instructional activities. This also goes for the school output which differs between and within (e.g. departments, divisions) schools. Interdependency is strongest within a specific subject-matter area, and for that reason most activities meant to coordinate activities are carried out within a subject matter area (e.g. within subject departments). Teachers teaching different subjects usually operate as loose segments; they coordinate their activities only to a small degree.

Of all forms of interdependence, this characteristic is strongest in the case of *reciprocal* interdependence; work is fed both forward and backward between employees. An activity's units output is the input for the next activity; every employee receives inputs from and provides outputs to others. Each activity/unit forms a contingency for the other. The following Figure visualizes this type of interdependence:

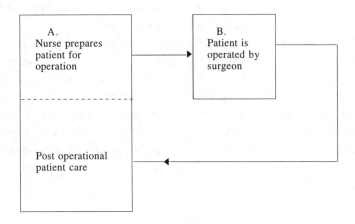

Figure 3.1: *Reciprocal interdependence*

The Figure shows the strong interdependence: B. is dependent on A. <u>and</u> vice versa. How the material/person to be transformed reacts to a certain form of treatment also influences the next action to a strong degree. An example from the world of vocational education: a student is first instructed and prepared for an internship e.g. in a company where (s)he gains new learning experiences. After the practical training period the student returns to school, where instruction ideally connects with the experiences students have gained during their practical training.

3.3.3 Complexity

The third and last technology dimension concerns its complexity which varies both between different types of organizations as well as within one and the same type of organization. McPherson et al. (1986) point to three criteria to judge the complexity of the applied organizational technology:

a. the variety in tasks;
b. the degree of specialization in tasks;
c. the number of locations at which tasks are executed.

Green (1971) has analyzed the *tasks* carried out by teachers. According to Green, teaching consists of logical acts (e.g. define, explain, compare, demonstrate, conclude); strategical acts (to teach students general skills being important in the long run like motivating, evaluating, planning and so on); and institutional acts (for instance collecting money, consulting students, home visits). Subject matter knowledge is important for logical acts; a student's nature is key for strategical acts. Considering the number and nature of the tasks a teacher has to fulfill, a teacher's job must be characterized as complex.

As far as *role specialization* is concerned as criterion for technological complexity, schools cannot be labeled complex. Most school staff are teachers (although different school types have different types of teachers); only a minor part of the staff of schools carries out other work like management activities, student counselling or work that is supportive of the teaching-learning process (e.g. by means of copying, cleaning).

If one views an educational system from a macro-perspective, education in a country is delivered in many different *locations* (= schools). The number of locations influences the coordination of work: the more locations, the more difficult it is to coordinate all activities taking place on different locations.

3.4 The primary process from an effectiveness point of view

Having analyzed the organization theoretical characteristics of the primary process and the operations technology applied, in the previous sections of this chapter, the relationship between the primary process and school effectiveness is now discussed.

The place where the action is
The impact of what takes place in classrooms on school productivity is stressed in research literature. Hill claims "Without question, there are strong empirical grounds for believing that schools and teachers can, and do, make a difference and that consistent high-quality classroom teaching can deliver dramatic improvements in student learning." (Hill, 1995, p. 14). On the basis of a review of school effectiveness research Hill concludes that the classroom is where -within the conditions set at school and context level- it happens, and that teachers are those who make it happen. The preconditions set at other levels are important but in themselves do not guarantee effective learning. Hill also points to the finding that much of the variation between schools is due to variation among classes. The unique variation due to schools over and above that due to differences among classes is small. Based on an analysis of data from nine countries, Scheerens et al. (1989) concluded that in many countries the size of the between-class differences exceeds 40% whereas school effects are significantly smaller (between 0-15%).
Within schools there proves to be significant effectiveness differences between subjects/departments. Schools tend to have strengths and weaknesses across the range of outcome measures. For example, Australian primary schools in the state of Victoria are by no means equally effective across core subjects and since these subjects are taught by one and the same teacher, teachers prove to be differentially effective in different curriculum areas. Hill claims therefore that the notion of an effective school needs to be treated with caution since most schools are effective in some classrooms and less effective in others (Hill, 1995).
It is probable that these between-classes/subjects differences have to do with the outcomes of the research of Rowan et al. (1993) who found that the extent to which teachers *perceive* variation in students (e.g. IQ, motivation) affects the extent to which their teaching becomes a non-routine task (section 3.3.1). The teaching of some subjects also proved more routine than others due to differences in the task knowledge (i.e. the rules to cope with variation and complexity) across academic disciplines. There is for example less diversity in the topics, goals and didactical approaches when teaching mathematics, than when teaching social studies. If teacher perceptions of student variation differ, as well as teaching strategies between teachers as a result of differences in the nature of subjects, this may explain (some) between-classroom effectiveness differences. Some teachers probably

apply more effective strategies than others in teaching a certain subject.

Empirical evidence on classroom factors that matter

Is there empirical evidence on the factors that matter in the primary process? Scheerens (1992) has summarized school effectiveness research and drawn conclusions concerning the factors that best account for variation in the rate of learning among students. Most of these factors concern aspects of the primary process. Multiple empirical research confirms that *structured teaching* makes a positive difference. This involves clear learning objectives, splitting teaching into manageable units delivered in a planned sequence, the frequent use of prompts and advance organizers, systematic monitoring and feedback as well as intensive remediation to overcome difficulties.

There is also substantial empirical support for the importance of *effective learning time* (time on task), which is influenced for instance by the length of the school day and school year, homework, and increasing the effectiveness of the time available.

There is also a reasonable empirical research base to show that:

- *opportunity to learn* (the match between what is taught and what is assessed) and;
- *pressure to achieve and high expectations of students* influence learning results.

Creemers (1994) attempts to explain differences in student achievement in an educational effectiveness model based on theoretical notions and findings from various research traditions. The model consists of a student-, classroom-, school-, and contextual level (Figure 3.2). According to Creemers the model has been tested to some extent (Creemers et al., 1996).

The results so far confirm certain aspects of the model: the central role of the classroom, and the crucial role of 'time for learning' and 'opportunity to learn' and the so-called consistency principle, which is elaborated below. According to Creemers there is moderate to strong empirical evidence for the influence of most *classroom factors* in his model, although differential effects occur in different schools depending on the student composition (cf. Hill, 1995). He also states that the empirical evidence of the *school factors* is also sufficient, although the factors at *contextual level* have as yet little empirical support.

An interesting point of Creemers' model is that it reserves a central place for the primary process by pointing to important classroom features, and by including those aspects of supra-classroom levels that have a direct bearing on what happens in the classroom. For this reason, the model deserves closer analysis.

Like Hill and Scheerens (Chapter 2, figure 2.3) Creemers stresses that educational effectiveness is primarily achieved at classroom level and that other system levels provide conditions for effective classroom instruction.

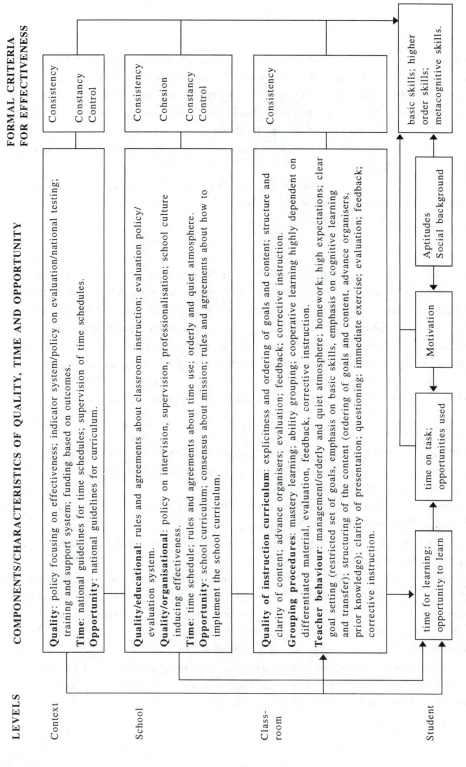

Figure 3.2: *A comprehensive model of educational effectiveness (Creemers, 1994)*

89

Although each model-component in itself contributes to learning, the combination with others is considered necessary for substantial effects. For example, more learning time means very little if the time is not spent on appropriate curricula, effective grouping of students and productive teacher behavior. This points to an important flaw in much school and teacher effectiveness research: the focus on *isolated factors*, when it is highly probable that configurations of student, classroom, school, and context level factors are decisive for school output.

Furthermore the model is based on the key concepts *quality*, *time* and *opportunity to learn* which are defined at all model levels. Only those factors that relate to one or more of these three concepts are included.

student level

The influence of the characteristics of the school, classroom and context on student achievement is mediated by two student-level features: 'time on task' and 'opportunities used'. Even if teachers accomplish high levels of 'time for learning' and 'opportunity to learn' in their classrooms, students decide how much time they really spend on school work and how many opportunities they take to learn. Therefore 'time on task' and 'opportunities used' are directly related to student achievement, which in turn is influenced by a student's aptitude and social background. The latter two factors also influence student motivation, which in turn influences 'time on task' and 'opportunities used'.

classroom level

According to Creemers the outcomes of education are determined by the time for learning, opportunities for learning and by the quality of instruction. He distinguishes three aspects of good teaching in classrooms:

- curriculum (e.g. clear goals, content, material for evaluation, feedback, correction);
- grouping (mastery learning, ability grouping, cooperative learning);
- teacher behavior (e.g. clear goal setting, high expectations, structuring content, clear presentation, evaluation).

The teacher's role is crucial since (s)he determines the time that can be spent on teaching and learning, ideally creates an orderly climate, keeps students on task, presents subject matter clearly, puts relevant questions, gives the right answers and feedback as well as having corrective measures for students who fall behind. Moreover, teachers decide on curricular materials and arrange grouping procedures in classrooms. Teaching material depend on the teacher, however certain ones can increase effectiveness like the extent to which they structure activities, the teacher's use of advance organizers, questions, student tests and additional instructional and exercise materials.

school level

Creemers stresses that most school level-factors are meaningless if not clearly linked to classroom factors, and for that reason only includes those school factors conditional for, and directly related to, the quality of instruction, time, or opportunity to learn at classroom level. Many school-level features in Creemers' model refer to the shared responsibilities and ideas of teachers who work in a team: a system of rules and agreements between teachers about classroom practices, and facilities to implement and control these. Creemers makes a distinction between educational (e.g. rules and agreements about curriculum material, student grouping, teacher behavior and consistency between them; and/or an evaluation policy and system), and organizational aspects of the quality of instruction at school level (e.g. a school policy on the coaching, supervision and training of teachers). The first group of aspects deal directly with what goes on in classrooms, the latter more indirectly but both are needed according to Creemers.

In addition to instructional quality, 'time' (e.g. a schedule) and 'opportunity to learn' (e. g. developing a curriculum or a school mission) are also important at school level.

context level

The concepts quality, time and opportunity to learn also play a role at context level. Quality refers for example to:
• a (national) educational effectiveness policy;
• an evaluation policy;
• training and support systems;
• outcomes based funding.

'Time' at context level can refer to national guidelines for school timetables, 'opportunity to learn' to (national) guidelines for curriculum development.

All levels of the Creemers model are synchronized by the concepts *consistency, cohesion, constancy* and *control*. The importance of a formal relationship between what takes place in and between classrooms, and between class and school level is stressed. Context features are conditional for school features, school characteristics for classroom features, and classroom features for student achievement. According to the consistency principle the effectiveness of classrooms, schools and contexts is enhanced if the features of these levels are in line with - and thereby support - each other. The levels should match as well as their components. The elements of a level should also receive equal attention, i.e. one should not be stressed more than another. In an integrated approach curricula, grouping procedures and teaching behavior adapt to and strengthen each other (synergy). If they are not in line with each other, the separate effect can be minimized or even disappear. In case of consistency, effects greater than the sum of the separate effects are possible.

If teaching staff assure consistency between components at school level teachers create cohesion. Constancy at school level is about continuity as a result of stable school rules and policies. The control principle refers to the plea for evaluating student achievement and teacher behavior, a quiet school atmosphere and teachers holding themselves and others responsible for educational effectiveness.

At classroom level consistency implies that curricular materials, grouping procedures and teaching behavior need to be synchronized. The need for constancy also implies that a specific grouping pattern should be continued across several grades, as should teaching objectives, methods, testing approaches, corrective measures and class climate. Consistency, constancy, and control are also important formal features at context level, emphasizing the importance of the same material characteristics over time and mechanisms that ensure synchronization.

Teacher development

It is not surprising that teacher development is assumed to be important for improving student results (Hill, 1995; Hopkins et al., 1994). Teachers have considerable discretion in the use of teaching strategies and thus can influence student achievement dramatically. Ideally they know about alternative strategies and are able to select from their repertoire the best strategy for a specific content area, and the age and ability of their students. In general, however, research evidence on improving teaching -and by that learning outcomes- is disappointing (Fullan, 1991; Joyce & Showers, 1988). According to Fullan the failure of in-service education results from the fact that such initiatives are poorly conceptualized, insensitive to the concerns of participants (wrong topics) and make little effort to help teachers relate what they have learnt to their classroom conditions (no follow-up support). Nevertheless, the fact that teacher training can be a powerful lever for improving classroom learning was shown in the Victorian Quality Schools project where a strong relationship between the professional development of teachers and effective teaching (Rowe, Hill & Holmes-Smith, 1994) was observed.

An important question in this respect is what the features of effective teaching are. According to Hopkins et al. (1994), a synthesis by Porter and Brophy (1988) indicates that effective teachers:

- have clear instructional goals;
- are knowledgeable about their teaching content and strategies;
- communicate with students on what is expected from them and why;
- use existing teaching material to devote more time to practices that enrich and clarify the content;
- are knowledgeable about their students, adapt teaching to their needs, and anticipate misconceptions in their existing knowledge;

- teach students meta-cognitive strategies and give them opportunities to master these;
- address higher and lower level cognitive objectives;
- monitor students' understanding by offering regular, appropriate feedback;
- integrate their teaching with that in other subject areas;
- accept responsibility for student outcomes;
- are thoughtful and reflective about their practice.

This is a global description of 'the effective teacher'. It claims that teachers have certain professional know-how and do many tasks that are described in general terms. It is for example not clear which teaching material teachers should use, *how* they should communicate with students, teach meta-cognitive strategies, reflect on their practice, etcetera. Moreover, the synthesis of Porter and Brophy is, logically, a generalization. What about the implications of differences between subjects and between teaching objectives? Does effective teaching for example include the same features if the objectives concern academic standards, personal development and social development, or is Porter and Brophy's 'picture' especially relevant to teaching basic skills?

Brophy (1983) presents a more specific characterization of teaching behavior, most closely associated with student achievement gains partly mentioned in reference to Creemers, Hill and Scheerens):

- content coverage (more covered, more learned);
- time allocated to academic activities;
- engaged time (time on task);
- consistent success (more learned if high success rates);
- active teaching (instead of students working on their own);
- structuring information (e.g. advance organizers, outlines, review of main ideas);
- frequently asking easy questions.

The question also remains here how teachers can acquire the skills and knowledge to enable them to teach in such a way that much content is covered, information is structured, success is consistent etcetera. The challenge is how we can upgrade poor classrooms into high performance ones. However, the process leading to effectiveness is unsure. Hopkins et al. (1994) suggest improving teaching practices via workshops (to gain understanding, attend demonstrations, and have the opportunity to practice in a safe context) and the workplace (as an opportunity for immediate and sustained practice, collaboration and peer coaching, as well as to development and implementation). In their opinion the models can be seen as informed advice that seems beneficial under certain conditions. Teachers should judge, experiment with, and test alternative teaching approaches (e.g. distinct models of teaching, cooperative learning, information-processing models) in their own classrooms and see them as a form of professional development. However, teaching to a certain extent is also a highly creative activity carried out in a personalized way. Next to planning, improvising is important because there are always unforeseen events. A successful teacher is able to respond and turn to advantage the unexpected. An interesting question is how 'artistic' teacher development can improve these teacher skills.

According to Hopkins et al. (1994) successful schools also create infrastructures for teacher development within their daily organization. In such schools social processes are a means of facilitating professional development and learning allowing teachers to reach beyond themselves and to let them learn through experience. Development in the form of curriculum development and implementation, discussing teaching approaches, observation sessions and on-site coaching is then a continuous process.

Organization theoretical primary process aspects in relation to school effectiveness

So far, it has been shown that what happens in classrooms causes effectiveness differences. The variables that have an empirically proven relationship with effective instruction (such as structured teaching, time, and opportunity to learn) have little interface with the organization theoretical aspects of the primary process dealt with in sections 3.2 and 3.3. There is very little research on organization theoretical features of the teaching-learning process, which confirms the claim made in the preface concerning the gap between school effectiveness research and school organizational theory. That gap is regrettable since integrating both perspectives will most probably increase our insight into the background of classroom and school effectiveness differences. What is missing is detailed information on numerous organization theoretical aspects of the operations technology and the primary process and their impact on student performance. There are some issues of interest in this respect.

It is highly unlikely that there is just one best operations technology. Best technologies probably differ across school types, school levels, and subject matter because of, among others, differences in the student population and the extent of task routinization within subjects.

The study of operations technologies, technological dimensions (their degree of uncertainty, interdependence and complexity in varying educational contexts) and their implications for educational effectiveness may clarify more what goes on in different types of classrooms, for what reason and with what result.

In section 3.2 it was claimed that mediating technology is probably dominant in education. However, as students within school types, school levels and lesson groups differ to some degree and students progress at different rates, an interesting question is to what degree there is room within this technology type for dealing with between-student differences. Are students really treated the same or is there room for diversity in mediating technology? If so, in what way, and what are the various effects of individualization for student achievement? Moreover, to what degree can the long linked and the intensive technology be observed in education, and what results do they produce?

Further study is also needed on the instructional conditions that make teaching routine (and thus lead to more similarity between teachers regarding their teaching) and the forms of coordination and control of instruction activities that best match more routine and non-routine teaching from the viewpoint of teacher and school effectiveness. What is the impact for instance of between-student variation, as perceived by teachers, for teaching strategies and their effectiveness?

The work of Rowan et al. (1993) is a good example of how research based on (school) organizational theory can benefit to increasing our understanding of school organizations and the relationship between school organizational features and the characteristics of the teaching-learning process. Where sensible this approach should be linked with the school effectiveness perspective to determine the impact of alternative organizational arrangements on student achievement.

One final observation concerning the search for an effective primary process. Although school effectiveness literature does not have roots in school organizational theory, there is some resemblance between the two. School organizational theory points to the uncertainty of the primary process. In the literature on educational effectiveness a plea can be observed for reducing such uncertainty wherever possible. Stressing the need for consistency between elements (e.g. at classroom level) and between levels (e.g. between the classroom and the school), continuity across grades, agreements between teachers, school teaching rules and modes of implementing school policy must be interpreted as a call for increasing coordination and technological interdependence between teachers. The assumption of the effectiveness enhancing impact of such an approach deserves a careful empirical test.

3.5 Summary

The preceding can be summarized as follows. The concepts 'primary process' and 'technology' have been analyzed from a general organizational theory point of view and have subsequently been applied to the context of educational organizations. Following Thompson (1967), a distinction has been made between: the long-linked, the mediating and the intensive technology. Each technology type could be seen to occur in education. Of these three, the mediating technology was considered most dominant in schools.

Subsequently, the technology dimensions: uncertainty, interdependence and complexity have been used to characterize the technology of educational organizations. The degree of uncertainty existing in the teaching-learning process of a school especially proves to be dependent on the extent to which students are considered to be similar by school staff and on the degree to which students are treated in accordance with that vision.

Three types of interdependence (pooled, sequential and reciprocal) have been discussed and translated to the area of education. Pooled interdependence can be observed in any organization, and there is also quite a lot of sequential interdependence in schools. However, the last type of interdependence is less strong there than in other organizations (e.g. mass-producing organizations).

School organizational complexity has been characterized on the basis of three criteria (tasks executed, role specialization, locations). The school has been evaluated as being complex as far as the number of and variation in teacher tasks and the number of locations are concerned. With respect to role specialization the school was not considered complex.

Primary process characteristics prove to matter for educational effectiveness. Variables that have an empirically proven relationship with effective instruction have been presented. There proves to be very little research on organization theoretical primary process features. Therefore, a plea was made for using school organizational theory as a basis for studying the features of the teaching-learning process.

• CHAPTER 4 •

Coordination and Control in Education

B. Witziers
University of Twente, The Netherlands

4.1 Introduction

Coordination and control in education are the central topics of this chapter. Section 4.2 of this chapter deals with the question of what these concepts entail and which means can be used to achieve coordination. In section 4.3 an in-depth look is taken at the characteristics and extent of coordination within educational organizations; three different perspectives are presented. Section 4.4 is dedicated to the relationship between coordination and school effectiveness. This chapter ends with a summary in section 4.5.

4.2 Coordination and control conceptualized

Background and definition
Organizations tend to divide their labor which leads immediately to the question how the different activities of organizational members must be integrated. For instance, within a manufacturing firm some employees are members of the sales department, while others work in the production department. Although both types of employees have their own responsibilities, it is obvious that their work should be, in one way or in the other, linked to run the organization smoothly. If sales representatives make promises to customers about delivery times, the production line should be notified about what and when to deliver.

Do educational organizations face the same problem? The answer to this question is yes. Although educational institutions are not the most differentiated organizations, within them staff perform different tasks, particularly in large schools. In these schools there may be, apart from teachers, laboratory technicians and specialists such as remedial teachers and counsellors and other non-teaching staff at work. Secondary schools should integrate the activities of the staff in such a way that their students are provided with a successful educational experience. Far more important, however, is that teachers' work is differentiated. In the typical case, teachers work either in one class teaching (almost) all subjects (in primary schools) or teach one subject in several classes (in secondary schools). In both cases, teachers' work should be interrelated. One reason for this is that students' learning often concerns a sequential process; teachers in higher grades depend on what students have learned in lower grades. Another reason is that if a school pursues a particular goal, this is achieved more effectively if all teachers contribute to this goal. If a school wants, for instance, to develop students' self-reliance, this goal can only be achieved properly if the activities of all teachers are directed towards this goal.

The same problem applies to the relationship between external administrative bodies (such as governments) and local schools. This relationship can be viewed in terms of a relationship between headquarters and divisions (the local schools). Headquarters is confronted with the task how to integrate the activities of each division/school (and of the various teachers within the schools) in such a way that the goals of the whole system are served best.

To sum up, people within organizations perform different tasks which need to be integrated. The concept of coordination refers to this process of integration. Hage (1980, p. 123) defines coordination as "the integrating of the various parts of an organization ..., so that there is a common output". Kieser and Kubicek (1983, p. 323) speak of coordination as "integrating different activities within an organization in order to reach organizational goals". Many authors state that coordination is essential for an organization. Hage (1980) for instance states that it is almost impossible to imagine an organization without any coordination, while Mintzberg (1979, p. 3) characterizes coordination as "the glue which holds organizations together". This is not only because coordination directs the activities of organizational staff towards the organizational goals, but also because it implies control.

The term 'control' is ill-defined in the organizational science literature. On the one hand the concept seems to deal with deciding what should be done and how things should be done within organizations. On the other hand it seems to refer to the employment of monitoring and checking devices and activities to ensure that all activities are performed as desired and that they generate the desired result(s). In general one could say that exercising control implies exerting influence over the behavior of other persons (cf. Simon, 1957). However, since this notion (exerting influence) is also central to the concept of coordination, it is not easy to make a distinction between both concepts. Like other authors (e.g. Mintzberg, 1979) these terms will be used as equivalents in this chapter.

Means to achieve coordination
An important theme in the organization science literature concerns how coordination within organizations can be achieved. One way to achieve coordination is through the

design of the organizational structure. An important step in designing this structure is the creation of departments, which are held responsible for their domain. A system of formal authority and a hierarchy are established, mainly through the appointment of managers for each department. The managers are responsible for the actions of their department staff and render account to higher level managers. In other words, a formal structure (the formal division of authority and tasks) is created which diminishes the overall need for coordination. The term structural coordination (Kickert, 1979; Torrington & Weighton, 1989) is used for this phenomenon. An example of structural coordination in educational organizations is the secondary school system, in which teachers are usually organized into subject departments, over which department heads, at least formally, exercise authority.

Opposed to structural coordination is procedural coordination. This type of coordination refers to what is actually being done in organizations to achieve integration. An influential writer on this topic is Mintzberg (1979, 1983), who distinguishes between several coordinating mechanisms.

The first mechanism is *coordination by mutual adjustment*. This mechanism refers to the process of informal communication. For instance, within a primary school mutual adjustment may imply that two teachers responsible for teaching third graders inform each other on what they teach, and thereafter adapt their individual lesson plans.

A second way to achieve coordination is by means of *direct supervision*. This implies that coordination is accomplished by one individual being responsible for, and supervising the work of others. An example in educational organizations is the work of principals, who are responsible for what is going on in their schools. More specifically, this mechanism refers to such activities as issuing orders and instructions, decision-making, delegation of tasks to and supervision of subordinates.

Work can also be standardized. Standardization can relate to three different work aspects. First, work processes can be standardized (*standardization of work processes*); that is, the content of the work is specified or programmed. Teaching methods are an example of this in the field of education, if one presupposes that teachers use them as blueprints.

Second, the desired work results may be specified (*standardization of work outputs*). For instance, many managers in business organizations are expected to realize certain profit and growth levels every quarter. How they accomplish this is left to their own responsibility. Within the field of education, national exams are a good example of this sort of standardization.

Finally, standardization can refer to the specification of the kind of skills and knowledge required to perform the work (*standardization of skills*). Mintzberg gives the example of an anesthesiologist and a surgeon working together in the operating room. They hardly need to communicate, since as a result of their respective training, they know exactly what to expect from each other. Translated to educational organizations, this would imply that teacher training is such that every teacher more or less applies the same teaching approach. Furthermore, this coordination mechanism refers to organizational socialization. This concept refers to the process by which newcomers in the organization acquire the perspectives, practices and goals of those within the organization (Lammers, 1983). Mintzberg suggests that if an organization can train (or indoctrinate) individuals to perform as required, there would be hardly any need for control. Since all members are trained thoroughly, it may be expected that they will perform in accordance with the goals and the established practices of the organization. In many organizations socialization of newcomers plays an important role. Apprenticeship programs within multi-national corporations such as Shell and Unilever are a good example. In the beginning of their organizational career newcomers rotate through various organizational divisions for brief periods, not only to learn the content of the work, but also to become imbued with the organizational culture. For educational organizations one can think of teacher inducement programmes.

The last mechanism Mintzberg discerns is *coordination by ideology*. The key notion here is that if workers think alike, they will act alike, thus ensuring that all activities are directed at the same goals. If teachers within a primary school, for instance, believe that teaching basic skills is at the heart of the educational enterprise, it is very likely that they all will emphasize these skills within their classrooms.

The question of which of these mechanisms discerned by Mintzberg to use in which situation is not easy to answer. In fact, most organizations mix (almost) all mechanisms. However, some authors stress that under specific conditions an organization will favor one coordinating mechanism over the others. Mintzberg (1979) for instance discerns, as has come to the fore in chapter one, several organizational structures (structural configurations), in which not only a different part of the organization is dominant, but also a specific coordinating mechanism. For instance, in the machine bureaucracy the most important coordinating mechanism is standardization of work processes, while in the professional bureaucracy the most import way of coordination concerns standardization of skills. In this sense Mintzberg is a typical representative of the contingency theory. Put briefly, researchers working under this label advocate the assertion that there is no one best way of organizing; those organizations will perform well that have a structure adapted to the prerequisites stemming from situational characteristics such as organizational size and age, environmental conditions and the technology employed (Mintzberg, 1979; Perrow, 1970). For example, if a company is small, the work can be coordinated by means of informal communication. However, as the number of employees increases, the organization must use more and more elaborate coordination devices, such as direct supervision and standardization, to perform effectively.

4.3 The nature and intensity of coordination and control in educational organizations

In the introduction of this chapter it has been stated that it is almost impossible to imagine an organization without coordination. This implies that coordination and control also take place in educational organizations. In the literature on school organizations there is no doubt that work in schools is coordinated and controlled. However, it is exactly after this conclusion that opinions start to diverge, in particular concerning the nature and intensity of coordination and control in educational organizations. In the following section three perspectives on this topic will be presented in chronological order.

In this way a more or less historical account is given of the way in which scholars have thought about educational organizations. This implies that attention will be paid, respectively, to educational organizations as bureaucratic organizations, loosely coupled systems, and as professional bureaucracies.

4.3.1 The school as a bureaucratic organization

Background

'Bureaucracy' is nowadays a word with pejorative connotations, suggesting impersonality, resistance to change, sluggishness and rigid rules. In the organization science literature, however, the word is used in a more neutral sense to describe a particular type of organization. The origin of this concept can be traced in the work of the German sociologist Max Weber (1864-1920). He was interested, among other things, in the development of western society. As one of the important aspects of this development, he considered the rise of a particular type of organization, the bureaucracy. This type of organization consists of the following characteristics (McPherson, Crowson & Pitner, 1986; Mintzberg, 1979):

1. The organization is arranged according to a principle of hierarchy with each lower office controlled and supervised by a higher one;
2. Conduct in office is governed by (usually written) rules;
3. Officials act within their own specified spheres of competence as part of a systematic division of labor;
4. Officials are selected on the basis of their qualifications;
5. Employment in this kind of organization constitutes a career, with promotion according to achievement;
6. Officials function impersonally without favoritism or arbitrariness;
7. Each official is subjected to strict and systematic discipline and control in the conduct of office.

From these characteristics one can readily assess that work in a bureaucracy is highly coordinated. Supervision plays an important role, as well as (written) rules with regard to work behavior. It is no surprise that some authors compare this kind of organization with a machine (i.e. Mintzberg): everything is designed and arranged in order to achieve certain specific goals in the most efficient way. This feature has also led to the use of the adjective 'rational', which is often added to the word bureaucracy ('rational' bureaucracy). Under rationality (McPherson et al., 1986, p. 76):

"The structure of the organization (........) is tightly articulated in terms of its goal directedness. Employees donate cooperatively to a clearly defined corporate product; the contributions of organizational members are closely monitored with efforts towards efficiency in goal attainment properly awarded; and career advancement opportunities (movement up the corporate ladder) are understood clearly to depend upon evidence of exceptional service to the organizations' stated purposes."

Noteworthy is that a worker in a bureaucracy, although constrained by rules, task specification and so on, in a sense is freed by this kind of organization, at least compared to more traditional forms of organization. One can think for instance of the fact that in a bureaucracy promotion is based upon more or less objective criteria ('exceptional services'), while in traditional forms of organization promotion may be based more on kinship or background. The same holds true for clients of the bureaucracy. They are not at the mercy of the whims of some potentate, as might be the case in an absolute state, but treated according to rules impartial to their background, political opinion and so on.

Another important scholar with respect to the bureaucracy is Frederick W. Taylor (1856-1917). Taylor is the founder of a movement known as 'scientific management'. At the heart of this movement is the idea that organizations can be managed in such a way that obstacles like antagonism between employers and employees and inefficiency could be overcome, thus securing maximum prosperity for both employer and employees. According to Taylor, this can be achieved by a systematic study of work to discover the most efficient method for performing the job. An example of his ideas is what Taylor calls 'the science of shovelling'. Taylor stated that, although shovelling seems to be an easy job, many factors affect the efficiency of this task. One can for instance think of the optimum load, the size of the shovel and the material to be shovelled. In his opinion it was the task of science to determine the most efficient way of shovelling. Applied to all organizational tasks, including managerial ones, science would lead to the most efficient organization. Another essential element in his thinking is the principle of maximum specialization. According to Taylor, efficiency is secured best when all workers concentrate on their specific task, implying for instance a sharp distinction between 'thinkers' and 'do-ers' within the organization (Schachter, 1989).

Both Taylor and Weber have been very influential. With regard to Taylor one can point to his influence on what is today called industrial engineering. Furthermore, to the fact that many organizations (particularly in the industrial sector) applied Taylor's ideas when designing jobs and tasks, thus giving impetus to the development of rational structures of organizations (Lammers, 1983; Schachter, 1989).

Whereas Taylor's work has been influential with regard to the design of organizational practice, Weber's work has been more influential in a scholarly fashion. His work has led to at least three developments (Mintzberg, 1979). First, it gave impetus to research the question whether organizations, as described by Weber, exist in reality. Or, in other words, do the aforementioned characteristics hold together in real organizations? This question was first addressed in the 1960s by Derek Pugh and his colleagues in the so-called 'Aston'-study. Pugh et al. (1976, 1977) discerned four dimensions, three of them based on the work of Weber. These three dimensions were specialization (referring to the division of labor), standardization (the level of regulations guiding work behavior) and formalization (the extent to which organizations make use of written rules). If bureaucracies exist, Pugh hypothesized, these three dimensions must be statistically related. And indeed, Pugh found in a sample of 46 organizations high correlations between these dimensions. He concluded that in reality a kind of organization could be discerned with a 'typical' bureaucratic structure: an organization putting great effort into structuring the activities of its work force.

After Pugh, many similar studies have been conducted, of which the studies of Burns and Stalker (1961) and Woodward (1965) are most notable. Both studies more or less confirmed the findings of the 'Aston'-study. Furthermore, they stressed the existence of a type of organization which can be seen as the antipode of the bureaucratic organization. In both studies this type of organization was called an 'organic' organization and was characterized by the dominance of loose and informal working relations, and the absence of (written) rules. Of course, this notion had already been implied in the 'Aston'-study. If there are organizations scoring high on dimensions like standardization, formalization and specialization, there must also be organizations scoring low on these dimensions. However, these studies took this notion a step further by stating that organizations can be placed on a continuum, with organizations with a bureaucratic structure on one end and on the other end organizations with an organic one. Furthermore, they claimed that the circumstances in which organizations operate are decisive in the determination of which organizational structure prevails. In short, bureaucratic-type structures can be found in organizations working in stable circumstances, while organic-type structures prevail in organizations working under conditions requiring organizational innovation and/or adaptation to rapidly changing environments.

Within another line of inquiry based on Weber's work the negative consequences of bureaucratic structures have been investigated. Scholars like Gouldner and Merton pointed to the dysfunctions of formalization. Gouldner (1955) stated that rules lead to worker apathy because they often imply minimum standards of 'good' work behavior. This encourages workers to achieve only what is required as a minimum. Merton (1952) pointed to the fact that the ever present demand for control in bureaucracies leads to a vicious circle in which rules are becoming increasingly strict, thereby causing growing resistance among workers. This in turn leads to dysfunctional consequences like rejection of innovative ideas, mistreatment of clients, turnover and even subversion of the operations of the organization. Distant echoes of these ideas can be found in the writings of scholars representing 'public choice' - theory (Boyd & Crowson, 1981; Niskanen, 1971). At the heart of this theory is the statement that public organizations, since they are often subject to tight regulations and in many cases are not awarded according to their achievement levels, often lack responsiveness to consumers' demands and the urge to perform efficiently.

Furthermore, Weber's work has influenced further thinking about what constitutes a bureaucracy. Discussions evolved, for instance, around the question of whether centralization or decentralization is an essential feature of a bureaucracy (Mintzberg, 1979). Finally, a scholar like Simon (1957) introduced the concept of 'bounded rationality', implying that a bureaucracy might not work as rationally as is often presumed. Instead, he argued that due to the limited capacity of man to handle information, the overwhelming complexity of organizational life and constraints, decision-making within organizations is only partially rational.

Schools as bureaucratic organizations

Despite some criticism and revisions of the bureaucratic concept, the rational perspective remains a powerful model for thinking about organizational behavior and administrative control. To show how an educational organization functions as a bureaucracy, a description borrowed from Firestone and Herriott (1982b) is given.

First, a rational bureaucratic educational organization is supposed to have *a single set of goals* that originates at the top. These goals are assumed to provide a clear guide for internal decision-making. Principals translate the general goals approved by the school board into sets of tasks to be implemented by department heads and teachers. It is assumed that subordinates share, or at least accept, these organizational goals. Thereby, responsibilities to carry out the tasks are clearly delineated for each role. Furthermore, organizational goals provide the framework for evaluation; administrators gather information on the organization's progress towards its goals, and when problems arise in this respect, policy alternatives are rationally examined and the one that is supposed to improve the school's performance most is selected.

104

Second, the educational organization as a bureaucracy is assumed to have *a formal control system*. This includes, besides the downward delegation of authority, the specification of required behavior through rules concerning the contents and/or results of the work. Within schools these rules are incorporated in curricula, timetables, school development plans, examination standards, budgeting procedures, personnel policies (rules concerning hiring, pay and rewards), sign in/sign out procedures and many more.

Third, educational organizations as bureaucracies are supposed to be *highly integrated*. Teachers, departments, administrators and others contribute in coordinated fashion to overall school performance. Principals are responsible for the overall coordination of departments, so there is a heavy emphasis both on vertical communication and centralized decision-making. School management controls the decisions regarding the educational process.

Finally, in the bureaucratic view the school is regarded to be a closed system, in the sense that there is a *dichotomy between 'politics' and 'administration'*. The bureaucratic school is a collection of employees which is protected from political pressures. Its efficiency and effectiveness stem from this isolation: principals and teachers perform their work free from political pressures.

Are schools really bureaucratic organizations?

An important question is whether or not educational organizations should be classified as bureaucratic organizations. Over the years many authors have tried to answer this question by focusing on the number of rules and regulations imposed on educational organizations by external administrative bodies such as governments (in most Western European countries), school districts (in the USA) and Local Educational Authorities (in the United Kingdom).

In general one can say that in Western countries the involvement of external administrative bodies with the educational system in general, and educational organizations in particular, has become larger and larger. In the Netherlands this development has been well documented by Idenburg (1975). In the years before 1960 he characterizes the role of the Dutch government as being 'passive' and mainly dedicated to the distribution of financial and other material resources to local schools. In the years thereafter, he characterizes the government's role as 'active' and 'constructive', that is, heavily concerned with the quality of education. Similar developments have occurred in other countries such as Belgium, France, Denmark, Norway and Germany (James, 1991).

Historically, a basic goal of this increasing governmental involvement has always been to increase student enrollment. Underlying this goal is the assumption that societies are better off with high levels of enrollment due to the positive externalties coming from education. That is, societies as a whole -including the people not receiving (many years of) education- benefit from a large number of people completing their education due, for instance, to the fact that a higher skilled work force usually implies higher productivity rates. A second goal behind the growth of governmental involvement has been the desire to raise the quality of education. Finally, in some countries, socialization for national unity (integration) and responsiveness to consumer demands have been motives for increasing state governmental involvement.

This increasing involvement from the national government with the school level has been manifested in many countries by a large increase in nationwide regulations aimed at controlling local schools. James (1991) mentions four reasons behind the rules and regulations. First, she states that this increase reflects a *'quid pro quo'*-approach. An increasing involvement also means that each year a larger portion of the national income is spent on education. This was true at least until the 1980s when due to financial problems, governments were forced to cut educational budgets. In return, governments demanded control over schools by establishing rules and standards which schools had to obey. Furthermore, she argues that rules enable governments to control educational systems financially. By specifying teacher salaries, for instance, governments are able to calculate, and thus to control teacher costs. Finally, she notes that governments were motivated to intensify the number of regulations as a result of the desire to increase the quality of educational systems, and to ensure equity. With regard to the former, one can point to rules regarding who is allowed to teach what subject. With respect to the latter point, one can think of the fact that specification of the content of exams ensures that all students, regardless of the schools they attend, are evaluated more or less equally.

Given the number of rules and regulations in many countries, it is not surprising that quite a few authors have stated that educational organizations have as a result become highly bureaucratized. Furthermore, these authors have pointed to the negative consequences of this feature. One frequently mentioned consequence is that schools, due to the number of rules imposed on them, have become unresponsive. Since they largely depend for their survival on following these rules, it is not really necessary for them to pay attention to the legitimate demands of other stakeholders (parents, the business community, etcetera) (Clune & Witte, 1990; Ingersoll, 1993, 1994; Van Hoof, 1986; Versloot, 1990). Another consequence is that (externally imposed) rules have a negative impact on teachers and teaching. Exemplary in this context is the work of Chubb and Moe (1990). They argue that within educational organizations, organizational qualities that are beneficial for school effectiveness are less likely to develop in a situation in which external authorities (board of educations, superintendents, district offices, governmental bodies) strongly regulate local educational organizations. They illustrate this by pointing at existing practices with regard to teacher recruitment. Given the fact that teacher collaboration and shared cultures are deemed to be important factors with regard to school effectiveness, Chubb and Moe state that it is important for principals to recruit 'mind like' teachers, that is, teachers committed to the values, norms and practices prevalent in the school. However, in a situation where teacher recruitment is under the control of bodies outside of schools, it is likely that teachers will be recruited more in accordance with bureaucratic criteria (educational attainment, certification and seniority) than with teaching philosophies in the particular school, thus impeding the development of a shared culture. Similar arguments are made by Chubb and Moe with regard to aspects like method choice, school objectives and curricula. For instance, if teachers have to deal with curricula developed outside the school, they might get demotivated since these curricular guidelines may imply goals and teaching practices that are in conflict with their own deeply felt convictions about what good education entails. Arguments in the same vein can also be traced in the work of other scholars (Bacharach, 1990; Murphy, 1991; Rosenholtz, 1989).

To support their viewpoint further, many of these scholars point to existing differences in school effectiveness between public and private schools. Many studies all over the world have shown that private schools in many cases outperform public schools (Scheerens, 1989). Since public schools, by nature, are more constrained by outside regulations than private schools, this is considered to support their contention that too much regulation is harmful for educational organizations' effectiveness. Needless to say, this contention is surrounded by controversy (for an overview of the discussion surrounding this issue, see Lee, Bryk & Smith, 1993 and/or Scheerens & Bosker, 1997).

Schools as bureaucratic organizations revisited

In the foregoing, some arguments are presented in favor of the premise that schools must be considered to be bureaucratic organizations. However, the question of whether schools are bureaucratic organizations or not has become more complicated due to changes in the relationship between external administrative bodies and local schools.

In several western countries, governments have tightened their grip on the educational domain within educational organizations. In the United States one can point to policy and reform measures taken in the early and mid 1980s. These measures were rooted in the deeply and commonly felt belief that American education was in a state of crisis. The influential report 'A Nation at Risk' (1983) stipulated for instance that children in other countries -in particular Japan- outperformed their American peers in almost all subjects. Since those countries also posed an economic threat to the United States, the deplorable state of education was supposed to endanger the economic position of the United States. Policy makers assumed that -among other factors, in particular teacher quality- the lack of coordination and control were responsible for the bad shape of American education. Therefore, they called for more accountability, evaluation and other policy measures aimed at 'tightening the ship' (Ingersoll, 1994, p. 151).

The message was picked up by most states and led to an increasing state legislation regarding curriculum (content and goals of teaching), academic testing and teacher improvement (through changes in teacher certification and evaluation). The rise of monitoring systems with the intent to tighten the organizational links between state and district goals, and what teachers actually do in their classroom is another consequence of this development (Douglas Willms, 1992). At the federal level one can refer to the development of nationwide educational goals and concomitant activities regarding evaluation and monitoring. 'Goals 2000', a policy developed by President Bush and the National Governor's Association in 1989 (and enacted by President Clinton in 1994) outlines educational goals to be reached by the year 2000 and implies the introduction of a national curriculum, although state adoption of these goals is voluntary (Stringfield & Herman, 1995). In sum, reform in the United States has attempted 'to intensify as exactly as possible the what and how of teaching' (Fullan, 1991, p. 7).

Similar developments have taken place in other countries. In many countries, the curricular and instructional domain of educational organizations (in particular in primary and secondary education) are now more than ever subject to rules and regulations.

Regarding other domains, however, today's schools may be less bureaucratic. In many countries, policies aimed at intensifying the what and how of teaching have been followed by measures directed at liberating schools from tight regulations and centralized decision-making, primarily by means of relegating decision-making power from central levels to lower levels within the education system.

In the Netherlands, intensification of regulations with regard to educational outcomes have gone together with deregulation. For instance, where the financing of schools was once subject to a complicated and detailed set of bureaucratic rules (Van Wieringen, 1987), schools today are financed on a 'lump-sum'-basis, thereby increasing their autonomy with respect to financial affairs. Moreover, many responsibilities have been delegated to municipalities (VNG, 1996). In the United States and Canada similar reform measures have been taken in some school districts under the heading of 'restructuring' (Murphy, 1990; 1991). Important goals of these measures are to increase educational organizations' autonomy and to enhance parents' influence over school affairs. An example with regard to the latter goal are policy measures aimed at liberating parents from restrictions with regard to school choice. Until recently in the United States many parents' ability to choose their children's school was severely limited. Nowadays, school choice has been liberated in many cases. These measures, at least potentially, increase parents' power, since schools, in order to attract a sufficient number of students, are forced to pay more attention to parents' demands and desires. Comparable reform measures have been taken in the United Kingdom. In this country parental choice was embodied in legislation. Furthermore, to help parents in making a proper choice, school examination results became public, at least in the case of secondary schools (Silver, 1994).

Given the developments depicted, one may say that contemporary scholars who emphasize that educational organizations are bureaucratic in nature seem to be only partly right. An educational organization's functioning may be heavily bureaucratized in some domains (e.g. curriculum and instruction), while it is not in others.

Whether rules and regulations really have the devastating effects some authors suppose, is another matter of debate. Although Rosenholtz stresses the negative effects of a bureaucratic mode of organization, she also concludes (1985) that formal rules reduce teachers' role ambiguity and uncertainty, factors that are inversely related to teacher satisfaction. Similar results are found in other research. Caldwell and Lutz (cited by Lee, Bryk & Smith, 1993) state that clearly established and consistently enforced rules are important factors in promoting teacher satisfaction. In this sense, one may even say that rules enacted by external administrative bodies are sometimes beneficial for educational organizations. The same point is made by other authors (Firestone & Herriott, 1982b; Marx, 1987) stating that these rules prevent conflicts within educational organizations, since all important decisions are already made elsewhere. To sum up, the question of whether rules are harmful or not may be more complicated than some scholars suggest.

4.3.2 The loose coupling perspective

Background

Many scholars have always asserted that the rational organization is the best answer to the question of how to organize large numbers of people in accomplishing large scale tasks. In the literature on educational organizations, the rational organization was the dominant frame of reference, both for research on school organizations and governmental policy-making regarding schools, until the late 1960s (Van Vilsteren, 1984).

However, the study of organizations has always been characterized by a tension between theoretical and applied models emphasizing rationality on the one hand and the reality of organizational life on the other. Organizational realities that correspond fully with the blueprint of the formalized, specialized, standardized structure were rare. Within the educational field one can refer to the work of Waller (1932) and Becker (1953).

During the 1970s this tension became stronger and stronger, in particular since a growing body of empirical data about the way educational organizations function became available which showed that educational organizations differ from the typical bureaucratic organization. In particular, one can refer to research into school organizations (Lortie, 1975) and research showing the failure of innovations attempted at the national level which were based on a rational perspective (Fullan, 1991; Wise, 1977).

These results led to a loss of confidence in both the explanatory power and the practical applicability of the classic Weberian model and to the ascendancy of a perspective stating that -some- organizations must be characterized as 'loosely coupled'. In general, this term applies to organizations lacking high levels of coordination and control (Ingersoll, 1993). The loose coupling perspective will be further elaborated now.

A closer look at the loose coupling perspective

Under this perspective three different, but interrelated, theories are usually subsumed (Ingersol, 1993, 1994; Tyler, 1988; Witziers, 1992). Each is discussed below.

The first theory stressing that (educational) organizations are essentially different from bureaucratic organizations was developed by Cohen, March and Olson (1972). This theory (*'organized anarchy and garbage can'-theory*) builds on Simon's concept of bounded rationality (Simon, 1957) and Cyert and March's (1963) work on the political character of organizational order. It points to the difficulties inherent in decision-making processes within organizations that appear to have unclear technologies and abstract goals. Within this theory it is argued that decision-making situations in those organizations often function as 'garbage cans' in which organizational members throw their personal (instead of organizational) problems and goals. Furthermore, within this type of organization important organizational decisions are often put off. Organizational staff fight over minor decisions without paying attention to their implementation, or only those decisions are made that neither threaten any participant, nor solve a particular problem.

Although Cohen, March and Olson themselves have not specifically developed their theory for educational organizations, other authors have stated that it can be applied to them very well (De Caluwe & Petri, 1985; Satter, 1981; Van Vilsteren & Visscher, 1987).

A second theory stressing that educational organizations do not resemble the bureaucratic organization was developed by Karl Weick (1976, 1982, 1984). He introduced the concept of *'loosely coupled systems'*, which refers to organizations composed of autonomous elements that are often unresponsive to each other, rather than rationally and hierarchically controlled. More specifically, Weick points to elements like the absence of regulations, the failure of superordinates to influence subordinates, employee autonomy, and a lack of goal consensus. In this view, educational organizations particularly are characterized by these features. According to Weick, these characteristics arise primarily from confusion surrounding the technology of teaching: how learning actually happens, what the best instructional approach is in a given situation, and the difficulties of predicting and measuring educational outcomes.

The *institutional theory*, developed by Meyer and Rowan (1983a), is the third theory stating that educational organizations deviate from the bureaucratic model. Meyer and Rowan state that although educational organizations do have a structure, it is not based on rationality, but rather on ideologies and traditions as to what particular organizations should be. In this sense, according to this theory, educational organizations appear to be tightly coupled: educational organizations do conform to demands stemming from the organizational environments to increase their legitimacy and their survival prospects. For instance, if primary schools are asked to generate plans to inform parents about how they work, many schools will do this in order to secure public trust in their organization.

However, this conformity does not imply that educational organizations are really tightly coupled. In fact, at the intraorganizational level they are loosely coupled. According to institutional theory, educational organizations refuse to adequately control their work processes. They do so to camouflage inconsistencies, irrationalities and inefficiencies which might undermine public faith in the organization. This theory more or less accuses educational organizations of 'window dressing'. Although external demands are met by educational organizations, these demands hardly affect what actually transpires inside the organization. For instance, educational organizations might appear to meet the external demands to optimize learning results, but actually not pay much attention to their productive function.

From the description of these three theories, it is hopefully clear why these theories are usually put under one heading. They all state that elements of the school organization are 'decoupled'; decision-making has hardly any relationship with what is actually going on inside the school organization (garbage can theory), the several elements of the school organization are unresponsive to each other (loosely coupled systems) and demands imposed upon educational organizations do not deeply affect internal school functioning (institutional theory).

Below will be checked whether there is some evidence for the premise that educational organizations are loosely coupled. For simplicity's sake an article written by Weick in 1982, in which he lists four characteristics of loosely coupled systems, will be used to organize the writing. In this article Weick contends that one (or more) of the following four conditions are absent in loosely coupled systems:

(a) a set of rules;
(b) feedback;
(c) evaluation;
(d) agreement of rules.

A set of rules

In section 4.3.1 it came to the fore that, particularly in western countries, quite a lot of external rules and regulations are imposed upon educational organizations. Furthermore, it has been shown, some authors claim, that these rules and regulations have a profound impact on school functioning.

However, the contention prevailing in the loose coupling perspective is that these rules and regulations do not exert a strong influence on what is happening in educational organizations. Meyer and Rowan even speak of 'ritual classifications' (1983a, p. 76). To illustrate this point they refer, among other things, to rules and regulations regarding teacher qualification. They argue that there are elaborate classifications of teachers; e.g. elementary teachers, physics teachers, college teachers, each with his or her own specifications and credentials. Furthermore, each teacher type has its own legitimate domain, for example, elementary teachers are not allowed to teach physics in colleges. Educational organizations have detailed rules delineating which individuals may teach in which type of classes and schools. However, once it has been observed that these rules have been taken care of, very little else is done to control teachers. What teachers really do is never controlled.

Similar arguments are used by Meyer and Rowan (1983a) with regard to what they call 'topic classifications'. Rules exist concerning which school is allowed to offer which subject, but there is little formal control concerning what specific topics teachers offer to students, how much time they spend on each topic, or to ensure that topics are taught in the same way. In sum, rules and regulations exist, but they are 'decoupled' from what teachers actually do.

Actual evidence for the existence of this decoupling phenomenon can be derived from the empirical work of Lortie (1975). He found that teaching is least controlled by specific and literally enforced rules and regulations. Further support for the phenomenon can be found in Dutch research on school work plan development within educational organizations. In the Dutch context school work plans are a legal requirement for every primary and secondary school and can be typified as plans which specify the intents, methods, goals and testing of teaching. In her research on this topic Van der Werf (1988) showed that, in as far as a detailed plan was available, it did not play a significant role in teachers' daily practices.

In this respect the phenomenon of 'goal displacement' should also be addressed (Etzioni, 1964). Many researchers have found that within educational organizations, rules and regulations are either ignored or bent for purposes other than those for which they had originally been designed. A striking example is the Dutch Educational Priority Policy. In accordance with the intentions of this policy, schools with a student population largely consisting of disadvantaged students (that is, students with a low socio-economic background and/or students belonging to minority groups) received extra resources to improve these students' educational achievement. Many schools did not use these resources for the intended purposes. Instead, they used them to pursue their own goals (Leune, 1985). Other examples of goal displacement can be found in the literature on school innovation. Fullan (1991) shows, for instance, that in Canada and the United States many innovation attempts have failed due to the fact that educational organizations adopted these innovations for financial reasons instead of school improvement goals. Overseeing all these research findings there is indeed some evidence for the statement that rules place few constraints on teachers' work.

Feedback

Within organizations there must be an understanding of what its various parts are doing, and whether these parts contribute to overall goal achievement. Therefore, a formal communication system is needed guaranteeing that information on these matters reaches the strategic apex of the organization. This information can be used to (re)assess existing organizational policies and practices. In other words, the collection of information provides feedback on organizational functioning.

Feedback plays an important role in the notion of cybernetic control in organizations which gained considerable influence on organizational thinking in the 1970s. Central to the cybernetic model is that the organization is considered to be a set of causally related variables that require close monitoring. The idea is to ensure that organizational performance stays in line with the stated goals (McPherson, Crowson & Pitner, 1986). An example in the context of educational organizations concerns student learning. Since it is assumed that many factors (e.g. students' aptitude and motivation, teachers' instructional strategies, homework load, student background) affect this variable, according to the cybernetic model, administrators should collect information on each of these matters in order to (re)assess existing organizational policies and practices. If the data show that there is a decline in student learning outcomes due to a change in students' aptitude, the school must use this information to solve this problem in a rational way. This might imply that the school decides to change its instructional strategies, so that the educational needs of the student population are addressed more properly, or it may decide to attract students of higher ability.

Is there any proof for Weick's statement that these processes do not play an important role within educational organizations? An unequivocal answer to this question is difficult to provide. On the one hand there is little doubt that educational administrators gather information about what is going on in their schools. In many schools, for instance, school leaders receive minutes of departmental meetings and engage in formal meetings with teachers, counsellors and so on (Van Vilsteren & Witziers, 1990). Furthermore, one can point to the increasing use of computer-assisted management information systems within educational organizations. The tangible advantages of computer use in terms of school efficiency and school effectiveness have led to the wide spread utilization of computer technology for the operation and management of schools, in particular in countries like the U.S.A., the Netherlands, Great Britain and Australia (Visscher & Spuck, 1991). Many of today's school leaders utilize spreadsheets, database management systems, and specific school administrative applications to handle activities that include budgeting and accounting, staffing, student enrolment, revenue projections, inventory control and student timetabling (scheduling). An international study conducted by Pelgrum and Plomp (1991) shows that the use of these systems has had a positive effect in many cases. Respondents perceive improvements concerning the quality of student administration, the amount of available information, the quality of teacher administration and the efficiency of school administration. As such, these systems seem to make a more grounded decision-making process possible with regard to school functioning.

However, whether this is really the case is questionable. Mintzberg (1989) states that managers rely most of the time on informal feedback channels (opinions, advice, anecdotes, hearsay, speculation and even gossip), prefer information related to problems and events at hand, and rely on information that supports their values and opinions. In other words, information-gathering by managers deals primarily with getting information rapidly, in order to solve problems at hand as soon as possible. This implies that managers do not operate as reflective planners. Managers are often thought of as stereotypical rational problem solvers, receiving relevant and reliable information and making decisions on that basis. This image, however, often proves to be false. Time consuming, profound problem analysis, the subsequent generation of alternative solutions and the elaboration of the most suitable solution prove to be rare.

The specific way of obtaining and dealing with information by managers also explains, according to Mintzberg, why formal information systems (such as computer-assisted management information systems) are only used in a limited way. The characteristics of the information that managers rely on are in conflict with most computer-assisted information systems that produce aggregated, precise, internal and historical information. Another problem with these systems is that they often lead to an information overload. Managers often receive more information than they need or even more than they can use.

The same message is conveyed in the literature on principals (Cuban, 1988; Imants, 1996; Kmerz & Willower, 1982; Leithwood, Begley & Cousins; 1990; Stoel, 1994) and the use of formal information systems within educational organizations (Visscher, 1993, 1996). The literature on principals shows, for instance, that principals are not the reflective planners they are supposed to be, and also suggests why this is the case. According to this literature, principals spend large portions of their time working away from their own desks, encounter frequent interruptions (e.g. from teachers, students, parents) and changes in the focus of their attention, and spend a lot of time solving 'day-to-day' problems. Illustrative in this respect is Table 4.1, which shows (excerpts of) an actual time log of a high school principal.

Table 4.1: *Time log of a High School Principal*

7:35 a.m.	Arrived at school. Picked up mail and communications. Unlocked desk.
7:36 a.m.	Looked for dean who wasn't in yet. Left word for him to see me.
7.38 a.m.	Looked at mail - Heart Association to promote a 'Heart Day.' Worked at desk, proof read two teacher evaluations.
7.47 a.m.	Secretary came in. Gave her evaluations of teachers for retyping.
7.49 a.m.	Checked with substitute clerk for absentees and late-comers (exceptionally foggy morning).
7:50 a.m.	Spoke briefly with arriving English teacher about his spelling bee and award certificates I had signed.
7.52 a.m.	Called five administrative offices, suggesting they check classrooms for possible late teachers.
7.54 a.m.	Gave secretary instructions on duplicating and distribution of material on change in graduation requirement.
7:55 a.m.	Saw dean about student who had called after school yesterday - threatened and beaten up by other students getting off bus.
7:58 a.m.	On way to staffing, stopped at attendance office to visit with parent who was in about son not doing well in school.
8:00 a.m.	Joined staffing with social worker, psychologist counsellor, therapist, parent, and student who had been removed from all classes for truancy.
9:10 a.m.	Left staffing to look for student who had been told to wait in outer office but had wandered off.
9:15 a.m.	Found student in hall, returned to staffing.
9:30 a.m.	Left staffing to keep appointment with candidate for maintenance job.
9:31 a.m.	While waiting for building and grounds director to arrive, gave secretary instructions for cover and illustrations for the open house printed program.
9:33 a.m.	While waiting read: Note from student needing early release. Bulletin from National Federation of Athletic Associations on college recruiting of high school athletes. Note from teacher upset over misbehavior in previous day's home room program. Staff absentee report for the day.
9:36 a.m.	Went to outer office to greet candidate and explain why we were waiting.
9:37 a.m.	Called building and grounds director and learned he wasn't coming over.
9:39 a.m.	Interviewed maintenance supervisor candidate.
10:00 a.m.	Took call from registrar - to be returned.
10:07 a.m.	Completed interview.
10:08 a.m.	Saw teacher who had pictures from German exchange program.
10:09 a.m.	Called for building and grounds director - busy.
10:10 a.m.	Returned call to registrar about purging of records of a dropout.
10:11 a.m.	Called building and grounds director to discuss maintenance candidate.
10:14 a.m.	Returned call to personnel director about administrator's in-service program next week. Agreed to make a presentation.
10:22 a.m.	Read:Two suspension notices. Plans of special programs coming up.
10:25 a.m.	Saw special programs coordinator in outer office. Approved her plans and discussed possible appearance of Navy Band in February.
10:27 a.m.	Saw dean to learn what he had done about yesterday's incident.
10:30 a.m.	Left for cafeteria - talked with counsellor in hall about Guidance Information Service (computer service for college selection).
10:31 a.m.	Stopped by to see psychologist to hear outcome of staff meeting.
10:36 a.m.	Stopped by health center to give nurses information from Heart Association about 'Heart Day.'

	Talked with nurse about her program at a PTSA meeting the previous day.
10:37 a.m.	Stopped in Audiovisual Center to ask director to prepare transparencies I had given him for in-service program.
10:40 a.m.	Stopped by athletic director's office to relate comments by parents about physical education that had come up at the PTSA meeting.
10:45 a.m.	Checked on the room where I was to have lunch with two students to come in for underclass pictures.
10:46 a.m.	Looked in on yearbook photographer who was waiting for students to come in for underclass pictures.
	Visited with student who had performed with choir previous day when students had misbehaved.
10:49 a.m.	Walked down to maintenance office to tell men about holes broken in wall of the student council office.
10:52 a.m.	Stayed around student cafeteria. Spoke with teacher who wants a school exchange.
10:54 a.m.	Stopped in faculty lounge to visit with three soccer coaches who were concerned about new play-off rules that eliminated our team.
10:57 a.m.	Picked up lunch and went to council office to meet students.
11:00 a.m.	Lunched with two students.
11:30 a.m.	Stopped and visited with a few students in the cafeteria.
11:35 a.m.	Returned to the office. On the way, stopped to visit with CVE teacher about cosmetology program and a student in the program.
11:38 a.m.	Visited with workmen installing new air conditioning units in office area.
11:40 a.m.	Made four telephone calls. No answer on two of them.
11:47 a.m.	Returned call from fellow principal, discussed graduation requirement proposal.
11:48 a.m.	Answered note from teacher.
11:50 a.m.	Reviewed minutes of previous day's principal's advisory committee meeting (principal is chairman and secretary).
11:51 a.m.	Read note from teacher about a student's early release.
11:52 a.m.	Looked up material needed for next day's athletic conference meeting.
11:58 a.m.	Read communications:
	Memo regarding special education student.
	Note from teacher about conduct in homeroom.
	Memo from special program coordinator about upcoming program.
	Board of Education summary.
	November homeroom calendar.

Source: Gilbert R. Weldy (1979), p. 65

Given their work conditions it is no wonder that principals behave as they do. In many cases there is no time to collect (and use) information in a more reliable and systematic way since many problems need to be solved immediately.

With regard to the use of a computer-assisted information system, one can point to the study of Visscher (1993) which showed that by and large schools did not benefit very much from the introduction of these systems to support policy-making. Leithwood and Montgomery (1982) state that principals experience difficulties using quantitative/statistical data because they are untrained and inexperienced with this type of data. This unfamiliarity makes it difficult for them to determine the quality of the information, and to interpret and use it for school improvement. This finding is in line with results from a study conducted by Riehl et al. (1992) showing that principals who are comfortable with quantitative data on student outcomes, who trust them, and are trained to interpret them, are more likely to use these data.

To sum up, there is indeed some proof for Weick's contention that feedback plays a limited role for policy-making at school level. Although principals and other administrators gather information on organizational practices, this does not always lead to more grounded and 'rational' decision-making. The literature on the use of computer-assisted management information systems indicates that the introduction of these systems, although they are widely used nowadays, has not changed this situation.

Evaluation

Many organizations evaluate how well their staff's actions meet organizational standards and expectations. As such, staff/personnel evaluation in general is an important device whereby administrators focus the attention of lower level employees; it leads participants to orient their efforts toward success on whatever criterion is selected to be measured (McPherson et al., 1986). According to Weick and other proponents of the loose coupling perspective, however, this is not the case within educational organizations. The following will explain whether this statement is true or not.

At first glance the literature suggests that evaluation does play an important role within education. Testing student progress, for instance, is a familiar phenomenon within schools. In his review on classroom evaluation practices, Crooks (1988) estimates that tests occupy students on average for 5 to 15% of their time. Furthermore, there is growing attention paid to student monitoring (Gillijns, 1991) and school-based evaluation (Hopkins, 1988; Voogt, 1989). Finally, in many countries principals are increasingly expected to observe and evaluate teachers (Crisci, 1991; Imants, 1996). Despite the growth in attention for evaluating student, teacher and school performance, the literature on educational organizations suggests that as a means for controlling educational organizations, evaluation is not the strongest of all available tools.

One reason for this is that, in education, the conditions required for the proper evaluation of staff are not met. In general one can say that in many organizations staff is evaluated according to the question of whether they achieve the desired output or not (output control). For instance, sales representatives are often evaluated on the basis of products sold per week. A problem with this approach occurs when personnel cannot be held responsible for the achieved output, or when no reliable and valid measures of the desired outputs are available. In that case, many organizations rely on evaluation procedures designed to check whether staff apply the right techniques (behavior control). It is not wise to evaluate a surgeon solely on the basis of whether or not a patient has survived an operation; many other factors beyond the control of the surgeon exert their influence as well. However, he/she can be evaluated on whether he/she has applied sound medical techniques or not. This type of evaluation is of course only possible if one knows what the right techniques are. It is obvious that this is in many cases a problematic endeavour. For example, although it is possible to specify how many articles a researcher must write, it is almost impossible to specify how this should be done. Finally, in some situations evaluation is not possible at all, since neither the outputs nor the work process are accessible to evaluation procedures. Painting is a fine example of this case. First, it is difficult to define a high quality painting. Second, there is no one best way to arrive at the desired goal. This not to say that in such a case organizations do not evaluate their staff at all. However, evaluation then must be considered to be a 'ritual': organizations then appear to act rationally, but they do not, since evaluation as a means to control staff has then hardly any consequence for the staff involved.

The foregoing paragraph is summarized in a matrix developed by Ouchi (1977). In this matrix (see Figure 4.1) three types of control are discerned. Furthermore, the matrix shows that the type of control employed by organizations is dependent on two dimensions, to achieve a desired result or outcome ('knowledge of the transformation process'): the availability of output measures, and the knowledge concerning the techniques to be used. With regard to the latter, a distinction is made between perfect and imperfect knowledge. Perfect knowledge implies that one is certain that if one applies a particular technique, the specified results will be achieved, while one is uncertain about this in the case of imperfect knowledge.

If in educational organizations evaluation is not the strongest of all available tools, following Ouchi's reasoning, there are problems concerning the availability of output measures, and the knowledge of transformation processes. Educational research has shown that problems indeed occur in both areas.

With regard to the availability of output measures, it may look like there are many quantitative output measures available in education. Examples are examination scores, the number of students graduated, student attendance rates and student job-placements.

		Knowledge of Transformation Processes	
		Perfect	Imperfect
Availability of Output Measures	High	Behavior control or Output control	Output control
	Low	Behavior control	Ritual

Figure 4.1: *The relationship between organizational structure and organizational control (source: W.G. Ouchi, 1977)*

118

However, this is not to say that there are no problems with respect to the output criteria. Some authors suggest that problems occur due to the fact that educational organizations do not have a set of clear goals. Scholars refer to the fact that schools, in fact, have multiple goals which may be incongruent or inconsistent (McPherson, Crowson & Pitner, 1986). The question then arises as to which goal, and which criterion must be used to judge the results of schools, in particular when some goals can only be achieved at the expense of others. For instance, schools are often confronted with the task to improve student achievement by raising standards, and to reduce student drop out. Which criterion should be used in this situation is very difficult to determine, since raising standards might go hand in hand with a growing number of drop outs. The statement that schools lack clear goals also refers to the fact that schools pursue goals that are abstract and vague (Meyer & Rowan, 1983a). An example concerns the previously mentioned study of Van der Werf (1988) on school development plans. She not only found that these plans do not play a significant role for teachers' daily practices, but also that, in many schools, intentions and goals were often stated only vaguely. In that case it is difficult to answer the question of whether or not schools have accomplished their goals. A related problem is that not all goals can be measured in a reliable and valid way. One can, for instance, use standardized tests in determining whether schools are effective in developing basic skills, but difficulties arise if one wants to answer the equally important question of whether schools effectively develop higher order thinking and creativity.

Finally, if reliable and valid output measures are available, their use is often problematic. If a principal wants to evaluate a teacher using exam scores and notices that the exam scores of the students taught by this teacher fall behind in comparison with other teachers, the question arises whether the teacher can be held responsible for the results at hand. It is possible that other factors beyond the control of the teacher have exerted their influence as well. It is possible that his students were far less motivated than students in other classes. Another factor may be that the students' aptitude was on average lower compared to other classes. In other words, it is not easy to determine which factors are responsible for the results in question. Similar difficulties are mentioned in the literature regarding the evaluation of overall school performance (Douglas Willms, 1992; Van Amelsvoort & Witziers, 1994).

In addition to the problems concerning the use of output measures to evaluate teachers (and schools), the literature also suggests that the knowledge of transformation processes in education is imperfect. To illustrate this statement one can refer to the difficulty of distinguishing between effective and ineffective teaching (Leithwood & Montgomery, 1982). There is no clear evidence that one teaching practice is superior to others; in many cases different practices lead to the same results. As a result it is very difficult to evaluate teachers concerning the question of whether or not they use the right techniques. Criteria regarding 'good' teaching are lacking and thus evaluation becomes more a matter of taste than of applying objective procedures. This is reflected by the fact that many studies on teacher evaluation show a lack of consistency among appraisers (Crisci, 1991).

In sum, the literature suggests that the use of output measures in education is problematic, and that our knowledge base concerning 'means' and 'ends' is imperfect. Referring once again to Ouchi's framework, we may state that although evaluation takes place within educational organizations, research supports that these actions must be considered to be more of a ritual than a way to focus teachers on what the organization deems important, and as a means of organizational control. Some studies (e.g. Wise et al., 1985) show that teachers are only evaluated infrequently and inconsistently, while other studies (e.g. Floden et al., 1988) indicate that teachers often are neither rewarded nor punished for (not) complying to rules concerning instruction. In other words, there is some evidence for the statement that evaluation plays only a limited role within educational organizations.

Agreement of rules

Weick suggests that there is no agreement of rules within educational organizations. Every organizational member (or subunit) has his own views on organizational, educational and pedagogical matters and tries to pursue his own goals. This contrasts sharply with the bureaucratic organization, where subordinates are supposed to share, or at least accept, the organizational goals (Firestone & Herriott, 1982b).

There is, indeed, some evidence in support of Weick's statement. Secondary schools can serve as examples in this respect. In these organizations it is not uncommon for members to be more committed to their department than to the school as a whole, potentially leading to many controversies and conflicts between departments about budgets, the allocation of resources and the educational path the school will follow (Lee, Bryk & Smith, 1993; Siskin, 1994). Within departments political struggles might also evolve around decisions about who teaches what, to whom, where and how. Ball and Lacy (1980, p. 151) for instance state in their study of British teachers, that:

'rather than being a cipher of subject knowledge for the teacher, the subject department is in itself an arena of competition in which individual social strategies are organized on the basis of biography, latent culture, and situational constraints.'

More support for the contention that education is a field in which many different views exist, can be deduced from the way policy-making proceeds at administrative levels other than the school level. Educational policy-making at state level is often considered to be difficult and conflict-ridden. This results from the fact that many stakeholders are involved, who have, based on different perspectives and values, diverging views on the goals and content of educational policies (Leune, 1985; Rossi & Freeman, 1993).

Some scholars have argued that as a consequence of all these differing perspectives, values and interests, decision-making processes within educational organizations proceed differently from those within bureaucratic organizations. Contrary to the bureaucratic model, in which organizational decisions result from the goals established in the strategic apex, the goals to be pursued within educational organizations are considered to be the outcomes of conflicts of preferences among organizational subgroups. This, in turn, implies that goals 'emerge' within educational organizations through processes of bargaining and negotiating rather than originate at the top of the organization. As a result it often takes a long time before any real action is taken, and that policy-making in a context of bargaining and negotiating often leads to vaguely stated, and sometimes even contradictory, goals (Leune, 1985).

Some scholars argue that the lack of agreement within educational organizations strongly relates to other aspects of school functioning. Rosenholtz (1989) argues that the lack of shared goals within educational organizations is closely associated with teachers' tendency to work independently from other teachers. This latter aspect has been shown in many studies of teachers' work life and in educational settings. Studies of Lortie (1975), Little (1982) and Prick (1983) highlight the fact that teachers show little concern for the professional needs of colleagues and tend to be primarily concerned with their own classroom affairs. This does not mean that teachers do not interact, but that this interaction is not centered around instructional and curricular matters. Since a shared culture partly depends on the level of interaction between organizational members, Rosenholtz argues that this 'egg-crated culture', where everyone only takes care of his own business, is a sincere impediment to the development of a shared culture.

Another important factor in this respect is the way teacher novices are socialized. There is ample evidence that schools do not offer new entrants direction in the details of practice. Newcomers must often rely, as Lortie (1975) has put it, on 'sink or swim socialization'. That is, when starting their teaching career, they have to sort things out without the help and guidance of fellow-teachers and/or principals. This practice is highlighted by the following quote of a teacher novice (Rosenholtz, 1989, p. 37).

"I couldn't answer you there. This is my first year in the school. I have stuck pretty much to myself. I'm really not on the grapevine so I just don't know. I'm just not really involved in this school. [Did others help you learn school procedures?] No. I more or less figured those things out for myself".

As a result, many schools continue to be fragmented entities, where teachers pursue their own interests. As Rosenholtz (1989) notes, teacher novices may observe a number of varied perspectives and practices within their school, thus encouraging them to develop their own views and practices and reinforcing the existing organizational reality of fragmentation and diversity.

Important to note is that in the literature the blame for the lack of agreement within schools is not put solely on educational organizations. In the foregoing it has been stated that the knowledge base with regard to education in terms of means-ends relations is quite weak. Furthermore, it has been stated that education can be considered to be a potentially conflict-ridden field; which educational goals to pursue and how to achieve these goals are subjects liable to debate and involving many different perspectives and values. These characteristics also pervade teacher education (Coonen, 1987; Fullan, 1991). As a consequence, within teacher education students are not confronted with a well-defined and uniform body of knowledge, thus making the development of a strong, coherent and shared professional culture within schools difficult.

Critique of the loose coupling perspective
The loose coupling perspective on educational organization may be criticized from a number of perspectives.
The most important critique is whether the advocates of the loose coupling perspective do not underestimate the influence of rules and regulations imposed on educational organizations and teachers. In this respect, one can refer to previously mentioned authors who stress that educational organizations should be typified as bureaucracies. This is not to say that these authors are by definition right. However, both the number of authors defending this viewpoint and the number of times schools have been depicted as bureaucracies in the last decades at least suggest that schools are more tightly coupled than terms such as 'ritual classifications' imply. Important to note is also that governments have taken many measures to ensure that schools are more controlled. Extreme examples are the publication of examination results (in England) and the rewarding of good schools (in some states in the USA). Although these examples are atypical, they nevertheless show that schools are now held more accountable for their results than ever before. In such a situation it is difficult to defend the proposal that schools are loosely coupled.
Furthermore, one can refer to research showing that teachers do not always ignore rules or bend them to fit their own goals. Rosenholtz (1987) and Wise et al. (1985) report, for instance, that teachers do alter the content of instruction to conform to the content of (changing) state tests, while Ax (1985) notes that external rules and regulations constrain teachers' autonomy regarding instructional goals and content, at least in some subjects. The constraint of teachers' autonomy is even stronger when other aspects of teacher behavior are taken into account, at least in the United States. Ingersoll (1993) mentions a strong control of critical and frank discussion of basic morals and norms, in particular those concerning sexuality, religion and political ideology.
Finally, one can wonder whether the loose coupling perspective does not place a too great emphasis on conflicting views and perspectives. Research in the Netherlands on

organizational problems as perceived by teachers show that many teachers experience organization-related problems only to a small degree (Hylkema, 1990; Schuit, 1994; Voogt, 1989; Witziers, 1992), suggesting that there is less conflict within educational organizations than proponents of the loose coupling perspective suppose.

4.3.3 Educational organizations as professional bureaucracies

The third theory addressing coordination and control within educational organizations is the professional bureaucracy theory. It has been developed by Mintzberg (1979), although some of the notions contained in his theory can be traced in the work of others (cf. Bidwell, 1965). Mintzberg emphasizes that some organizations -among them schools and universities- award their workers with considerable autonomy. Decision-making power concerning work affairs is relegated to the workers themselves. This is done because the tasks to be performed in this kind of organization are professional in nature. That is, they require considerable expertise, judgement and creativity. The term 'professional' refers to these aspects.

When professionals carry out their work there is little room for both collegial (e.g. mutual adjustment) and bureaucratic controls (e.g. standardization and direct supervision of the work). The job of administrator mainly consists of handling disturbances (e.g. dealing with difficult clients) performing maintenance (e.g. capacity planning) and boundary-spanning (e.g. negotiating with sponsors). Consequently, it is hard for administrators to control the work of the professionals, even when they function poorly.

Although the role of collegial and bureaucratic control is a limited one within professional bureaucracies, that is not to say that coordination and control do not play a role at all. According to this theory, coordination is mainly achieved through the standardization of skills; all professionals are thoroughly trained and socialized in the required knowledge, skills and norms, which more or less ensures that professionals work alike. Control in the professional bureaucracy is accomplished by the codes of behavior, regulations and norms which professional groups impose upon the work of their members. In this respect, the work within these type of organizations is essentially bureaucratic in nature: what and how things are done is predetermined by rules and procedures.

One can say beforehand that these phenomena do not apply very well to education. As it has been shown in the previous section, teacher training does not provide entrants with a uniform body of knowledge, while socialization is such that schools do not offer them direction in the details of practice. In this respect Mintzberg's statement (1979, p. 373) that the standardization of skills is 'a loose coordination mechanism at best, failing to cope with many of the needs that arise in the professional bureaucracy', seems to be particularly true for educational organizations. Furthermore, professional associations in

123

the field of education develop standards, but these standards are almost never obligatory. Textbooks may be taken as an example. Teachers use them, of course, but never as a blueprint for action. Nevertheless, this model is often referred to when scholars write about educational organizations (Scheerens & Van Vilsteren, 1988; Smets, 1985; Van Vilsteren, 1984).

Are educational organization really professional bureaucracies?

The model of the professional bureaucracy, first and foremost, highlights the question of direct supervision. This concept, introduced in section 4.2, refers to the capability of exercising power by the virtue of the fact that an individual occupies a hierarchical position within a social institution. This position enables him (or her) to perform activities such as issuing orders, delegating tasks, controlling and evaluating subordinates and many more.

With regard to school organizations, this concept means that actors like school boards, principals, vice-principals and department heads come into sight.

The assertion made in the professional bureaucratic model is that direct supervision is not a strong feature of educational organizations, this in contrast to, for instance, a bureaucratic organization. At first glance it seems that this assertion is not right. The literature on educational organizations clearly shows that the formal relationship between principals and teachers is hierarchical in nature. In the United Kingdom the teacher is legally an 'assistant', who is contractually required to perform tasks set by and subject to review by the head (Kogan, 1986). In the Netherlands, the task description of the principal states that he is either responsible for organizational, educational and domestic affairs on behalf of the school board, or formally and legally mandated to carry out these responsibilities (Hermans, Backx & Pors, 1993). In this respect educational organizations can formally be conceived of as being hierarchical by nature, thus in fact reflecting a bureaucratic mode of organization.

However, the literature also suggests that this does not imply that educational organizations can be equated with bureaucratic organizations. Kogan (1986, p. 34) states that, although hierarchy is a dominant feature of most school organizations in the United Kingdom, formal lines of hierarchy are frequently 'criss-crossed by collegial styles and matrix structures', implying that many school decisions are relegated to subsystems (e.g. departments) or made by teacher committees. In a similar vein, Firestone and Herriott (1982b) address principals' authority in American schools. They state that major decisions in American schools often require discussions with school office staff, teachers and, in secondary schools, department heads. Furthermore, they argue that important decisions are often delegated, made by committees, or guided by formulae in ways that limit the principal's discretion to shape the school organization. In other words, school leadership in these countries is in many cases rather more collegiate than hierarchical.

In The Netherlands this seems to be even more the case. Since the 1920s, partly due to the pressure from teacher unions, principals have been part of the teaching team and are obliged to consult with their teachers with respect to school affairs in general, and educational matters in particular. In other words, leadership within Dutch schools has become democratized, thus clearly affecting the relationship between teachers and principals. This relationship evolved from a relationship based on hierarchy and authority into one more characterized by collegiality and equality (Van Wieringen, 1989). This is reflected in present Dutch legislation stating that teachers in primary schools are responsible for school work plan development, while in secondary schools teachers should be consulted in this matter. Hermans, Backx and Pors (1993) note that this legislation de facto implies that educational decisions are made by teachers. Another consequence concerns that a principal is primarily considered by (fellow) teachers to be a primus inter pares ('first among equals'). For the delegation of tasks in primary schools this implies, for instance, that delegation is largely dependent on the willingness of teachers to perform the task at hand (Stoel, 1994). These matters show that school organizations do not resemble bureaucratic organizations in this respect. Although hierarchy is formally embedded in the structure of schools, principals can not be equated to leaders in, for instance, business organizations.

This absence of strong hierarchical relationships within educational organizations seems to be strongest in the curricular and instructional domains of schools. With regard to the Dutch situation, it has been noted already that teachers in primary and secondary schools are de facto responsible for decisions concerning educational matters. This is illustrated by Table 4.2, showing the results of a Dutch study (Witziers, 1992) on, among other aspects, the influence of different actors within secondary schools on curricular and instructional decisions.

Principals and middle managers, like department heads, prove to be hardly influential with respect to what teachers do in their classrooms; this is largely determined by teachers themselves.

Table 4.2: *Influence of different actors in secondary schools on curricular and instructional decisions (source: Witziers, 1992)*

	school manage- ment	depart- ment head	depart- ment	teacher	others
teaching philosophy	2.50*	1.54	2.33	2.20	1.86
teaching goals	1.40	1.63	3.24	2.62	1.27
choice of text book	1.11	1.73	3.82	2.08	1.04
teaching content	1.07	1.63	3.45	2.66	1.05
ways of teaching	1.23	1.42	2.34	3.57	1.11
discipline	1.48	1.33	1.87	3.64	1.27
grading of tests	1.04	1.35	2.92	3.12	1.03
content of tests	1.01	1.36	2.92	3.21	1.04
frequency of tests	1.65	1.39	2.80	3.03	1.17
nature and content of exams	1.29	1.44	3.15	2.64	1.04
homework	1.22	1.17	1.74	3.80	1.12
frequency of meetings	1.71	2.48	2.93	1.76	1.15

*Mean scores based on data provided by 378 teachers in 103 schools; scale ranges from 1 (=not influential at all) to 4 (=very influential)

This finding applies not only to the Dutch situation, but is corroborated by studies in many other educational settings, even in settings in which the position of principals is formally stronger with respect to educational affairs than in the Netherlands. In a classic study on teachers' work life in the United States, Lortie (1975, p. 73) found:

'that acceptance of the principal's authority is coupled with definite ideas on how that authority should be deployed. They agree that it should be mobilized to serve teacher interest; parents should be buffered, troublesome students dealt with and chore-avoiding colleagues brought to heel. Most respondents seem to favor a light rein for themselves; some, however, prefer the principal who checks them closely and carefully. Our respondents stand ready, it seems, to award deference and loyalty to principals who make their authority available to teachers; that authority can help them achieve working conditions which favor classroom achievement and its rewards.'

This quote highlights that teachers do not question the authority of school leaders in itself, but restrict this authority mainly to matters outside the classroom; school leaders should use their authority to facilitate teachers' work ('providing good administration') and their activities must not interfere with classroom affairs, including the evaluation of teachers' work.

Another reason for the weak role of evaluation within educational organizations is being mentioned here. Crisci (1991) argues that this weakness is closely related to the strong tradition of awarding considerable personal autonomy to teachers in the instructional domain, thereby emphasizing the existence of an adversarial rather than a collaborative relationship between teacher and principal. This relationship implies that teachers will resist evaluation, in particular when evaluation is viewed as a means to increase control over what they do. Research on teacher appraisal suggests that when appraisal is perceived as a weapon for fault-finding rather than as a group process for problem-solving, teachers will resist it. This distrust is further fed by teachers' feelings that principals are out of touch with what occurs in classrooms, in particular with the mitigating circumstances that prevent teachers from being successful.

What has been said about principals, can also be translated to other officials and bodies within school organizations, such as school boards, which are officially clad with decision-making power concerning school affairs. School boards are responsible for the proper functioning of schools in administrative, financial and educational respects, which implies the possession of many formal competencies. Despite these formal competencies, research results suggest that many school boards are only remotely involved in school affairs, thus hardly making use of their formally established decision-making power (Hofman, 1992).

Summarizing, principals and school boards are in a legally established position which enables them to exercise power over others. However, in reality the exercise of power is largely constrained, in particular in the curricular and instructional domain of schools. In this respect, the professional bureaucracy model seems to give an accurate account of educational organizations' functioning.

Critique of the professional bureaucracy

Although there is some evidence in favor of the professional-bureaucratic model, this does not imply that it is above criticism. One matter of debate is whether teachers should be considered to be professionals. Hanson (1979) states that educational organizations consist of two zones, one administrative and one instructional. The former is the domain of educational administrators, the latter the domain of teachers. With respect to these zones, he states that both are unreconcilable in the sense that each group is responsible for its own zone and does not allow interference from others. Hanson's account closely resembles the school as a professional bureaucracy model by stressing the strict division of labor between educational administrators and teachers, although he also distinguishes a third zone (the 'contested' zone) in which both administrators and teachers try to exert as much influence as possible. However, he also states that this division of labor is based more on tradition and teachers' ideologies than on the professional status of teachers. Similar statements have been made by other authors (Niederberger, 1984; Van Vilsteren 1984) who point to the fact that teachers as an occupational group, lack many of the characteristics of the 'true' professions (lawyers, doctors). Teachers, for instance, lack a code of professional behavior. While doctors can be suspended or even expelled from their professional group as a result of the verdict of a jury of their peers, such a mechanism is lacking in education.

Another matter of debate is the question of whether principals are really as powerless as is often suggested. Principals put pressure on non-conforming teachers, while highly respected principals can persuade teachers to act as required (Van Vilsteren & Witziers, 1990). Furthermore, principals influence a number of key decisions. Ingersoll (1993, 1994) summarizes a number of American studies showing that principals have a great influence on decisions concerning staff hiring and firing, overall curricular design, student discipline, building arrangements and the school schedule. Ingersoll suggests that principals also have a number of key levers with which they can control teachers. For instance, teachers are vulnerable to administrative power because of their limited disciplinary authority towards students. As a result, teachers depend on being 'backed up' by principals in discipline problems with students or in dealing with angry parents. It is clear that this dependency can be used by principals to control teachers. Another example concerns the school budget. Principals have a great influence on the allocation of financial resources which can be used to steer teachers (or departments) in the 'right' direction.

4.3.4 What kind of organization are schools?

In the introduction of this chapter it has been stated that coordination and control take place in every organization. Educational organizations are no exception to this rule. However, this not to say that there is no controversy regarding this issue. In the foregoing sections it has been shown that at least three perspectives can be distinguished. First, there is a strong tradition stating that schools are overly coordinated and tightly controlled. Second, there is a stream of literature claiming that the reverse is true. Finally, a third perspective states that coordination and control take place within educational organizations, but in a rather restricted sense, that is, primarily through training and socialization. More specifically, these perspectives differ widely on a range of issues. For instance, proponents of the first perspective emphasize the detrimental effects of rules and regulations imposed on educational organizations, while advocates of the second perspective state that the rule perspective is not the best way to understand educational organizations. To add to the confusion, one has to admit that all these perspectives have their merits. There is some empirical evidence for each perspective.

Given this confusing array of perspectives and research results, no unequivocal answer can be given to the question of how educational organizations should be typified in terms of coordination and control. Answering this question is further complicated by at least three other factors. The first factor is where one looks; instructional and curricular aspects may be tightly coupled, while other aspects may be loosely coupled. There are also differences between educational settings; secondary schools may differ from primary schools, while there may also be large differences between countries. Finally, even within the same setting, there may be large differences between educational organizations. Research on effective schools shows, for instance, that in some schools principals do get directly involved with educational affairs, while in other schools they refrain from these activities. The same confusion seems to surround the theme of coordination and school effectiveness. This theme will be further explored in section 4.4.

4.4 Coordination and school effectiveness

In one of the foregoing sections it has been stated that many scholars believe that educational organizations lack high levels of coordination and control. Some scholars have argued that such a system has its advantages. Weick (1976) mentions the following advantages of 'loosely coupled' systems:

(1)   they are capable of flexibility of response; some parts of the organization can adapt to environmental changes, while others persist as they are;

(2)   the possibility of localized adaptation affords a loosely coupled system a strong potential for change and innovation;

(3)   within loosely coupled systems there is a reduction of costs in terms of both money and conflicts;

(4)   within such systems actors can act autonomously, which might enhance their sense of efficacy.

In spite of these advantages, however, a common thread through the literature on educational organizations is that improving levels of coordination and control will enhance educational organizations' performance. This contention comes particularly to the fore in the work of researchers and scholars in two interrelated lines of inquiry.

The first line of inquiry, 'school effectiveness research' investigates whether there are substantial differences between schools with regard to organizational and teachers characteristics in particular, and whether these differences are related to the outcomes of schooling - academic achievement in particular (Scheerens & Bosker, 1997). One of the main results of this strand of inquiry is that principals' involvement with the curricular and instruction domains of schools is related to students' academic achievement (Hallinger &

Heck, 1996). Other results point to the importance of monitoring and evaluation, consensus and cohesion among staff and school development planning for improving schools' effectiveness (Cotton, 1995; Levine & Lezotte, 1990; Sammons, Hillman & Mortimore, 1995; Scheerens & Bosker, 1997). These results have led several scholars to the conclusion that coordination and control matter. For example, Scheerens and Bosker (1997) note that, given the results of school effectiveness research, a plea can be made for formalized and highly structured educational programs, supported by structures that emphasize order, coordination and unity of purpose.

The second line of inquiry primarily concerns itself with the question of which factors are responsible for the successful implementation of school innovation efforts (Fullan, 1991). The contention that coordination and control are important comes within this line of inquiry to the fore, for example, in the following statement made by Dalin (1988, p. 88):

"The change process will unfold quite differently in loosely coupled schools (with or without innovative experiences), in 'Project schools' that have successfully implemented changes in projects in various departments and sections of the school, and in schools that have a common vision, have a common ideology and norms and are used to coping with change as an organization."

In spite of the more or less generally held belief that more coordination and control make schools better, differences exists between scholars and policy-makers with regard to how coordination and control within educational organizations can be improved. One can discern two viewpoints on this issue.

The first emphasizes the need for improving coordination within educational organizations by strengthening 'direct' means of coordination. The underlying argument is that since research has shown that within educational organizations, educational leadership, monitoring and regulations with regard to goals and content are lacking, these elements should be strengthened. Not only to increase control concerning what educational organizations and teachers actually do, but also to improve students' academic achievement.

A typical elaboration of this perspective, apart from the actions taken by governments aimed at strengthening their grip on educational organizations as described in section 4.2, has been the development and implementation of in-service training programs for principals in the United States (Hallinger, 1992). These programs were based on the assumption that principals have to act as instructional leaders to improve schools' effectiveness. This implies that they were expected to be knowledgeable about curriculum and instruction matters, and able to interact directly with teachers and students. More specific, according to the designers of these programs, principals should have high expectations of teachers and students, supervise classroom instruction, coordinate the school's curriculum and closely monitor student progress. Another elaboration concerns innovative programs aimed at evolving schools into 'high-reliability' organizations, in which there is -among other things- an emphasis on hierarchy, the implementation of highly structured educational programs, supervision and monitoring and evaluation (Stringfield, 1995).

The second viewpoint stresses the need for improving coordination within educational organizations by strengthening 'indirect' means of coordination. The work of Little (1982) is sometimes considered to be the starting point for this way of thinking. She argues that effective schools are characterized by teachers who have given up their autonomy and operate as part of a team, thereby constantly focusing on improving their school's educational system. It has been this study, among others, that has led scholars such as Purkey and Smith (1993, p. 442) in their review of school effectiveness research to the conclusion that an effective school "is best characterized as one that promotes corrolarily planning, collegial work and a school atmosphere conducive to experimentation and evaluation." Similar notions can be found in other publications on effective schools (Ashton & Webb, 1986; Hargreaves, 1995; Little, 1988; Rosenholtz, 1985; 1989), in the literature on staff development (Joyce & Showers, 1988; Lieberman, Saxl & Miles, 1988) and on school improvement (Fullan, 1991; Hopkins, Ainscow & West, 1996). All these authors focus on the school culture and state that it should change into a 'collaborative' one that stimulates teacher learning and enhances the problem-solving capacity of educational organizations. These aspects are conceptualized most explicitly by Lee, Bryk and Smith (1993), who have introduced the term 'communal organization'. This type of organization is characterized by a system of shared values, a common agenda of activities and collegial relations among teachers coupled with a 'diffuse' teacher role. According to Lee et al., shared values provide a set of clear expectations to motivate and guide the behavior of staff and students, while a common agenda of activities unites school members both physically and spiritually. A diffuse teacher role brings teachers into frequent contact with other teachers and students in settings other than the classroom.

An important role in creating such a school organization is assigned to the principal. Rosenholtz (1989) states that principals must primarily perform their task by means of techniques like 'management by walking around' and creating a decision-making structure which involves all teachers, thus allowing them to have a say in matters traditionally belonging to the authority of the principal or other school officials. This notion is also reflected in other literature on school leadership. A frequently used term in this respect is 'transformational' leadership (Leithwood, Tomlinson & Genge, 1996; Murphy & Seashore Louis, 1994; Sergiovanni, 1990), implying that one of the main tasks of principals is to initiate processes and structures within the school that enable teacher collaboration and participative decision-making.

'under conditions of loose coupling one should see considerable effort devoted to constructing social reality, a great amount of face work and linguistic work, numerous myths and in general one should find a considerable amount of effort being devoted to punctuating this loosely coupled world and connecting it in some way in which it can be made sensible (Weick, 1976, p. 13).'

It should be noted that the viewpoint stressing the need for improving coordination within organizations by strengthening 'indirect' ways of coordination is deeply intertwined with the perspective that educational organizations are overly coordinated and tightly controlled. As shown in section 4.2, proponents of this perspective assume that the bureaucratic structure of educational organizations impedes the development of school-effectiveness-enhancing aspects such as shared cultures and teacher collaboration. Furthermore, it is assumed that bureaucratic structures diminish teachers' commitment. Hence, authors stressing the importance of 'indirect' means of coordination often plead to abolish the bureaucratic structure of schools (Rosenholtz, 1987; Rowan, 1995). Finally, given the efforts aimed at relegating decision-making power from levels outside the school to lower levels in the education system (see also section 4.2), it might be concluded that, to a certain extent, these pleas have been successful.

School improvement revisited

It is not easy to determine which perspective on school improvement is most valid. A sincere complication concerns the fact that, although both perspectives build on results from studies on school effectiveness, there is no empirical evidence which clearly favors one of them over the other. One must also remain aware of ideological overtones. However, it seems safe to state that both viewpoints contain valid arguments and that the answer to the question in which direction educational organizations should go in order to improve their performance lies in integrating both perspectives. An example of this can be found in the work of Scheerens (1992), who states that in order to improve educational organizations' performance, both direct and indirect means of coordination should be enhanced. Scheerens makes another important point when he argues that the road to increased effectiveness does not simply run via more integrated educational organizations. Instead it requires more differentiated answers to decide how much and in which part-systems of educational organizations coordination is needed. This point is also made by Astuto and Clarke (1985). However, one must acknowledge that the existing knowledge base is still weak, and confess that the following statement made by Cuban more than a decade ago still holds true today:

"None of the richly detailed descriptions of high performers can serve as a blueprint for teachers, principals, or superintendents who seek to improve academic achievement. Constructing a positive, enduring school climate remains beyond the planner's pen. Telling principals what to say or do in order to boost teacher expectations of students or to renovate a marginal faculty into one with esprit de corps remains beyond the current expertise of superintendents or professors. Road signs exist, but no maps are for sale yet" (Cuban, 1984, p. 132).

4.5 Summary

This chapter deals with the issue of coordination and control in educational organizations. In the introduction it is stated that it is almost impossible to imagine an organization without coordination, implying that coordination also takes place in educational organizations. Although the literature on school organizations no doubt states that work in schools is being coordinated, it is after this that opinions start to diverge. An important point of discussion concerns the nature and intensity of coordination within school organizations.

One perspective states that schools are overly coordinated and controlled. In essence, this perspective states that there are far too many rules and procedures, in particular at the cross school level, governing the work of principals and teachers. As a result, teachers may get demotivated, thus endangering school effectiveness. Furthermore, due to these rules and regulations, school organizations have become too complex, inert and unable to respond to developments within their environment and to righteous demands of parents and other stakeholders.

Another perspective tells us that educational organizations should be seen as rather 'loose' organizations lacking mechanisms of coordination and control. This perspective points, for instance, to teachers conducting their work without the need to render account to either colleagues or principals, and to the absence of evaluation practices and formalization.

Finally, a third perspective argues that coordination takes places, but in a rather limited way. Although coordination is achieved through means of training and socialization, it is questionable whether these means are sufficient to cope with many of the needs for coordination that arise in educational organizations.

With regard to the question of which perspective is right, one can state that an unequivocal answer is very difficult to provide. One reason is that there is some empirical evidence in support of each perspective. A second reason is that the answer to this question is largely dependent on where one looks. Educational organizations might be tightly coupled in one domain and loosely coupled in another. A third reason is that there are strong differences between educational settings (type of school, country). Finally, educational organizations also differ within the same setting; some schools are more tightly coupled than others.

In the last section of this chapter, the relationship between coordination and school improvement is dealt with. It is stated that, in general, scholars believe that if educational organizations put more effort into coordination and control, their performance will improve. A closer look, however, revealed that, again, two different perspectives can be discerned. The first one stresses the need for enhancing 'direct' means of coordination and control (hierarchy, formalization, evaluation), while the other one emphasizes the need for strengthening 'indirect' means of coordination (the importance of a school's cultural system: teacher collaboration, shared goals). With respect to the question of which approach is preferable, it is stated that the answer to this question lies in integrating both viewpoints.

• CHAPTER 5 •

Teacher Motivation and Commitment

H.W.C.H. van Amelsvoort
University of Twente, The Netherlands

5.1 Introduction

The standing, competence and motivation of the teaching force are at the center of public discussion in many countries (OECD[1], 1990). In this chapter the reader is introduced into issues concerning the motivation and commitment of teachers. Motivation refers to the desire and willingness of a person to take some action in pursuit of some goal, while commitment refers to involvement and the emotional linkage between the individual employee and the organization. At present, it is widely claimed that the teaching profession is demoralized and suffers from diminished job satisfaction and decreased commitment. In this chapter motivation and commitment are discussed briefly from the perspective of the (inter)national level of education systems. The major part, however, focuses on the organizational level, as it deals with commitment within schools.

First, the political relevance of the subject is illustrated by describing important aspects of the teaching profession as well as problems encountered by teachers when practicing their profession. Second, an elaboration on the concepts of motivation and commitment is given by presenting some current theories. The third part of the chapter deals with factors affecting commitment. Special attention is given to school features that may inhibit commitment, and characteristics of the life cycle of teachers that could influence commitment. Next, several remedies are discussed for the problems that hinder the motivation and commitment of teachers within the Dutch context, as proposed by the Dutch Committee on the Future of the Teaching profession (CFT). Finally, the chapter is summarized and some conclusions are drawn about teacher motivation and commitment.

---

[1]Organisation for Economic Co-operation and Development

5.2 Political relevance of teacher motivation and commitment

Some figures may underline the political relevance of a well-performing teaching force in a country from a financial-economic perspective. Five and a half percent of the labor force is employed in education. According to the OECD (1996a), 2.8 per cent of that total consists of teaching personnel. In The Netherlands, where education is provided to approximately 4 million students (Commissie Toekomst Leraarschap), six per cent of the labor force is employed in education. This means that the country has some 210.000 teachers and about 40.000 other employees working in the sector. The total budget for education in OECD countries encompasses on average 12.3 per cent of the total public expenditure (OECD, 1996a). Teacher salaries represent some 60 per cent of education spending (OECD, 1996b).

The teaching profession currently faces some important issues and problem areas:
1) a sense of profound dissatisfaction within the teaching body, 2) the perception of the key role of teachers in the pursuit of quality in education and the increased demand for accountability, 3) the problems of adequate teacher supply (OECD, 1990). Successful educational policies are needed to influence these trends and to tackle these problems of the teaching profession.

5.2.1 Dissatisfaction within the teaching force

Teachers are expected to have a calling for the profession they have chosen and to be very devoted to their jobs. Recently, however, many complaints can be heard from teachers about the low standing of the profession, the lack of career opportunities, the high workload and the inadequate compensations. According to Prick (1990) teachers are less satisfied in their profession and suffer from more stress than people in comparable professions. The magnitude of staff absenteeism is relatively high in education, although it is mainly caused by a small group of -mostly elderly- teachers. Gallup (1989, in Hill, 1994) reported that 23 per cent of the primary teachers who responded to a telephone survey, seriously considered leaving the profession, with stress and workload being the most commonly cited reasons. *Burnout*, the phenomenon of being physically and mentally exhausted, is considered a severe threat to many well- functioning teachers. It is the main factor that causes demotivation according to Van Ginkel (1985). It arises from a combination of factors, but difficulties with students are considered to be one of the main sources, or at least the crucial element that sets it off (Huberman, 1993).

Two groups of factors increase the demands on teachers and are likely to lead to teacher burnout. *Primary factors* are those factors which have a direct effect on the teacher in the classroom and which may result in tension connected with negative emotions. Examples of such factors are lack of materials, inadequate working conditions due to institutional limitations, increased violence within schools (Esteve, 1989), the use of modern information technology in school, the integration of special and regular education, more individualized tuition, and the influx of cultural minorities in schools (Neave, 1992; Scheerens, 1995). Workload is not only related to the number of working hours, but also to the tasks to be performed in those hours. The amount of time a teacher has to spent on teaching is regarded as an indication of the workload; more teaching hours are associated with a higher workload.

Table 5.1: *Teaching time and working time of teachers (public lower secondary education)*

Country	Teaching hours per annum		Teaching weeks per annum	Teaching time as a percentage of working time
	1991/1992	1993/1994	1993/1994	1993/1994
Austria	747	651	39	41
Belgium	720	720	37	-
Denmark		750	40	45
Finland	798			
France	632	660	36	-
Germany (West)	761	712	40	42
Greece		569	36	38
Ireland	792	735	33	100
Italy	612	612	34	74
Netherlands	954	954	40	60
New Zealand	897	869	39	-
Norway	666	611	38	36
Portugal	648	681	39	46
Spain	900	900	36	62
Sweden	576	576		33
Switzerland		1056	39	-
Turkey	1080	996	36	92
United Kingdom	669			
United States	1042	964	36	
Country mean	781	766	37	56

Note: Some countries have no data on official working time   (Sources: OECD, 1995, 1996a)

Table 5.1 provides international information on the number of hours (60 minutes) per year a public junior high school teacher teaches a group of students according to the formal policy (school years of reference: 1991/1992 and 1993/1994). Furthermore, some figures on the formal length of the school year are presented.

Across countries there appears to be a considerable variance in teaching time (OECD, 1995, 1996a; Van Amelsvoort & Scheerens, 1996). The average number of teaching hours across all countries is 781 in 1991/1992 and 766 in 1993/1994. The range goes from 576 hours in Sweden to 1080 hours in Turkey (1991/1992), and from 569 hours in Greece to 1056 hours in Switzerland (1993/1994). The proportion of the working time teachers devote to teaching is presented in the far right column and is on average 56 per cent.

Countries vary quite substantially with respect to this proportion, which could be interpreted as an indication of the differences in teacher workload. The highest workload of teachers can be found in Turkey (92%) and Ireland (100%), while the lowest workload can be reported for the Scandinavian countries. In Norway and Sweden teachers have to spend only 36 per cent and 33 per cent of their working time on teaching activities respectively. Teachers spend on average 37 weeks per year on teaching.

Secondary factors are more indirect and may diminish teacher motivation, involvement, and the effort he or she is willing to put in the job (Esteve, 1989). There have been, for instance, changes in the role of the teacher and of the traditional agents of social integration (family, community): teachers are expected to take part in a greater part of primary social integration. The societal attitude toward teachers has also changed: teachers get part of the blame for vandalism and for the many deficiencies of the education system, support of parents is no longer unconditional, teachers are held as responsible for unsuccessful pupil careers and the status of their profession has declined (as a result of low payment and deterioration of the image of the teacher). Immobility, in the sense of no career options and working too long within the same organization, is regarded as an important cause for teacher absenteeism in education (Prick, 1990).

Furthermore, some secondary factors are related to the modernization of the teaching job. They can be interpreted negatively in the sense of an increased burden, but they can also have a stimulating effect on teachers. An example of such a factor is the increased decision-making power provided to teachers, which implies that they have to invest more time in school policy-making and in contacts with parents and external constituencies (Scheerens, 1995).

Teachers are compensated for their efforts in various ways. Among them intrinsic motivation as a result of contact with youth can be regarded as very important (Huberman & Grounauer, 1993). Other forms of compensation are salary, immaterial rewards, career opportunities and, in principle, public recognition for the teaching job.

Table 5.2 shows the average gross salaries of teachers in public lower secondary education at the middle of their career, i.e. after 15 years of experience. It also provides information on the number of years it takes to grow from minimum to maximum salary. Salaries have been converted into purchasing power parity (PPP) rates (an international conversion measure) in order to make comparisons among countries meaningful. Teacher salaries can be related to the gross domestic product per capita (per capita GDP; an index for the national welfare level) to get an idea of the status of the teaching profession in a country.

Table 5.2: *Mid-career salaries of teachers in* **lower secondary** *public education (in equivalent US dollars converted using PPP's (price level 1992; 1994)), GDP per capita, and number of years from minimum to maximum salary*

Country	1991/1992			1993/1994		
	GDP per capita (1992)	Gross salary 15 years of experience	Years from minimum to maximum salary	GDP per capita (1994)	Gross salary 15 years of experience	Years from minimum to maximum salary
Austria	18 096	25 497	34	20 210	25 533	34
Belgium	18 195	25 514	27	20 166	27 997	27
Denmark	-	-		20 548	28 096	14
Finland	14 545	24 049	20	16 208	22 727	20
Germany (West)	20 435	33 516	22	19 675	36 213	21
Greece	-		-	11 315	14 946	32
Ireland	12 391	27 697	24	15 212	34 248	24
Italy	17 482	23 864	40	18 681	23 133	40
Netherlands	17 023	26 712	25	18 589	28 191	25
New Zealand	14 434	25 631	9	16 248	22 511	8
Norway	17 756	21 336	14	21 968	21 806	14
Portugal	9 766	26 529	29	12 335	30 079	29
Spain	12 853	25 520	45	13 581	26 955	42
Sweden	16 590	19 698	15	17 422	20 413	20
Switzerland	-		-	23 942	49 095	21
Turkey	3 728	8 964	29	5 271	7 172	27
United States	23 215	31 258	16	25 512	29 577	16
Country mean	15 465	24 699	25	17 464	26 394	24

(Sources: OECD 1995, 1996a)

There are fairly large differences in salaries for teachers across countries as well as substantial differences in the number of years required to obtain the maximum salary (OECD, 1995, 1996a; Van Amelsvoort & Scheerens, 1996). Although many teachers have faced contracting education budgets during the eighties, Table 5.2 indicates that teacher salaries have risen after 15 years of experience between 1991 and 1994 and that they are above the GDP per capita in all countries.Interesting is the salary (increase) relative to (increases of) the GDP per capita. The mean ratio 'salary to GDP' is 1.6 1991/1992 and 1.5 in 1993/1994, indicating no substantial shift in teachers' standing. The status of Irish, and Portuguese teachers is relatively high, as their mid-career salaries are far above GDP per capita in both years. The standing of teachers in 1993/1994 is also relatively high in Switzerland (ratio 'salary to GDP' = 2.05). Teachers' salaries after 15 years of experience are relatively low in Norway and Sweden.

On average teachers grow from their starting salary to their maximum salary in 24 years. In Sweden the number of years to reach the maximum salary has grown from 15 to 20 years. In most countries the figures for 1991/1992 do not deviate from the 1993/1994 figures with respect to the number of years required to progress to the maximum salary.

Dissatisfaction can easily emerge when there is no longer a balance between the professional competence and commitment, the professional demands, and the professional recognition in terms of either status or financial compensation or both. Obviously, some distortions in this balance have appeared. Educational policies aimed at maintaining this balance cannot neglect any of these aspects if they are going to be successful (OECD, 1990).

5.2.2 The role of teachers in the pursuit of quality in education

The second reason for paying attention to teacher motivation and commitment is the alleged role of teachers in the pursuit of quality in education. Improving the quality of education is at the policy agenda of most governments. High motivation and strong commitment to work are essential requirements for effective schooling (Sergiovanni, 1987). Although the role of teachers in and of itself cannot guarantee the quality of education, it is considered the most necessary factor in providing a sound education (OECD, 1990).

Indeed, if we look for teacher variables that might influence the quality of education from a holistic perspective, teacher motivation and satisfaction frequently rise as factors that matter. Empirical findings resulting from school effectiveness research indicate that teacher effects are more important than school effects (Luyten & Snijders, 1996). However, the results of looking for specific teacher variables (i.e. teacher characteristics) that have shown empirically to have a significant positive association with educational attainment, are rather disappointing. Teacher preparedness in the sense of subject matter knowledge and in the sense of pedagogical knowledge, have shown empirically to matter as far as achievement is concerned. Teacher's intentions, objectives and expectations also seem to matter in constituting appropriate instructional behavior (cf. Brophy & Good, 1986).

Yet, looking from the effectiveness perspective not only at descriptive characteristics of teachers, but at the *actual functioning* of teachers in the classroom, the instructional effectiveness research results (cf. Creemers, 1994) underline three basic elements of the teaching process that can be influenced by teachers on the one hand and may improve students' achievement on the other: 1) optimizing instructional time, 2) giving students the opportunity to learn in the sense of correspondence between content taught and content assessed, and 3) providing structured teaching, characterized by setting clear instructional objectives, frequent review and questions, and feedback and correctives (Scheerens, 1995). Consequently, teachers have to stay motivated and committed to play their role in the pursuit of quality adequately. Effectiveness-enhancing conditions of schooling that are indirectly connected to teachers' functioning are according to Levine and Lezotte (1990): a productive school climate and culture, characterized by faculty cohesion, collaboration, consensus, communication, and collegiality, and by faculty input into decision making. Furthermore, teachers should be supported adequately by both outstanding leadership and the availability and effective utilization of instructional support personnel.

Closely related to the issue of the role of teachers in improving the quality of education is the trend of the increased demand for accountability. Educational policies tend to become more output-oriented. Schools have to account for their performances and so do teachers. Some countries have even introduced merit pay to stimulate, although such measures have sometimes been known to be contra-productive. In general, accountability requirements are likely to increase some teachers' sense of an environment that poses even higher demands.

5.2.3 Adequate teacher supply

Demographic developments affect both the magnitude of the student population and the teaching force, although predictions about the future demand for teachers cannot simply be deducted from demographic developments. After a large recruitment of teachers during the seventies when the 'baby boom' generation was at school, a dramatic drop in the number of births from the beginning of the sixties and the subsequent decline of enrollments of students in most western European countries made the demand for teachers fall and led to an over-supply of teachers during the eighties and early nineties. This over-supply has deteriorated the employment prospects of teachers in the sense of more temporary and part-time appointments, a decrease in external teacher mobility, and a blocking of career

Table 5.3: Gender distribution of public **primary** teachers within age groups as a percentage of all teachers in public primary education

Country	Age < 30 male 1991/1992	1993/1994	Age < 30 female 1991/1992	1993/1994	Age 30-39 male 1991/1992	1993/1994	Age 30-39 female 1991/1992	1993/1994	Age 40-49 male 1991/1992	1993/1994	Age 40-49 female 1991/1992	1993/1994	Age 50-60 male 1991/1992	1993/1994	Age 50-60 female 1991/1992	1993/1994	Age > 60 male 1991/1992	1993/1994	Age > 60 female 1991/1992	1993/1994	Total male 1991/1992	1993/1994	Total female 1991/1992	1993/1994
Austria	2	2	21	19	5	4	34	33	7	7	20	25	3	3	6	6	1	1	1	0	18	17	82	83
Belgium	3	3	13	13	9	7	23	25	18	12	20	22	8	9	6	9	0	0	0	0	38	30	62	70
Denmark		1		2		9		15		19		27		11		12		2		1		42		58
Finland	1		4		9		20		9		20		12		18		3		4		35		65	
France	2	2		10		9		23		9		30		5		13		0		0	24	24	76	76
Germany	0	0		6	1	2	29	20	3	6	30	36	3	6	18	22	1	0		1		15		85
Italy	2	2	8	8	1	1	29	27	3	3	30	34	3	3	18	19	1	1	5	4	8	7	93	93
Netherlands	2	2		12		11		25		15		22		5		8		0		0		33		67
New Zealand	2	2	12		5		24		21		16		5		14		0		2		20		80	
Portugal	1	2	8	7	3	7	25	25	2	6	24	33	2	3	18	14	1	1	15	2	9	18	91	82
Sweden	2	2		4		4		11		9		34		5		24		6		1		21		79
Switzerland	5	5		19		10		21		10		20		5		9		1		1		31		69
United States	1	2	6	10	4	3	19	18	6	6	34	36	4	3	20	19	0	0	6	3	15	14	85	86

Sources (OECD 1995, 1996a)

developments. Clearly, these effects have made the teacher profession less attractive.

Today, youth cohorts are starting to rise again. We also face the problem of a greying teaching force: a large number of teachers will be reaching retirement in the next two decades (OECD, 1996b). At this moment about 40 per cent of European teachers in public primary and secondary education are between 40 and 49 years of age (OECD, 1995; Van Amelsvoort & Scheerens, 1996). The number of teachers under 30 fell in the European Community from 18 per cent in 1985 to 11 per cent in 1993 (OECD, 1996b).

Table 5.3 provides insight into the age and gender distribution in percentages of the total teacher force at the level of public primary education. Empty cells indicate data inavailability.

In public primary education teachers are predominantly female. A relatively high proportion of male teachers can be found in Belgium (38% in 1991/1992) and Denmark (42% 1993/1994). For some countries the gender distribution can be compared over the two years. The percentage of male teachers in Portugal has increased while in Belgium it has decreased. Looking at the gender distribution within age groups, the highest proportion of female teachers is between 30 and 49 years of age.

Due to both an assumed overall decrease of younger people entering the work force and into teaching combined with the abolishment of many facilities for early retirement the teacher aged 40 to 49 is expected to stay in the profession until these teachers are about 65 years old (Prick, 1990). Research by Van Ginkel (1985) in the Dutch educational context shows, however, that only one of four teachers stays in his/her profession until he or she is 65 years old. Therefore, from a political point of view, it is necessary to keep these teachers motivated. A high level of teacher burnout is not acceptable and can easily lead to supply problems. Additionally, countries will have to recruit new teachers, an effort whose success depends highly on the attractiveness of the teaching job. This implies big challenges for both national educational policies and the management of schools in dealing with issues such as the status of teaching, compensation and job prospects.

5.3 Theories on commitment and motivation

After an explanation of the policy relevance of the issue of teacher motivation at the level of a country's education system as a whole, some intrinsic aspects of teacher commitment and motivation within school organizations will be focussed on. First some motivation theories will be presented in section 5.3.1. Several definitions of the concept of commitment emphasize the linkage between the individual and the organization. Commitment implies motivation, agreement on goals, loyalty and effort. Referring to Mowday, Steers and Porter (1979), Reyes (1990) states that commitment leads to a) a strong belief and acceptance of the organization's goals and values, 2) a willingness to exert considerable effort on behalf of the organization and 3) a strong desire to maintain organizational membership. From a perspective of exchange, commitment can be regarded as a function of a cognitive evaluation of the costs and benefits of maintaining organizational membership. From a psychological perspective, people's need for stability leads to an identification with the goals and beliefs of the organization. In this view commitment arises to the extent that organizational experiences help to attain goals of mastery and support. The sociological perspective posits that commitment is a central process by which the personality system and the social system become articulated. Theories about commitment will be presented in section 5.3.2.

5.3.1 Motivation theories

The concept of motivation is closely related to satisfaction. A widely used conceptualization of job satisfaction is Herzberg's (1966) 'two-factor theory'. He distinguishes between 'satisfiers', which are factors that give rise to job satisfaction and that are intrinsic to the job, and 'dissatisfiers', which are contextual factors that cause dissatisfaction, but cannot in and of themselves bring about satisfaction. Intrinsic motivation arises from satisfiers as achievement, recognition, work itself, responsibility, advancement and possibility of growth. Examples of demotivating dissatisfiers are company policy and administration, supervision, working conditions, status, personal life, security and salary (cf. Hill, 1994).

Although Herzberg's distinction has been subject to considerable criticism, several research results underline the importance of intrinsic job factors as sources of job satisfaction of teachers (cf. Conley & Levinson, 1993; Hill, 1994; Huberman, 1993; McPherson et al., 1986; Sergiovanni, 1987). Following the well known need classification scheme of Maslow (1954, 1970), White (1959, in Sergiovanni, 1987) examined the competence motive - the desire for mastery over one's environment. He concluded that the need to be competent is intrinsic and is aroused when individuals are faced with new challenges rather than in response to external matters such as increased pay or directives.

According to Atkinson and to McClelland (1964, 1961, in Sergiovanni 1987), who developed a social motives theory, teachers come to work with different mixes of the need for achievement, power-influence and affiliation. Appropriate environmental circumstances are necessary to activate this motivational potential and turn it into motivational behavior. Only recently, Kottkamp (1990, in Conley & Levinson, 1993) reported a noticeable shift among teachers in the relative valuation of classroom-based (intrinsic) rewards in relation to extra-classroom-based (extrinsic) rewards.

A useful motivation theory for complex organizations such as schools concerns the expectancy theory (cf. Miskal, 1982; Vroom, 1964). It suggests that the effort people put into their work will depend on a) their expectations of the results that are likely to occur, b) the values they place on the expected rewards associated with these results and c) the probability that such rewards will actually be received if the work is done. So, results or rewards should be perceived as being desirable, individuals need to know what needs to be done to obtain the outcomes and need to be confident in their own ability to perform adequately (Sergiovanni, 1987).

5.3.2 Theories on commitment

This section draws heavily on the reviews of McPherson cum suis (1986) and Reyes (1990) and presents some theories on commitment from the sociological and psychological perspective.

According to *Kanter* (1968) commitment is mainly an investment of the individual in the organization and is associated with individual solidarity to the organization. She distinguishes between three forms of solidarity. The first form, called continuance commitment, is characterized by cognitive, rational commitment. Individuals believe that their interests are sustained by participation in the organization. They know that personal sacrifices are necessary to remain members in the organization and that their investments give them the right to future gains. Commitment arises from the feeling that participating within the organization provides more benefits than leaving the organization.

The second form is more relationship oriented and is called cohesion commitment, defined as the individual's affective solidarity with a group. Organizations engage in symbolic activities to develop psychological attachments to the organization. On the other hand individuals have to renunciate outside relationships that may disrupt group cohesion and harmony. Moreover, individual separateness has to be relinquished and replaced by identification with the collective whole. This 'communion' leads to a "we-consciousness" within the group.

The third form is called control, by which a more evaluative commitment of the individual to the organization is meant. Individuals become attached and obedient to the norms and values of the organization, which, on the other side, become an important guide to suitable behaviors. Control commitment involves both mortification and surrender. Mortification refers to the submission of individual identity to social control, whereas surrender refers to an attachment of decision-making prerogatives to a greater power. Although both processes may be experienced by teachers, particularly during the start of their teaching career, they are not assumed to play a big role in schools.

In summary, Kanter finds commitment in the sacrifices that are imposed upon the members of the organization. Socializing practices like mortification, renunciation, communion, and surrender bind the individual firmly and comfortingly to the social group (McPherson et al., 1986, p. 156).

Etzioni (1975) conceptualizes commitment as a compliance relationship between the organization's application of control and the type of employee involvement within the organization. In contrast to Kanter, Etzioni views commitment more as an exchange relationship than as mere response to behavioral requirements. Commitment, or involvement, is exhibited in three forms: 1) moral, 2) alienative and 3) calculative. Organizational power is correlated with these forms of commitment and is distinguished in 1) normative power, 2) coercive power and 3) remunerative power.

Moral involvement refers to a strong positive orientation toward the organization, in other words, to a high commitment. The individual internalizes the goals, values, and norms of an organization and identifies with the authority structure. In organizations in which moral involvement is high, normative power is supposed to be the reward for this commitment. Normative power can be associated with the use of esteem, prestige, and other symbolic rewards to obtain employee compliance.

At the other end of the continuum, alienative involvement is found. Alienative involvement represents a negative orientation toward the organization, a very low level of commitment. In this case coercive power, which refers to threats of physical harm or punishment, is used to secure compliance and to obtain commitment. Etzioni recognizes that individuals are seldom either fully committed to or alienated from their organizations.

Calculative involvement is less intense than moral involvement, and largely based on an exchange relationship. Individuals become committed to the organization because of the benefits and the rewards they receive from the organization and respond calculatively to those in power. Remunerative power fits to this form of commitment. It refers to control of the allocation of material sources and rewards to secure compliance. Examples of such material means are salaries and wages, commissions, fringe benefits, services and commodities.

Summarizing Etzioni's theory of commitment, McPherson cum suis (1986, p.158) state that some individuals serve within the organization at a higher level of involvement than others. For these people symbolic rewards will do, while others, less involved, may require harder rewards and sanctions of money, power, or threat of punishment.

After these sociological theories, a more psychological approach to commitment will be discussed, in which the nurturing of employee behavior is regarded as the key to commitment. While recognizing the important role of the individual in building commitment, *Porter and Miles* (1974) suggest that what happens to the individual in the work situation is also a centrally motivating force. They approach the concept of commitment the other way around by focusing on the organization's commitment to its employees, guided and displayed by the attitude and the behavior of the organization's manager. This theory is largely based on motivation theories (cf. Herzberg, 1966; Maslow, 1970; Vroom, 1964) that play an important role in the human-relations view on management.

Porter and Miles developed a classification system of variables involved in the management of employee motivation as nurturance, variables that can -more or less- be affected by educational administrators in order to influence teacher commitment. These variables are 1) individual attitudes, such as expectations of employees, 2) job characteristics, such as the accessibility of individual performance, degree of goal clarity and degree of job challenge, 3) work environment characteristics, such as personal significance reinforcement, stability of expectations and reference group experiences and 4) external environmental characteristics, such as demographic, economic, technological and political characteristics.

As McPherson cum suis (1986) summarize, administrators can nurture employees toward commitment through socialization processes and efforts to manipulate job characteristics, reward systems, and aspects of the external environment.

5.4 Teacher commitment in schools

Throughout this chapter several factors likely to affect commitment in schools have been mentioned. In section 5.2.1 primary and secondary factors that increase the demands on, and the workload of teachers have been presented. Additionally, the variables being worthwhile to be subject to nurturance according to Porter and Miles and factors from motivation theories, can be regarded as factors that might affect commitment. First, an overview of all factors that have been found to be related to organizational commitment, and, in addition, to educational organizations is presented in section 5.4.1. The section then focuses on certain features of schools that form constraints for teacher commitment (5.4.2). The third section deals with the life cycle of teachers, which is considered an important factor in affecting commitment (5.4.3).

5.4.1 Factors affecting commitment in educational organizations

Reviews of Mowday, Porter, and Steers (1982) and Reyes (1990) present a number of factors as affecting organizational commitment.

Table 5.4 distinguishes between personal characteristics, role-related characteristics and structural and work experience characteristics as groups of correlates to commitment.

Noticeable in this list of merely positive correlates is the negative correlation between educational level and commitment, and between commitment to the profession and

Table 5.4: *Factors affecting commitment*

---

1. Personal characteristics as correlates to commitment
- longevity   +*
- age   +
- gender (woman)   +
- sense of competence   +
- achievement motivation   +
- higher order needs   +
- educational level   -

2. Role-related characteristics as correlates to commitment
- commitment to profession   -
- role conflict   -
- role overload   -
- job scope   +

3. Structural and work experience characteristics as correlation to commitment
- formalization   +
- decentralization   +
- worker ownership   +
- participation in decision making   +
- degree of perceived organizational support   +
- feeling to be needed   +
- positive environment (co-workers)   +
- opportunities for promotion   +
- perceptions of fairness of promotion process   +

(Source: McPherson et al., 1986)

* + and - symbols indicate positive or negative correlations

organizational commitment. As the educational level of a teacher rises, commitment decreases, the higher the commitment to the profession, the lower organizational commitment.

In addition to this list, regarding outcomes of commitment, Reyes (1990) concludes from other studies that commitment has been significantly negatively associated with turnover, and to a lesser extent, with other withdrawal behaviors, such as decreased performance and increased absenteeism and tardiness (cf. Steers, 1977 in McPherson et al., 1986).

The research on teacher commitment is rather limited in size and unsystematic in the sense that it is based on different theoretical foundations. Reyes (1990, p. 153) developed a more or less eclectic model of teacher commitment in which the research findings on this subject have been included. He uses the following definition of teacher commitment:

"a psychological identification of the individual teacher with the school's goals and values, and the intention of that teacher to maintain organizational membership and become involved in the job beyond personal interest".

Reyes' model is presented in Figure 5.1.

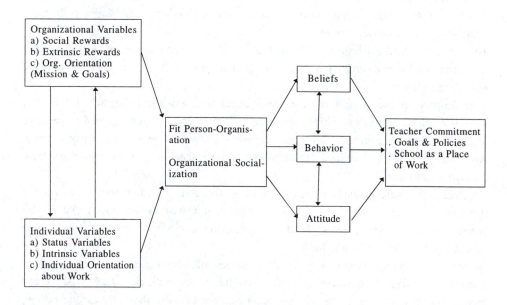

Organizational Boundaries

Figure 5.1: *Model of Teacher Commitment to an Organization (Source: Reyes, 1990)*

Within the box *'Individual variables'* the first group of variables concerns status variables. Status variables comprise tenure in an organization (greater tenure leads to more commitment), age (older teachers are more committed than younger ones), teaching experience (more experience, higher commitment), educational level (higher educational level, lower commitment) and sex (women display higher levels of commitment than men).

Intrinsic variables, the second group, form characteristics of the job tasks that positively affect commitment: 1) the extent to which worker expectations are met by job tasks, 2) the opportunity for optional social interaction in completing tasks, 3) the extent to which teachers are involved in planning and making decisions about their jobs, and 4) the amount of authority teachers have in order to make decisions about their immediate surroundings.

Finally, the individual overall work orientation of teachers affects commitment. For example, teachers who prefer materialistic rewards exhibit lower levels of commitment than teachers preferring normative rewards.

In the box *'Organizational Variables'*, three groups are also distinguished. Social reward variables include relationships with the supervisor, co-workers, and students. If these relationships are positive, they enhance commitment.

The extent to which extrinsic rewards, such as pay, benefits and promotion opportunity are used by a school to motivate teachers also correlates positively with teacher commitment according to Reyes.

With respect to the overall organizational orientation, empirical research shows that schools emphasizing the normative aspects and affective goals of schools tend to generate higher levels of commitment than those emphasizing career ladders or merit pay systems. Also, schools with well-defined organizational cultures tend to generate higher levels of teacher commitment.

Organizational socialization concerns a factor in the box *'Person-Organization Fit'*. It represents the match of individual and organizational values. It was found that private schools generate high levels of teacher commitment because of the similarity in the school's and the teacher's orientation.

In his model Reyes (1990) suggests four stages of commitment. First there is an interaction between the organizational values and the values to the new teacher. At the end of this exploratory stage the teacher may find a match between these values: the person-organization fit, the second stage. The process of organizational socialization then starts and, depending on the strength of the person-organization fit, this socialization will lead to the development (the third stage) of specific beliefs, attitudes and behaviors, which determine the level of teacher commitment to his/her workplace and to the school's goals and mission.

5.4.2 Features of schools that influence commitment

The nature of education and educational organizations puts some special constraints on teacher commitment. McPherson cum suis (1986) subsequently discuss: 1) the tension between the professional and the bureaucratic loyalty, 2) the relationship between commitment and job performance, 3) the inadequate level of reward, and 4) the object of the teacher's allegiance.

Schools are often characterized as professional bureaucracies, in which relatively autonomous professionals, i.e. teachers, are responsible for the learning processes of the students (cf. Mintzberg, 1979). Professional teachers at higher levels of education are known for their primary loyalty to their academic disciplines, and their secondary loyalty to the institution they work in. Educators are professionally trained individuals who work in bureaucracies. There are typical tensions between professional values and bureaucratic goals, as well as between professionally nurtured images of behavior (e.g. individual autonomy) and bureaucratically established definitions of role (e.g. responsiveness to supervisory directions). The length and nature of professional training tend to correlate negatively with bureaucratic loyalty. In the instrumental view of many teachers the primary function of the school as an organization is to serve the professional. Therefore, a professional's loyalty or commitment to an organization can be regarded as depending on the adequacy of its support according to McPherson cum suis (1986).

Furthermore, policies created in order to mandate and implement a highly structured, prescriptive and standardized curriculum that result in an increased bureaucracy in the classroom can be regarded as contradictory to teachers as professional decision-makers and may diminish motivation and commitment. School organizational patterns that encourage isolation, privatism, and lack of social interaction among teachers are also a severe threat to teacher commitment according to Sergiovanni (1987).

The second constraint on teacher commitment concerns the rather weak relationship between commitment and job performance that has, until now, emerged from studies of commitment. Even though it has to be admitted that it is very hard to measure teacher effectiveness, it cannot be stated, at this moment, that the committed teacher is the better teacher (McPherson et al., 1986). Although, section 5.2.2 states that teachers are indeed considered to be the key to educational performance, teacher effectiveness has been studied merely through instructional effectiveness criteria.

The inadequate level of compensation is mentioned as another constraint for teacher commitment, i.e. the reward structure of education does not include incentives to honor commitment. Teachers are paid on the basis of a standard salary schedule based on years of experience rather than quality of teaching (cf. Van Amelsvoort & Scheerens, 1996), and on accumulation rather than application of training. Still, immaterial rewards that follow from working with students are important to teachers and to their feelings of satisfaction. However, the general feeling is that the simple joy formed in teaching has diminished in recent years due to the experienced higher workload. Financial rewards, as well as opportunities for upward mobility and task differentiation within a context of job enlargement within schools have failed to keep pace with the increased work burden and therefore have failed to compensate for the increased work load. Section 5.5 discusses some organizational solutions for this problem in the Dutch context.

A final constraint for teacher commitment due to the features of educational organizations concerns the uncertainty about the object of commitment according to McPherson cum suis (1986). Should teachers be committed to the organization, to the students, or to the profession? Although teachers should be committed to their students first, some teachers, particularly those at working in high schools are more subject-centered than student-centered. Additionally, when the focus is on the student, opinions differ with regard to which students merit what kind of and how much attention. Moreover, the object of commitment seems to change during the teaching career. This issue is further elaborated in the next section, when the relation between the life cycle of teachers and commitment is discussed.

5.4.3 The life cycle of teachers

Huberman (1993) studied the human life cycle and focused his own research on the lives of teachers and the career paths of secondary school teachers in particular. Although typical sequences can be found, (cf. Brekelmans & Wubbels, 1994; Buchanan, 1974 in McPherson et al., 1986) the development of the teaching profession is not a linear process at all and it does not develop in the same way for all teachers. For that reason the distinct phases depicted in Huberman's model in Figure 5.2 should merely be regarded as central tendencies. The figure shows multiple branches at mid-career. These branches are to be interpreted as optional courses of events.

1. Career entry
Entrance into classroom life is somewhat uniform among beginning teachers and is often characterized as a period of both survival and discovery. Survival aspects accompany, for example, the encountered reality shock in teaching, the continuous trial and error processes, the mental state of self-absorption and the experienced distance between ideals and daily classroom realities. Teachers may also experience the beginning of their career as a period of discovery, from an enthusiasm of beginning a career with experimentation, from a feeling of pride of having one's own students and programmes and from the feeling of being part of a professional guild.

2. Stabilization phase
After the exploration phase, a period of stabilization and responsibility starts. An important characteristic of this phase is the strong emergence of commitment: the decision to commit oneself to the order of teaching, which means an elimination of other professional possibilities. Independence or autonomy plays a significant role in this stabilization phase. Stabilization also relates to pedagogical mastery; one is less preoccupied with oneself and much more concerned with instructional and pedagogical matters. With increased pedagogical mastery a being comes at ease with one's performance in the classroom.

Years of experience   **Career phases**

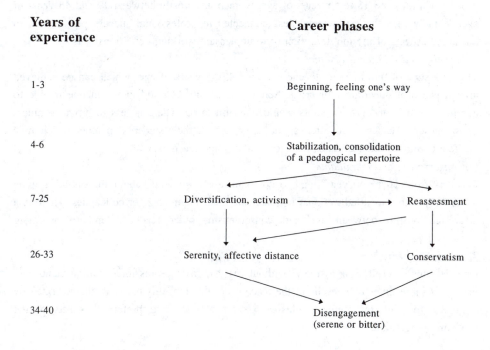

Figure 5.2: *Trends in the life cycle of teachers (Source: Huberman, 1993)*

3. Experimentation and diversification

After this stabilization a phase of diversification can sometimes be observed. Pedagogical consolidation leads to personal experiments by diversifying their instructional materials, methods of evaluation, modes of grouping the students, and/or instructional sequences. It can be the most highly motivated and dynamic phase. The motivation can translate into heightened personal ambitions (more authority, responsibility, prestige) through access to administrative slots. The teacher sets off in search for new challenges, new stimulations, new ideas and new commitments.

4. Reassessment

After the diversification stage a phase of self-questioning may follow, although reassessment can also follow the stabilization stage. This is a period of self-doubt and routine, or perhaps a period of disenchantment with the outcomes of successive reforms. It occurs at 'mid-career', generally between the ages of 35 and 50 or between the fifteenth and twenty-fifth year of teaching. There appears to be a different experience between men and women in this period (Prick, 1986 in Huberman, 1993). While men go through this phase when they are 36 to 55 years of age, women are mostly between 39 and 45 years of age. With women the crisis seems less connected to professional success per se than to unwanted aspects of the job definition or to unpleasant working conditions.

5. Serenity and relational distance

This is a state of mind among teachers around 45-55 years of age, which can be achieved after a phase of uncertainty or crisis. Serenity is a state of mind in which one is able to accept oneself is and not as others would like him to be. There is less to prove to others or to oneself. Teachers are often at the same age as their students' parents which may create a communication distance between students and teachers.

6. Conservatism and complaints

Teachers from 50 to 60 years tend to complain about students, about the public attitude toward education, local educational policies, and about their younger colleagues. There is a clear relationship between age and conservatism; older teachers tend to be more conservative.

7. Disengagement

One detaches oneself progressively, without regrets, from professional commitments and one takes more time for oneself. In the teaching profession, this phase is characterized by a greater focusing on preferred classes, preferred tasks, and preferred aspects of the academic programme.

Teachers' career paths may follow different streams, as the arrows indicate. A highly harmonious sequence would go from diversification, via serenity to serene disengagement. The two most problematic trajectories, according to Huberman, would be either from reassessment to bitter disengagement or from reassessment via conservatism to bitter disengagement.

Is there any evidence for a relationship between the life cycle of teachers and their motivations, their satisfaction, their commitment?

Contradictory results with respect to the dominant motives to *enter* the teaching profession appear from the research literature. In addition to professional motives, such as love of subject matter, contact with young people, and the desire to 'serve' others, also material motives, such as job security, salary, and long vacations, are mentioned. Secondary school teachers, however, appear to be predominantly motivated to the profession through the subject matter. Huberman and Grounauer (1993) investigated the initial motives and distinguished between active motivations - which suggest a deliberate choice -, material motives and passive motives. Active motives are predominant and among them 'contact with youth' and 'love of the subject matter' form the greatest part (see Table 5.5).

To measure their satisfaction at the *middle* of their career, teachers were asked whether they would choose teaching again if they could make a new start with a professional career. Fifty per cent of the teachers firmly answered 'Yes', thirty per cent answered 'Yes, but with qualifier', eight per cent answered indifferently and twelve per cent answered 'No'.

To determine how satisfied primary head teachers are with their jobs and careers, Hill (1994) asked them whether they would encourage their sons and daughters to follow in their footsteps. Their answers were not that positive; more than half of them declared that they would encourage neither son nor daughter to follow them into teaching.

Table 5.5: *'Active' motives for entering the teaching profession (n=156)*

Active motives*	Number of responses	Percentage of all responses
• Contact with youth, at ease with young people	50	12**
• Love of the subject matter	45	11
• Discovery, success with initial substitute teaching	39	9
• Desire to share one's knowledge	35	9
• Modelling: influence of a former teacher or of parents who were teachers	27	7
• Desire to influence young people socially	24	6
• Success as a pupil; desire to remain in an academic environment	16	4
• 'Natural inclination' as a result of prior studies and choices	14	3
• Power: a desire to 'direct' others	7	2
• Compensate for a perceived educational deficit; desire to 'do better than one's own teachers'	4	1

Source: Huberman and Grounauer (1993)

* This table only contains active motives
** Interpretation: 12% of the total number of motives that have been mentioned

Furthermore, Huberman & Grounauer (1993) found that more satisfying career *ends* are associated with 1) positive starts, 2) the evocation of a period of chance, of diversification or renewal and 3) diverse conditions of stabilization during all stages of the career, such as an enduring commitment to the profession, 'manageable' classes, in which one can maintain good relations with students, good relationships with colleagues and a balance between school and home life/personal interests.

Summarizing his research, Huberman (1993) concludes that the relationships with students are at the heart of most motivations, but also at the heart of the preoccupations, difficulties, crises or dissatisfactions experienced by the teachers. In addition, he states that men put more emphasis on their career than women, who maintain other professional lines. Professional satisfaction for women appears less emotionally charged. This attitude contributes to the maintenance of a constant level of commitment throughout their careers. Men generally pursue full-time positions and depend heavily on the pedagogical and institutional parameters for their self-esteem. Male and female teachers both endure intense moments of self-doubt, but women seem to emerge from them more quickly. The results from the research of Hill (1994) confirm these differences between men and women with respect to job satisfaction. Difficult moments in the career, related to motivation, are: 1) at the start, 2) after 8-15 years of experience, the moment at which reassessment often occurs, and 3) after the failure of a structural reform in which one has invested.

In the view of Huberman, teachers' relationships with the institution change with the career phases and the way in which these phases are experienced by teachers. The overall picture is one of teachers feeling that their efforts are seldom, if at all, recognized institutionally. Teachers demand: 1) more personalized relationships within the hierarchy, 2) administrators on whom they could lean in times of necessity, 3) diversification of professional paths available to them and 4) a more flexible intra-career mobility (Huberman, 1993).

The management of educational organizations taking the maintenance and improvement of teacher commitment seriously should create time for professional reflection and relate the management of human resources to career phases.

5.5 Policy recommendations to improve teacher motivation and commitment

In The Netherlands, the Committee on the Future of the Teaching profession (CFT) has recently developed advice for the Dutch government in which it analyses the role, position and appreciation of the teaching profession and develops some proposals for improvement (Commissie Toekomst Leraarschap, 1993). The CFT observes a number of problems that have to be solved to make the teaching profession more attractive: 1) the internal mobility (within a school) and external mobility (to/from other organizations) for teachers are very limited and make them feel trapped; 2) their job size and burden, absenteeism due to illness and incapacitation are high, whereas payment is relatively low and the status of the teaching profession is controversial; 3) teachers' professional development is very limited. Schools do not pay much attention to teacher performance evaluation, career development, coaching and in-service training.

In accordance with what has been pointed out earlier, the analysis of the CFT shows that it is the disruption of the balance between professional competence, professional demands and professional recognition that causes dissatisfaction, decreased commitment and withdrawal behavior.

The CFT attributes these problems to characteristics of the educational system and to features of school organizations. Regulations from the national governmental level have become very detailed, leaving very little room for human resource management at school level. The straitjacket of central regulations has made schools passive implementators of what is determined at the national level. Human resource management in schools is still in its infancy. Most schools do not consult with staff about their level of performance, nor draw up a long term staff planning. Job differentiation and career development have developed very little. Furthermore, the CFT points to the professional autonomy of teachers; behind the classroom door they decide and are responsible for what happens. Few, if any other, occupations place such faith in the organizational unit of the solitary professional. It is not well understood by people outside education how tiring teaching in front of a class actually is.

In the opinion of the CFT solutions for these problems lay in transforming schools into modern professional labor organizations that act strategically. Instead of the national government, the school boards should become the employers and develop personnel policy and human resource management by means of personnel selection and job allocation, reward structures, performance evaluation, training and development. Schools need more room for human resources development enabling a more flexible, efficient and varied staff input. It should include teacher career development, a self determined appointment and gradual development from junior teachers (limited teaching load and intensive coaching) to senior teachers (full teaching task and more independent).

The CFT is of the opinion that more differentiation in teaching jobs is needed, combined with more co-operation between teachers in order to solve problems in a multi-disciplinary way. Such an approach asks for an open school organization characterized by co-operation and a shared responsibility between staff, which would enable the exchange of knowledge, staff mobility and the freeing of teachers from an extremely isolated and very demanding position. Career development is hardly possible now because job differentiation within schools almost does not exist, although teachers fulfill many different tasks. Schools can create more possibilities for teacher mobility by creating more different jobs: e.g., coordinator of extra-curricular activities, supervisor of a number of grades, counsellor of junior teachers, head of department, career counsellor, supervisor of student counselling and tutorship. When teachers experience more variation in their work and when their expertise can be used better, their job satisfaction will probably be higher, which also may result in a better teaching-learning process quality (cf. Van Ginkel, 1985).

Finally, teacher education needs to be revised. Teachers enter a school after graduating from university or a teacher training institute, and although they often receive some initial coaching from colleagues, in most cases this ends when they receive tenureship. The CFT maintains that schools should plan the teacher career and determine the career path of a teacher in accordance to the development of a teacher's professional skills. Developing school policy should be a joint matter of teachers and school management. Teachers must be stimulated to innovate education. However, increasing the policy area of schools by decreasing central governmental regulations makes it necessary for schools to develop quality control instruments into order to determine their results and to correct undesired effects according to the CFT.

5.5.1 Towards a national policy for the teaching profession

The Dutch government responded positively to the CFT report and incorporated many of the recommendations in a new national education policy for the teaching profession (Ministerie van Onderwijs en Wetenschappen, 1994). The main policy components are: 1) policy measures to turn schools into professional labor organizations, 2) relaxation of the qualification requirements, 3) improvement of teacher education.
In order to facilitate the process of turning schools into professional labor organizations the new national education policy focuses on the primary process (less 'red-tape', i.e. less bureaucratization, more didactical support for teachers, government responsibility for setting the global goals). Second, more decentralization from government to school level with respect to terms of employment is being planned. Furthermore, the government intends to provide schools with opportunities to establish job differentiation, performance evaluation and reward structures. However, it remains the responsibility of the national government to set the frames for both a system of performance evaluation and teacher salary levels. Creating opportunities for job differentiation is meant to improve school internal mobility. External mobility (to other organizations) is supposed to be stimulated by developing a more flexible system of teacher training. A few concrete policy-measures have been taken in the area of working conditions: starting salaries have been raised by up to 35 percent and working time has been reduced by 3 percent. For secondary school teachers, the formal teaching time has been reduced from 28 to 26 hours per week. Also, initiatives on continuing education of teachers are stimulated: schools have a budget for in-service training, can develop their own internal policy on in-service training, about 10 percent of teachers' working time may be devoted to training and education, teachers' performance and investments in in-service training are becoming a criterion for salary and career development and extra resources are spent on sabbatical leaves that are devoted to training and development.
The need for relaxing the qualification requirements, the second policy component, is still

a hot item according to the CFT. Not only formal qualifications of teachers (diplomas, certifications), but also, the actual skills (e.g. as a result of having executed a profession for years) should play a role in recruiting and appointing teachers. The government, in line with this, has started the development of a system of competence requirements for teachers apart from the existing qualification requirements. This system is meant to guide employers in executing an adequate recruitment and human resource development policy. This system of teacher requirements is based on profiles of the profession from which starting competencies for teachers are derived. Basic principles are the description of the profiles of the profession by educational labor and board organizations, a focus on the different roles teachers are assumed to play and measurable requirements in terms of skills. The starting competencies of teachers will get a legal basis and will be renewed every five years. Sitting teachers will also be forced to meet these requirements in order to be subscribed to the newly established Teacher Register.

The third component of the new policy focuses on the improvement of teacher training and education. At this moment the fit between teacher training and labor requirements is considered to be insufficient. The new policy aims at introducing a dual teacher education system, where student teachers work in practice during their training. This measure is meant to reduce the 'reality shock' of beginning teachers, and to provide useful feedback to teacher training programmes. In primary education, an initiative has been taken with the introduction of the so-called LIO's, i.e. student teachers who have not completely finished teacher training college, but get the opportunity to teach at schools under the guidance of an experienced teacher. As a second measure to improve the fit between teacher education (e.g. the development of a common curriculum, the establishment of regional alliances) and teacher practice, better co-operation between organizations participating in teacher education and the development of job-profiles is stimulated by government.

In summary, it can be stated that in the Dutch educational context, schools are expected and stimulated to play a greater role in creating optimal labor conditions for teachers: conditions for good education and for professional development.

5.6 Teacher motivation and commitment from a school effectiveness point of view

There is strong empirical evidence that teacher behavior is an effectiveness enhancing factor (Creemers, 1994). Teachers are considered to be the key to educational performance. However, teacher effectiveness has been studied merely on the basis of instructional effectiveness criteria. Teacher motivation and teacher commitment do not show up as teacher characteristics investigated in school effectiveness research. Characteristics that have been empirically shown to have a positive association with educational attainment are teacher preparedness in the sense of subject matter and pedagogical knowledge (Fraser et al., 1987), and teachers' intentions, objectives and expectations (Brophy & Good, 1986). Teacher motivation and commitment have been studied in relation to job performance, however there is no clear evidence yet whether motivated teachers are better teachers (McPherson et al., 1986; Reyes, 1990).

In this chapter the link between the individual and the organization has been emphasized as the core of the commitment concept. Commitment implies motivation, agreement on goals, loyalty and effort. According to Reyes (1990) commitment leads to a strong belief and acceptance of the organization's goals and values, a willingness to exert considerable effort on behalf of the organization and a strong desire to maintain organizational membership.

The presence of commitment among staff can be regarded as a prerequisite for an effectiveness-enhancing school climate. Several features of such a climate related to commitment have been shown to matter for school effectiveness. In the review of Levine and Lezotte (1990), several aspects of a productive climate and culture that are closely connected with the features of commitment are identified. These include the presence of faculty commitment to a shared and articulated mission focused on achievement, as well as faculty cohesion, collaboration, consensus, communication and collegiality. This shared vision of goals, demonstrated through unity of purpose, collegiality and collaboration, has also been underlined by Sammons et al. (1995) as an effectiveness enhancing condition of schooling.

The idea of commitment as a prerequisite for organizational effectiveness can also be grounded on the perspective of teacher autonomy. Teachers are very autonomous in making decisions regarding instruction. Without commitment and a shared view on the purposes of the organization, chaos is more likely to occur than achievement of organizational objectives (cf. Bomers, 1990).

5.7 Summary and conclusions

In this chapter teacher commitment is regarded mainly as the linkage between the individual and the organization, implying motivation, agreement on goals, loyalty, involvement and effort. This linkage is obvious - with a changing emphasis - in the sociological commitment theories of Kanter and Etzioni, the psychological commitment theory of Porter and Miles and the theory of Reyes, in which several research findings on teacher commitment have been integrated. The concept of motivation has been associated with job satisfaction. Although Herzberg claims that job satisfaction is a function of work features alone, others maintain that it is an outcome of the interaction between the job and the individual.

Dissatisfaction and a decreased commitment within the teaching force is regarded as an important problem, which is likely to result in high levels of teacher absenteeism and even burnout. At the national level these effects of dissatisfaction can easily lead to financial-economic problems in education and to future teacher supply problems. Furthermore, teacher dissatisfaction and decreased commitment of teachers are supposed to negatively affect the quality of education. Teachers are at the heart of the instructional technology for achieving the goals of educational institutions. The quality of the educational process is to a high degree dependent on their expertise, efforts, motivation and commitment. However, considering the role of teachers in the pursuit of educational quality from a narrow effectiveness perspective, i.e. looking for teacher characteristics that have shown to improve student achievement, has not yet yielded clear evidence that teacher motivation and commitment directly affect student achievement. The results of research on effective instruction (Brophy & Good, 1986; Creemers, 1994; Luyten & Snijders, 1996) indicate that teachers play a more indirect role with respect to student performance, namely in providing effective learning conditions to their students. In other words the necessity of nurturing and maintaining teacher motivation and commitment for educational quality stays beyond discussion.

Several reasons for the diminished satisfaction and the decreased commitment have been mentioned: the high workload, the lack of career opportunities, the inadequate compensations and the low standing of the profession. The high workload can be associated with intrinsic job factors and in particular with the contacts with youth. Youth has become more difficult to deal with. Here we face the dilemma that on the one hand this contact with young people seems to be at the heart of most intrinsic motivations of teachers, while, on the other hand, their relationships with students seem to cause many difficulties, crises and dissatisfactions. Successful policies to decrease the workload, therefore, cannot neglect this aspect and should consist of policy measures supporting teachers in their contacts with students. Aspects of the career phase of the teacher should also be taken into account. It seems to make sense to diminish the number of teaching hours for older teachers in order to lower their workload.

The other reasons for teacher dissatisfaction (e.g. inadequate compensation) can be considered indirect or extrinsic factors. It is not clear how much effect on motivation and commitment may be expected from improving these secondary teacher labor conditions only. Conley and Levinson (1993), for instance, investigated the relation between teacher work redesign and job satisfaction. They conceptualized job satisfaction as a function of (teacher participation in) work redesign, rewards (intrinsic and extrinsic benefits), values (wants, desires, seeks to attain from the job) and experience. Their main finding was that participation in work redesign is only associated with job satisfaction among more experienced teachers. Furthermore, they found intrinsic rewards to be in general strong positive predictors of job satisfaction, whereas extrinsic rewards proved to be predictors for job satisfaction for less experienced teachers. The authors conclude that work rewards tap slightly different aspects for more and less experienced teachers. Addressing policy-makers, they recommend the development of policies that increase entry-level salaries as a magnet for less experienced teachers. Later in the teaching career, work redesign schemes that allow teachers to use their special and individual abilities are considered to be a sensible magnet to the profession.

In the policy-measures included in the Dutch policy concerning the teaching profession, little attention has been paid to the elaboration of policy-measures to support teachers in the primary process of teaching. Most attention is paid to transforming schools into professional labor organizations, and thus especially to improving mostly the secondary work conditions.

• CHAPTER 6 •

Leadership in Schools

C.A. van Vilsteren
University of Twente, The Netherlands

6.1 Introduction

Every school has its leaders: a principal, vice-principals, department heads, heads of house, course coordinators, a head of student deans. As is the case in every organization, leaders seem to be necessary in schools, too. The fact that a school requires leadership, and the way in which this leadership is conducted are not trivial matters. This conviction is shared by practitioners, as well as school leadership theorists and researchers.
This chapter presents a selective overview of different ways in which leadership scholars have tried to reach a better understanding of school leader behavior and its impact. Although our understanding of school leadership is growing, it needs much more analysis, theorizing and research.

In the field of educational administration no consensus has been reached on definitions of the terms 'leadership' and 'management'. In this chapter the terms 'leader' and 'leadership' will be used predominantly. The terms 'manager' and 'management' will be allocated to a specific domain of leadership activities: legal matters, finance and budgeting, personnel regulations, employment conditions, time scheduling, availability and maintenance of accommodation and facilities, and the functioning of the accounting and clerical school office. These activities are concerned with the more technical aspects of daily life in a school organization. One should be aware, however, that in much of the literature the term 'management' is also used as a catch-all term for all kinds of leader behaviors. The core elements and processes of a school organization are the teaching and learning activities, the curriculum, student guidance and counselling, the long term school strategy, and the learning results and school performance. As far as school leaders are concerned with these core aspects of school life, however, the use of the term 'leadership' is preferred. It is stressed here that in the literature on leadership, the terms 'leader' and 'leadership' are used with different scopes and meanings; they are also used there as overall terms for all kinds of leadership behavior. For this reason the specific teaching and learning directed behavior of school leaders is often labelled as *'instructional leadership'*.

The title of this chapter (Leadership in schools) is a well considered choice. In everyday language, a leader is currently characterized by the object of his or her leader activities: e.g. the principal *of* school X; the head *of* the mathematics department; the coordinator *of* the computer technology course. As a consequence of this, the chapter title would have been "Leadership *of* schools". However, this title would result in too narrow a scope in which leadership is, in essence, limited to the organizational leader of a school: the rector, principal, head or director. It is the explicit intention of this chapter to present 'leadership' as an activity which is carried out at different levels and in various areas of a school organization, namely: school level, course level, classroom level, and department level, or curriculum, student guidance, instruction, testing and evaluation, and teacher supervision areas. However, this chapter does not include 'classroom management' as part of leadership in schools. The central focus will be on 'leadership in schools beyond the classroom'. The literature about school leadership demonstrates a great bias toward leaders in the hierarchical top of a school. As a consequence of this bias, the school rectors, principals, heads or directors unavoidably have a central position in this chapter. But, where reasonable and suitable, leaders on other levels and in other areas of a school will be presented to facilitate a better understanding of the leadership phenomenon in schools.

The next section (6.2) presents an overview of the main issues of school leadership, including some criticisms. The third section is dedicated to the main leadership theories and their relevance to the management of schools. Because the cognitive perspective on leadership seems to be a promising new approach for a better understanding of what school leaders do and why they behave as they do, this approach is given special attention in section 6.4. The chapter ends with a section (6.5) about an exclusive school leadership topic, the so-called instructional leadership. This kind of leadership is regarded as necessary by many school leaders, but is hardly carried out in practice.

6.2 School leadership

6.2.1 Introduction

The practice of management and leadership in schools has developed differently in various countries and educational systems. Its manifestation nowadays is still divergent, as is illustrated below. The impact of research and theory-building on the practice of school leadership, has generally been weak. However, this theory-practice relationship is not the same in all countries. In educational systems where the school leader is perceived to be a distinct resource and center of power in a school, the impact of theoretical concepts on the work and the training of school leaders seems to be relatively large. In systems where the head master and school principal are merely seen as good teachers with some limited leadership responsibilities, the impact of leadership theories on leadership practice is smaller. The latter is the case in most European countries, whereas the former situation is characteristic of many North American school systems. Bolman & Heller (1995) have presented an elucidating analysis of the development of thinking about leadership practice in the United States. An interesting element of their description is the regularity they found in the way in which leadership theories entered into the practice of school management, and in the training of school managers. Succeeding organization and management theories were applied first in the private and business sectors. Educational administration specialists then initiated trials to implement these concepts, procedures and instruments into school management practice. The university training programmes for school principals were used as vehicles for doing so. The history of American school leadership-practice has shown that the consequence of this process has been that elements of the 'big' management theories can be detected. For instance, when schools were growing during the first decades of the 20th century, school districts took over the command-and-control model of management (labelled as 'scientific management'), which was very popular after the turn of the century in the theory and practice of organizational leadership. This transfer of ideas and techniques from the business and private sector was not the case in the management of European schools until about a decade or two ago. When school management became a growing issue of training, consultancy and research in Western European school systems, this happened not primarily by transferring experiences and instruments from other organizations into school organizations, but mainly as a reflection of the overall societal changes in the role of authority, in power relations, and in the growing mutual dependency between people for reaching common goals. School management, together with the management of other types of organizations, is a reflection of the societal culture and habits in its use of authority and power.

6.2.2 Different kinds of leaders and leadership

6.2.2.1 Leaders

"Take us to your leader!" demanded the man at the front of the group of explorers when they met a group of natives. Since there was no immediate response, the command was repeated more loudly; something often thought to be an effective method when strangers do not understand you. Then something extraordinary happened. The group of natives

165

drew together and talked with one another. Turning back to the explorers they said in unison: "We are the leader". This hit the explorers very hard, because the natives had said something very mystifying. "Well, men", said the man at the head of the group, who had learned the art of consultation during his university training, "what do you make of it?" "I don't believe them", said one of the youngest explorers, joining this type of field work for the first time. "I bet behind that hill we'll find a guy sitting in a big hut giving out the orders". "Or else some smooth laddie who moves around from clan to clan whispering in their ears", added another group member, experienced in management-by-walking-around. Without much discussion, the natives gathered loosely together in their customary way and moved off towards the hill. The explorers stepped off boldly behind the seemingly disordered group, convinced they were being taken to a leader. In fact, they were simply being led into a new territory.

This short story has been taken (with small adaptations) from Clive Hopes' introduction to his synthesis of ten case studies from OECD countries about "The school leader and school improvement" (Hopes, 1986). The story is illustrative in three respects: observations of leader behavior are coloured by one's concepts of what a leader is; leaders differ depending on their position in an organization; and leaders want something to do with people.

Biased observation

The passage first clearly demonstrates the pitfall of biased observation and interpretation of events and situations one is not familiar with. As a beginning school management student, for example, one has perhaps only a common sense idea about leadership: where two or more people meet and join their interests, capacities and capabilities there will be or should be one person who is called 'the leader', otherwise, nothing useful will happen! Or, a middle-aged person who has had discouraging experiences with covert leader strategies could be inclined to interpret the lack of overt leader behavior in a small primary school as an indication that the school has a bad principal. However, it may be that the principal avoids 'behaving as a leader' because it would not fit in with the pleasant, informal team climate that characterizes the school. After all, this school is small, its lines of communication are short, and the teachers employed there are highly visible. Because leadership is related to power relations and dependencies between persons, the observation and study of leaders is vulnerable to highly subjective expectations, assumptions and experiences. Studying leadership, therefore, requires rational, objectivity-advancing measures and procedures.

Kinds of leaders

The story is also indicative of a variety of meanings and interpretations given to the term 'leader'. Most people use the term to refer to an official who is in charge of responsibility for the work, the quality and the well-being of a group of two or more persons, frequently referred to as 'the boss'. In the literature about management and leadership, starting with Taylor during the first decades of this century (cf. Taylor, 1915), several types of 'bosses' have been distinguished. These distinctions are based merely on different types of authority relations between leaders and their workers or group members. A differentiation in the following three work-directed authority relations has proved to be useful for the analysis of leader-subordinate relations in work organizations.

The *hierarchical* boss has authority because of the power connected with his hierarchical position to make decisions about the appointment, the transfer, secondment, and the promotion of employees. He coordinates personnel assessment and supports management development.

The *functional* boss has authority over the work methods and instruments used by the organization's staff and over the maintenance and availability of knowledge and skills. He draws his power from his expertise to make decisions about the best working methods, and about the way the available resources are used. He draws up the required competencies and skills, as well as the staff's work capacities and work force.

The *operational* boss has authority to divide and schedule tasks. He has the executive and logistic power to make decisions about task assignments, task priorities, the coordination of tasks and control of the results of the executed tasks.

Teachers in some schools call their school leader 'the boss'. In most cases it is meant as an informal expression of acknowledgment that someone is 'leading', 'commanding', and 'directing' them. That does not mean, however, that school leaders, principals, head teachers, directors, etcetera, operate in basically the same way. Many common sense and caricatural expressions typify the 'head' mainly as a hierarchical boss. That stems perhaps from our early, childhood experiences with the head master as 'the big person 'who sees and knows everything and everyone because he or she teaches the highest class.

Leaders aim at goals with people

In the short illustrative story 'the man at the front' commands the group of natives. Some explorers have assumptions about the goals of non-visible group leaders; the explorers follow the withdrawing natives with an expectation. Leaders want to influence others. Although the terms and labels used in the literature to denote 'leadership' are varied, two main features prove to be characteristic for leadership: leadership is a social phenomenon based on the interaction between two or more persons, and can be further characterised by those interactions through which the 'leader' exerts deliberate influence upon the 'followers'. This deliberate exertion of influence by leadership or management can be conceived as a 'controlling' or 'steering' activity. Influence can take several forms and can be directed at different goals (cf. Scheerens & van Vilsteren, 1988). In section 1.3.2.3 of chapter 1 of this book, the so-called 'control paradigm' is presented and explained. This paradigm, also labelled as 'steering paradigm' in the management literature, presents a framework for distinguishing the ways in which leaders exert influence, depending on the goals of the leader: routine steering, adaptive steering, or goal steering (De Leeuw, 1982).

6.2.2.2 Explanations for leader differences

Leaders differ in many aspects of their behavior. The bias in leader observation and the different kinds of leaders concern two different issues, illustrated by the short 'native explorers' story. Leadership is a real life topic about which people have divergent opinions and expectations; it can have various objectives and be a manifestation of various kinds of power. Leadership is a multi-faceted phenomenon, both in subjective as well as in objective meaning. A multitude of alternative explanations for diversity in leader behavior exists and will be developed in the future. They will be explored later on in this chapter.

In this section special attention will be given to a rather strong context factor for the school leader: the way in which the governing and authority of education and schooling are structured, regulated and formalised in a certain country, state, province or region. This determines the authority and the free space of a school leader. In that regulatory systems for education differ, we must conclude that school leaders in different countries operate within different regulatory and authority contexts. Those regulations determine the position, authority, responsibilities, and also the role of a school leader. This is illustrated below in two ways. First by using the contemporary differences between the educational authority systems of various countries (cross cultural); then through the analysis of changes over time within country-bound systems (longitudinal).

Cross cultural comparison

In Sweden, a principal has to rely on his teachers as a dominant party in the school's decision making, while his French colleague has to act as a civil servant of the Minister of Education, formally isolated from the teachers in his school. The American high school principal is expected to behave as a kind of unit manager under the authority of the school district management and superintendency, while the principal of a high school in the Australian province of Victoria is mainly directed by and responsible to the School Council of her school, of which she also is a voting member. A Canadian principal has to cooperate with one or two vice-principals whose management tasks are mainly decided upon by the Local Board of Trustees. The Dutch high school principal has the option of installing a number of assistant principalships with self determined areas of responsibility. The Italian Head Master needs the advice of an elected advisory group of two to four teachers for his decisions. His Dutch colleague, in contrast, by law needs advice, or in the case of strategic decisions, even the approval of the Participation Council. This body is elected by and from teachers, parents and students of his school. As is the case in many countries, the path to principalship in England and Wales is open to everyone with teaching experience, without the requirement of any formal school management or leadership certification. Many American states require a university Master's degree in Educational Administration as a basic qualification for their principals, similar to Sweden where training is also made compulsory for most school principals. To become a principal in Italy, an experienced teacher has to pass a state examination with strong selection criteria, resulting in placement on a list of qualified candidates. In France, a place on such a list is based on personal and professional evaluation by the regional and the 'Paris' officials, and is also a 'conditio sine qua non' for a head teacher position. Once on that list, a candidate has access to the central training courses for future French head masters. The so-called 'local cultural fit' is an important selection criterion in many US-states and in Italy, whereas the decisions to appoint Swedish principals are very often made on political grounds. This means that preference is given to candidates who support the ideas of the dominant local, regional or national political parties. Swedish, American and Italian principals legally do not have teaching duties, whereas the Canadian primary school heads have a significant teaching task, as is also the case in most Dutch primary schools.

One can conclude that in almost all countries the principal is ultimately and legally the boss responsible for the whole school, although most principals share this responsibility with other persons or bodies outside or inside the school building. The way in which this sharing of responsibilities and authority is executed depends largely on the educational governing structure of a country or region. This cross cultural analysis makes clear that school leaders depend on their decision making environment in their work.

Longitudinal changes
Guthrie (1990) has presented insight into the development of the dominant orientations and strategies of leadership in the public sector during this century, including school leadership. From his analyses he concludes the following flow of practice and thinking about leadership. School leadership started as an *authority*-oriented construct, based on

existing power relations in society. Later, it was transformed into a *rule*-oriented, bureaucratic style of management. As schools grew larger and teaching and learning processes became more complex, more regulation, coordination and control were needed. Accordingly, leadership changed from direct action of one person into levels, or cascades, of authority influence. As the societal expectations of schooling grew higher and broader, schools became more dependent on the professional qualities of their teachers and leaders. They therefore needed more discretion concerning their own work. The rules and procedures were experienced more as constraints than as support. The leadership of schools, as a consequence of this, changed into an *employee*-oriented style. The intensifying relationship between schooling and its end users, customers and clients, recently prompted a further change in the leadership orientation of school leaders. These market groups at the output side of a school create a new kind of authority that influences the school organization. In reacting to this new external power, school leadership has adopted characteristics of a *market*- and client-oriented style. Guthrie explains this development as a school-oriented representation of shifts in the role of power relations, and in the views on individual development and motivation. These developments in headlines can be traced in all western educational systems. Differences result from specific cultural, societal and/or political differences between countries.

In his comparative analyses Clive Hopes also came to the following conclusion: there is an overall shift over time from centralized to decentralized governing and policy-making in education and schooling. This change has been accompanied by a development from the above mentioned bureaucratic (hierarchical) leader behavior up to educational (functional) and organizational (operational) school leadership and management. An emphasis on the maintenance and smooth running of schools has gradually been replaced by attention paid to the improvement of teaching and learning in schools. Even in the hierarchical and centralized bureaucratic French school system, the installation of school councils indicates a growing decentralization of decision making. The involvement of a principal in the teaching activities in his school, until recently nearly forbidden by French teachers and teacher unions, has quietly become accepted in a growing number of schools.

'School based management' is a new slogan in American and British educational administrative practice and literature. The process behind this slogan is the increase of school autonomy, as compared with the centralized authority of the American School Districts and the British Local Education Authorities (LEAs). In such countries as the Netherlands an individual school has traditionally possessed substantial jurisdiction in such matters as the choice of textbooks and other teaching and learning materials, the selection of teachers, student evaluation, teacher and parent participation, budget estimation, allocation and spending of funds. Even in these countries, decentralization to the regional and school level is broadening and the number of central governmental regulations has been decreasing. In the Dutch educational governing structure, this process is meant to make schools more responsible for the organization and quality of their educational work. The movement to more autonomous schools requires a number of other changes. One is that school leaders must display a pro-active, policy making and future-directed style of leadership, which unavoidably pushes the school leader to become intensively involved in the core school activities: learning and teaching. It would seem likely that not all principals should survive this enormous change in leader orientation. The hierarchical boss has to become a functional boss. As a hierarchical boss the head teacher could hide his decisions behind the regulations and mandates of the Minister of Education when teachers grumbled at him about the lack of teaching resources. As a functional boss, the same head teacher is now blamed by the same teachers, as it is he who is now held responsible for the resource priorities and availability.

These changes in the governing context of schools, and the corresponding changes in required leader behavior illustrate how school leaders are influenced by the characteristics and dynamics of the relevant school environment.

The external governmental context of schools is part of the leadership environment of a school leader. School leaders are influenced by this context and are held accountable for the specific public responsibilities in their schools. It also implies that school leaders are expected to influence the external environment in appropriate ways which benefit the maintenance and the quality of their schools. There is a two-way action between a school leader and the relevant external (governmental) environment.

A school leader has two other relevant environments, which are often labelled as 'internal environments', since these regard aspects of the school organization itself. One includes the professional teachers, who in schools are a major quality determining factor of the basic activities of teaching and learning. These professional workers should be involved by school leaders in decisions on the curriculum, instruction and student guidance. In doing so, the teachers are given the opportunity to influence their school leaders. To enhance the quality of education, however, the work of the relatively autonomous teachers requires direction and coordination. For this reason, leaders must influence teachers and the teacher work groups in their schools.

The other internal environment of a school leader concerns the functioning of the school as a goal-directed organization. This contains the 'managerial' aspects of a school organization, as delineated in the introductory section of this chapter. Due to their position, school leaders are held responsible for these aspects of school life. Their relation to this internal environment, therefore, is basically one-way in nature, originating from the position of the school leader (see the one-way arrow in figure 6.1). Others can be given a voice in the decision making process of the leader, as far as the leader deems it helpful.

The three school leader environments form a basis for the following depiction of the so-called 'responsibility environment' of a school leader. This environment consists of three parts: public responsibility and accountability, instructional responsibility, and managerial responsibility.

This threefold responsibility of a school leader is characterized by competing interests which can lead to internal role-conflict. The principal who gives priority to his instructional responsibility, for instance by initiating curricular changes and emphasizing his teachers' professional orientation, risks his public responsibility and neglects the constraints of work load and lack of available time of his staff. The school head who pays great attention to the neat and obedient use of the school's limited financial resources runs the risk of being considered by his staff to be a knight of the budget-slashing Minister of Education. The school director who puts emphasis on clear and smooth school regulations and processes, perhaps by the Inspectorate, may be considered a neat principal of a school in which nothing will change from an educational point of view. Is the best school leader he who is able to maintain a balance between instructional leadership, public leadership and managerial leadership? Or should, as a consequence of the primary task of a school, instructional responsibility be given the highest priority by school leaders? One's answer to this question will be different as a result of the kinds of criteria that are chosen.

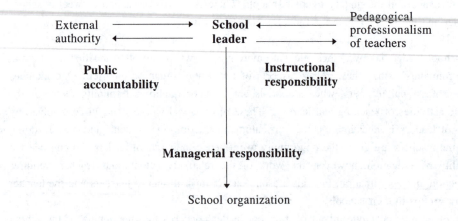

Figure 6.1: *School leader responsibility environment*

6.2.3 The leader as an organizational function

So far the term 'leader' has been used in the sense of a functionary: an occupant of a certain position in an organization. When using the term in relation to the organization 'school', it means the leader in the top of the school organization (although there are also other leading people at other levels within a school). We can hardly imagine that an educational institution could exist and fulfil its goals without having one ultimately responsible person at the top. Yet, such schools do exist! In some Swiss cantons (provinces), primary schools do not have a formal school director. The bulk of the leadership activities is done at canton level by means of a director of education and a rather intensive supervisory system. Each school has its meetings and conferences of all teachers (the Plenary Teachers Conference). At community level there is a Communal School Board, a body that in cooperation with the school Teachers Conference functions as the formal 'school leader'. Individual board members are held primarily responsible for specific tasks, in most cases without final decisive authority.

Another example of collective leadership until recently could be seen in the management and governance of Dutch universities; the system now is changing to a more entrepreneurial style of management. As a consequence of the 1968 Paris student revolt, the governance of universities in the Netherlands was transformed from an autocratic into a broad democratic system. This was demonstrated in the decision making structure and the distribution of authority in Dutch universities. This can best be characterized with the labels 'collegiate boards' and 'co-governing councils'. The first label means that each university and each faculty was managed by a board of 3-5 temporarily appointed persons who made their decisions in a collective way; the board chairman was not an autonomous, ultimately responsible functionary. The councils were elected bodies with seats available for scientific staff, support staff and students. They controlled the decisions of their corresponding boards. The councils had final jurisdiction about budget allocations and matters of strategic planning. At departmental level, within a faculty, the main policy decisions fell under the authority of the Conference of Permanent Department Staff Members, which also included some elected students, and was chaired by one of the department professors. In this system, no person could be held individually accountable for the decisions made and for their consequences. This setup did, however, enjoy a rather broad base of acceptance, stimulated commitment, and a broad participation of many interest groups within a university. This structure of shared responsibility and democratic decision making has been in place for more than twenty years.

Non-individualized leadership of educational institutions has proven to be a feasible and effective option. In other words: 'Good leadership is possible without individual leaders at the top'.

173

This non-individualized leadership practice introduces a new understanding of the role and dynamics of leadership in organizations. Instead of viewing leadership as a role or task of one person or group of persons, leadership is conceptualized in this new approach as a characteristic of the system called 'organization'. Leadership is seen as a systemic feature and as an organizational quality. Communication, decision-making, coordination and organizational culture are four other systemic characteristics. They are system-inherent variables with differing dynamics and qualities. Although leadership is also an inherent aspect of organizations, it should not be regarded as the exclusive task of one or some persons.

When leadership is considered to be an organizational feature, the point of view from which leadership is observed and analyzed is influenced by one's conception of organizations.

Ogawa et al. have recently contributed to the theorizing about leadership in school organizations by looking for a broader and system-bound conceptualization (Ogawa & Bossert, 1995; Pounder, Ogawa & Adams, 1995). They, too, relate the understanding of leadership to the perspective one has on organizations, and on that basis distinguish between a technical-rational theory of organizations, and an orientation that stems from institutional theory, the former being the dominant view.

Ogawa & Bossert's frame of reference attends to four dimensions of leadership, independent of the concept of leadership used: function, role, individuals and culture. The function of leadership is that it should always influence the performance of an organization. Leadership is connected with certain roles in an organization. It is given shape by individuals with specific attributes and ways of behaving, and it operates within an organizational culture. The way these four leadership dimensions are interpreted is rooted in one's own conceptualization of organizational leadership.

The ways in which each of these four dimensions is operationalized determine the conceptual difference between the above mentioned technical-rational and the institutional view on leadership. This will be taken up in greater detail below.

The technical-rational view on leadership in organizations
In the technical-rational view, leadership is considered to be the influence of individuals in specific areas of the organization, as exercised through their traits and actions, on the culture and performance of an organization. The primary task of an organization in this approach is the attainment of specific predetermined goals. In support of that task, adequate ways of coping are adopted or developed. Rules and procedures are designed which aim at steering the behavior of organizational staff towards the goals. Normally this is done by or within the authority of the top leader of the organization, as he has the

authority and overviews all organizational activities. In general, formal power is the preferred vehicle used by these school leaders.

In this view the dominant *function* of leadership is influencing the performance of the organization, i.e. the degree to which organizational goals are achieved. The leadership actions are connected with *roles* in the top of an organization. In most countries this concerns the role of the principal. These *individuals* conduct their leadership by establishing goals, and by designing organizational structures that support goal attainment. In the educational context, these school leaders manifest instructional leadership and an initiating style of leadership (these terms are explained further on in this chapter). Leaders work in an organization with a certain *culture*. They will try to influence the staff's interpretations of what is going on in the organization in line with the dominant values, behavioral norms and habits (Bolman & Deal, 1994; Sergiovanni & Corbally, 1986).

The institutional view on leadership in organizations

This perspective on organizations is guided by "A general institutional theory of social organization, which explains that the behavior of actors, both individual and collective, expresses externally enforced institutions rather than internally derived goals. Institutions are general, societal rules that take the form of cultural theories, ideologies, and prescriptions" (Ogawa & Bossert, 1995, p. 231). This theory stresses the importance of the organizational environment for the structure of an organization. The primary organizational performance goal is the survival of the organization in its environment. This is particularly the case in organizations with unclear and uncertain operations and technologies (see Chapter 3), and with little competition with regard to the recruitment of clients. The former is still a reality in schools: the scientific knowledge base on which solid relations between instructional goal and instructional technology in teaching and learning can be grounded, though it is growing, is only partly available. The factor of low client competition can still be applied to the situation of public schools, depending on the degrees of freedom they have in recruiting students for their schools. These regulations for recruiting differ between countries and sometimes even among states or provinces. Based on these criteria Meyer & Rowan (1983b, 1983c) characterize (American) schools as 'highly institutionalized organizations'. Schools are dependent for their survival on the fit between their organizational structure and society's explicit and implicit theories, beliefs and values about schooling and schools; they are continuously in pursuit of legitimacy. As an illustrative example of this dynamic legitimizing process, Ogawa and Bossert (1995) describe the drive of American school districts to implement 'school based management', through which they expect to gain more legitimacy, despite the lack of evidence about its impact on student achievement. In many cases, such an innovation is implemented only superficially, to the extent that window dressing is enough to be convincing that the change has occurred.

How do the four leadership dimensions look from an institutional view of school organizations? The performance directed *function* of leadership is the advancement of external social legitimacy of the school. To achieve that goal, school participants try to influence the thoughts and actions of the school constituents, both individually and through the committees, decision bodies and meetings in which school related thinking and activity takes place. Institutionalized organizations act in a network of *roles*. Leaders focus on the maintenance of such networks for the survival of their schools. Every role has access to different resources. Thus, leadership is not embedded in particular roles, but in the relationships between members filling different roles. Every *individual* controls individual resources with the consequence that every school member can potentially lead. Principals, teachers, parents and students, all contribute to their school's total leadership. Leadership is relational; both the leaders and the followers are important. Leadership can flow through the school organization, regardless of formal rules and procedures. The previously described non-individualized leadership in Swiss cantonal schools and in Dutch universities are successful examples of this organic way of leadership, because the distribution of leadership power has been regulated for the long term. Ogawa & Bossert hypothesize that more effective institutional leadership requires a more flexible, ongoing flow of leadership through a school organization. The shared opinions and values of organizational staff help constitute an organization's *culture*. Leadership makes up part of that culture, even as it tries to support the shaping of that culture in an organization.

6.2.4 Review of the section

This section started with the explanation of the rationale for the chapter title: leadership is and will be exercised at different levels, and by various participants in a school organization. Leadership is viewed as an organizational property, and not only as the activity of the so-called 'top' of an organization. Due to a lack of convention about terms, the distinction between management and leadership has been described. Leadership is connected with vision, strategy, and the central processes of teaching and learning (this form of leadership is often labelled as instructional leadership). Management is dedicated to the more technical aspects of organizations (such as finance, personnel and facilities), and must act in support of the central teaching and learning tasks of a school.

The next section (6.2.2) focused on differences among (school) leaders. The grounds for these differences are myriad. Differences based on school system have been illustrated by a cross-national comparison. The developments over time in some systems illustrated that the underlying culture within a school system can change, mainly as a reflection of changing values in society. This indicates that cultural differences can also explain part of

176

the differences between school leaders. Within a school organization factors can also be traced as sources for differences in leader behavior. Some of these factors are: the personality characteristics of leaders, the kind of leadership which is expected from a specific leadership position, and the characteristics of the organization members who are to be led. Apart from the leader's individual characteristics, all of these internal and external factors together create the so-called 'leadership environment' of a school leader. Different environmental domains imply different responsibilities of school leaders: public, instructional and managerial responsibilities.

In the third section (6.2.3) a difference in conceptual, scientific-analytic view on leadership has been explained: a rational or an institutional one.

In the next section an overview of the research and the literature on leadership in general will be presented and will be applied to educational organizations. The main point centers on the basic question: "What do leaders have in common, and in what sense and why do they differ from each other?" As it has been analyzed earlier in this section, explanations for differences between them may be found in the leaders themselves, in the situations the school leaders have to work in, and in the 'followers' they have to lead and manage. Those three potential causes for differences between leaders are used as the framework for section 6.3.

6.3 Leadership: perspectives and theories

The leadership and management of task groups and organizations have been the subject of much theorizing and research in the past several decades. Various 'schools' of leadership theories have succeeded one another, although the newer theories have often not swept out the ideas of their predecessors. The succeeding theories tend to create a process of conceptual enrichment and growing understanding.

In this section the milestones of this developmental process are presented. The primary focus will be on an analysis of the relevance of different theoretical perspectives on leadership in order to understand its place in the leadership and management of school organizations. All thinking, theorizing and research about school leadership start from the assumption that leaders are necessary and important for schools.

6.3.1 Leadership theories

Leadership is one of the oldest topics in the study of administration, government and management. McPherson, Crowson & Pitner (1986) in the leadership chapter of their educational administration text book, "Managing Uncertainty", distinguish between three theoretical perspectives on leadership which have been prominent over the past years.

In the first perspective, the traits, behavior and style theories, the personality and the behavior of the leader are given central attention as those characteristics are considered crucial for success in leadership. Leaders are seen as people who possess specific traits which are lacking in non-leaders.

The second perspective, consisting of the situational theories, stresses the impact of the context and the situation of the leader on effective leadership. According to this approach there is no one best way of leading a group or an organization; behavior that is appropriate in one context can be irrelevant in another environment.

In the third theoretical perspective on leadership the decisive role of the followers of leaders is the central focus. To be considered a leader, leadership qualities must be attributed to someone by others, be they followers or observers. Leadership cannot primarily be found in the attitudes and behaviors of the leading persons, but in the attitudes and behaviors of those who follow them. For this reason McPherson et al. label these theories as follower theories.

6.3.1.1 Traits, behavior and style theories

Trait theories

Reviewing the early (pre 1950) literature about characteristic traits of leaders, it turns out that a few traits frequently correlate with what is judged to be good and effective leadership (cf. Stogdill, 1948). Good leaders are intelligent people whose intelligence does not differ greatly from that of their subordinates. It is theorized that too great a gap in intelligence may decrease their influence. Leaders take initiative, are self-confident, energetic and active, and possess knowledge over the task at hand. They are also skilful interactors, want to have influence, and are performance oriented. This means that their primary interest is productive task fulfillment. The effective leader is able to adopt a helicopter view, by means of which he may oversee the overall situation; he is not focused on details which can distract him from the big picture.

Interest in the personal traits of effective leaders diminished after the nineteen fifties. The trait theorists were considered to be too rigid in their proposition that traits of effective leaders are innate, which means a good leader is good in every situation. This group denied for too long the growing conviction in the field of psychology that traits can develop through practice if such traits are called for. Such a development can result in various behaviors and styles, based on the same innate personal traits. Conversely, we may also postulate that though the innate traits of leaders are different, they can result in the same leadership behaviors and styles.

178

Despite this criticism, and as a result of the more flexible attitude exhibited by recent researchers, attention to the traits of leaders has returned because, as House & Baetz (1979) suggest, "the magnitude of the correlations between leader traits and criteria of leadership are as high and often higher than correlations between leader behavior and leadership criteria" (p. 352). In an interview study of successful executive leaders Bennis (1982) found five common leader characteristics:

- they have a clear and strong vision of the future of their organization, and are outcome-oriented;
- are able to communicate their vision to their subordinates, and make creative use of-sometimes indirect-ways to do so;
- are persistent persons who stay on the chosen path, but who also see failures and mistakes primarily as opportunities to learn;
- always find ways and means to implement changes in their organization, also because they conceive change as a way of organizational learning, and
- are able to create an organizational climate and environment that empowers workers to do their best, because they are considered central to success.

Overviewing these features of effective leaders, it is remarkable that they all have a 'can-do'-character. This means that a psychological trait is not crucial in itself, but only through the abilities and skills based on these traits which a leader predominantly exposes in his leadership work. In other words, in the recent leader traits studies, more attention is given to trait patterns over time and to something like a behavioral style of good leaders. This shift from a trait-centered to a behavioral-style centered interest in leadership passed smoothly. It is remarkable that during the last 15 to 20 years, starting in North America and spreading in the nineteen eighties through western countries, a specific selection approach of administrators has been developed: the so-called Assessment Center technique. This approach is based on trait-related characteristics, in combination with the paralleling abilities and skills. It is increasingly used in the selection of school leaders and other top and middle managers in educational organizations. The growing use of this traits- and attributes-centered technique demonstrates the practical usefulness of this theoretical perspective on leadership.

Gender differences between school leaders have received little attention from either the pre 1950 leader trait investigators, or from contemporary researchers. The research that has been done on this theme, however, reveals some interesting results (Adkinson, 1981; Meskin, 1979; Shakeshaft, 1987). Women prefer and demonstrate a more democratic leadership style, they provide more instructional leadership and are judged by their teachers as better primary school leaders. Kruger (1994, 1996) carried out a study on the factual differences between men and women in instructional leadership in Dutch secondary schools and schools for vocational and adult education. In secondary schools this study demonstrated no substantial differences between male and female principals with regard to the way they lead their schools, except for the difference in orientation to the primary processes of teaching and learning. Male and female school leaders are equally convinced that they ought to give more attention to instructional and learning matters in their school, but the female school leaders put this conviction into practice significantly more than their male colleagues. Because this is not the case in vocational schools, Kruger concludes that gender differences between school leaders correlate with the school culture. Women tend to be effective leaders when they have the possibility to exercise their instructional leadership in a culture that matches their gender. Leaders in 'masculine' or large school cultures are not expected to be involved directly in educational affairs, but rather to give strong attention to the organizational management of their schools. In such school cultures an insufficient appeal is made to the instructional leadership power of female school leaders to become supportive for the effectiveness of a school; their potential impact is neutralized. For that reason, Kruger (1996, p. 39) gives warning to the Dutch central educational policy-makers about their policy of increasing the Dutch school size. These big school organizations tend toward a masculine culture, which she conceives as being less appropriate for effective instruction-directed leadership.

Behavior and style theories
Instead of looking for individual traits and abilities of effective leaders, researchers became more interested in the specific behavioral styles which distinguish stronger leaders from their weaker colleagues. Strong and weak here reflect the degree to which the goals of a school organization are attained.
Although there is little agreement upon the specific behavioral traits of effective leaders, there is a dominant dichotomy of leadership styles in the various studies. These two major styles can best be characterized as a task and organization centered style, to be distinguished from a people and interaction centered style of leadership. Disagreement exists with regard to which of the two is most effective, and also concerning the specific behaviors that are considered to be indicators of each style.

The studies, aimed at finding style features in the behaviors of organizational leaders, can best be reviewed on the basis of three different research groups: the Ohio State Leadership Studies initiated by John Hemphill, the Michigan Studies of Rensis Likert and the Managerial Grid Studies of Blake & Mouton (cf. McPherson, Crowson & Pitner, 1986). These three leadership 'schools' are delineated below.

In the *Ohio State Leadership Studies*, which started in the early nineteen forties, the development and use of the so called Leader Behavior Description Questionnaire (LBDQ) for measuring leader behavior has played a central role. The LBDQ contains twelve scales to measure various aspects of leadership behavior which are clustered in two dimensions. These two dimensions, 'initiating structure' and 'consideration', function as the focal points of the Ohio studies. A consideration-type leader has the primary focus of his attention on the needs, wishes, contributions and well-being of the workers in his organization; he facilitates and supports people and gives much attention to relations between people. The typical initiating structure type leader is primarily directing and steering; he gives the greatest attention to the organizational goals and outcomes, likes to work on the basis of clear expectations, and he designs the work structures along which the tasks should be carried out. The Ohio theorists take the position that effective leaders combine these two styles of leadership.

In many studies on school administrators the LBDQ has been used as a framework for collecting research data. This nearly exclusive North American research reveals that school leaders demonstrate relatively little initiating structure behavior. A plausible explanation could be the relatively weak knowledge base about effective instructional processes and learning activities. Directive structuring by school leaders lacks the necessary solid and agreed upon 'how to' knowledge. This research also reveals that school leaders seldom combine the two styles; "they take either a facilitative or a directive role" (McPherson et al., 1986, p. 227). Both styles seem to have a positive effect upon the satisfaction of teachers in their work. Despite their beloved and maintained attitude of professional freedom in their teaching work, teachers like a principal who both cooperates with them on instructional matters, as well as gives them clear rules and workable structures. But, on this point a movement can be established, in which teachers increasingly prefer to work 'under' a task and structure directed leadership style. The so called 'effective school studies' also indicated that school leaders should play a more directive and relatively less facilitative role regarding the central tasks of teaching and learning in their schools. As has been mentioned earlier in this chapter, the activities of a school leader constituting this task directed style are qualified as 'instructional leadership' (see section 6.5).

In the *Michigan Studies*, which were carried out around 1960 by Rensis Likert and his colleagues, the supervisory behavior of leaders was studied with special attention paid to the way they behave with their subordinates. The researchers concluded that effective, highly productive managers distinguish themselves from less-productive managers in four respects. They:

• demonstrate supportive behavior, through which they give subordinates the feeling of being respected as important group members;

- emphasize reaching the group or organizational goals, which motivates the employees to accomplish the work leading to the expected outcomes;
- facilitate the work of their subordinates mainly by removing constraints;
- facilitate the interaction between group members with the intent of developing group cohesion and building productive teams.

The person versus task dichotomy from the Ohio studies is also apparent in these four factors of Likert's model of productive leadership (Likert, 1961). However, the emphasis is more on the consideration than on the initiating structure type of leadership. In order to be effective, a leader should give much attention to the human side of work in an organization and especially to team building. Leadership behavior is also explicitly guided by the expectations, opinions and interpersonal skills of his staff. Power and responsibilities are required and inherent dynamics for an effective organization, but they have to be shared with the people who work in that organization. If a leader does so he will advance the cohesion and team spirit in his organization.

Likert has elaborated on this concept of leadership in several ways. The most interesting one concerns the Linking Pin model. The following representation of overlapping triangles illustrates this model. In Figure 6.2 each triangle represents a work unit with its own domain of decision power and responsibility. At the top of each work unit a leader is positioned.

The different levels of the triangles are placed in an expressly hierarchical relation. The underlying concept of the linking pin function is that organizational groups are coupled by means of the interactions of the group leaders on different organizational levels. In those interactions 'influencing' is the crucial activity. The sharing of power and responsibilities in an organization assumes that people in leading positions have sufficient and recognized influence over the decisions made by their superiors. The control of a group leader over the work of his group members depends substantially upon the influence that the leader is able to exert upon his work group and the leaders who are hierarchically positioned above him. McPherson et al. (1986) formulate this cohesion improving dynamic as follows: "The capacity to exert influence upward is essential if one is to exercise leadership successfully downward" (p. 229). If this is not the case, the linkage of a group with the organization is not sufficient which can have negative effects upon the performance of that group. The

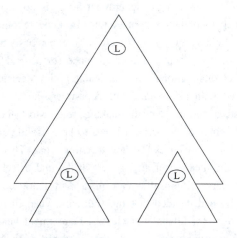

Figure 6.2: *Likert's Linking Pin model*

Linking Pin concept has remarkable relevancy when applied to school organizations.

Schools are often characterized as 'loosely coupled' organizations, related to divergent subject specialties of groups of teachers in a school, and in some schools to rather different study programs and curricula offered by the same school. If a school looks to develop more cohesiveness despite its loosely coupled structure, decision making and communication in a linking-pin like structure would be useful. However, the implementation of such a decision making structure presumes the subgroup leaders to have formal leadership authority which gives them real decision-making powers concerning their work units. In most current school systems, leadership positions subordinate to the school principalship exist only on the basis of informal agreements. The heads of department, heads of house, grade and year coordinators, and study programme leaders are active functionaries in schools, but they lack formal authority on relevant issues, including the related employment conditions and salary scale regulations. The British school system is one of the exceptions to this picture. In British schools most of these functions are distinguished formal posts, and part of the career ladder in the educational system by which the formal competency of lower level leaders is met. In a study of Dutch secondary school principals' activities aimed at improving the work of the subject departments in their schools, researchers could track a shift over time from a fully informal to a more formal and deliberate role of department heads in the schoolwide decision making processes (Van Vilsteren & Witziers, 1990). The impact of this development in schools is illustrative for the formal linking pin position of group leaders in a school organization. Although 'department head' is not a formal school management position in the Dutch secondary school system, in some schools the researchers observed the principals communicating on a somewhat regular basis with the joint department heads. In one school this setup had been in place for several years as a kind of school policy council for all instructional and curricular policy decisions. In another school the rector communicated with an assembly of department heads several times a year, as if those meetings had a formal decision-making role. Most teachers in the departments considered these meetings of department heads to be a useful source of information for the rector with no direct consequences for their teaching work. That discrepancy did not create any problems until the meeting of all teachers at the end of school year, where the rector announced that after careful consultation with, and in nearly complete agreement with the department heads, he had decided that the following year all departments would need to organize common tests for all parallel classes. Department heads who had not consulted their departmental members beforehand were charged with breach of confidence and misuse of their role. Two of them were immediately dismissed from their position of department head by their colleagues. The implementation of common tests for all departments had to be postponed by the rector. Here the linking pin construction was effective upwards, but lacked the acknowledged grounds to also become effective downwards, and finally it did not work at all. In terms of formal management levels, schools have a weak middle management structure. This empirical finding is in line with the relatively limited importance of the middle line in the professional bureaucratic type of organization to which schools belong (Mintzberg, 1979).

In countries with highly centralized school systems, be it at district level in the United States, or at national or regional level in France, the principal of a single public school can best be conceived of as a middle manager. The main policy and curricular decisions are made in the district office or in the ministries of education, and the school head is expected to manage the implementation of those decisions in the local school. Analysis of this situation from a linking pin point of view reveals that principals can rarely use their Linking Pin position to influence external superiors in relation to their particular schools. In more decentralized school systems, where individual schools have more formal authority power and ownership, schools must also comply with external 'superiors', embodied in governmental regulations and policies, labor market expectations, local tax decisions or school board decisions. The school leader who makes better use of his linking pin position in favor of effective influence upon these external 'superiors' increases the probability of being taken seriously by his teaching staff when he makes proposals to improve instruction and learning in his school. Therefore, one of the main criticisms of the so-called 'school effectiveness research' is (see 6.5.2) that it pays hardly any attention to the external actions of school leaders in promoting quality.

Studies in the third group of leader style research have been carried out by Blake & Mouton. In 1964 they published *"The Managerial Grid"*, in which they presented their leadership typology. Their research was focused mainly on the management of higher education institutions in the United States (cf. Blake & Mouton, 1981). They also make use of two style dimensions which are similar to the 'consideration' and 'initiating structure' dimensions in the Ohio studies.

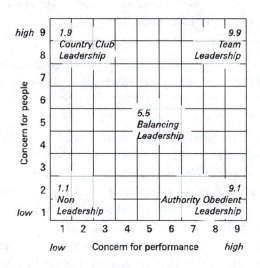

Figure 6.3 *The Managerial Grid*

Blake & Mouton distinguish between concern for people and concern for institutional performance. Leaders of the former kind give priority to relationships between people and to the needs and self-worth of subordinates. The latter type of leader is merely interested in the achievement of the organizational goals and outcomes. Each of these dimensions can be placed on one of the two axes of a grid. In that grid a multitude of combinations of the two style dimensions can be plotted (see Figure 6.3). The assumption that no leader is purely people or purely outcome oriented gives Blake & Mouton's model a realistic and down to earth character.

Table 6.1 presents the features of the three studies above described on the behavioral styles of leaders at one glance.

Table 6.1 *Studies of effective behavioral styles of leaders*

Label	Styles	Most Effective
Ohio-State (LBDQ)	-▸ consideration -▸ initiating structure	combination of both styles
Michigan (LIKERT)	-▸ worker directed -▸ task directed	worker directed style
Managerial Grid (BLAKE & MOUTON)	-▸ people concerned -▸ performance concerned	combination of the maximum of both styles

Reviewing the trait and the behavioral style theories -which are based on a vast amount of research- reveals some problems. The main problem of these theories is that they assume that one leader trait or style is superior, regardless of the specific kind of organization, and the kind of circumstances in which leaders work. In the first section of this chapter it is shown that cultural differences between school types and school systems create a differentiated picture of the characteristics of an effective school leader. That empirical finding alone should arouse suspicion about theories that make a plea for a single best leadership orientation. It was precisely this pretension of the trait and style theorists that motivated scholars to explore the interaction between leadership behavior and leadership context. Most of them made use of the behavioral style instruments and categories for analyzing the behaviors of leaders. However, they changed the rigidity of 'the one best leader style' into an attitude more receptive to the possibility that a leader's behavior is prone to situational factors in being more or less effective, and that some leader's behaviors have the capacity to change specific situational elements in such a way that their behavior will become more effective.

6.3.1.2 Situational theories

No one leadership style can be expected to be effective under all situational conditions; this is the baseline statement of the situational theorists on organizational leadership. Their research efforts are focused on the exploration of so-called if-then regularities in the interaction between leader behavior and situational features: if the leadership context is or has X, then leader behavior B has proven to be most effective. These types of theories in organization and management science are commonly typified as the contingency theory. In this theory, leader behavior and situational elements are considered as concurring and interacting. Both can change resulting in some kind of mutual adjustment between the two that reveals the best possible outcome. If this is the case, leader behavior and leadership situation are contingent. Most of the earlier situational leadership theorists viewed this contingent relationship from a deterministic and correlational point of view. That means that the if-then relationships exist independent of the cognitive processes and capabilities of the leader. What the leader knows, thinks, analyses, and interprets in relation to the leadership situation is not taken into account in the understanding of the effects of leadership. As we shall see later on in this chapter (section 6.4), new insights from cognitive psychology have presented arguments for a cognitive approach to organizational leadership in which the 'internal cognitive processes' of the leader are given a central role in pursuit of understanding leader behavior. In essence, however, this cognitive approach is still situational or contingent in nature.

Following McPherson, Crowson & Pitner (1996), several theorists are presented in this section whose studies give grounded reasoning for the conclusion that a better contingency between leader and situation results in more effective leadership. The theorists vary in two aspects. One group of situational theorists assumes that leaders are able to influence people and processes in the group or organization they lead. Another group is critical of that assumption, and has found little or no empirical support for this point of view. They conclude that characteristics of the leadership situation are the main, or sole, determinants of what is going on in an organization. The first group of theories is labelled 'hierarchical', the latter 'non-hierarchical' situational leadership theories. Within the first group some theorists assume that leader behavior is immutable, whereas the situation has to be changed somehow; others take the opposite position. For the second group of theorists, the ability of the leader to change is not of interest. They consider the situation to be the main determinant of what is going on in a school organization.

These two distinctions are used below as organizing labels for the descriptions of relevant theories.

Hierarchical situational theories

Fiedler's theory

Fred Fiedler developed his contingency theory on leader effectiveness in the mid nineteen sixties (Fiedler, 1967). In accordance with the stylistic dichotomy of the behavior style theories, he distinguishes between two styles of leadership: the task-directed versus the social-emotionally oriented leadership style. The first one is labelled as the 'initiating structure' style, the latter one as the 'consideration' style. These labels are often used in the literature on leadership and management. The crucial new element in this theory is the conviction that some characteristics of the leadership context determine whether an opportunity for leadership becomes effective or not. His research revealed three critical dimensions of the leader situation:

- in the relations between the leader and his subordinates, the latter trust the leader and are willing to please him;
- a clear task structure in which the leader knows precisely what he should do and how he should go about doing it;
- the leader is in a powerful enough position to afford him freedom to deal out rewards and punishments.

These are favorable conditions for effective leadership. It is the interaction between the leadership style of the leader and the degree to which the situation is advantageous for effective leadership that determines the ultimate actual effectiveness of the behaviors of that leader. Initiating structure type leaders seem most effective in both very favorable and in very unfavorable situations. A moderately favorable/unfavorable work context makes a consideration type of leader more effective.

Fiedler considers someone's leadership style as being almost intransient. If the leadership style and the critical situational conditions are not compatible with each other, Fiedler prefers to try to change the situational conditions to realize a better fit with the style of the present leader. If this is not possible, the organization should ultimately look for a new leader who is better suited to the context conditions for leadership.

The professional autonomous attitude of teachers is strong, and the available 'how to teach' knowledge is still relatively weak. This makes that the tendency of teachers to obey the wishes of the school leader, the existence of a clear task structure and of rewards combined with the authority for effective punishments are obviously less present in school situations. However, according to Fiedler, the critical situational conditions are present -to a certain extent- in school organizations; although schools vary in this respect.

The effective contingencies suggested by Fiedler can be illustrated in a school which has to implement an externally imposed change. In Dutch schools, for instance, this has often been the case during the last twenty years in nearly all facets of the educational system. The implementation of these rather complex, school-wide innovations, creates mistrust and refusal or hesitation of teachers to cooperate with the school principals. It also makes teachers uncertain, both about their usual way of teaching, as well as about the nature of the new practices they are supposed to introduce. Implementation of these innovations in practice demands a significant extra effort on the part of the teachers, which can usually not be rewarded by the principal. Because of the relatively high job security legally afforded to Dutch teachers, effective punishment of non-cooperating teachers is nearly impossible. Such change-directed school contexts can be characterized as unfavorable, and as Fiedler would propose, are best suited to a highly task-oriented principal. Research on the change-supporting role of school principals also demonstrates that 'initiating' and 'structuring' type school leaders tend to be most effective in the support of innovation implementation in their schools (cf. for instance Fullan, 1991; Leithwood & Montgomery, 1986). Experiences from the practice of external support of schools-in-change present firm indications that esteemed, friendly and responsive school principals who have effectively managed the ongoing processes in their schools for many years become far less successful once they try to manage a change process in their schools. Their social-emotional style of leading a school was effective in the favorable conditions of a steady state school organization. This effective contingency, however, is roughly disrupted by the altering conditions caused by the imposed changes. Consequently, a turnover in the principalship of an innovating school would probably be judged by Fiedler to be a rational and wise decision.

Vroom & Yetton's theory

In contrast with Fiedler's ideas, Vroom & Yetton assume the possibility of a leader to adjust his style to the conditions of the leadership situation. In the early 1970s they developed their normative theory about effective leader decision making (Vroom & Yetton, 1973). They define effective leadership as knowing when, how and to what extent subordinates should participate in decisions that have direct or indirect consequences for themselves. Thus, they define leader effectiveness as decision-making effectiveness. Effective decisions are characterized by the following three elements:

• the quality of the decision, indicated by what the decision yields for the organization;
• the acceptance of the decision, depending on how important acceptance is for the implementation of the decision;
• the time needed to reach the decision, indicated by the relative importance of properly made decisions against quick decisions.

Organizational leaders diagnose a specific problem in their organization by a systematic, checklist-like investigation of the presence of defined problem attributes, which are related to the three elements of effective decisions presented above. That diagnosis is the basis for the decision making style the leader will choose to reach an effective decision, in terms of an effective solution to a problem. Leaders are observed to differ with respect to the decision making style they prefer. However, what Vroom & Yetton label as 'style' could also be considered a deliberately chosen decision strategy in which the overall individual decision-making preference of the leader is one of the key determinants. Sometimes an autocratic decision is most effective, whereas in other problem situations an intensively participative decision-making strategy is called for.

In spite of Vroom & Yetton's narrowed interest on leader decision making, their model has relevance for school leaders. Because of the partly non-routine character of many school processes, school leader activities can best be viewed as problem solving activities (see also section 6.4 on the cognitive approach). Problem solving implies a chain of different kinds of decision making activities. The normative decision model of Vroom & Yetton implies that the kind of problems that exist in a school organization are important features of the leadership situation of a school leader. Thus, the problem-focused bias of the Vroom & Yetton theory fits with the problem dominated work of school leaders.

The contingency between the leader's decision making style and the kind of problems to be solved, which Vroom & Yetton consider to be a pre-condition for effective decision making, implies that a specific kind of problem demands a specific style of leadership. In schools, problems can be typified depending on to whose responsibility domain they belong (cf. Hanson, 1979; Lortie, 1977). Some topics -for instance classroom management, subject curriculum, instruction modes- are considered by teachers as theirs, whereas other topics such as finance, discipline, public relations, building are regarded as belonging to the discretion of the principal. In the latter case, an autocratic leadership style is probably effective. If instructional or curricular affairs are at hand, a consultative and participatory kind of leadership should be chosen by the principal to reach the desired outcomes. The advantage of this view is that the rigid belief in participation of teachers in all kinds of school decisions, frequently considered as a prerequisite for quality schooling, deserves a thorough reconsideration.

Non-hierarchical theories

All leadership orientations presented so far have shared the common assumption that leadership is based on the hierarchical higher position and responsibility of the leader. Some researchers, though they accept the formal hierarchical position of the organizational leader, conclude that those leaders at a higher organizational level have only a supplementary role in reaching organizational goals (e.g. House, 1971). Others argue that the potential leader impact on the processes and outcomes of their organizations is partly neutralized or substituted by other actors or dynamics in the same organization (Kerr & Jermier, 1978).

The path-goal theory

House and his colleagues belong to the group of theorists and researchers who suppose that leaders can only supplement the goal-directed work of their subordinates. Because their leadership theory is heavily based on the expectancy theory of worker motivation (see the explanation of this theory in Chapter 5 about commitment and motivation), they also assume that the leader's situation influences the impact of his behavior upon the work motivation of subordinates. Their Path-Goal model considers the fit between a leader's behavior and situational variables (e.g. characteristics of the subordinates, task characteristics) as a conditio sine qua non for effective leadership. However, the production of the organizational outcomes in House's theory is basically not dependent on the activities of the leader. He can only facilitate the work, and show ways to desired rewards. Leaders may do this in different ways, the effectiveness of which is determined by the contingency with situational factors. For that reason, this theory is placed under the umbrella of situational leadership theories.

In the context of school organizations, the great attractiveness of this model is that it basically accepts the core role of the professional teachers in a school, including the complementary position of the principal. The latter should not be interpreted to mean that the role of the principal is unimportant for school effectiveness. Without a school leader teaching and learning processes will continue with sufficient outcomes. However, technical-administrative, logistic and coordinative problems will after some time produce negative teaching and learning effects. House argues for a more people-directed style of leadership. Task-directed instructional leadership by a school principal, in contrast, is judged by House and his colleagues as a possibly useful, but in most situations rarely effective leadership style.

Substitutes of leadership theory
Kerr & Jermier (1978) became interested in the supplementary character of organizational leadership, and hypothesized that under the conditions of clear goals and known means, motivating and directing leader behavior is not needed. Under such conditions people do not need leadership for reaching their desired goals. (Kerr & Jermier take an organizational goal perspective that is broader than the direct outcomes an organization has to realize) In this case leader activities become redundant as other conditions in the organization function as moderators of leadership. Kerr & Jermier distinguish between two types of leader moderators:

• substitute conditions functioning in the place of leader behavior, and
• neutralizing conditions counteracting or minimizing the impact of leader actions.

The substitute or neutralizing conditions in organizations turned out to have three possible alternative kinds of characteristics: features of individuals working in the organization, features of the tasks to be performed, and features of the structure of the organization. The following scheme presents an overview of these conditions.

A. Conditions in individuals
- long experience and high training level and competence
- professional orientation
- indifference towards rewards from the organization

B. Conditions in the task
- structured, routine task
- feedback integrated in the task
- intrinsically satisfying task

C. Conditions in the organization
- high level of planning formalization and formal responsibilities
- inflexible rules and procedures
- specialist staff functions and isolated leadership position
- strong cohesive work groups
- lack of leader control over rewards from organization

Kerr & Jermier (1978) assume that these conditions have various substituting and/or neutralizing effects, consistent with the type of leadership a leader exhibits: a task-directed, instrumental style, or a worker-directed, supportive style. Strong cohesive work groups function as a substitute for both types of leadership, whereas rigid rules and procedures especially neutralize instrumental types of leader behaviors. Tasks that satisfy workers intrinsically possibly act as a substitute supportive leader behavior, while an isolated, non-communicative leader position neutralizes both supportive and instrumental actions of leaders.

Because schools exhibit many of the characteristics of a professional bureaucratic type of organization, both the singularities of professionals, as well as the peculiarities of bureaucratic rules and procedures can influence school leadership. Therefore, the ideas of Kerr & Jermier have been investigated empirically in research projects in schools, not only at institutional level (Pitner, 1986), but also at subject department level (Freeston, 1987).

Table 6.2 *Overview of situational leadership theories*

		Behavior	*Situation*
hierarchical	Fiedler	fixed	changeable
	Vroom/Yetton	adaptable	given (problem)
non-hierarchical	House	supplementary	core
	Kerr	redundant	given

An interesting conclusion from these studies is that, at school level, cohesive subject departments function as substitutes (and possibly also neutralizers) of principal interventions. The impact of a department head upon his colleagues is mainly diminished when high teacher competence and professional orientation are brought in the power game taking place in a department.

"Many things a leader tells others to do were suggested to him by the very people he leads. ... this sometimes gives the impression that he is a rather stupid fellow, an arbitrary functionary, a mere channel of communication, and filcher of ideas. In a measure that is correct. He has to be stupid enough to listen a great deal, he certainly must arbitrate to maintain order, and he has to be at times a mere center of communication. If he used only his own ideas, he would be somewhat like a one-man orchestra than a good conductor, who is a very high type of leader". This quotation from Barnard, more than 40 years old (1952, p. 84), sounds like a modern leadership adage, because it expresses a conception of leadership in which subordinates or followers are considered as co-determining actors in a leadership arrangement instead of being seen as mere objects of leader actions. His followers influenced a leader's behavior to a substantial degree, which explains the use of the term 'follower theories'. Chaleff views followers as courageous persons, who stand up to and for their leaders (Chaleff, 1995).

6.3.1.3 Follower theories
A third group of theories brings into focus the role of followers' perceptions as an added element to our understanding of leadership. 'Attribution theory' and 'symbol management' are dealt with below as examples of this follower perspective.

Attribution theory
An attribution is an evaluative opinion about the reasons for another person's behavior. This evaluation is subjective in nature since it is determined by the expectations or ideas human beings have about the behavior of others. These expectations can be rather self-fulfilling, as Rosenthal & Jacobson (1968) have illustrated with their research finding that teacher expectations about the learning capabilities of their students influence the achievements of those students. The expectations and ideas also seem to be related to personality characteristics of individuals. Introverted persons tend to blame themselves for their failures. Women seem to do the same, and also tend to attribute their successes preferably to external circumstances. Men tend to do the opposite. These findings imply that attributions of behaviors and their effects are biased. This conclusion has specific consequences for the understanding of subordinates' perceptions of their leaders. This will be explained in view of the leadership context of school organizations.

In general, the expectations of teachers about the behavior of their principal are that principals should support them when conflicts with students or parents are at hand, but that they should not intervene in classroom matters; they should also demonstrate mediating behavior and skills between teachers and the authorities above their school. If a principal does not behave in accordance with one or more of these expectations, he will be judged by his teacher-followers as bad or ineffective. An effect of that judgement may be that the teachers are no longer willing to follow this principal. Teachers are willing to follow or obey a principal when it is possible for them to attribute explanations for the behavior of that principal that are consistent with teachers' own ideas. In all organizations -but especially in schools- the problems of middle managers can be better understood if their position is analyzed by means of the attribution concept (see also the Linking Pin model, explained earlier in this section). Those middle managers, such as year coordinators, division leaders, faculty deans, department heads, and in some systems head teachers themselves, work in varying organizational positions. Their position varies with the divergent audiences or target groups they interact with, because each type of audience or group connects its own specific attributes to those middle managers with whom they work. Tight cooperation with the top management of the school is not expected by teachers, but judged as effective by superiors. To ardently look after his group's interests is not what his superiors expect him to do, but is nearly the only quality that teachers attribute to an effective boss. The middle manager himself runs a big risk of entering into internal role conflicts and to suffer from a so-called 'Janus-head' syndrome. Good and healthy middle managers -especially in schools- are able to play the game in a field of divergent attributions. The leadership behavior of these school management functionaries can only be understood, if one understands the perceptions of their followers, too. Teachers tend to appreciate their principals when they can explain the principal's behavior in terms consistent with their ideas about good leadership. However, attribution can also be broadened when teachers are confronted with phenomena they value as positive, but which they cannot explain clearly. If a school produces better exam results as compared with earlier years or with other schools, this is appreciated by the teachers. If the principal of that school is judged to be a good school leader, the teachers are more likely to attribute that success to their principal than would be the case in a school with similar progress but with a principal who is perceived by the teachers as functioning poorly and ineffectively. In a study on the phenomenon of leadership attributions in organizations, Meindl, Ehrlich and Dukerich (1985) concluded that external observers of an organization as well as organizational staff members attribute good or poor organizational performance to the leader. The authors characterize this as 'the romance of leadership'. This attribution phenomenon has a peculiar consequence for the methodology of school leadership research. Data on the behavior of school leaders and their effectiveness are frequently based on teachers' opinions about their school leader. Knowing the biased character of attributions, one must be skeptical of the validity of those data and about the analyses and conclusions based on them.

Symbol management

"The greater significance of leadership lies not in the direct impact on substantive matters but in the ability to exert control over the meanings and interpretations important constituencies give to whatever events and occurrences are considered relevant for the organization's functioning" (Meindl et al., 1985, p. 99). Central in this statement is 'the control over meanings and interpretations'. These are considered to have a substantial influence on the cohesiveness of the organization and the well-being of its members. It proves to be difficult for an organizational leader to influence the opinions and interpretations of his followers in a directly rational or cognitive way. Those kinds of influences stuck in the dominant cognitive culture of schools, and do not reach the basic level of staff's personal opinions and interpretations. The 'important constituency' in professional school organizations is made up of the teaching staff. The myths, symbols, stories and images of teachers in and around a school organization are a representation of their meanings and interpretations. Together they create a kind of map that guides the thinking, talking and acting of the school team. Good leaders -school leaders included- are effective to the degree that they succeed in influencing the thinking of their subordinates, which creates their maps. Those leaders neither suggest standardized rules, nor command operating procedures, nor do they try to channel communication. Rather, they spend much time simply walking around in their school, talking with students and teachers, and observing classroom practice (cf. Sergiovanni, 1984). In doing so, the principal can strengthen signals and symbols that are in line with his vision on schools and schooling. He can also suppress stories, images and practices that are indicators or symbols of deviating visions. For that reason this kind of leadership is called 'symbol management'. The followers perspective is at stake, because it is they who create the map of opinions and interpretations (values, priorities, expectations) that functions as the invisible guide for a school organization.

The overview of leadership theories makes it clear that to understand organizational leadership means to understand the character and the dynamics of three crucial factors: (a) the individual leader, (b) the leadership context, and (c) the influence of the followers. Yet, as McPherson et al. (1986) state, "the subject of leadership in education remains poorly understood and only marginally useful in the day-by-day management of schools". School leadership scholars interpreted this evaluation as a stimulating starting point for new ways of searching for the 'hows' and 'whys' of leader behavior. In the next section one approach to that subject will be explored: the cognitive perspective on school leadership.

6.3.2 Review of the section

After reviewing the literature on organizational leadership, one can conclude that its central focus is on the traits and behaviors of leaders. As depicted in this section, research and theorizing during the last 35 years have presented a dynamic and still developing picture of leadership. Substantial are the shifts from traits-research to the behavioral inquiry of leaders, and from the recognition of behavioral styles of leaders to the situational contingencies of leadership. Each of these shifts has resulted in the recognition of new factors which are relevant for the understanding of leadership, and they have also generated -and this is important for the study of leadership- competing explanations of leader outcomes and effects. The shifts in thinking about and explaining leadership did not imply that the findings, methods and questions of the preceding theoretical perspective have been totally overruled and wiped out by the 'next wave' of leadership theories. The theories focusing on leadership behaviors and styles have accepted leader traits and personality characteristics as useful variables that potentially color or constrain leader behavior. The theorists oriented towards a situational understanding of leadership and leader behavior have, in essence, broadened their earlier concepts. In fact, most contingency researchers make use of the behavior style framework and research instruments to describe and analyze the actions of leaders. As such, they rely on the work of their 'behavior biased' colleagues. The substantive newness that the situational leadership theorists introduced was an exploration of the impact that the concrete context of a leader can have on the suitability and contingency of analyses leader behaviors or leadership styles.

As a result of this broadened perspective of leadership studies, a substantial knowledge base on leader behavior has become available. We know a lot about what leaders do, and to a lesser extent about the effects of their actions. Stated in theoretical terms, we are now able to make grounded statements about effective, personally embedded and contextualized leader behavior. However, we still have a relatively poor understanding as to why leaders act the way they do.

In section 6.4 a rather new point of view will be described as a potential answer to that poor understanding: the cognitive perspective on leadership. As will become clear in that section the cognitive perspective can best be labelled a situational theory with an accent on a leader's individual cognitive processes directed toward the specific situation in and around the leader's organization. Those 'internal' (cognitive) processes explain why a leader acts the way he does in a particular situation. Though this perspective could have been handled as a part of the situational theories it is described in its own section because of the newness of this approach.

6.4 The cognitive perspective on educational leadership

Why do principals act as they do? A promising and comprehensive impetus toward answering this question has been presented by Kenneth Leithwood, Philip Hallinger and Joseph Murphy (Hallinger, Leithwood & Murphy, 1993; Leithwood, 1995). After in-depth research that lead to useful behavioral categories of school principals (cf. Leithwood & Montgomery, 1986), these researchers were looking for ways to further the development of quality-supporting leader behavior. For that purpose they needed a solid explanatory framework for understanding the behavioral differences they had found between school principals. They made the deliberate choice for a theoretical framework which fits within the body of available knowledge from cognitive psychology. Leithwood et al. are aware of the individual bias underlying this approach. They recognize that the behavior of a school leader is also influenced by power balances and conflicting interests, both being part of the environment in which he or she tries to lead a school in a certain direction. They also know from their own practice and research experiences that the ways in which schools organize their work and their staff are partly determined by laws and formal regulations, and partly by financial and human resource constraints. Thus, the school leader has only a rather small degree of freedom for creating a work organization that best fits his personal images about the way it should ideally be. However, one should avoid interpreting this conclusion too straightforwardly as being a strong argument for the idea that school leaders are unable to have any impact on their schools. Even though the latitude for school leader impact is restricted, the power of that impact can be relatively strong. Though aware of these other influences on school leader practice, Leithwood et al. have started their search for the explanatory roots of leadership practices of school leaders. Coming from a dominant descriptive-analytic and correlational research background, they now look for a more explanatory, causal model of leader behavior that is grounded in strong theory.

6.4.1 The cognitive approach to school leadership

In the mid nineteen eighties Leithwood and his colleagues had already taken up the so-called 'information processing theory' as a strong explanatory theory for their empirical findings on school principals. (Leithwood & Montgomery, 1986; Leithwood & Stager, 1986). This theory offers a framework for answering three questions:
• Why do people attend to some aspects of available knowledge in their environment and not to others?
• How is knowledge stored, retrieved and developed?
• How is knowledge used in support of the solution to problems?
Based on this framework a 'multi-component model of administrative problem solving'

has been developed, and is presented in this section. This approach is grounded in the so-called 'cognitive perspective': an application of scientific knowledge from cognitive psychology to the practice of individual leaders. The main assumption is that the actions of a school leader depend on what she or he thinks. In this approach the actions are considered to be 'problem solving activities'. The thinking (the cognitive activity) of a school leader depends on his expertise. In the view of the cognitive perspective 'school leaders are problem finders and problem solvers with varying levels of expertise'. Leithwood labels the thinking processes of a leader as 'Internal Processes', that determine the overt behavior of a school leader. The cognitive processes of a leader are not just one influence, among many others, upon leader behavior, but exclusively determine the leadership practice. These are the internal processes in the mind of a school leader that are subject to environmental influences, both from the inside as well as from outside the school organization. By this we mean that the leader's mind treats, analyses, and interprets external influences which are handled as pieces of information which determine the factual behavior of the leader. The quality of information treatment of a leader is a crucial determinant of the quality of the leader's actions. The quality of information treatment depends on the expertise of the leader. The leader's actions are directed toward followers (e.g. teachers, parents) who, in true, also treat them as relevant external pieces of information. The treated or processed information also determines the professional practice of these actors. Teachers are an important target group of school leader practices since their main activities in a school determine the way students are instructed and guided during their formal learning career. The quality of their teaching work is heavily influenced by their processing of information from relevant contexts, and the quality of their information processing depends, in turn, on their expertise with regard to those specific contextual factors. Leithwood views this causal chain around leadership practices as depicted in Figure 6.4 below.

As has been stated earlier, the 'internal processes' of a leader -understood as 'information processing'- constitute the crucial elements of the cognitive approach. Congruent with the information processing theory Leithwood et al. distinguish four dimensions of leadership practice: goals, factors, strategies and decision-making. Leithwood, Begley & Cousins (1992) used these dimensions as a structuring vehicle for their research review about concrete overt "what do you observe they do in their day-to-day work?" behavior of school leaders (not about roles, behavioral patterns and leadership styles). School leaders want to reach specific *goals* in their schools. Therefore, in their view, specific *factors* have to be influenced (e.g. changed, strengthened, weakened, removed), because they are considered relevant for goal attainment. A choice is made from available *strategies* in order to influence some factors. The school leader tracks a way of decision-making about the goals to be reached, the relevant factors to be influenced, and the strategies and

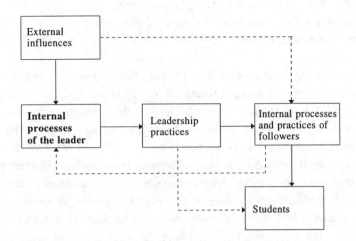

Figure 6.4:   *The place of Internal Processes in a conception of the nature, causes and consequences of school leadership (Leithwood, 1995, p. 117)*

procedures that will be used. Those tracks include the specific roles of the school participants.

The four dimensions together constitute the conceptual structure of the information processing theory, which the authors deem to be strong enough to develop a real understanding of the cognitive processes of school leaders. They consider these four dimensions to be the components of a problem solving process, which they label as 'administrative problem solving'. This will be explained further in this section.

6.4.2 The school leader as problem solver

Leithwood et al. base their model of administrative problem solving on the dimensions of the information processing model. The 'internal processes' are viewed as problem solving processes. Every leadership activity of a school leader starts with screening for the existence of a problem. If a problem is observed, he will initiate trials to solve that problem. A school leader has at his disposal the expertise of a certain quality level for the benefit of both the identification and definition of a problem, as well as for the creation of a solution. The knowledge base for that level of expertise has been developed through preceding practical experiences and learning processes. These experiences and processes bring so-called 'cognitive schemes' into being in what cognitive psychologists call the leader's long term memory. These schemes are partly based on declarative ('is'-)

knowledge, and partly on procedural ('how to'-) knowledge.

In the solution of a problem, two sub-activities are distinguished:

• understanding the problem, and

• solving the problem.

Both activities draw upon information from the long term memory of existing knowledge. A school leader is more or less able to make use of this knowledge: the stored declarative knowledge is used to develop an understanding of the problem information, and the procedural knowledge is used to advantage the solution to the problem. The closer the available cognitive schemes can be connected to new information about a problem or problem context, the higher the leader's expertise is in relation to that problem or problem context. A high level of expertise usually brings with it an increased effectiveness and efficiency in the problem solving process. However, the *amount* of domain or problem specific knowledge is not the only determining characteristic of a leader's long term memory; the way that knowledge has been *organized* is also important, especially in terms of the accessibility of the stored information.

Expertise means the possession and use of complex skills and knowledge to accomplish goals. Thus, an expert school leader has at his disposal a high level of knowledge and skills, and is able to use them in a deliberate way. This means that an expert school leader is most probably an effective leader. However, this is not automatically the case. Due to circumstances (e.g. illness, legal and formal regulations, constraints from higher level officials) external to the high quality of 'internal processes' his potential expertise cannot become effective. The opposite situation can also be the case: he is judged to be an effective school leader only because his actions as a school leader correlate with the desired outcomes of those who judge him. Whether this happens based on expert cognitive processes or intuitively is not considered to be relevant. In this respect the cognitive process approach differs from the correlational approach of most school leadership research. The latter tries to detect a relationship between behavior and results; the cognitive approach tries to explain and understand a relationship between leader activities and outcomes.

Expert, experienced school leaders possess a larger body of domain-related, declarative and procedural knowledge and their cognitive processes operate more effectively than those of novice problem solving school leaders (cf. Glaser & Chi, 1988; Yekovich, 1993).

6.4.3 The process components of problem solving by school leaders

To understand and solve a problem a school leader makes use of his available knowledge, as it is stored in his memory. That use of knowledge is expected to be a fixed, direct connecting flow between the characteristics of the problem and the relevant information the leader has available in his mind. Six factors can be distinguished that make the problem of directed knowledge use a more complex and not fully predictable activity.

These six process components are explained below, and the impact of each component is illustrated with examples from the research findings of Leithwood et al. (1993). The components are divided into three groups according to their primary relevancy for either problem understanding, problem solving, or for both.

6.4.3.1 Understanding problems

Two components of the problem solving process are of primary importance for understanding a problem: problem interpretation and goal clarity.

Problem interpretation

A school leader tries to understand the problem information by comparing it with the relevant knowledge (cognitive schemes) in his long term memory. For an expert problem solving school leader, the present situation, the goal situation and the solution path between these two are familiar from prior (learning) experiences. If this is the case, then the problem is a routine one that is well-structured, and there is full clarity about the relevant cognitive schemes to be used. However, many leadership problems in education lack such full clarity. This can come as a result of the weak knowledge base on problem causes, or because school leaders are confronted with their own unclear or missing relevant knowledge. As a consequence of this, school leaders have a lower level of expertise. When the present situation, the goal situation, and/or the solution path are unclear, the problem is non-routine and ill- structured. Such a problem is interpreted by looking for the best corresponding problem category; these are mostly categories of a type like 'curricular problems', or 'strategic problems'.

Expert educational leaders seem to develop a clearer understanding of the problem before attempting to solve it, and view a presented problem in its relationship with the broader mission and problems of an organization.

Goal clarity

Understanding an ill-structured problem (which is, as said before, often the case in education and educational administration) demands that the problem will be broken down into manageable parts. This can be done by analyzing such a problem within a set of more precise problem solving targets and related goals. Those target goals have a better chance of being connected with the information stored in the head of the problem solver.

Expert school leaders adopt a broader range of goals for problem solving as compared with their less expert colleagues, and more often establish staff development as an explicit way of solving problems in groups.

6.4.3.2 Solving problems

Two other components of the multi-component problem solving model developed by Leithwood and his colleagues are substantially relevant for the solution of a leadership problem: constraints and process modalities.

Constraints

The larger the number of constraints (limitations and hindrances), the more a problem will be of the ill-structured type. The constraints can have the form of a lack of what is required, of actions with inappropriate or no results, or of deviations from the problem solving route. In terms of the four previously described dimensions of administrative information processing, constraints should be considered to be negative factors that disturb progress towards the stated goal.

On the basis of their research, Leithwood et al. suggest that expert educational administrators more effectively anticipate many of the constraints likely to arise during problem solving, and show a greater tendency to plan, in advance, how to address anticipated constraints.

Process modalities

Processes are created by taking deliberate steps to achieve goals. These steps are the result of looking for relevant procedural schemes in a leader's long term memory. The relevant information-processing dimension, as distinguished earlier in this section, is labelled 'strategies'.

Three modalities of procedural schemes can be distinguished:

- scripts: elaborated chains of actions of a leader who possesses all relevant problem knowledge to solve well-structured problems;
- plans: a description of available choices that are used in support of the solution of less- or ill-structured problems for which the leader possesses substantial relevant knowledge;
- heuristics: general, problem domain independent procedures (e.g. brainstorming, working with analogies and metaphors) deemed possibly useful for the problem-solving process when problem-related, procedural knowledge is not available at all.

The studies of Leithwood and Steinbach (1991, 1995) on group problem solving by principals suggested that expert principals have well-developed plans for collaborative problem solving, prepare and organize clearly the problem solving meetings, clearly indicate their own view on the problem without intimidating or restraining others, and use problem-relevant knowledge in their problem solving.

6.4.3.3 Understanding and solving problems

Two other components Leithwood et al. distinguish in their multi-component model are relevant for both the understanding and the solution of problems by educational leaders: values and moods.

Values

Values concern enduring beliefs about preferred actions and means which guide one's actions and thoughts with respect to the desired goals as well as to the activities to reduce the gap between the current and the goal situation. Values provide a kind of perceptual filter for the administrator to see and hear what he wants to. They can become part of one's long-term memory, and are tacitly embedded in existing knowledge schemes to be used by leaders. They can also develop further into an independent value system, becoming a kind of value structure, and can channel the behavior of problem solving school leaders (Hamrick & Brandon, 1988).

Expert educational administrators seem to be aware of their values, use their values regularly in solving ill-structured problems, and use values as substitutes for knowledge which they lack when solving ill-structured problems.

Moods

Moods may influence the degree of cognitive flexibility that one can exercise in a problem solving process. Strong moods can reduce that flexibility to such a degree that they inhibit the goal directed problem solving processes.

Leithwood and Steinbach (1995) and Stager and Leithwood (1989) indicate that expert principals are able to control strong moods and remain calm during problem solving, are self-confident about their ability to solve ill-structured problems, and are likely to be reflective about their behavior, thoughts, and moods.

6.4.3.4 Review of the section

The content of this section on the 'cognitive perspective' can best be reviewed by presenting a schematic overview of the elements of the 'Multicomponent Problem Solving Model' of school leadership. The cognitive approach of leadership has just recently been used seriously as a framework for school leadership research. It has been presented here in more detail as it is expected to be a fruitful gateway into a real understanding of the behavior of school leaders.

This model functions as a map for understanding the 'internal processes' of school leaders.

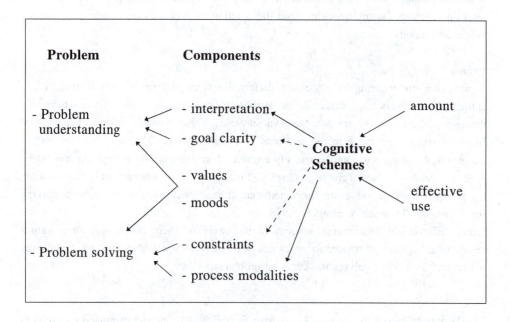

Figure 6.5: *The Multicomponent Problem Solving Model of Leadership*

6.5 Instructional Leadership

In order to guarantee that schools perform their educational tasks in an accountable way, governments and parliaments have made, and continue to pass educational laws and rules. They also install and maintain a school inspectorate. In line with this societal control of educational organizations, school leadership has traditionally concentrated on law and rule implementation, and on the daily management of resources (staff, finance, equipment and facilities) which schools received from the government. The quality of education was left mainly in the hands of professional teachers. The teaching process, as such, was no major issue of head teachers, principals and school directors. School leaders did not, and in many schools still do not, play the role of educational or instructional leader. However, a growing number of them take the view that they should take up that role for the betterment of their school.

The theoretical perspectives on leadership that were explained in sections 6.3 and 6.4 suggest that the task and outcome-directed leader, who has an expert leadership capability for solving educational problems in his school, fulfills the prerequisites for instruction-directed school leadership best.

6.5.1 The need for instructional leadership

About a decade or two ago, three powerful movements placed the instruction-directed task of school leaders on the educational front page.

First was the *School Improvement* movement (Van Velzen et al., 1984). In reaction to the disappointing results of many innovative projects -many of which had their origin outside the school and had been developed at too great a distance from real school life-educational scholars made a plea for giving the school organization itself more control over the quality of school work. As a consequence of this strategic change, the school leader himself should become more concerned with the curriculum, the teaching and guidance of teachers, and the learning and well being of students. In the earlier literature on change processes in schools, the crucial role of the principal had already become a fixed theme. Researchers who analyzed the activities of principals in school innovation projects even detected different change-facilitator styles of school principals (e.g. Hall et al., 1984).

The second push for an increase in the interest of school leaders in the teaching and learning processes in their schools stems from the *Effective Schools* research and development activities. British and North American researchers observed that some primary schools were achieving better learning results than others, although the individual and social background characteristics of students could not sufficiently explain that difference. One of the differences they found between more effective and less effective schools concerned the attitude and the activities of the school leader. The leaders of effective schools:

• show direct involvement in their school's education and students;
• repeatedly evaluate classroom work of their teachers and the learning progress and
  results of the students;
• promote an orderly work environment and a school climate in which every child is
  expected to be able to learn (Scheerens, 1992).

Replications of this type of research in European countries, and meta-analyses of the relevant North American research reports do not give uncontestable support to these findings, although a positive relationship between instructional leadership of American school leaders and the learning outcomes of their schools cannot be denied. (Bosker & Witziers, 1996). The picture of the effective school leader who leads curriculum and instruction has been painted by the effective schools research movement, and since then covers the mental wall of many educational policy makers, developers, consultants and management trainers.

The third motor driving the way to educational leadership concerns the trend of *Decentralization and Autonomy of Schools*. Central governing authorities gradually became convinced that their centralized efforts to improve the quality of education in schools did not have the desired effects, and sometimes resulted in feelings of alienation on the part of school teachers and principals. In addition, it became increasingly clear that central initiatives could not accommodate the specific problems and needs of local school organizations. It seemed to be more appropriate to delegate the responsibility for the quality of public education to the local school level. The decline in public funding of schools in almost every western country accelerated this process, because it was assumed that the maintenance of quality with lesser resources could be better looked after within individual schools. The central governmental offices tended to be allotted the task of controlling the quality of organization, processes and outcomes of individual schools. In most cases, the transfer of responsibilities to the school level in fact means the transfer to the school leader; the result being that he will act more as an instructional leader. This process of decentralization of accountability for quality is considered in several countries to be a prerequisite for the maintenance, or even an increase of quality. For instance, the underlying statement of the decentralization policy in the Dutch higher education system was: "Autonomy and Quality".

The three movements described, separately and together, demand leaders who devote a lot more of their time, energy and knowledge to teaching and learning issues in their schools. It sounds reasonable that the shift from mainly externally governed and controlled schools to more autonomous, independent and thus more self-responsible institutions, would correlate with the shift from individual leadership dominated by technical rationality, to institutional leadership where sharing and networking are the preferred vehicles. Yet, in the vast majority of research and literature on instructional leadership, this school leadership task is still restricted to the principalship: leadership is principalship.

6.5.2 The reality of instructional leadership

A principal who intervenes in curricular and instructional affairs is often considered to be someone balancing on a narrow wall with barking dogs on both sides beneath. When he intervenes too much and too intensely in the zone of control which the teachers consider to be theirs, he will be blamed for not recognizing their professional autonomy and expertise. As the reader may remember from the first section of this paragraph, a French primary school head in so doing will fall prey to his complaining teaching staff. If, however, the principal leaves all educational decisions to the professional teachers, he runs the risk of being accused of neglecting his school leader duties by parents and school board members.

Through instructional leadership activities a school leader enters the decision making domain which belongs to the teachers. Teachers have successfully mastered high level teacher training, both in their subject matter and in instructional activities and didactics. Because of their proven competence to deliver adequate instruction to a group of children, they are employed in a school. The school leader has to respect the professional autonomy of his teachers.

As indicated before, instructional leadership is part of the role of a so-called functional boss. This type of boss derives his authority primarily from his specific knowledge and expertise. As far as content expertise is concerned, the principal lacks specific knowledge, except with respect to the subject he teaches. The curricular, instructional and didactic expertise of a school leader serves a broader scope, assuming that his knowledge has sufficient quality to be recognized by his teachers.

Ultimately, all leadership activities in a school are intent upon the best possible learning outcomes for all of the children who attend that school. However, some of a leader's activities (finance, facilities and accommodations, conditions of employment and labor relations, school's office of clerical work, catering, security, and external relations) have non-educational targets. All of these management tasks are executed under the ultimate responsibility of the head teacher or school director, and must be carried out in the most efficient and rational way. The other part of a leader's activities has a direct bearing on teaching, learning and student guidance. The primary focus of these leader activities is education, as such, and they together constitute the instructional leadership of a school.

A large number of research projects during the last 15 years have tried to find answers to questions on aspects, processes and effects of educational leadership. Because of the poor and various definitions of instructional leadership used by researchers, and as a consequence, the different operationalizations and research items, the knowledge about effective instructional leadership lacks cohesiveness. As a result several research instruments are available for determining the instructional leadership attitude and activities of school leaders. Most of these instruments have been developed for the specific context of primary or secondary schools, because the researchers expected substantial differences in instructional leadership between these two levels of schooling. One of those instruments is the 'Principal Instructional Management Rating Scale' (PIMRS), developed by Hallinger & Murphy (1985). Their initial definition of instructional leadership has been developed for use in secondary schools and consists of ten indicators spread over three dimensions: (a) defining a mission of the school, (b) managing the curriculum, and (c) boosting a learning-oriented school climate. There is reason to expect that instructional leadership differs in accordance with the differences between parts of school systems and the administrative cultures of various countries. The research done by Kruger (1994, 1996) to explore differences in the instructional leadership orientation and activities between male and female Dutch secondary school principals gives rise to such a cultural impact. The questionnaire she developed to collect data about the instructional leadership of the principals in the study was based mainly on the indicators and dimensions Hallinger & Murphy used as framework for their PIMRS-instrument. However, the analysis of the Dutch data did not reveal the originally underlying structure of the PIMRS-based scale-instrument. Kruger detected quite a different meaningful structure. Earlier in this section we denoted that the overall central position which is attributed to American school leaders with respect to the development and quality of teaching and learning in their schools has not been found to the same extent in European schools (cf. Bosker & Witziers, 1996). There are real cultural differences between school systems, with relevance for the possible influence and central targets of instructional leadership activities. Despite this cultural bias there is in some respect congruence between school leaders in their activities towards learning and teaching in their schools.

What do school leaders who behave as instructional leaders do?
Several research reviews have been published on instructional leadership, both summative and evaluative ones. An overall picture of instructional leadership activities is presented below. These activities are clustered under eight headings, and are presented as they have been observed to be effective by school organization and leadership researchers

a. Management of curriculum and instruction
The leader translates his view on schooling and student learning into concrete school goals and final attainment levels. He makes policy decisions on curricular and instructional matters, and directs the choice of clear instructional objectives. He gains staff support for his policy decisions and choices, and for that reason is concerned about value consensus and practical coherence in the teaching staff. He maintains the support of the staff by being consistent in his decision-making and directing orientations, which give his staff a sense of security and builds confidence. He gives a lot of attention to the evaluation of students and teachers, develops quality control systems, uses information on student progress in his policy making, and looks for systematic longitudinal information on the students' results. He initiates innovations in the areas of instruction, curriculum and student guidance. All school participants can observe that the principal devotes much of his attention to teaching, learning and student affairs.

b. Cooperation with teachers on curricular and instructional issues

He makes intensive use of instances where teachers and leaders meet for final curricular and instructional decision-making. He frequently initiates contacts with teachers, nurturing a trust based relationship with them. He extends a lot of influence to the teachers in educational affairs, basically limiting himself to coordinating their decision making. In many instances his involvement in teacher decision-making has great impact. He actively participates in text book selection, discusses the student learning results with the teachers, informs them about new developments and does not hesitate to exploit specific qualities and capacities of individual teachers in benefit of the whole school.

c. Encouragement and reward of teachers

He holds the teachers responsible for their teaching behavior, and clearly communicates his expectations with them. He takes the personal aspirations and wishes of his staff members into account. He supports teachers in their attempts to improve the effectiveness of their instructional work, pushes the development and use of specific instructional programmes, and when asked for, demonstrates instructional procedures and techniques. He stimulates cooperative problem solving and rewards improved outcomes and innovative efforts. At the same time he does not avoid critical messages to teachers, and if necessary, points mistakes out to teachers.

d. Supervision and control of teachers

He visits teachers during their classroom work for the purpose of evaluation and recommendations for improvement, and he likes to give personal feedback and coaching. He is concerned that every teacher be afforded free opportunity to bring up his instructional problems in teachers' meetings. Occasionally, he controls the instructional planning of teachers. Conduction of performance reviews with individual teachers is a regular part of his responsibilities.

e. Advancement of teachers' skill, expertise and professionalism

He expects a high level of professionalism by teachers, and a high learning performance on the part of students. He controls quality and continuously pursues quality improvement regarding the educational work of his school. He asks that problems, once detected, be investigated, and tries to enhance the problem solving capacity of his team. For that purpose, he organizes staff development sessions to improve their knowledge and skills. He develops an in-service training policy, and looks for adequate in-service opportunities and facilities.

f. Provision of resources, facilities and conditions for quality education

In his management duties concerning the non-educational domains of his task, the quality of education, the professional improvement of teachers and the maximum learning facilities for students are the top criteria in his bargaining and decision-making processes. He appoints the best qualified teachers available. The school organization is clear and effective, and he prefers organizational arrangements in which teachers have to cooperate with each other. He creates time and support facilities for temporary and permanent work groups, and buffers the staff from strong external pressures.

g. Promoting an orderly and stimulating work climate

He encourages a safe work environment and tight relations in his school, expresses high expectations with respect to the learning results of the students, and pays attention to their discipline. He tries to install educational routines that fit with the existing culture and climate of the school. Innovative initiatives are welcomed by him, and he looks for ways to support their implementation.

h. Personal characteristics, traits and behavioral styles

Although personal features do not concern leader activities, some traits and styles of instructional leaders are mentioned repeatedly in the literature about instructional leadership. The instructional leader is both task- and person-oriented. He is present, visible and accessible to his teachers and demonstrates an 'enablement' style of support giving. He has solid, non-specialized knowledge on curricular and instructional issues, and thinks in an expert way. He is a carrier of values and norms and models them in his own behavior. He has a relatively broad repertoire of intervention methods at his disposal.

6.5.3 The effects of instructional leadership

As has been stated before, it was the Effective Schools Research movement that prompted the relevance of the instructional leadership role of school leaders for the learning achievement of the students. This was accomplished by comparing data from effective and from less effective schools. These research findings were mainly of a correlational type, and did not explain the relationship between leadership and effects.

During the early nineteen eighties, parallel to the initial effective schools research activities, a group of researchers and educational developers from the Far West Laboratory did a longitudinal research project in which they analyzed the behavior of 17 school leaders within the context of their school organizations. They concluded two important things:

(a) the effectiveness of the instructional leadership behavior of school leaders is influenced by antecedent and context variables that they themselves are rarely able to change (i.e. personal characteristics, elements of the formal educational context, characteristics of the local community);

(b) the impact of educational leadership behavior of school leaders on student learning results is mainly of an indirect kind, instead of a direct one. (Bossert et al., 1982).

These findings focused the attention of theorists and researchers on the primary area of concern of a school leader: the school organization. Which aspects or elements of the organizational level of a school can be influenced by a principal in such a way that the learning processes and outcomes will change in a positive direction? Bossert hypothesized that both the school climate and the instructional organization at school-level should be the main vehicles for school leaders to influence teaching and learning processes and outcomes in classrooms. This shift from classroom level to the level of the school as an organization, proved to be an important one in fostering a better understanding of the ways in which school leaders can influence the effectiveness of their schools.

Hallinger & Heck (1996) published an important contribution by way of a thorough analysis of the research literature on instructional leadership published since the review of Bossert et al.. For their analysis, they used a framework of five different conceptual models. Starting with the 'old' direct-effect model they further developed the Bossert model by putting gradually more antecedent and intermediate variables - separately and combined - in their conceptual research models.

The more complex models seem to have a greater capacity to present more useful results that are capable of clarifying the complex reality of school organizations.

Nevertheless, it continued to be difficult to find non-trivial effects of school leader behavior on student achievement. Bosker & Witziers (1996), from their statistical meta-analysis of European research projects, could not conclusively identify such a school leader influence. For American primary school schools they could account for some differences in learning results based on school leader behavior.

Further research into effective American school leaders generated two common features of the behavior of these school leaders:

(a) they are remarkably concerned with and active in the mission, the goals and the outcomes of their schools;

(b) they give substantial attention to the cohesiveness of the teaching-learning process, mainly by making basic curricular decisions and by improving coordination and communication between teachers (cf. Hallinger & Heck, 1998).

In a growing number of recent research projects (i.e. the cognitive-approach based studies by the Leithwood group of the principal as expert problem solver (par. 6.4)), the school leader's expertise on educational and instructional matters has been pointed out as an important characteristic of effective school leaders. Perhaps these educational expertise qualities should be considered as prerequisites for a school leader's influential concerns about school goals and teaching and learning matters.

6.6 Summary

This chapter directed the reader's attention to the leadership function in school organizations. Although leadership is executed on different levels and within various tasks of organizations, the main theoretical and research interests till now have focused on the roles, the activities, the context and the effects of principalship.

Because of the public duty of schools, their leaders will have to balance between their external and their internal leadership responsibilities - a dynamic that is a characteristic of professional bureaucratic organizations, such as schools. Within the school, leaders have to combine their managerial duties with their overall instructional responsibilities. For the latter, they depend highly on the instructional quality of the teachers. Principals in their instructional leadership role are trying to improve the teaching of teachers in support of the learning improvement of the students. The positive effects of these influencing behaviors of principals, however, can not be proved definitively.

School leadership should profit from the general leadership knowledge, which has mainly originated from research in organizations other than schools. The history of leadership theory and research can be depicted as a succession of theoretical movements. Over time, this development can be characterized as a progressive flow: traits, behavior, styles, situation, and followers of leaders. This progression has taken place because a growing new movement has criticized the preceding one; not by substituting, but mainly by broadening and somehow integrating the foregoing conceptions and research findings. The development of leadership knowledge thus far has really been progressive and will continue to be so.

Because of the relatively recent entrance of school organizations into the interest of leadership researchers, especially in continental European countries, school leadership thinking and practice could profit from this already broadened and more integrated leadership knowledge. The recently developed cognitive approach to school leadership originated from researchers who have been working mainly in the context of teaching, learning, cognitive development and problem solving - the core business of schools. That development has created new opportunities for a better understanding of the leader behaviors of school principals and other leading figures within school organizations.

• CHAPTER 7 •

Aligning the Organization with its Environment

A.A.M. Wognum
University of Twente, The Netherlands

7.1 Introduction

Aligning the organization with its environment refers to the interrelationship between educational institutions and the environment in which they are embedded. It concerns determining educational goals and strategies in interaction with this environment. In former years, this interrelationship was not an important issue in the field of educational organization and management. School leaders could manage their schools from a closed-system approach by focusing mainly on internal principles of structuring and functioning. The external environment was stable, and changes were predictable. It is common knowledge nowadays that the external environment is changing rapidly and significantly since the late nineteen fifties. The environment has become dynamic and changes are less predictable. The impact of all kinds of environmental forces on educational activities has increased, and it has become imperative that schools understand and reckon with their environment. The closed-systems approach has proven itself to be inadequate for dealing with the problems of educational administrators (Boyd & Crowson, 1981). The interrelationship with the external environment has become an important issue for schools. This new open-systems perspective is essential for the viability of schools.

The relevant literature shows that this process of adjusting to environmental change, and maintaining an effective alignment with the environment while efficiently managing internal interdependencies, is much more complex than usually assumed (Levin, 1993). Much variation exists in the school-environment interaction process. In part of the literature, the idea has been articulated that organizations constructively manage their environment. Other authors indicate that schools merely adjust to externally imposed changes. In other publications it is still argued that the relationship between organizations and their environment is two-sided, meaning that the interaction between schools and their surrounding environments is reciprocal (see section 7.5). This chapter explores the different kinds of interactions between schools and their environments, in other words: aligning strategies. Before discussing these relationships and the ways in which policy-makers in organizations can take environmental features into account, it is important to address the changing perspectives on the school-environment relationship, and to conceptualize the idea 'environment'. Sections 7.2. and 7.3, respectively, deal with these topics. Environmental management is crucial for achieving an appropriate relationship with an organization's external environment and to choose the right aligning strategy. Section 7.4 discusses three aspects of environmental management, i.e. environmental scanning, the problem of boundary and boundary spanning. In section 7.5. three categories of aligning strategies are presented and analyzed. Section 7.6. pays some attention to the significance of environmental characteristics from a school effectiveness point of view. The chapter ends with a summary in section 7.7.

7.2 Changing perspectives on the school-environment relationship

Pröpper (1993) indicates that Taylor and Fayol, in the second decade of the twentieth century, did not mention the environment as an important factor for the structuring of an organization. In 1921 Weber even stated explicitly that organizations must be guarded against the environment, and also in the Human Relations theory of Mayo (published in 1933), and the decision-making theory of Simon (published in 1947), only internal principles were regarded as critical for the functioning and change of an organization. The interaction between an organization and its environment received very little attention from these authors. Educational administrative theory and practice were based on these theories, assuming that education could be walled off from community pressures. This closed-systems perspective was physically manifested in schools by high placed classroom windows and high walls surrounding the school.

Before the nineteen sixties, the environment of schools was quite stable and clear. Change occurring, for example, in the financial funding of the school or in the flow of students was slow and fairly predictable. For this reason, schools could act without seriously taking their environment into account. Internal principles of structuring and functioning, such as the reward and motivation strategies, the hierarchical organizational structure, and the organizational decision/coordination mechanisms, received much more attention than aligning the organization with outside elements (McPherson, Crowson, & Pitner, 1986). Schools could count on their professional ability and working procedures, and only minor changes were made.

A few decades ago, the environment began to change with an increasing effect on schools. The pressures placed on schools led to a number of far-reaching changes. Many examples of these pressures are noted in reports on education (Levin, 1993). For instance, because of legal requirements and constraints around education, schools must explain and justify

214

their goals and methods, and to involve parents and other stakeholders in part of their school's decision-making. Because of decreasing student numbers and smaller budgets, schools have become more competitive and are obliged to mobilize resources.

All these factors, and more, link schools with their environments, ultimately increasing the impact of the external environment on school's internal functioning (Goldring, 1995a). Today's schooling has become more permeable, more open to, and even actively seeking the influence of the wider environment. Only schools with sufficient aligning capacity will flourish in the new environmental realities.

Related to this, the literature moved from a closed-systems perspective to a perspective emphasizing the interrelationships between organizations and their environments, and stressing that this interchange is essential for organizations to survive and be effective. Selznick was the first author who, in 1957, paid attention to the important role of the environment (Selznick, 1984). Katz and Kahn (1966) and Pfeffer and Salancik (1978) followed him by pointing to the open-systems perspective. The relationship between the school organization and its environment has grown in importance since then. Schools have become more open systems, interacting with their environments.

7.3 Conceptualizing the environment

An understanding of the environment concept is extremely useful in any effort to explain the process of interaction between an organization and its environment. The term 'environment' is complicated and "has been used with considerable variability in the literature" (Levin, 1993, p. 6). An 'organizational environment' is no homogeneous entity, but composed of a complex combination of various aspects. Organizational theorists have identified numerous environmental features that have a bearing on the organization. Some of these features are more critical to the organization's operations than others are (Miles & Snow, 1978). The impact of global warming, for example, is less critical for schooling processes than the increased use of computers in society, which forces schools to alter their curricula in favor of information technology.

According to Levin, a variety of categories has been developed to describe the features of the organizational environment. However, usually, three main categories are distinguished:

• external elements;
• external characteristics;
• external areas.

These categories, which are not mutually exclusive but rather complement each other, are explained in the sections 7.3.1 up to and including 7.3.3.

7.3.1 Elements of the external environment

A well known approach is to interpret an organization's environment in terms of "all elements that exist outside the boundaries of an organization" (Bolman and Deal, in Levin, 1993, p. 7). These elements concern all external forces and groups affecting a school's functioning (Kotler & Fox, 1985). Figure 7.1. depicts the school environment in terms of these external forces and groups. The forces are usually categorized into demographic, social, economic, ecological, technological, political, and cultural forces. They shape opportunities for and pose threats to the institution (Kotler & Fox, 1985). Examples of external groups affecting the schools' functioning are, among others, students and other consumers and stakeholders, such as parents, competitors, legislative bodies (federal, state, local), suppliers and donors, publishers, business groups, unions, media personnel, government agencies, accreditation organizations, and the local public (Boyd & Crowson, 1981; Keuning & Eppink, 1993; Kotler & Fox, 1985).

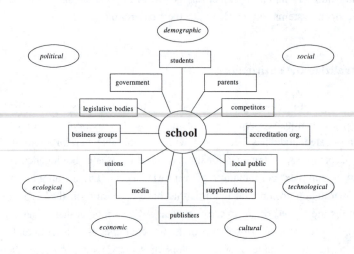

Figure 7.1: *The school environment in terms of external forces and groups*

It is beyond the scope of this chapter to discuss all these external forces and groups. A few examples will be mentioned to gain more insight into their impact on the goals, processes, and outcomes of educational institutions.

External forces
A first example concerns the increase in the proportion of minority groups in society. This

216

demographic development has caused a growth in the proportion of minority children in schools with the resulting increase in different cultural heritages and in the number of foreign languages in schools. Sometimes, school leaders assume that this growing proportion of minority children hinders them from realizing high performance standards. They then perceive this demographic development as a threat to their school's functioning. It is ,however, also often considered an opportunity for innovation as this growing number of minority children encourages significant shifts in curricula, school structures and internal schooling processes. It enables schools to initiate, for example, specific classroom arrangements for multicultural education and/or minority language and culture teaching. A similar example of a demographic force concerns the immigration of thousands of Russian immigrants to Israel. This development resulted in a changing enrollment pattern in Israeli schools. In reaction to this force, some principals have started to market their schools to take advantage of this new influx. Others, on the contrary, could not accept all those who have moved into their neighborhoods (Goldring, 1995a). A diversity of reasons may lead them to the exclusion of those new immigrants, for instance, by making the student admission procedure more strict.

The extension of primary education to pre-school education is an example of a political development. This legal requirement resulted in mergers between nursery schools and elementary schools. A similar example of a legislative measure concerns the introduction of a national core curriculum for the first three years of secondary education (implemented in the Netherlands in 1993). This forced schools to adjust their curricula to the new governmental requirements. This change coincided with the reduction of interference from central government into the details of education and the devolution of financial and managerial responsibility to schools since 1992.

Changes in family structures and parental work patterns are examples of social changes. An increase in the divorce rates brings more children under emotional pressure than before. A high unemployment figure causes social and financial problems in children's homes. These developments brings children with more emotional or social needs into schools (Goldring, 1995b) which may result in learning and behavioral problems. In these cases, schools will be urged to provide tailored education and integrated services, like out-of-school care and extracurricular activities.

Another example of a social development is the decline in tolerance for authority in society, which has also created a revolution in authority relations in schools (Boyd & Crowson, 1981). Students consider their teachers more and more as their equals and treat them likewise.

Changing economic characteristics (an example of an economic force) will influence the extent of financial parental contribution, and diminish the fundings and budgets for education. This will force schools to tap new financial sources which may be acquired by delivering educational activities to companies and other institutions who pay for these kind of activities to enhance the performance of their employees.

A last example of external environmental forces concerns various kinds of technological changes. The ever increasing trend toward the application of computer technology will force schools to include computers in the curriculum, and challenge teachers to use computer-assisted instruction in at least part of their lessons.

External groups

As indicated above, many groups outside the school and outside the teaching profession have an impact on schools' functioning (see Figure 7.1). An increased influence in school affairs by these groups has changed their roles and relative power. Stronger educational demands from new students and other stakeholders, (e.g. parents, business groups, the government, and schools of higher education) force schools to be more aware of and more responsive to their needs, rights, and likely contributions (Goldring, 1995b). Parents and other constituencies urge schools to involve them in their school's decision-making processes in order to assure themselves of this kind of school responsiveness.

Competitors force schools to increase the popularity of their curriculum (McPherson et al. 1986) by making their courses more attractive. Schools may be pushed by their rivals to improve their marketing and communication strategies, to strengthen their market position and to attract and keep students (Witziers & De Groot, 1993).

The government, another important influential group, can demand that schools implement new educational acts. An example is the implementation of Public Law 94-142 (The Education of All Handicapped Children Act) in Massachusetts. This law forces schools to coordinate testing, to write individualized programs, and to hold meetings to discuss these programs. The time needed for these activities reduces the time that can be invested in other activities like instruction (McPherson et al., 1986).

The demand for league tables of school performance and the publication of school inspection reports are also examples of the influence of the government. Schools are asked to provide a range of information for publication that can be used to compare and rank the performance of schools (Woods, Bagley and Glatter, 1998).

A final example of how external groups can affect a school's functioning concerns the influence of business groups. Companies encourage schools to 'produce' a better-educated workforce. They therefore provide schools with equipment and supplies which are unavailable through regular budgetary routes. Schools, however, have to ensure that the influence business groups bring to bear on the kind of instruction and services schools provide to students does not become too large.

Although many external forces and groups tend to influence a school's functioning, schools cannot predict the impact of all these external influences. Sometimes the behavior of certain groups can be predicted. For example, in 1970 the Columbus public schools foresaw a lack of funds provided by suppliers and donors. This forced them to eliminate some additional courses from their elementary schools as a precautionary measure. However, the unforeseen severe energy shortages in the winter months of 1977 however forced to close their school doors suddenly (McPherson et al., 1986). Schools can buffer themselves against the impact of some external forces or groups. Severe fluctuations in the flow of students, for example, can be avoided through establishing networks between primary and secondary schools. Secondary schools are then ensured of a continuous enrollment of students leaving their main feeder primary schools.

7.3.2 Characteristics of the external environment

A second perspective on the environment complements the external elements view in some way. It concerns the analysis of the external environment in terms of its characteristics. Important attributes of environments center around four dimensions (Goldring, 1995a, 1995b; Hrebiniak & Joyce, 1985):
• capacity (abundant-scarce resources);
• clustering (structured-anarchy);
• volatility (stable-dynamic);
• complexity (simple-complex).

Table 7.1: *External characteristics and environmental uncertainty*

dimensions	low environmental uncertainty	<---------->	high environmental uncertainty
capacity	resource-abundant	<---------->	resource-scarce
clustering	structured	<---------->	anarchy
volatility	stable	<---------->	dynamic
complexity	simple	<---------->	complex

Each dimension, together with its characteristics is explained below. A combination of these dimensions characterizes the specific environment with which the school leader must contend, and indicates the level of environmental uncertainty. Attention is also paid to this

219

environmental characteristic. Table 7.1 depicts, to some extent, the relationship between the characteristics of the external environment and (the level of) environmental uncertainty.

Capacity

Environmental capacity refers to the extent to which those resources used to sustain organizational activities are available from the environment (Goldring, 1995a & 1995b). A distinction can be made between such intangible resources as good will and public trust, and more tangible ones like budget, students, and talented workers (McPherson et al., 1986). If resources, including the intangible ones, are scarce, competition between schools within the same environment will increase. For example, schools need parents to volunteer in their schools. Parental participation is subject to pressure due to an increasing number of working mothers. This requires all schools to search for alternatives for this type of assistance. As a result, they become competitors with one another (Goldring, 1995b).

Capacity also dictates whether or not there is room for expansion and growth. Organizations in resource-rich environments can expand with relative security (Goldring, 1995a). Establishing an auxiliary branch in a new housing estate with young families presents nearly no risk for elementary schools because of the growing number of potential students.

Clustering

Environmental clustering indicates the extent to which the environmental elements are organized and structured, rather than being randomly distributed in a disorderly fashion (Goldring, 1995a). The degree of clustering affects the functioning of schools. An anarchic, unstructured and relatively disorganized environment demonstrates little coordination between environmental elements. To achieve a greater fit with these sorts of surroundings, schools have to interact with each important element (such as separate business groups, distinct schools, or individual parents) to become aware of major changes and educational needs. Clustered environments are more organized. Elements in such environments are more coordinated and coupled, which facilitates their exchanges with educational and other institutions. A network of schools, for example, can minimize the inter-school competition and maximize the level of cooperation, the exchange of information and the acquisition of financial and other resources. All Catholic schools for primary and secondary education may, for instance, have made some agreements on the recruitment of students and the enquiring of parents and other stakeholders. In such a clustered environment schools can participate in these and other kinds of networks in order to gain the benefits of network agreements.

Volatility

Environmental volatility refers to the extent to which environmental elements are stable or dynamic. Stable environments remain more or less the same over a period of years. In case of change, for example in the financial funding of the school or in the flow of students, it is slow and predictable. However, under unstable conditions, environmental elements shift in abrupt and unpredictable ways (Daft, 1992; Hoy & Miskel, 1982). Instability can occur, for example, if the percentage of prospective students choosing for another school increases, or when companies quite suddenly require new knowledge, skills and attitudes, related to their fast changing production processes and business strategy. Other causes for instability can be found in new legislative regulations, or in competitors acting with aggressive moves in terms of advertisements, new courses and other student-attracting activities.

Complexity

Environmental complexity indicates the degree to which environmental elements are simple or complex. Simple environments are homogeneous, with more or less uniform elements. Complex environments include many heterogeneous elements, which all interact with and influence the organization in their own way (Daft, 1992). For example, the environment is simple when all parents come from similar socio-economical and ethnic backgrounds (Goldring, 1995b), or when there are a few relatively similar companies. The environment is more heterogeneous and complex when parents represent different social classes with various educational demands, or when companies demand highly skilled graduates of myriad specialties. Schools have to deal with these different guests, each asking for effective education.

Environmental uncertainty

Environmental uncertainty refers to the amount of information on environmental features a school needs to collect in order to function effectively and efficiently (Goldring, 1995a). The level of environmental (un)certainty is indicated by the combined scores on the dimensions that have been explained above. One extreme concerns stable, organized, simple, and resource-abundant environments in which it is easy to work (see Table 7.1). There is little uncertainty since only a few fairly stable external elements have to be coped with. Managers are easily able to collect the necessary information on these few elements for managing their schools. An example may be the school leader of a rural elementary school who has only to deal with a stable group of parents, a few secondary schools and one industrial company. Because no radical changes are to be expected, he can rely on his routine way of interacting with this group of stakeholders. He has an adequate perception of their educational demands and knows how they will respond to school initiatives. The provision of education by his school will be satisfactory for a period of several years.

A shift in one dimension creates more uncertainty and complexity and changes the relationship between a school and its environment. In a stable but more complex environment for example, the school faces a large number of environmental elements, which all need to be analyzed and acted upon. In a commuter village, for example, the parental community has become more heterogeneous than before. The original inhabitants are relatively homogeneous with more or less the same kinds of interests and cultural habits. The new residents, on the contrary, are characterized by a diversity of professions and interests. This different group of parents send their children to the same rural school. The school leader has to communicate with all these parents to assess their different needs and their reactions to school initiatives. The environment is stable because these groups of parents do not change rapidly or unexpectedly regarding their way of life and their educational demands.

More uncertainty is felt in the simple, unstable environment. Rapid changes create uncertainty for school leaders. Even though the organization has a limited number of external elements, they are hard to predict. How, for instance, will the usual group of parents react if the Catholic school is obliged to cooperate with a school of another religious denomination because of financial or legislative reasons? The school principal has to predict the parental reactions and assess possible impacts on his school.

A school in a complex, unstable, resource-scarce and unstructured environment has to deal with most uncertainty. When several environmental elements change simultaneously the environment becomes turbulent. Most school organizations currently face uncertainty. A large number of frequently shifting elements simultaneously impact on educational institutions. Many of the forces and developments mentioned in the preceding sections occur simultaneously, like the changing demographic features of students and parents, new legislative initiatives, economic constraints and labor force conditions.

In these complex and dynamic environmental realities it is imperative that schools stay in close interaction with all relevant elements of the surrounding environment. School managers have to collect information on how these elements will impact their individual schools. Related to this, they must determine the changing educational demands of relevant stakeholders and inquire about their reactions to new educational initiatives. If they lack this kind of information, they may not know which actions are best to respond to the rapidly changing environment.

7.3.3 External environmental areas

A third approach to interpreting an organization's environment is to divide the external environment into areas or sectors. A distinction is often made between the general and the specific environment (Gross, in McPherson et al., 1986). The internal environment is also mentioned often in the pertinent literature. It consists of the school organization, itself, with its internal staff and strengths and weaknesses regarding the organizational structure, culture and processes. Figure 7.2 depicts the three environmental areas. The general and the specific environment are discussed below. The internal environment is not discussed in this chapter, as attention has been paid to it in the preceding chapters of this book.

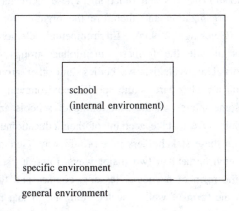

Figure 7.2: *Areas in the school environment*

General environment

The general environment, often called the macro environment (Kotler & Fox, 1985), or the contextual environment (Emery & Trist, 1969), consists of those forces and influences by which the organization is affected without the possibility to act upon or to control them. The earlier mentioned political, economical, social, cultural, technological, and demographic forces are situated here. These forces are constantly changing nowadays. They affect the educational institution far more than the institution affects them. The following examples indicate that an organization has to take full account of the consequences of these forces.

Schools cannot, for instance, affect the downturn in the number of college-age youngsters (an example of a demographic force). However, this downturn will have immediate effects on most higher education institutions in a nation (Kotler & Fox, 1985). Schools can also hardly be expected to act upon the level of unemployment, which partially determines the economic situation in a country. However, more unemployment usually causes a longer stay of students in schools for secondary education. The unavoidable trend of automation and technological innovations leads to major changes in the school curricula as new skills are needed. An example of legislation affecting schools concerns the fixed student enrollment numbers which limit the number of students they can admit. This political action has forced schools to reconsider their acceptance and dismissal policies.

Specific environment

Other labels for the specific environment are the task environment (Daft, 1992), the immediate environment (Gross, in McPherson et al., 1986), or transactional environment (Emery & Trist, 1969). It is comprised of those environmental elements that are critical for executing the organizational tasks and functions. These elements have immediate and direct relevance for the organization and therefore the organization interacts with them closely and directly (Goldring, 1995a). Environmental elements in the specific environment of schools include the formerly mentioned groups of students, parents, suppliers, and competitors. Unions, legislative bodies, and other groups and organizations concerned with education are also part of the specific environment. These constituencies and stakeholders have some interest in the functioning of schools and make demands on their performance. Schools have to take account of their educational needs, but they can also exert an influence on these stakeholders in a certain way. Generally, the organization is bound to its specific environment in two major ways. First, it uses the environment to deliver its products in the form of curricula, lessons, courses and the outcomes of these educational programs in the form of well educated students. In that respect it tries to live up to its own educational standards and to the demands of important stakeholders and constituencies. Second, it uses its specific environment for recruiting potential students and teachers, and for acquiring financial resources and other materials to continue their educational programs. This can be achieved through communication linkages and an exchange relationship with stakeholder groups and other constituencies in the organization's specific environment.

In this third approach to interpreting the organization's environment, both of the preceding perspectives (the environmental elements and environmental characteristics approach) become visible. The examples given in the previous sections deal to some extent with the impact of environmental forces on various groups in the specific environment. As an example, the increasing pressure of global competitiveness could alter the notion of achievement held by parents and business groups for instance, encouraging views that see achievement less in academic terms and more in vocational and practical terms (Woods et al., 1998).

Simultaneously changing developments in the general environment will cause more complexity and instability in the specific environment. To be effective, school managers have to monitor their environmental areas, stay in close interaction with all relevant elements of the surrounding environment and collect all information critical for the structuring and functioning of school organizations. Some aspects of this environmental management process are taken up in the next section.

7.4 Environmental management

The previous section dealt with the issue of characterizing a school's external environment. This section addresses some aspects of environmental management, namely:

- environmental scanning activities which permit school leaders to monitor their environment and take account of the most important environmental features;
- the problem of boundary;
- the fundamental elements of boundary spanning.

The sections 7.4.1 to 7.4.3 explain these strategies in more detail.

7.4.1 Environmental scanning

Information is needed to assess the impact of environmental changes and developments on the organization and to determine their influence on the functioning of a school. Environmental scanning is a method of environmental information-gathering utilized by organizations in order to prepare for likely environmental changes, opportunities or threats (Hodge & Hankin, 1988). If school leaders fail to keep themselves abreast of environmental trends and characteristics, they may, for instance, find themselves faced with the need to make major changes at a time when the required tangible or intangible resources are unavailable.

The more uncertain the environment, the more information is needed for policy-making and for planning processes in organizations. School leaders have to decide which information is most important and critical for the functioning of their schools. They also have to decide on which groups of stakeholders and constituencies they are willing to exert influence. School managers must therefore identify their surrounding environments in terms of the aforementioned environmental areas, elements, and characteristics. For that purpose they have to draw 'demarcation lines' or boundaries (see the two lines in Figure 7.2: the boundary between the internal and specific and the one between the specific and general environment). Boundaries have many important functions. According to Goldring (1995a, p. 285), among others, they "help insulate schools as organizations from their environments, so that a balance is reached between the constantly changing external environment and the need for stability in the school's internal functioning". They also divide the organization's external environment into the specific and the general external environment and enable school leaders to 'span the boundaries'. Section 7.4.3 addresses the process of boundary-spanning. The next sub-section deals with the problem of boundaries.

7.4.2 The problem of boundary

A clear delineation between the organization, itself, and its specific environment is sometimes difficult to draw. Where does one establish the boundary? Are parents and students, for example, part of the specific environment as clients and consumers, or are they members of the internal environment of schools? The answers differ. The following examples illustrate that drawing boundaries depends on the school's activities, in accordance with the goals and objectives the school manager has in mind.

At the present, parental meetings are popular. During these meetings parents are informed about the kind of education their children receive or will receive. In addition, parents are asked to share their views on the education the school offers, and to support the school emotionally and financially. In this case, parents are part of the specific school environment. The school interacts with them in order to develop good courses for their children. When parents, as members of a school's participation council, discuss the school's educational goals or processes with representatives from the local authority, they belong to the internal school organization. If schools want to influence the donations from companies and other constituencies in their specific external environment, they can use the parents of their students as advocates. In that case, parents are also part of the internal environment of schools. If schools have to develop new courses and curricula based on students' educational needs, they must first identify those needs. In this case, students comprise one of the elements of the specific environment.

The delineation between the specific and general environment is also difficult. Sometimes the government belongs to the general environment, because legislative measures may be mandatory and have a strong impact on schools. Sometimes schools can interact with the central governmental authorities to influence specific policy measures (for instance, to be selected as an experimental school in a pilot project). In those cases the government belongs to the specific environment of these schools.

These examples illustrate that organizations differ in the permeability of their boundaries (Katz & Kahn, 1966), mainly in the extent to which parents and other stakeholders participate in or influence organizational activities.

7.4.3 Boundary spanning

The term 'boundary-spanning' is used to describe school leaders' activities to manage some kind of organization-environment relationship (Daft, 1992; Goldring, 1995a; McPherson et al., 1986). It is primarily concerned with defining the boundaries and detecting the key elements in each environmental domain which are important for the functioning of these leaders' schools. Boundary spanning is the process by which an organization receives input in terms of information and resources from these key elements. It enables school leaders to separate information critical to decision-making from information concerning non-schooling affairs (Goldring, 1995a).

Conversely, the organization may exert some control over these elements by sending information to the elements to establish a positive image and enhance the level of guaranteed financial and other input (Boyd & Crowson, 1981; Daft, 1992). Boundary spanners are thus concerned with promoting their schools and informing their stakeholders and other constituencies, which indicate that strategic planning and marketing are part of the environmental management process.

The example of parental meetings (described in section 7.4.2), illustrates this kind of boundary spanning. During these meetings parents are informed about the education their children will receive. They are asked to express their educational demands and give their view on the type of education the school offers. They are also invited to support the school emotionally and financially. Parental meetings are therefore an excellent means for supporting school leaders in managing this part of the organization-environment relationship.

The outlined aspects of environmental management are important for detecting the most suitable environmental areas, and with that, the most critical elements and characteristics influencing the goals, processes, and outcomes of school organizations. They are also crucial to achieving an appropriate relationship with a school's external environment and to choose the relevant aligning strategies. Section 7.5 deals with these aligning strategies.

7.5 Some strategies for aligning the organization with its environment

Schools have to align their organizational structuring and activities to the kind of environment in which they operate. Some educational institutions, for example, respond to the fact that today's students are more career-oriented and serious about their vocational futures than before. They require more vocational training and applied forms of education. Universities and colleges with more traditionally oriented courses which do not react to this new situation will probably experience problems.

At issue is whether schools and other educational organizations are manipulated by their environments, or conversely, that schools have the power to manipulate and control their environment. Perhaps there is a balance that "affords schools both the necessary resources and relationships that require a certain level of environmental dependence while achieving enough interdependence to adapt and ensure changes" (Goldring, 1995a, p. 286). Organizational leaders can employ various strategies to respond to their environments. The literature shows that these aligning strategies are, in most cases, grouped into three

categories (Goldring, 1995a; McPherson et al., 1986):
• environment directed strategies;
• management directed strategies;
• organization and environment directed strategies.

Miles and Snow (1978) and Hrebiniak and Joyce (1985) add a fourth category: performing a passive strategy, and waiting for external changes. Managers using this category do perceive changes and uncertainty in their organizational environments, but they are unable to respond effectively.

Because of internal constraints, they seldom make adjustments and can be said not to be following an aligning strategy. "Organizations apparently exhibit no coherent strategy to take advantage of fortuitous environmental conditions" (Hrebiniak & Joyce, 1985, p. 342). They are more laissez-faire in their approach to their environments (Bagley, Woods & Glatter, 1996). This is problematic in a complex, resource scarce and dynamic environment. Such organizations experience great problems in merely surviving. If they want to be effective, they have to restructure their internal strategy-structure relationship and overcome their internal weaknesses and constraints. If they succeed in doing so, they can follow one of the three aligning strategies mentioned.

Each of the three perspectives influences, in its own unique way, the relationship and interaction process between the organization and its environment. An environment directed aligning strategy leads to the adaption of organizational structures and processes to environmental constraints. In a management directed strategy, school leaders challenge themselves to create the kinds of environment that best support their goals and values. In an organization and environment directed strategy, the organization-environment interchange is reciprocal.

In the sections 7.5.1 to 7.5.3 these three aligning strategies are discussed. A clear notion of these perspectives is required for understanding the strategies school leaders employ to respond to their external school environment. Table 7.2 summarizes these aligning strategies and their main characteristics. Attention is paid to features like: the basic principle and central actor of each aligning strategy, the central perspective on the organization-environment relationship, the theoretical basis behind the aligning actions, some key concepts guiding the aligning behaviors, and the main incentives that force schools to act or react.

Table 7.2: *Aligning strategies and their characteristics summarized*

aligning strategy	basic principle	central actor	central perspective	theoretical basis	key concepts	main incentives
environment directed	natural selection	environment	organizational adaption to the environment	• population ecology approach • resource dependence approach	• niche • distribution of available resources	external conditions and constraints
management directed	rational selection	school manager	redefining the specific external environment	public choice or political economy approach	• merger • contracting • cooptation	• organizational reward structure • supply and demand characteristics
organization and environment directed	strategic choice	environment and school management	reciprocal interaction and dynamic equilibrium between organization and environment	political systems theory	• strategic marketing • market segmentation • needs analysis • voluntary response • buffering	need for equilibrium between environmental demands and organizational objectives

7.5.1 Environment directed strategies

The user of the strategies in this category assumes that organizations are the creatures of their environments. It is the environment which is the central actor. Conditions and constraints in the environment guide organizational behavior (McPherson et al., 1986). The external environment asks for adaptation to environmental demands. Proponents of this view argue that an organization must adapt to the characteristics of its context in order to be effective. School organizations have to connect their internal structures and processes to environmental forces, including the cultural norms and rituals surrounding each societal institution. If some environmental group of parents or other stakeholders forces schools to offer some specific programs, or to group the students in some particular and experimental way, schools have to accommodate these groups, "however obstreperous or erratic its representatives may be" (McPherson et al., 1986, p. 196). Organizations have to adapt or otherwise they are out. "Adaptation is determined from without, as the environment selects organizations and allows only those forms with appropriate variations to remain" (Hrebiniak & Joyce, 1985, p. 338).

The organizational ecology model fits this strategy. "The approach borrows heavily from notions of natural selection in biology and incorporates concepts of competition, the struggle for existence, adaptive variation and retention, cultural habitat (or niche), and species mortality" (McPherson et al., p. 1986, p. 195). The ecology model adds that institutions, like living organisms, must undergo adaptive efforts, or die. The structure and function of an organization, and in particular the formation of internal decision-making processes, reflect environmental contingencies, because the environment creates the conditions for intra-organizational behavior.

Alchan (in Miles & Snow, 1978, p. 19) has demonstrated that some organizations, by chance alone, will develop characteristics more compatible with emerging environmental conditions than will their counterparts. Those organizations fortunate enough to have the 'right' structure will perform best, forcing their competitors to emulate these structures or cease to exist. Goldring (1995a) points to research documenting the congruence between an organization's structure and its external environment. Organizations facing relatively stable environments resemble mechanistic structures, characterized by rigid task defini-tions, formalization of authority, vertical communication patterns, and centralized control mechanisms. In contrast, organizations in rapidly changing, dynamic environments resemble organic structures characterized by flexible task definitions, low formalization of authority, lateral communication patterns, and diverse control mechanisms (Goldring, 1995a).

According to McPherson et al., (1986) within this aligning strategy category a distinction can be made between two alternative approaches. Organizations can be studied as populations with common characteristics (population ecology approach), and as separate organizations, with attention to their internal adjustments to resource dependencies (the resource dependence approach). Both theories are discussed now.

The population ecology approach

In the population ecology approach, species of organizations are studied (e.g. all public schools, all universities, all schools for lower vocational education). New organizational forms occur "as the result of environmental constraints, through a tendency among all organizations to vary with, select from, and retain that which best fits them (vis-a-vis their environment) for survival" (McPherson et al., 1986, p. 196). A cluster of these kind of schools should be isomorphic with and optimally adapted to the expectations of stakeholder groups in their environment. Their structural patterns reflect their particular circumstances. The government for instance regulates by law the organizational structure and processes of all school communities or regional training centers. Only those forms of organization effectively adapted to their environment can be expected to survive.

The idea of a niche is a key concept in this approach. A niche is a domain of unique environmental resources and needs (Daft, 1992). It defines a population of organizations that face similar environmental constraints. The concept can be useful in explaining why some organizations specialize while others generalize. Research on niches suggests that narrow niches tend to support specialist organizations whereas wider niches support generalist organizations (Daft, 1992). For example, narrow niches in terms of certain populations of students like minority children, low educated and unemployed women, or populations with a preference for Montessori education support specialist schools, whereas more diverging communities support schools with all kinds of vocational education or with a regular approach to learning. The population is tied to a given niche and considers adaptation to other niches impossible because of entrance barriers and resource constraints (Hrebiniak & Joyce, 1985), related to different values and expectations in their social environments. If a niche is not available, the organization will decline and may perish. In the population ecology approach management has a minimal role in the aligning process. Strategic choices and deviant organizational behavior are difficult because of this dependency, resulting in strong environmental control over the organization.

The resource-dependence approach

In the resource-dependence approach, an organization is most critically attentive to those elements in its environment that provide the resources important for its survival. The demands from these elements, such as the few wealthy parents with specific educational demands for their children, or the families with children who will do well in examination, will receive most attention. School managers spend a lot of time and energy on these target groups, and changes in school organizations are being brought about with these specific groups in mind (Bagley et al., 1996; Van de Ven & Drazin, 1985). In this approach, the relationship between the organization and its environment is more interactive than in the population-ecology approach. School administrators try to alter their environment in order to manage external dependencies and to ensure organizational survival. Following this perspective, schools change their specific environment (see section 7.3.3.), if necessary, by focusing merely on these groups of resource-rich stakeholders or other constituencies. There are indications from the Parental and School Choice Interaction study of schools choosing to be responsive to those parents with middle-class backgrounds with academically able children, to keep or improve the standing of the school in the academic league table (Bagley et al., 1996).

7.5.2 Management directed strategies

In the previous section a natural selection process of alignment was central. Other theories indicate that the relationship between the organization and its environment is not simply one of organizational adaptation. Organizations can reach out and change the external environment, although they depend upon the external environment for resources vital to their survival and success. This section deals with the rational selection approach to alignment. The rational selection process asserts that while environmental conditions largely determine the efficacy of different organizational structures and processes, managers of successful organizations efficiently select, adopt and discard environmental elements (Miles & Snow, 1978). School leaders can manage the external environment by redefining their specific environment (Daft, 1983). They determine the best fitting task environment, for example, by seeking affluent parents and other stakeholders and resource-rich institutions. They can also redefine their student admission policy hoping to enroll more students, or develop new courses in domains with little competition. Schools for higher education in the Netherlands, for example, search for new student target groups because of the decreasing number of regular students. They not only focus on students leaving secondary school, but also on inquisitive adults who are eager to further their education. Goldring (1995a) calls this 'strategic manoeuvering', method of influencing the nature of the environment in which an organization is situated. "These strategies endeavour to afford the organization more autonomy and less dependence on the present task environment" (Galbraith in Goldring, 1995a, p. 301). Goldring describes an example for schools, in which strategic manoeuvering is achieved by defining new missions, such as changing into a so-called 'magnet' school. This strategy allows the school to attract a totally new type of student, extra educational support and enhancement of governmental subsidies. In 1991, a 'magnet' school, the Leonardo da Vinci-school, was opened in

Amsterdam, the Netherlands. To enhance integration between black and white students, both black and white students were accepted without restrictions. Because of the explicit attention to art, music and information technology, many parents, including 'white' parents, were interested in sending their children to this school. The money needed for the extra activities was donated partly by the national government and partly by the local government.

To influence others in their common or newly defined task environment, school leaders can establish favorable linkages with key elements in the environment, by using strategies such as (Daft, 1983; Goldring, 1995a):

• merger;
• contracting;
• cooptation.

Merger is the most effective linkage strategy since it removes all dependency on an external element that influences the organization. If the number of students entering the school organization is uncertain because of other competing institutes, merger with these institutes will remove that uncertainty (Daft, 1983).

Contracting reduces uncertainty through a legal and binding relationship with another organization. Contracts can provide long-term security for both parties on issues that are important for the task environment and which cannot be managed through independent actions or implicit cooperation (Goldring, 1995a). An example of contracting concerns a school system making arrangements with specific agencies to provide services, for instance, for students with special needs.

Cooptation concerns another possible strategy for school organizations to adapt to their external environment. It bears upon "the process of absorbing new elements into the leadership or policy-determining structure of an organization as a means of averting threats to its stability or existence" (Selznick in Pröpper, 1993, p. 180). This means that a school organization may absorb elements from its environment to reduce threats and exert more control over the environmental element. Cooptation occurs when influential leaders from important domains in the specific school environmental area are brought into the organization. For example, schools may appoint managers of companies with potential trainee posts to the school board. They also may invite affluent and influential parents to become members of the school's governing body. As a board member, they have an interest in the organization and become more aware of the needs of the school. As a result they are emotionally and/or financially more committed in school affairs, and will probably tend to include the school's interest in their decision-making (Daft, 1983).

Public choice or political economy approach

A theoretical approach that incorporates elements of the above mentioned rational selection process is the public choice or political economy approach. This approach finds educational organizations guided by the self interest of individuals (Boyd & Crowson, 1981, McPherson et al., 1986). These individuals try to accomplish their own purposes by manipulating the external environment. The public choice theory provides the diagnosis of instances of organizational ineffectiveness such as goal displacement, overproduction of services, purposefully counterproductive behavior, making work (i.e. officials creating work for each other), hidden agendas and time- and energy-consuming schisms between subunits (Scheerens & Bosker, 1997).

The individual actions (even when undertaken in cooperation with others) determine the ways in which schools respond to their environments, and provide the basis for understanding the organization. One of the merits of this approach is that the rational choice perspective pays attention to the difference and tension between the formal goals of organizations (e.g. concerning the reading performance of elementary school students) and the goals of individuals (e.g. maximizing their own welfare or benefits). In this perspective, individuals may use the organization to acquire more power, upward mobility, or job security, or to arrange better collegial contacts. As a consequence, this approach may provide a rational explanation for much that otherwise appears irrational or pathological in terms of the announced goals of (school)organizations (Boyd & Crowson, 1981).

Following this approach, there are two important groups of incentives for individual school leaders as they make decisions on the organization-environment relationship. The first group of incentives results from the organizational reward structure, the second group from the supply and demand characteristics.

The first group (the organizational reward structure) focuses on the utility-maximizing (self-interested) behavior of individuals or groups. The following example illustrates that the organization's responsiveness to its environment is closely tied to its reward structure.

The formal goals of a specific school concern the 'production of excellent student learning outcomes'. With such goals it tries to satisfy the educational demands of all stakeholder groups. Financial support, however, comes from the government rather than directly from satisfied clients. For that reason the school principal tends to address governmental demands and conditions to maximize the school's budgets, and to motivate and reward his teachers and other staff, rather than to satisfy students, their parents, other clients and constituencies as much as possible. Besides, it is easier for school leaders to respond to governmental regulations than to demonstrate organizational effectiveness to students, other clients and interest groups in their own terms. According to Freeman (in McPherson et al., 1986), this results from the fact that the central instructional technology is poorly understood. Which techniques work, and why, is not clear. As a consequence, school managers respond to their individualized rationality which relates to their work pressures and their understanding of institutional incentives (McPherson et al., 1986).

Regarding the second group of incentives (the supply and demand characteristics), schools have to take into consideration the demands of external stakeholders when delivering educational activities. From this perspective, if a considerable group of parents asks for experience-based education, the school has to react with some form of experience-based education. If it does not, this will raise collective actions from the stakeholders who may collectively decide to remove their children from this school, or to withdraw their financial or emotional support. This kind of environmentally determined constraints upon educational institutions guide and restrict the educational organization's exchange with its environment. In this view school managers contribute to an organization's adaptation to important and relevant environmental groups.

7.5.3 Strategies directed at the organization and the environment

Miles and Snow ask: "If the natural and rational selection views of the alignment process are not accurate, how then do organizations align themselves with their environments?" (Miles & Snow, 1978, p. 20). In their view the most accurate way of conceptualizing this process is the strategic choice approach. In this approach the organizational structure is only partially preordained by environmental conditions, with a heavy emphasis on the role of the top decision-makers who serve as the primary link between the organization and its environment. Managers are considered to be in a position not only to adjust the organizational structure and processes when necessary, but also to attempt to manipulate the environment itself in order to bring it into conformity with what the organization is already doing (Miles & Snow, 1978). In other words, they point to an organization and environment directed strategy aimed at reducing the dependencies between organizations and their environment. This kind of strategy is possible for organizations facing a pluralistic environment in which movements within and between niches or market segments are not severely constrained by exit or entrance barriers (Hrebiniak & Joyce, 1985). In this perspective the organization-environment interchange is reciprocal. "Organizations not only adapt and change in response to their environments, they also act upon and change their environments" (Trice & Beyer, p. 301, in Goldring, 1995a).
Several approaches related to this kind of interchange are mentioned in the literature (Daft, 1983; Goldring, 1995a; Kotler & Fox, 1985; Miles & Snow, 1978). They concern the following key concepts:

- strategic marketing;
- market segmentation;
- educational needs analysis;
- voluntary response;
- buffering.

Some of these approaches become very important, especially in highly uncertain environments. The five concepts belong to the so-called 'political systems interpretation' of organizations and their environments. Before addressing the political systems theory in the remainder of this section, each concept is described briefly.

'Strategic marketing' refers to the effective management by an institution of its exchange relationship with its various markets and publics, regarding environmental opportunities and threats (Kotler & Fox, 1985). The institution has to systematically seek information concerning events and relationships in its environment (i.e. it has to engage in environmental scanning and forecasting activities). It must further analyze possible trends and developments, and identify them as opportunities or threats for the functioning and performance of the organization.

'Market segmentation' and 'educational needs analysis' are important for identifying the most relevant clients and other groups of stakeholders or constituencies, and to assess their problems and educational needs in order to develop the most appropriate educational programs.

'Voluntary response' refers to the response of an institution to elements of its task environment in a way which surpasses what is considered necessary or generally expected. According to Goldring (1995a) voluntary responses often arise out of a sense of social responsibility, for example when schools maintain the hiring of all school aids from within the community. This strategy is meant to establish groups or constituencies in the environment that depend on the organization. It adds to the satisfactory feelings of environmental groups for the organization, and increases organization-environment interdependencies (Goldring, 1995a).

'Buffering' seeks to isolate organizational aspects (e.g. core technologies) from environmental influences (Daft, 1992). Principals usually achieve this by creating formal procedures to respond to external demands and requests, for instance by insisting that local groups contact them before approaching teachers (Goldring, 1995a).

Political systems theory
The political systems interpretation of organizations and their environments has had a far-reaching impact upon our understanding of organizations. It depicts a reciprocal

interaction between organizations and their surrounding environments. In short, this means that the environment provides inputs in the form of both demands upon and support for the organization. These inputs are converted by the organization into decisions, actions and policy measures, which in the form of outputs and outcomes (for instance in the form of well-educated students and high-skilled graduates) provide feedback to the larger environment. Stakeholder groups and other constituencies may react to these outputs with new educational demands, or more financial support with which the organization must contend (McPherson et al., 1986). For educational systems one can imagine that the demands concern the expressed expectations and preferences regarding curricula, staffing, educational objectives, outcomes and so on. Aside from financial support, support can take the form of good will, educatable children, voluntarism and supportive services. The demands from stakeholder groups in the school environment (parents, neighbors, local government, secondary schools, companies, etc.) are often in conflict, or at least potentially conflicting. Companies may ask for graduates with more specific knowledge and skills in vocational and practical terms, while the government or post-graduate institutions need graduates with a more general level of proficiency. Parents appreciate a general increase of the quality of education.

Obviously, schools cannot react to all educational demands and expectations from their constituencies. Moreover, instead of increasing funds, most governments reduce funds due to declining financial resources. All these inputs force schools, as political systems to undertake balancing, adapting, or compromising actions which feed back into the creation of new demands and new support (McPherson et al., 1986).

In the political systems approach, 'interaction' and 'equilibrium' are the two most important aspects of this theory of the organization-environment relationship. Organizations have to engage in a continuous and reciprocal interaction: to become aware of the demands and educational needs of the environmental groups and the possible support they are willing to give (inputs), and to assess the environmental reactions to the delivered outputs and outcomes. They have to strive constantly for a dynamic equilibrium between the goals and objectives of the organization itself (or single schools and sub systems within schools, like classrooms) and the demands of the environmental group which, as mentioned before, sometimes conflict. Related to this, an important role is reserved for the selection and decision-making capacity of schools, in order to satisfy the most important educational needs with respect to the institution's mission. McPherson et al. speak of a 'dynamic tension', because there is 'an ebb and flow to the distribution of interests and to the power that accompanies demand and support communication' (McPherson et al., 1986, p. 186).

7.6 Environmental features from a school effectiveness point of view

This chapter states that the external school environment constitutes an important factor regarding goal attainment and school effectiveness. Schools depend on their environments to survive, and only those schools with sufficient aligning capacity will flourish in new environmental realities. Therefore, an integrated school effectiveness model has to address internal as well as environmental factors influencing school effectiveness.

Most research on effective schools, however, has focused mainly on internal school characteristics that promote effectiveness. These include educational leadership, an orderly and safe atmosphere, high expectations of student progress, and frequent evaluations (Fidler, 1996; Scheerens, 1992). Context variables were long considered unimportant by many scholars (Teddlie, 1994). External conditions that may stimulate school performance and school effectiveness have not been the object of many empirical studies. However, since the mid nineteen eighties, some environmental factors have been included in school effectiveness research.

7.6.1 Environmental factors in school effectiveness research

Teddlie (1994) refers to a number of studies in which variation in contextual and environmental conditions have been shown to influence some effectiveness-promoting school characteristics. These environmental features mainly concern three groups of contextual variables that account for variance in school effectiveness (Teddlie, 1994): the socioeconomic status (SES) of the student population, the grade level of schools (i.e. primary, secondary or high schools), and the urbanicity of schools (i.e. rural, urban, suburban or inner-city schools).

Moreover, a limited number of effect studies have focused on specific variables that may account for variance in school effectiveness: the governance sector (public versus private schools), the denomination of schools (here it concerns Catholic versus non-Catholic private schools) the ethos in school districts, and administrative control by school boards. These seven (groups of) contextual variables are briefly explained below.

1. Socioeconomic status (SES)
Teddlie (1994) refers to the results of two studies, one conducted by Hallinger & Murphy (1986) and one by Teddlie & Stringfield (1985, 1989). These studies pointed to a number of interesting differences between effective middle- and low-SES schools, revolving around six areas: promotion of educational expectations, principal leadership style, the use of external reward structures, emphasis in the school curriculum, parental contact with the school, and the experience level of teachers. According to Teddlie, effective middle-SES

schools were significantly different from effective low-SES schools in strategies employed in each of these areas. For example, school leaders in schools with a relatively low socioeconomic status appeared much more obviously as initiators of educational reform than leaders of effective schools with a middle-SES composition - who tended to be good managers. Other illustrative results of these studies (drawn from Scheerens and Bosker, 1997, pp. 287-288, and based on Teddlie et al., 1989, Teddlie, 1994, and Teddlie & Stringfield, 1993) are:

- a shorter-term orientation towards educational expectations in effective low as compared to middle socioeconomic status schools;
- a more pronounced external reward structure in effective low as compared to high socioeconomic status schools;
- invitational versus a more careful (sometimes even buffering) attitude toward parents in effective middle as compared to effective low socioeconomic status schools;
- controlling educational leadership with respect to instruction and task orientation in effective low socioeconomic status schools as compared to low or moderate controlling leadership in these areas in effective high socioeconomic status schools (Hallinger & Murphy, cited by Teddlie, 1994).

2. Grade level of schools

Teddlie (1994) refers to various authors when stating that most school effectiveness studies have examined elementary schools, while some have examined secondary levels exclusively and have made comparisons with previously reported research from elementary levels. Two studies included samples of both elementary and secondary schools. Teddlie concluded that secondary schools differ from elementary schools on a number of important dimensions, including a shift from a child-centered towards a knowledge-centered curriculum. Firestone and Herriot (in Scheerens, 1992) have established that in secondary education, the 'accent on basic skills was more broadly interpreted than in primary education in the sense that effective secondary modern schools had an explicit mission to excel in all subject fields' (Scheerens, 1992, p. 93). In effective elementary schools, the emphasis was placed on academic goals as compared to both personal as well as educational goals in secondary schools (Teddlie, 1994).

3. Urbanicity of schools

In a few studies, urbanicity has been investigated as a factor influencing school effects. Levine and Lezotte state (in Fidler, 1996) that differences in urbanicity (i.e. inner-city working-class schools or middle-class suburban schools) make a difference for, among other things, the curriculum, leadership, and teaching methods in schools. Teddlie (1994) points to the results of the handful of studies and reviews that have looked at rural school effectiveness, related to resource allocation and cohesiveness. Rural schools are, in general, characterized by more scarce resources than urban schools (Buttram & Carlson, 1983, and Stringfield & Teddlie, 1991, in Teddlie, 1994). Rural schools typically have smaller student bodies that are more culturally homogeneous and are therefore more likely to be cohesive (Conklin & Olson, 1988, and Lomothey & Swanson, 1990, in Teddlie, 1994). This leads to strong educational leadership being required for success in urban elementary schools, whereas a managerial leadership style often proves successful in suburban elementary schools. An 'intermediate' between manager and initiator has been seen to work best in rural elementary schools (Teddlie, 1994).

4. The governance sector

Coleman & Hoffer (1987) conclusions support the existence of positive private-sector effects. Private schools generally produce higher student achievement than public schools for comparable groups of students. There is, however, still debate and controversy regarding this conclusion (Teddlie, 1994). Coleman et al. claim that Catholic schools in the United States are superior because they assign more homework, maintain better discipline and require advanced courses (Coleman et al. in Scheerens, 1992). This may be facilitated by the more or less homogenous school population in Catholic schools compared to the more diverse characteristics of students and their parents in public schools. In the view of Hallinger and Murphy, parents in private environments are more supportive and active in promoting the well-being of the school than parents in public school environments (Hallinger & Murphy, in Scheerens, 1992). Coleman and Hoffer attributed the positive private sector effects to two quite different orientations to schooling. Public schools 'represent an orientation that sees the school as an instrument of the society to free the child from constraints imposed by accident of birth. Private schools represent an orientation that sees the school as an agent not of the society but of the family, with authority vested in loco parentis' (Coleman & Hoffer, 1987, p. xxvi).

5. Denomination

According to Coleman & Hoffer, Catholic private schools are more effective than non-Catholic private schools in raising the academic achievement of subpopulations who traditionally achieve at lower levels (such as blacks, children from families that provide lower levels of parental support, and children from families with lower socioeconomic standing (Coleman & Hoffer, 1987). In their opinion, these differences can be attributed to differences in the orientation of the families who send their children to Catholic or non-Catholic schools. Catholic families see the school not primarily as an agent of the family, but as an agent of the religious community of which the family is a part. The other groups of parents, with children attending independent private schools, see the school as a direct agent of the family in a very individualistic sense. Parents send their child to that school which is most closely aligned with their values.

6. Positive ethos

Coleman & Laroque studied the ethos of school districts. This included, for example, emphasis on instructional issues, accountability, managing change and improvement, securing the commitment of professionals to shared beliefs and agreed-upon practices, treating members and clients with consideration, and gaining community support. They concluded that a positive ethos can be seen as a distinction between high-performing and low-performing districts (Coleman and Laroque, 1990). In successful districts there is an emphasis upon 'monitored autonomy' for schools, and upon co-management at the district level, with superintendents modelling norms of accountability and consensuality (Coleman & Collinge, 1991). The apparent relationship between positive ethos and district performance was brought about largely through influence of school boards on principals and through them on teachers. They also found that responsiveness to parents, which is notably different for high performing districts than for others, is an essential component of a positive district-ethos.

7. Administrative control

Hofman studied characteristics of, and administrative control by, school boards in the Netherlands, operating at the level above the school (Hofman, 1995). She found that school board characteristics do explain variance in cognitive achievement. In other words: characteristics of the functioning of school boards make a difference. School boards that involve school teams and parents (committees) in their decision-making process manage schools with relatively better results in the cognitive domain.

7.6.2 An environment framework for school effectiveness research

The previous section described various contextual factors that have been studied in school effectiveness research. It confirms, to some extent, the importance of the external environment regarding goal attainment and school effectiveness. The examples presented point to the impact of parent-group characteristics, such as their SES, religion, and stimulating attitudes. The examples also point to school characteristics, such as governance sector, grade level, urbanicity, and denomination. In most cases, however, these factors were studied separately, while a combination of these factors are probably of crucial importance for school effectiveness. The importance of these variables for school effectiveness will undoubtedly vary across different kinds of environments. For instance, the effects of SES backgrounds of a rural school with a changing parental community and no competing schools in the specific environment will differ from the effect of SES backgrounds of a heterogenous but stable parental community in inner-city schools with various competitors.

Adding the notion of the environment, as described in this chapter, to school effectiveness studies will provide those researchers with a framework for studying the various environmental characteristics in concert. This framework will help to divide the external influences into classes of factors. It will draw specific attention to the impact of environmental forces on the various groups in the specific school environment. It will also call attention to the level of environmental uncertainty, which is indicated by the combined scores on the capacity, clustering, volatility and complexity dimension (section 7.3.2.). Second, the classification of the contextual factors already studied will reveal some blank spaces in the search for effectiveness-enhancing external conditions. School effectiveness research in the future has to fill in these voids.

7.6.3 Aligning strategies in school effectiveness research

It is stated in this chapter that only schools with sufficient aligning capacity will flourish in new environmental realities. The examples presented in section 7.6.1. confirm, more of less, that school effectiveness depends on the different strategies school managers deploy to respond to environmental conditions. Effective managers align the structuring and functioning of their schools to some extent to the kind of environment in which they operate. In order to explain variance in school effectiveness, it is important to search for patterns in the specific school-environment-aligning behavior. Morgan (in Coleman & Collinge, 1991) points to the importance of the political systems' view for examining and restructuring the relationship between organizations and society. In his view, this theory provides a framework within which representatives make public choices among competing values. Scheerens & Bosker (1997) mention the public choice theory as a strategy that provides the diagnosis of instances of organizational ineffectiveness.

In this chapter, the alternative theoretical perspectives are categorized into three different kinds of aligning strategies. Each of them approaches the relationship between the organization and its environment from its own point of view. Incorporating these three aligning strategies into future school effectiveness research may help to find out which strategy is the most effective under specific environmental circumstances.

7.7 Summary

This chapter treats the interrelationship between educational institutions and their external environments. This topic has become important since the late nineteen fifties, due to many environmental pressures. School managers have to take account of these pressures and their impact on the functioning of their schools. They have to align school policy-making and other educational activities with the environment in which they operate. Only schools with sufficient aligning capacity will flourish in new environmental realities, since strong alignment will increase the performance of their schools. The kind of environment determines the margin for an aligning strategy. It is therefore important to characterize the school's external environment in terms of the degree of environmental uncertainty. School leaders have to monitor their environments in terms of the forces, groups and characteristics critical for the structuring and functioning of their schools. Environmental scanning and boundary spanning are relevant strategies for detecting the delineation of the most suitable environmental areas, and to assess the most critical elements and characteristics in each specific area.

The features of the environment alone do not determine the margin for the aligning strategy; the prevailing environmental perspective is also important. School organizational staff differ concerning this perspective. School leaders employ various strategies to respond to their environments. They differ in the kind of goals and objectives they stress, and the extent to which they pursue these goals and objectives.

In this chapter three categories of aligning strategies have been explained. In all strategies the environment is closely tied to the school organization, but each strategy does so in a different way. On the basis of their main aligning direction, a distinction is made between three categories of strategies:

- 'environment directed', characterized by an adaptation of the school organization to the external conditions and constraints in the surrounding environment;
- 'management directed', characterized by a reshaping of the environment to the advantage of all school staff, and promoted by internal reward and supply characteristics and external demands;
- 'organization and environment directed', characterized by a dialectic and dynamic adaptation between organization and environment.

The main characteristics of each aligning strategy have been summarized in Table 7.2: the basic principle and central actor of each strategy, the central perspective in each category, the theoretical basis behind the aligning actions, some key concepts guiding the aligning behaviors, and the main incentives that force schools to (re)act.

An environment directed kind of strategy leads to the adaptation of organizational structures and processes to environmental constraints. The school leader strives for the creation of an environmentally adapted organizational structure in order to achieve the externally imposed goals and specific objectives.

In a management directed strategy, school leaders challenge themselves to create the kind of environment that can best support the schools' professed goals as well as the goals of individual school members. Schools following this perspective are effective to the degree to which they succeed in realizing these internally derived goals.

In an organization and environment directed strategy, the organization-environment interchange is reciprocal. Consensus between the organization's goals and objectives and those of relevant groups in the external environment is the guiding principle. In this category of aligning strategies, schools are effective if they succeed in the attainment of their agreed upon goals.

Searching for patterns in the specific school-environment aligning behavior leads to a better understanding of the assessed level of school effectiveness. However, the environmental factor has not been an important element of school effectiveness research. Most of this research studied only internal school factors associated with school effectiveness. Since the mid nineteen eighties, some environmental factors have been included in school effectiveness research. However, these factors were studied separately, while a combination of these factors will probably be of crucial importance for school effectiveness. The notion of the environment as outlined in this chapter provides future school effectiveness researchers with a framework that includes various environmental features that characterize a school's external environment, as well as the strategies that characterize the school-environment aligning behavior.

· CHAPTER 8 ·

Human Resource Development in a Corporate Setting from an Organizational Point of View

S. Tjepkema & A.A.M. Wognum
University of Twente, The Netherlands

8.1 Introduction

After leaving school, the workplace provides a major source for further learning for most people. Learning from work experience, in an informal way, is an important way for employees to acquire new skills and knowledge. Most companies also provide formal schooling activities for their employees. We refer to the learning which takes place within corporations as *corporate training and development* or *Human Resource Development (HRD)*[1]. A proactive and efficient HRD function enables companies to keep abreast of new developments and market challenges. In the current business reality of many companies this is extremely important, since the environment of many corporations is marked by continuous and very rapid change.

Section 8.2 contains a description of the field of HRD. The section will provide a definition, an overview of different kinds of HRD activities, an explanation of the main differences between corporate training and education in schools and a description of what is called 'the HRD function'. Large organizations often provide many training activities in-house; they have a specialized HRD department which is responsible for planning, organizing, developing and conducting HRD activities for employees. Smaller companies usually employ the services of external agencies to provide HRD activities. Section 8.3 addresses this and other topics related to the organization of HRD within companies. Section 8.4 provides a brief overview of current trends and developments within the area of HRD. Section 8.5 looks into the effectiveness of HRD activities. In section 8.6 the question is answered how the corporate HRD approach can be applied to schools. The

---

[1] Corporate training and development is also often referred to as Human Resource Development (employees are the human resources -or 'human capital' of an organization). This term was coined by Nadler, around 1968 and has gained widespread acceptance since then. In this chapter the terms 'corporate training & development' and 'Human Resource Development (HRD)' will be used as synonyms.

chapter ends with a brief summary in section 8.7.

8.2 Human Resource Development: exploration of the field

In many situations, formal education in a school setting provides adequate preparation for the fulfillment of a job for the initial working period (although there are jobs for which the necessary knowledge and skills can only be acquired in practice; Kessels & Smit (1989) mention the job of air traffic controller as an example). However, it can also be the case that the knowledge and skills learned in school are too general in nature, or too theoretical to be directly applied in the workplace. If that is the case, the employee needs to acquire some company-specific, or job-specific knowledge and skills in order to perform adequately.

After the initial working period has been completed, the knowledge and skills acquired in school almost always become outdated. This may be because a new tool or technology has been developed, or a new product invented. In some organizations knowledge becomes outdated more quickly than in others. This depends on factors such as the speed of technological innovation. In each case where qualifications acquired through school education are not, or are no longer sufficient for satisfactory job fulfillment, employees need additional training in order to perform adequately. Qualifications can be defined as the sum of all knowledge, skills and attitudes which enables employees to fulfil certain tasks (Kwakman, 1992).

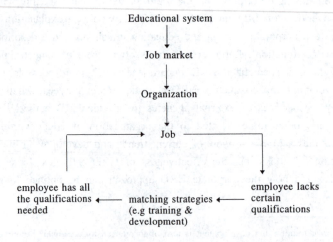

Figure 8.1: *Relationship between educational system and corporate training and development (based on Kessels & Smit, 1989).*

Most organizations face this situation (a mismatch between the qualifications desired and those available) on a regular basis. This concept is depicted in Figure 8.1.

Figure 8.1 shows that after having acquired certain qualifications in school, people leave the educational system and enter the job market. They then move on to a specific job within an organization for which employees with their specific qualifications are needed.

For several reasons, a lack of fit may exist, or arise in the course of time, between the knowledge and skills of the employee and the qualifications needed for proper job fulfillment. Some examples are when:

- an employee starts to take on more difficult tasks for which he has not yet received any schooling (e.g. an organization consultant who initially only works on projects acquired by colleagues, who later must also approach clients in order to acquire new projects for the company);
- as a result of an organizational restructuring, an employee has to perform new tasks, which were previously not part of the job description (e.g. a client service employee who formerly only had to help clients with questions on product X, now also has to answer questions on products Y and Z);
- qualifications become outdated as a result of technological innovations or scientific discoveries (e.g. when a new treatment for a certain tooth disease is discovered, dentists have to learn to apply that treatment).

Organizations may employ several methods to eliminate such mismatches between qualifications desired for the job, and qualifications available in the employee. In Figure 8.1 these alternative solutions are referred to as *matching strategies*. One of these strategies is Human Resource Development, by means of which the employee can acquire the knowledge and skills which he or she lacks. Other 'matching strategies' are, for instance, firing the employee and hiring someone new who does possess the necessary qualifications, or transferring the employee to a different, more suitable job within the organization (where his qualifications match the demands of the job).

This section deals with HRD as a matching strategy. First, a definition of HRD is provided in section 8.2.1. Section 8.2.2 describes the different kinds of activities that belong to HRD. Section 8.2.3 looks into the main differences between HRD and education in schools. And section 8.2.4, finally, describes what is meant by the 'HRD function' of a company.

8.2.1 Definition of HRD, or corporate training and development

There is no single generally accepted definition of Human Resource Development. HRD has been defined by different authors in various ways. A comprehensive definition is:

HRD activities are:
- *facilities that fit within the general company policy,*
- *which aim to realize specific learning processes in employees,*
- *which, in turn, are intended to, directly or indirectly, enhance current performance,*
  as well as the development of both employees and the organization as a whole.
  (based on Mulder, Akkermans & Bentvelsen (1989, p. 16); Thijssen, 1996).

In the following, each of the elements of this definition will be discussed more elaborately. In turn, attention will be paid to:
- what is meant by the phrase 'specific learning processes';
- the relationship between specific learning processes (knowledge and skill acquisition) and performance improvement;
- objectives of HRD activities (development of both individual employees and the organization as a whole).

Specific learning processes: the difference between learning and training
For most people, learning takes place on a daily basis. We learn in many ways, in many different places, at many different times, often unexpectedly. In fact, some of the most meaningful learning experiences occur as the result of an error or stupid mistake we make. There is a huge difference between this kind of learning, on the one hand, and training on the other. Only those learning experiences that have been deliberately planned and organized can be called 'training' (see Nadler & Wiggs, 1986; Kruijd, 1988; Rothwell & Kazanas, 1989). Training activities are often referred to as *formal learning*, whereas the spontaneous, unplanned learning which occurs every day is called *informal learning*. Informal learning is not part of Human Resource Development. HRD activities, by definition, concern learning that occurs deliberately, and is aimed at specific learning objectives.

In recent years, however, companies have also been increasingly trying to facilitate and stimulate the informal, spontaneous learning. They try to transform the workplace into a place 'fit for learning', by, for instance, stimulating deliberate experimentation with new work routines and creating teams in which employees work together instead of on an individual basis (thus sharing their knowledge and skills, and learning from each other). The underlying rationale is that in order to keep up with the many developments in their external environment, organizations need to become 'learning organizations': organizations in which employees continuously learn from their own work and apply those new insights to improve existing products, services, processes (Senge, 1990; Nonaka & Takeuchi, 1995). HRD departments in many cases also try to facilitate informal learning in the workplace and thus support the development of companies into learning organizations.

Two examples of such activities in which HRD departments stimulate informal learning are:

- setting up an 'open learning center' that employees can visit at any time to look up information, to leave questions for experts, or to follow a computer-assisted training program;
- establishment of a mentor system, whereby a mentor is assigned to each employee in order to assist this employee in day-to-day learning in the workplace.

HRD departments are still experimenting with new ways to facilitate informal learning in the workplace. These 'learning facilities' can be considered to be part of the field of Human Resource Development because, though it is not planned in space or time, learning is deliberately stimulated and the learning content is influenced. This element of deliberate intent distinguishes these learning facilities from truly informal learning. Because they are not as formalized as training is, it can be argued that they form a 'grey area' between informal learning on the one hand and training on the other. The field of Human Resource Development covers both training and this 'grey area' between training and learning (learning facilities), but does *not* include the purely informal, spontaneous learning which occurs on a day-to-day basis. This approach to HRD entails an important change of focus: HRD used to be directed mainly towards training, but it increasingly aims to also facilitate informal learning. From this point in the text, whenever the words 'training & development' or 'HRD' are used, these refer to both *formal training activities* and *learning facilities*.

Learning processes and performance improvement
As the definition states, corporate HRD activities are aimed at provoking learning processes, which will, in turn, enhance performance of both individual employees and, eventually, of the organization as a whole. This is depicted in Figure 8.2 (from: Kessels & Smit, 1989). The acquisition of knowledge and skills is not a goal in itself; it is a means to reach performance improvement and/or organization development. In this respect, corporate training differs from education in a school setting. In schools, the main focus is on student development, while corporate HRD activities are aimed at solving or preventing performance problems, and/or to assist in reaching organizational targets. A course in French cooking will seldom be arranged within the scope of corporate HRD as it is irrelevant for organizational success (unless, of course, the organization is a French restaurant). Sales techniques, on the other hand, are a good example of a common topic of HRD activities, because a skilled salesforce is often a prerequisite for reaching the (financial) targets of a company.

A point which is important to emphasize is that the goal of teaching new skills and knowledge is to bring about the *possibility* of performance improvement (see Thijssen, 1996). New qualifications do not automatically lead to improved job performance. There are many cases in which it does not, for instance when:

- the newly learned skills cannot be applied on the job due to a lack of adequate equipment;
- poor performance was not caused by a lack of knowledge and skills in the first place, but, for instance, by a lack of time to perform all tasks in an adequate way (Nadler & Nadler, 1989).

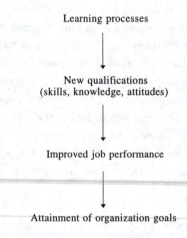

Figure 8.2: *Intended relationship between learning processes and attainment of organizational goals*

Likewise, a direct link between job performance and the degree to which organizational goals are met is not always present either. Sometimes the relationship between the two is quite clear, such as when a sales representative improves his sales techniques, and as a result sells more products. In many cases, however, the relationship between individual and organizational performance is much less direct. In those instances, training activities may improve individual performance, but have little visible effect on how the organization as a whole functions. For instance, when the bookkeepers and other members of the financial department attend a word processor course, this may result in a more effective use of the personal computer by these people. This may result in a decrease in the time needed to write up financial reports, and it may lead to a more professional lay-out of these reports, but it will hardly be seen to affect the performance of the organization as a whole.

Even though the link between HRD activities and the attainment of organizational goals is not always water tight, HRD activities are always undertaken with the objective of fostering the attainment of these goals. Because of this strategic focus, corporate HRD is called a *'tool of management'*. It is one of the instruments management employs to reach organizational objectives. For example, training is often one of the interventions used by management to facilitate the smooth implementation of organizational changes (such as changes in jobs and work processes) which follow from changes in company policy. Training is then used to prepare employees for these changes and to assist them in their implementation (Bergenhenegouwen et al., 1992).

Human Resource Development objectives

Next to a 'tool of management', HRD can also function as a *'tool of personal development'*. From this viewpoint, development of the individual (and not of the organization) is the overriding aim of HRD. Achieving personal growth and improving individual and/or organizational performance can go hand in hand. Most organizations strive for a good mix between these two approaches; they use training mainly as a means to reach organizational targets, but deliberately take an individual employee's wishes into account. This twofold function can be recognized in the definition, mentioned earlier, in which it is stated that HRD activities are ultimately aimed at enhancing current performance or development of individual employees, and the organization as a whole.

Thus, HRD can have one or more of the following objectives (Van der Krogt & Plomp, 1987; Gilley & Eggland, 1989):
- personal development: advancement of employees' knowledge and skills for personal and professional use.
- career development: support the professional advancement of employees to jobs at a higher level in the organization by providing them with the necessary qualifications.
- organizational development: performance improvement in order that the organization as a whole can benefit.

The combined use of HRD as both a tool of personal development and a tool of management is especially apparent in those instances where training takes place in the context of career development.

Implicitly or explicitly, training and development activities sometimes serve additional objectives, such as (Kessels & Smit, 1989):

- a break from the day-to-day routine;
  In some cases training is regarded more as a chance to do something other than 'work' for a day or two rather than as an opportunity (or necessity) to improve performance. In this view, training is mainly 'fun', a distraction.
- reward or punishment;
  Sometimes when a department performs very well, its employees are sent to a training program which is not needed because they lack certain qualifications, but is organized as an implicit reward for outstanding performance. In this case training is also regarded as 'fun'.
- criterion for promotion;
  In some organizations, employees need to follow specific courses as a prerequisite for promotion, regardless of whether they need the additional qualifications or not. Following the training program is considered 'regular procedure'.
- support for the status of a function;
  In some corporate cultures, a highly valued function 'demands' an elaborate and highly esteemed educational background. It happens, for instance, that managers in a certain position attend an MBA course with which they gain an official title, even though they do not need (all of) the new qualifications.

In some cases these additional goals are justifiable, in others they are not, as may have become clear from the illustrations provided. In any case, these *additional* objectives can never be the main goal of HRD as it is defined in this chapter.

8.2.2 Kinds of HRD activities

After having defined what is meant by HRD, and having explored, briefly, the main reasons why companies provide HRD activities for their employees, it is now time to look into the different types of HRD activities organizations can provide. The nature of HRD activities can differ considerably. A widely used criterion for classification concerns the scope of the activities. A classification which has gained widespread acceptance is the one developed by Nadler & Nadler (1989). It distinguishes between three types of HRD activities:
- training: directly focused on the present job;
- education: focused on a future job;
- development: general growth, not focused on any specific job.

Training is typically aimed at short term goals, education is focused on medium term goals, whereas development activities serve a long term goal. The latter are also not specifically related to any job, but set up in order to facilitate growth of the employee or the company in general. Important to note is that the three terms (training, education and development) are often used in ways other than those mentioned above. As a result, when a particular training and development activity in a company is labeled 'training', this does not necessarily mean it is an activity focused on a present job. In fact, many companies reserve the word 'training' for practical, skill-oriented courses. It is therefore recommended to check on the meaning a specific company attaches to these terms.

A very important classification of HRD activities concerns the classification on the basis of the place where HRD activities take place. It is common to distinguish between *on-the-job* and *off-the-job* training. On-the-job training activities are offered in the actual workplace. Sometimes the actual work process has to be interrupted for these learning processes. However, it is also possible to combine training and working at the same time, for instance when a new employee learns to operate a machine with the help of a workplace instructor. The work process can continue during this learning activity. The advantage of on-the-job training is that the learner can apply the new skills directly. Off-the-job training takes place outside the workplace, in a separate classroom within the company, a hotel or conference center, or at home (self study). The advantage of this kind of training is that it is very suitable for explaining theoretical concepts. It is also possible to learn and practice (in a workshop) new skills that are not yet needed in the present job, and thus cannot be practiced in the workplace. In off-the-job training there is also less chance of interference in the learning process. With on-the-job training, the learning process is often disrupted because of phone calls, urgent meetings, work that has to be finished that day (which leaves no time for training), and so on. The downside of off-the-job training is that there is often a huge gap between the theory explored and the skills practiced within the classroom setting, and the practice of the daily work situation in which the employee has to apply his knowledge and skills. This is called the problem of *transfer*.

With regard to the classification of Nadler & Nadler, it can be stated that training activities often take place on-the-job, and if that is impractical (for instance because it is dangerous to practice certain tasks on the workfloor) off-the-job. Education and development activities are usually provided in an off-the-job setting. Usually these activities have a large theoretical, as opposed to practical, component and they are aimed at future work situations, which makes it difficult to learn new knowledge and skills on-the-job. To prevent the 'transfer of training' problem, many HRD departments choose to alternate learning off-the-job and working (applying the knowledge and skills learned on-the-job in specified assignments, which are reviewed afterwards in an off-the-job setting).

Other classifications of HRD activities also exist. One that is also used quite often is based on the *learning goals* of training activities. This qualification distinguishes between HRD activities aimed at cognitive, psychomotoric, or attitude-related learning goals (e.g. Rijkers, 1991). Many HRD activities, of course, focus on a combination of these three kinds of goals. Another commonly used classification criterion concerns the *number of employees*: are the training activities aimed at one individual, a group of employees or are they implemented organization-wide? Although this provides a useful criterion in some instances, it does not provide much information with regard to the goal and content of the HRD activities.

8.2.3 Differences between corporate training and education in schools

In exploring the topic of corporate HRD in the previous sections, several differences between HRD and public education have become apparent. Thijssen (1988) identifies seven of these differences, each of which will be briefly discussed below. This overview serves mainly to illustrate the specific qualities of corporate HRD.

Degree of specificity
In schools, students are being educated for a wide variety of jobs. This is of course especially the case in general education, and holds less true for the more focused vocational education. However, in either case corporate training activities are far more specific than education in a school context. Corporate training is often aimed at a clearly defined group of employees with similar jobs, and usually deals with a clear set of skills and knowledge to be acquired. Quite often, corporate training activities are concerned with company-specific qualifications which cannot be taught in schools (because schools have to prepare students for a variety of jobs and companies).

The problem of choice
Whereas education is a primary activity in schools, in companies it is only used to support the primary process (such as production) companies. In most cases companies have to choose between different alternatives to support this primary process optimally (e.g. McLagan, 1983) while bridging the gap between desired and available qualifications. Training is but one of the options available. Alternative measures include hiring new employees or redesigning jobs (the 'matching strategies' in Figure 8.1). The fact that training is not a goal in itself for work organizations also has implications as to when training is considered to be a success. In schools the focus is on good learning results. The goal is reached when students do well on a test, and master the subject matter. In companies, good learning results are also important, but most important is an improved

job performance and, as a result, the attainment of organizational objectives.

Type of participants
In schools, the student group consists of children or young adults with more or less homogenous backgrounds. Participants in corporate training activities are nearly always adults who usually all have very different (educational) backgrounds.

Length of training
Training in schools normally takes a number of years, whereas training activities in a corporate context usually take only a few days, because they are far more specific in nature.

Transfer problem
When a participant of a course within the context of corporate HRD uses the newly acquired skills and knowledge on the job, transfer of training has taken place. This is considered extremely important in a corporate setting. In schools the topic of transfer is not unimportant, but receives much less attention. Of course schools strive for acquisition of relevant knowledge and skills, especially in vocational education, but schooling is almost never directly aimed at one specific work situation in which these qualifications have to be used.

Organization
Great variety exists in the way corporate training activities are organized. For instance, training can take place on the job or in a classroom, groups can be very small or large and teaching and working can be combined or separated, to name but a few options. In school settings, educational activities are usually organized in a much more uniform way (namely classes of approximately 20-30 students).

Governmental concern
In many countries, the amount of governmental concern with regard to education in schools is considerable. An extensive set of rules and guidelines (with regard to lesson tables, teacher qualifications, exams, etcetera) that have been set at central governmental level, determine operations within the school to a large extent. In corporate training, these kinds of governmental rules and guidelines are almost absent.

Table 8.1 summarizes the aforementioned main differences between education in a school setting and corporate training and development.

Table 8.1: *Main differences between education and corporate HRD*

	Education	Corporate HRD
Degree of specificity	general	specific
The problem of choice	non-existent, schooling is the primary process	existent, training is used to support primary process of the company
Type of participants	mainly children and young adults	mainly (older) adults many differences in backgrounds
Length of training	long	short
Problem of transfer	receives little attention	important topic
Organization	uniform	much variation
Governmental concern	high	almost absent

8.2.4 The HRD function

The processes of planning and executing HRD activities in companies, as well as the people involved in it, are referred to as the corporate HRD function. In some companies, only training professionals are part of the HRD function. Nowadays, in most companies, however, line managers and other employees also fulfill certain tasks with regard to HRD, and are thus part of the HRD function. At this point, a brief look is taken at the kinds of processes which jointly form the HRD function. Section 8.3 will deal with the organization of the HRD function in greater detail.

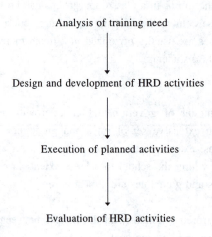

Figure 8.3: *Phases in the process of organizing HRD activities*

The process of organizing HRD activities basically consists of four phases (Van der Krogt & Plomp, 1987; Bergenhenegouwen, Mooijman & Tillema, 1992), as is depicted in Figure 8.3.

Phase 1: Analysis of training need

The analysis of the need for training is a very important activity. Corporate training activities are expensive, and therefore have to be used as effectively as possible. In this respect, a thorough analysis of the existing training need is imperative for success (Kessels & Smit, 1989). A needs analysis may consist of an analysis for one specific case in which performance improvement is needed, but may also stretch to the development of a general HRD policy. Such a general HRD policy states the way in which the organization plans to fulfill its present and future needs for well qualified employees by means of HRD activities. Other matching strategies (such as hiring and firing, or job redesign) are not included in this plan, only the contribution of HRD to a well qualified workforce is discussed. A company's HRD policy contains decisions concerning the goals, focus and organization of the HRD activities within the company.

The corporate HRD policy can be used as a guideline for the analysis of training needs in specific situations. In considering whether training provides a suitable answer to any specific performance problem, the question of whether the proposed training fits within the general HRD policy is one of the criteria that can be used to decide on whether or not to deliver a training activity as a solution to the problem at hand.

Examples of other questions which should be considered when analyzing the need for HRD activities are:

- does the employee lack certain qualifications which are required for a certain (current or future) job?
- does this result in performance problems?
- is training the most efficient way to obtain the lacking qualifications?

Phase 2 and 3: design, development and delivery of training

After certain training activities have been decided upon, these have to be developed and delivered. It is quite common for organizations to make use of the services of an external training institution for both development and delivery of training, as both tasks are quite time consuming, and often do not have to be performed on a permanent basis (which makes it inefficient for the organization to hire full-time in-house experts on course development and specialized trainers). Only some (very) large organizations employ their own specialists for these activities.

Phase 4: evaluation

The last phase entails comparing results with the initial goals of an HRD activity. Evaluation can take place at different levels (Kirkpatrick, 1987):

- evaluation of learning results (have the participants learned what they set out to learn?);
- evaluation of performance improvement (has the anticipated improvement in performance taken place as a result of the acquisition of new skills and knowledge?);
- evaluation of organizational development (has the anticipated organization development occurred, as a result of the training?).

The appropriate level of evaluation depends on the goals of the HRD activities. In general, however, one can state that an evaluation of learning results is not enough, because acquiring new knowledge and skills is never the ultimate goal of corporate HRD (as has been mentioned earlier in this chapter). Evaluating performance improvement is necessary to ascertain whether transfer of training has occurred (that is, whether the knowledge and skills learned are applied on the job). There are many reasons why employees sometimes do not apply their new skills (for instance, because they do not have the right equipment). Evaluation at performance level is also important to decide whether the newly acquired skills actually lead to performance improvement.

Evaluation at organizational level is usually very difficult. The attainment of (or failure to attain) organizational goals is dependent on so many different variables, that it is hard to determine the contribution of any specific HRD activity in this process. Therefore, evaluation at this level is quite rare.

8.3 Organizational characteristics of the HRD function

There is no one best way to organize the HRD function. The optimal structure depends on the organizational context in which it is embedded. Section 8.3.1 describes this organizational context, and explains which contextual elements are important for the organization of the HRD function. The sections 8.3.2 up to 8.3.4 address the structure, technology and management of the HRD function.

8.3.1 Context of the HRD function

As Figure 8.4 shows, the HRD function is embedded in an environment in which two levels can be distinguished:

- the *macro environment* surrounding the company for which the HRD function works;

- the specific *company* for which the HRD function provides training and development activities.

Both levels and their specific characteristics are discussed below.

The HRD function is situated within the specific company. In most cases this function is formalized as an internal HRD department. As mentioned in section 8.2.4, the internal HRD department often cooperates with an external HRD institution for the development and delivery of training activities. This external HRD institution is located in the macro environment. The cooperation between both the internal and external part of the HRD function is visualized by the dotted line in Figure 8.4.

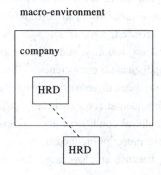

Figure 8.4:*The context of the HRD function*

The macro environment

The macro environment consists of all forces which affect the company, such as demographic, social, economic, ecological, technological, political and cultural forces. Some of these forces also have a direct or indirect impact on the HRD function (American Society for training and development, 1994; Streumer & van der Klink, 1996). It is impossible to mention all of these forces. A few examples will be mentioned to gain more insight into their impact on both the company and the HRD function.

A first example is the decline in the birth rate. This demographic development leads to a smaller number of young entrants on the labor market some 16 to 20 years later. For a company, this may result in a difficulty in hiring new staff, which in turn may increase the need to train older employees in new competencies. An increase in foreign members of the national population (another demographic development) may result in a more multicultural workforce in companies. This in turn may force the HRD staff in some companies to develop language courses for the changing workforce.

A change in life style characteristics and work ethics, or changes in employees' expectations towards working conditions are examples of social or cultural developments. These may force organizations to respond with measures such as flexible working hours or variable employment contracts. This in turn may necessitate such things as individualized and computer-assisted HRD programs, or programs delivered at less traditional hours in the day.

Reducing the expenditure on organizational products and services (an economic force) will affect the financial results and profit margin of the organization. When facing unfavorable economic conditions, many organizations are inclined to save money by reducing the HRD budget and HRD efforts of their organization (see also Sredl & Rothwell, 1987).

Other important developments concern various kinds of technological changes. The ever increasing trend toward automation, robotics, and other applications of computer technology requires workers with sophisticated competencies. The HRD function is forced to deliver HRD programs which provides these workers with the required competencies.

A last example of macro-environmental forces concerns strict environmental prescriptions or demands. This political or cultural condition forces companies to adapt their production processes in order to meet these prescriptions and demands. In some cases this may affect the content of HRD activities, because employees need more knowledge on environmental issues.

The company

The company forms the direct environment of the HRD function. In this section some important characteristics of companies, which exert strong influence on the HRD function, are discussed (and summarized in Table 8.2). Examples of these characteristics are (Rothwell and Kazenas, 1989; Carnevale, Gainer & Villet, 1990; Ford, Major, Seaton & Krifcher Felberc, 1993; Blakely, Martinec & Lane, 1994):

- the trade of industrial sector;
- the organizational technology;
- the organizational size;
- the organizational structure;
- the organizational culture;
- the organizational strategy;
- work force characteristics.

• *Trade or industrial sector*

The trade or industrial sector refers to a group of organizations producing the same kind of products or delivering the same category of services, i.e.: agriculture, transportation and communication companies, wholesale and retail trade organizations, insurance companies, service providing organizations (Van Hulst & Willems, 1992). The trade characterizes, to some extent, the kind and complexity of a company's core processes (Mulder, Akkerman & Bentvelsen, 1989; Van Hulst & Willems, 1992; Dekker & Wognum, 1994). Evidently, the work to be done in the primary process of, for instance, a service company differs from the work in the automobile manufacturing industry.

Differences between trades can be observed both with regard to the *amount* and the *content of HRD activities* (Mulder, c.s. 1989; Wognum, 1995). In some trades (e.g. construction) companies offer hardly any HRD activities, while other trades companies are very active in the field of HRD (e.g. insurance). One of the factors which may influence this trade-related difference in the amount of HRD activities is the rate of innovation in a trade. Companies which constantly develop new products and services need a lot of HRD activities to support employees in activities such as producing and selling these new outputs. Concerning the content of HRD activities, the banking trade, for instance, was found to offer significantly more HRD activities on marketing and public relations (in 1993) than the transportation trade or industry trade in the same year (Wognum, 1995). This is probably the result of a new client-centered approach adopted by the banks. This approach calls for more marketing and public relations skills. Likewise, the manufacturing industries in 1993 offered more HRD programs on production processes, health and security (Wognum, 1995). Complex and drastic changes in their manufacturing production process and related machinery probably called for these kinds of HRD interventions in order to enable employees to operate the new machinery safely and effectively.

• *Organizational technology*

The organizational technology encompasses all knowledge, skills and techniques used to transform input into output (McPherson et al., 1986). As indicated in chapter 3, "included are as well techniques applied to analyze the relevant features of the raw material (the input for the organization) as techniques for designing the transformation process (input into output) itself, and all kinds of arrangements made on the shop floor to realize the desired output". In the automobile industry, for example, a standard production method with routine assembly line work is used to transform steel and other materials into cars. Organizations in the medical sector need a different kind of organizational technology to 'transform' people with health problems into mentally and physically sound persons. Each kind of organizational technology calls for *specific technology related HRD interventions*. The technology used in car factories typically calls for HRD activities focused on skills in using machines in the car production process. The organizational technology in a psychiatric hospital calls for HRD activities on topics such as treatments, medications, and social and communication skills. So, the kind of organizational technology used in a certain company influences the content of HRD activities to a great degree. Changes in organizational technologies influence the content of HRD activities as well, because these changes demand workers with other and often more sophisticated qualifications. Both employees and managers in these changing organizations need to be retrained and 'upgraded' continuously via specific HRD activities since it is difficult to find employees with the required competencies in the labor market.

• *Size of the organization*
The number of employees of a company is another important organizational characteristic which strongly influences the HRD function. The company size influences the following elements of the HRD function:

HRD policy: In companies with more than 500 employees, a more explicit training policy is usually formulated than in smaller companies (Mulder et al., 1989). In organizations with less than 500 employees, HRD activities are more dependent on the actions of the individual employees.

Structure of the HRD function: larger companies are more likely to have an HRD function formalized as an HRD department. In small companies, there is usually only one person in charge of all 'people' issues like hiring, payment, counselling, and HRD matters (Wexley and Latham, 1991). Large companies often have a centralized group of people controlling all training programs and other HRD activities.

Content of HRD activities: In general, larger companies need other skills and attitudes need to be trained or educated than in smaller organizations. For example, companies with more than 1000 employees seem to offer significantly more programs on marketing skills than companies with less than 1000 employees (Wognum, 1995). This may be caused by differences in the number and variation of products and services.

• *Structure of the company*
With regard to the company structure, the amount of organizational (de)centralization exerts great influence on the HRD function. It affects, for example, the *number of HRD activities aimed at top management*. Research shows that centralized companies (with only a central structure) typically offer less HRD activities for top management than companies with decentralized structures (Wognum, 1995). This may be due to the specific situation in decentralized companies, where a set of more or less autonomous entities (generally called units or divisions) are coupled together by a central administration or headquarter. Top managers in those companies have to communicate and negotiate with a number of unit

managers in order to implement the organization's strategy in each unit. HRD interventions can help them to acquire the necessary communication and negotiation skills and attitudes.

The degree of (de)centralization also affects the *organization of the HRD function*. In decentralized companies it is very common to divide the HRD responsibilities over a central HRD department (located at the central staff), and several decentralized HRD officers or trainers (Wexley and Latham, 1991). The central HRD department monitors the quality, provides consultation, support and coordination of the HRD activities in the various divisions. Occasionally, central staff develops special training programs, to be conducted by trainers at decentral and divisional level (London, 1989). Companies with a centralized structure often organize their HRD function in one central department.

• *Organizational culture*

Sredl and Rothwell define organizational culture as 'the relatively enduring pattern of beliefs, norms, and values internalized by employees and managers (Sredl and Rothwell, 1987, p. 32). Some aspects of the corporate culture affect the HRD function (see among others Frissen & Van der Putten, 1990). The attitude of managers towards training is an especially important aspect of the corporate culture (Ford & Noe, 1987; Wexley and Latham, 1991). It may affect their *involvement* in HRD activities, if they consider HRD interventions as typically intended for employees in the operating core. A negative attitude of managers towards HRD will influence the *level of self-assessed training needs* of employees. It usually results in a denial of any need for training, because a stated training need is equated to admitting personal failure. Managers' attitudes towards training and development are also expressed in the *level of financial support* for HRD activities (Rothwell & Kazenas, 1989). If HRD is not regarded as being an important means to reaching organizational targets, then it is very often regarded as being a cost, rather than an investment for the future. The resources which management then wishes to spend on training will be significantly less than in situations where management does regard HRD as an essential prerequisite for a company's success.

• *Organizational strategy*

The strategy of an organization can be defined as "the broad-scale plan for operating in a competitive environment to achieve organizational goals" (Carnevale, Gainer & Villet, 1990, p. 159). This overall strategy has an impact on HRD, since HRD activities always have to fit within this general policy, as is expressed in the HRD definition given in section 8.2. As Carnevale et al. (1990) point out, this overall or 'umbrella' strategy influences several HRD issues, such as the choice of *specific HRD target groups*, preferences for some *specific training content* or *new HRD interventions* in traditional and new training areas. It is impossible to make an inventory of all possible cause and effect relationships between the general company policy and its HRD function; the number of relationships is almost infinite. To give an illustration, however, in the following paragraphs a few examples are given of how four common types of general company policies can influence the HRD function. Carnevale et al. (1990) distinguish between four categories of 'umbrella strategies': concentration, internal growth, external growth, and disinvestment.

Concentration means that an organization focuses on doing what it does best, within its established markets, using essentially the same technology and marketing approach, based on the known competencies of the organization and depending on the use of existing resources, both human and material. Concentration is essentially an attempt to maintain the status quo. The implication of this strategy for the HRD function is 'that the organization already has what it needs to develop and implement training, but those resources must be molded and organized so that they are more effectively and efficiently used' (Carnevale et al., p. 178). In other words: the company aims at optimizing existing HRD practices.

A strategy of internal growth means that an organization actively fosters innovation, expands its markets, develops new products, or teams up with another organization to strengthen its competitive position. Such a strategy typically leads to a large number of HRD activities, which are meant to assist employees with the implementation of organizational changes, and the production and selling of new products or services.

An external growth strategy means that an organization attempts to expand its resources or fortify its market position through the acquisition or founding of new businesses. For the HRD function, it usually means that top management becomes an important target group for HRD activities, as they will need new management skills and attitudes to manage the new organization.

An organization with a disinvestment strategy faces economic and financial difficulties and moves to pare down its operations. Disinvestment is accomplished by reducing or eliminating operations. HRD in these instances is very often used to support outplacement of superfluous employees, for instance by means of courses in interviewing and writing application letters.

• *Workforce characteristics*
The workforce is the last major influence on the HRD function to be discussed in this section. The specific characteristics of the workforce influence factors such as the way in which HRD is delivered, and the topics on which HRD activities are focused.

The *mode of delivery of HRD activities* is directly influenced by workforce characteristics. An important aspect here is the language, because many organizations employ a multilingual workforce which mirrors the multicultural society. If a considerable proportion of the workforce consist of Turkish employees, for instance, it may be necessary to provide some basic courses (e.g. on safety regulations) in Turkish.

Age is another example of an influential workforce characteristic in this respect. The workforce nowadays is older on average, as a result of demographic developments. Older employees prefer different teaching and training methods than younger people, e.g. more 'learning by doing' and 'learning-on-the-job' activities and less traditional off-the-job courses (Rhebergen & Wognum, 1996).

The *content of HRD activities* is also influenced by workforce characteristics. If the workforce contains a large proportion of older employees, it may become necessary to provide basic computer skills, for example. Related to this, the educational level of employees is an important characteristic, because it determines the kind and complexity of the knowledge and skills learned in courses.

Overview of important company characteristics

Table 8.2 provides an overview of the mentioned company characteristics and their impact on some aspects of the HRD function. It is important to state that there are no one-on-one relationships, in the sense that each change in a company characteristic automatically leads

Table 8.2: *Company characteristics and some related HRD aspects*

company characteristic	some related HRD aspects
trade of industrial sector	• number of HRD interventions • content of HRD interventions
organizational technology	• content of technology related HRD interventions
size of the organization	• HRD policy • structure of the HRD function • content of HRD activities
structure of the company	• number of HRD activities aimed at top management • organization of the HRD function
organizational culture	• management involvement in HRD activities • level of self-assessed training needs • degree of financial HRD support
organizational strategy	• specific HRD target groups • specific HRD interventions
workforce characteristics	• mode of delivery of HRD activities • content of HRD activities

to a certain development in the HRD function. Only some general insight is provided into how certain organizational elements can influence some HRD characteristics.

Though this inventory does not attempt to be complete, it does show that there is no one best way to organize the HRD function. The HRD function is influenced by many factors in the specific company of which it is a part. In the following section the structure of the HRD function is discussed in more detail. Two important characteristics will be discussed, i.e. the position of the HRD function within the company (i.e. central, decentral or a combination of both), and the division of HRD tasks (i.e. the tasks of internal professionals and external institutions, related to the number of HRD professionals).

8.3.2 Structure of the HRD function

The structure of the HRD function varies enormously across companies. For instance, small companies may have one person charged with HRD activities, while larger companies may employ as many as 200 or more HRD professionals. Sometimes HRD staff report to decentral line management, in other cases they are located in the corporate headquarters and report to top management. Some HRD professionals perform various kinds of roles, whereas in other organizations they have only one predominant role, such as trainer or purchaser of training programs. In this section some possible variations in the structure of the HRD function or department are described with regard to the following topics (Sredl & Rothwell, 1987):

- the position of the HRD function within the organization, or in other words: where on the organizational chart is the HRD function located?
- the organization of the HRD function: who is involved in HRD, and how are tasks divided among the persons involved?

Position of the HRD function

The HRD function may be positioned in the central part of an organization, or in decentralized units or divisions. In companies with a centralized structure, the HRD function is often formalized as an autonomous staff department, standing outside the flow of the formal line of authority. This kind of HRD departments is sometimes concentrated at the top (Figure 8.5.a), serving the whole company and falling under the direct responsibility of the top managers of the company. In other cases the HRD function is attached to a personnel department (Figure 8.5.b) and falls under the responsibility of the Personnel or Human Resource Manager. In some companies the HRD function is attached to one or several departments, such as production, marketing or sales. It serves more or less local

266

needs and is linked closely with the executive managers of these departments (Figure 8.5.c). In this case the company's customers are also an important target group for training, since these customers may need new knowledge and skills to handle the purchased products or delivered services (Addison & Haig, 1994). In companies with a decentralized structure, the HRD department is often positioned in the central staff departments as well as in the decentralized divisions or units (in most cases as a staff department and/or part of the personnel department (Figure 8.5.d). As indicated in section 8.3.1, in these cases the HRD responsibilities are distributed among both parts of the HRD function.

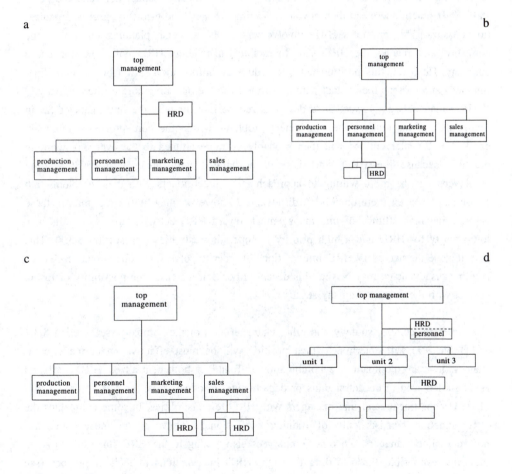

Figure 8.5: *Several possible positions of the HRD function in companies*

The position of the HRD function within the organization has an impact on the kinds of employees who normally take advantage of HRD activities. A centralized department normally covers the whole organization, whereas a decentralized department may cover only part of the organization (London, 1989). A centralized department also directs its activities to top and middle management levels in the company, while a decentralized department most of the time focuses on a company's divisional and operational level (Wognum, 1995).

There are some advantages and disadvantages to each of the portrayed positions of the HRD function. Placing HRD responsibility in a central staff department facilitates, among other things, a more structured consultation between company management and the HRD staff. Staff practitioners can then devote more time, money, and effort to specific organizational issues. This promotes HRD involvement in the strategic planning process of the company, and enables the HRD staff to establish a coherent HRD policy for the entire company. However, this position tends to reduce the information flow from several 'line' functions and loosens the contact with departments in the operating core of the company.

If HRD managers are located in a decentralized position or near the line manager (as in Figure 8.5.c), this enables them to detect problems within the core processes relatively quickly. HRD interventions will then probably be more attuned to the everyday working practice, because the HRD staff is well acquainted with the workplace. Operating employees will be more willing to approach HRD practitioners with their problems and action can be taken more quickly. A disadvantage, however, may be the fact that, in these cases, a negative attitude of line management toward HRD activities usually results in a low priority for HRD and a high priority for operating activities (see section 8.3.1). This may impede the necessary HRD interventions in order to solve some operational problems. Another disadvantage may be that this decentral position increases the possibility of losing contact with the overall company strategy.

The structure, culture, strategy and other characteristics of the company (see section 8.3.1 and Table 8.2) will determine which position will be most effective under the circumstances. In many companies, a combination is found of both centralized HRD staff and HRD staff placed in decentral units or departments. In other cases, there is a combination of HRD departments and line managers with HRD responsibilities. In some companies the HRD function consists only of training professionals. However, in most companies nowadays line managers and other employees also belong to the HRD function; as such, they are responsible for providing the right HRD interventions to their employees (see section 8.3 for more detail). A coordinating task between the central office and the decentral HRD staff, or between HRD staff and other employees with HRD related tasks is then necessary to overcome the disadvantages of separate positions, and to align the overall HRD strategy with decentral HRD activities.

Organization of the HRD function

The organization of the HRD function concerns the division of tasks, duties, and responsibilities between individual functionaries (Van Dam & Marcus, 1980; Sredl & Rothwell, 1987), which is affected by the primary process of the HRD function. This process encompasses all knowledge, skills and techniques used to perform the HRD function in companies. It consists of four areas or phases of HRD activities (as described in section 8.2).

Not all four kinds of activities are executed by every HRD department or function (Van der Krogt & Plomp, 1987). As mentioned before, the HRD function can be situated *inside* the company, mostly formalized as an HRD department, but also *outside* the company. In the latter case, external institutes or HRD agencies provide training and development activities for the company. This is usually the case with smaller organizations. These external institutions are often specialized in one particular area, e.g. management development, technical training, or communication. Of course, in many cases, a combination can be encountered. The HRD function is then organized internally, but collaborates with external institutions (this is visualized by the dotted line in Figure 8.4). In general, it can be stated that any company's specific situation determines which elements of the HRD process are the most important ones to be performed in-house. In dynamic organizations (e.g. in the automation business or in the service industries), HRD staff will usually stress the HRD policy-making and evaluation phases, especially when changes occur in the business policy, structure, or in the production and delivery processes. Large, less dynamic companies (e.g. in the automotive or steel industry), focus in most cases on developing and executing HRD activities, because these companies usually need to train large numbers of employees in company-specific technical topics.

The number of appointed HRD professionals influences the *division of the HRD tasks* the HRD employees have to perform and are responsible for. Tasks can be divided over several hierarchical levels, e.g. over staff at higher, middle and lower level in the HRD function. This is called 'vertical task differentiation' (Van Dam & Marcus, 1995). In large HRD departments with several HRD functionaries some vertical differentiation is perceived. In those cases, the HRD department usually consists of the HRD manager, some group or project leaders at middle and first-line management levels, and several teachers or trainers at operational level. In most cases, there is also a support staff. If there

269

are only a few HRD functionaries and there usually is very little vertical differentiation. One member of the group often functions as HRD manager, as a 'primus inter pares'.

Two other forms of task division are the so-called horizontal differentiation and horizontal specialization (Van Dam & Marcus, 1995). 'Horizontal differentiation' concerns the grouping of similar kinds of tasks or functions. In large HRD departments, horizontal differentiation is a common principle for task division. Differentiation is usually based on the already mentioned four phases of the HRD process: a large HRD department may employ needs analysts, training developers, instructors and evaluators. In small HRD departments, most of the work is done by a single functionary or a few HRD function-aries, cooperating with line managers, business employees and/or external institutes. These functionaries, usually charged with all 'people' issues (Wexley and Latham, 1991), function primarily as training brokers.

'Horizontal specialization' means that tasks are being grouped related to output (products, markets, or geographic areas). For an HRD department, this implies that all members of the department perform activities regarding most, or even all phases in the HRD process. However, all of them do so with regard to only one specific market or group of employees (e.g. middle management, operators, supporting staff), specific geographic area (e.g. the northern part of the country, or another country/continent), or specific HRD product (e.g. sales, communication, or technical training).

8.3.3 Technology of the HRD function

The operations technology of the HRD function encompasses all knowledge, skills and techniques used to 'transform' employees with inadequate or insufficient sets of qualifica-tions into employees with the required skills, knowledge and attitudes for satisfactory job fulfillment by means of HRD activities. As indicated in chapter 3, it includes the methods applied to analyze features of the raw material (the input) as well as techniques used to design the transformation process itself, and all of the arrangements made to attain the desired output.

The HRD technology encompasses the expertise of the HRD staff, training materials, and the methods used to transform input into output. The raw material concerns the employees with some (anticipated) deficiency in qualifications. The transformation process itself concerns the training and development process, basically consisting of the four phases described in section 8.2.2:

- analysis of the specific training needs which leads to the definition of the HRD goals the company wants to achieve by HRD interventions;

- design and development of training activities;
- the training process itself;
- evaluation of the training results in terms of new acquired knowledge, skills and attitudes.

The output of the HRD function concerns the trained employees, who are equipped with the necessary qualifications. As stated in 8.2.1, knowledge and skills acquisition is not a goal in itself. Corporate HRD activities are meant to improve job performance, solve or prevent organizational problems, and achieve organizational targets. Output information thus concerns information about the degree to which job performance is improved, problems are solved and organizational goals are met as a result of the HRD activities.

8.3.4 Management of the HRD function

The roles and responsibilities of the HRD manager vary considerably from industry to industry and even between organizations in the same industry (Addison & Haig, 1994). However, in each organization it is the task of the HRD manager to manage - to a certain extent - all HRD activities, foster the integration of HRD into the organization, and secure the alignment of HRD activities with the company's problems, developments and main processes. Just like all other management activities, HRD management comprises four categories of tasks on four different management levels (Snellen, 1981):

- strategical HRD management;
- tactical HRD management;
- operational HRD management;
- institutional HRD management.

Figure 8.6 relates these four management levels to the technology of the HRD function, discussed earlier. HRD managers need all kinds of information on this process to ensure that all four categories of management tasks are intended to optimize the HRD process within the organization.

If HRD management is really effective, the HRD process provides employees with new knowledge, skills and attitudes. The trained employees are then equipped with the necessary qualifications to improve job performance and, eventually, to achieve the targets of the company they work for or solve/prevent organizational problems. Therefore, HRD management is not an isolated activity. It has to be aligned with the entire company of which it is part. This is visualized in Figure 8.7, where the left side of the figure represents the HRD function with three management levels, and the right side represents the

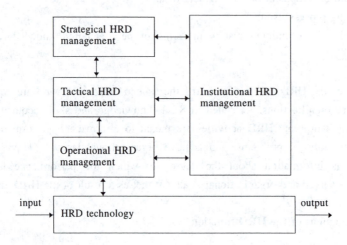

Figure 8.6: *Categories of HRD management tasks (adapted from Snellen, 1981)*

same three management activities in the company. Strategic HRD alignment is visualized by the three arrows, representing the interaction between (strategically oriented) HRD managers and representatives of the three company levels (Wognum, 1994). The institutional management tasks are not included in Figure 8.7, because (as explained below and also visualized in Figure 8.6) these tasks create the conditions for all strategical, tactical and operational management activities.

Strategical HRD management
Strategical HRD management concerns policy-making processes with regard to HRD, performed by the HRD manager or HRD staff with management responsibilities. Put more specifically, strategical HRD management concerns the development of the mission and long-range strategy of the HRD department. The HRD mission statement should reflect the reasons for existence of the HRD department such as, for instance, supporting the company's mission and strategy, solving a company's problems and/or supporting the company's developments. By analyzing business problems, developments and other issues, HRD specialists should identify these needs, which serve as a starting point for HRD processes in the company. A good fit between strategical HRD management and the company to which the HRD function belongs, is thus an important condition for providing employees with the right competencies at the right time: strategical HRD management has to be aligned with the company. Toward that aim, information is needed on the company's mission statement and strategy, but also on performance problems, important develop-

ments, and perceived HRD needs. Organizational problems and developments and their related training needs can arise at the strategical, tactical and operational level of the organization (see the right side of Figure 8.7).

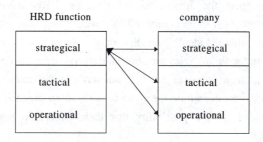

Figure 8.7: *Levels of strategical HRD aligning*

The first level at which relevant stakeholders and their training and development needs can be identified is the strategical level of the company, with a company's top management as a primary stakeholder. At this level top management can decide to change the organizational structure, strategy or production process, or to approach new markets. This may cause some new training and development needs. At the company tactical level, middle managers are the primary stakeholders for HRD. At this level, problems may arise concerning the coordination and cooperation between organizational departments and units, which may call for HRD interventions. At the operational level, lower executive management and other employees in the operating core are the primary stakeholders. HRD interventions at this organizational level are mainly meant to support performance problems of individual workers and operational departments.

Strategic HRD management at all three company levels includes the identification of potential HRD needs. These needs are related to the performance levels and business results to which stakeholders are striving. Fulfilling these needs will support them in reaching these levels and results. HRD interventions will only be effective if the results of these interventions match the needs of all relevant stakeholders. Mutual involvement of both parties (HRD management and primary stakeholders) is vital to assess HRD needs and to determine the goals of the necessary HRD interventions. This 'strategic partnership' Robinson & Robinson, 1989) creates the conditions for HRD effectiveness (see e.g. May, 1987; Rothwell & Kazanas, 1989). It creates a supportive work environment to gain the desired performance and business results. In case a supportive work environment is missing, the newly acquired competencies will soon fade away after the training.

Research findings support the importance of strategic HRD aligning processes and stakeholder involvement at all three organizational levels (Wognum, 1994). HRD programs are often developed without identifying the most relevant stakeholders. Mutual and interactive consultation with all relevant stakeholders in order to detect the actual real training needs, did not seem to occur on a regular basis in the cases studied. As a result, HRD interventions may not constitute the right answers to an organization's problems and developments. This leads to the possibility that their effects do not match the effects desired by the company.

Tactical HRD management

Tactical HRD management concerns the creation of favorable conditions for effective implementation of HRD activities. Formulated more specifically, it concerns the translation of general HRD policies, goals and strategies (as a result of the strategical HRD management processes) into more specific procedures. It includes the allocation of HRD staff, budgets and other resources to the required HRD interventions, to realize those HRD interventions. Coordination and structuring of staff and other needed resources is also part of tactical HRD management. In large HRD departments, this work can be carried out by group or project leaders at the middle management level. Most HRD departments, however, are relatively small, and for that reason, tactical HRD management in those cases is mostly part of the work of all HRD functionaries.

Operational HRD management

HRD management at the operational level refers to the management of the HRD core processes. It concerns, among other things, the management and control of specific HRD activities (like time schedules and other detailed arrangements, and final selection of employees to be trained or educated). It also includes the formulation of standards for desirable practice and of intended learning results. In large HRD functions, this work is done by some principals at first-line HRD management level. In smaller ones, it is part of the work of all HRD functionaries present.

Institutional HRD management

Finally, HRD management at the institutional level is part of the broader strategical HRD marketing process, and includes establishing a positive HRD image, both within the company and in the macro environment of the organization. It thus creates the conditions for the strategical, tactical and operational management tasks. Among other things, this can be done by providing important stakeholders (such as top executive management, supervisors and potential trainees) with information on HRD effectiveness and efficiency and Return On Investment of HRD investments (ROI). A positive attitude towards HRD in companies will lead to a higher level of involvement and partnership in HRD activities, specifically in needs analysis and goal-setting procedures. It can also foster an improved agreement on HRD goals and objectives, shared HRD responsibility, more support for the transfer of HRD results to the workplace, and more tangible resources (for instance in the form of higher training budgets). Institutional management tasks are therefore the primary responsibility off all HRD staff.

All four categories of HRD management tasks create the conditions and set the standards for all four phases of the HRD process (as described in section 8.2.4). However, as explained below, the emphasis on each of these categories varies. In former times, an emphasis on tactical and/or operational HRD management level could be observed in companies. The needs for a more focused approach to training and development in companies leads to a stronger emphasis on strategical HRD management, that is aligned with the entire company. Section 8.4 describes this and other important developments in the field of HRD.

8.4 Important developments within the field of HRD

This section identifies some major trends in the field of HRD. Of the many developments and challenges HRD professionals face, the following ones can be considered as being the most influential ones:
- the trend towards a focused approach to training and development;
- the importance of workplace learning;
- the focus on performance (support);
- the increasing use of information technology.

The subsections 8.4.1 to 8.4.4 will look into each of these trends. Subsection 8.1.5 will briefly explore the changes in the division of HRD tasks which these trends provoke.

8.4.1 Towards a focused approach of HRD

In recent years, a trend towards stronger integration of the HRD function in the company as a whole has been observed. More and more organizations find the gap between the HRD department and the rest of the organization too large. Among other things, this becomes apparent from a low involvement of HRD managers in company policy-making. It is quite common for HRD departments to be informed of changes in an organization's strategic course or changes in design of the work processes only long *after* these decisions have been made. This lack of interaction between policy-makers and the HRD function makes it difficult to support organizational changes with a proactive HRD policy. The somewhat isolated position in which many HRD departments find themselves, hinders these departments in making a visible and clear contribution to organizational success. Therefore, in many companies, both parties (HRD departments as well as line/top management) strive for a better integration of the HRD function in the organization.

In an overview of different approaches towards HRD, Barham & Rassam (1989) call this the 'focused approach'. It contrasts sharply with more traditional views on training and development, which Barham and Rassam describe as the 'fragmented' and the 'formalized' approach. To gain a better understanding of the focused approach, these traditional views on training are sketched briefly below, before describing the essence of the focused approach.

Traditional views on training: the fragmented and formalized approach

In 'the fragmented approach', training is a peripheral activity within the organization. Training is regarded as being the responsibility of specialized professionals who provide courses which are typically highly directive in nature (no active role for the trainee) and delivered on a 'take it or leave it' basis. This means that line management is hardly involved in deciding which training activities will be offered by the HRD department; line managers and employees choose courses from the catalogue which is compiled by the HRD department. This lack of communication between the HRD department, line management and employees usually leads to a very weak link between training and the wider objectives of the organization, and, to limited practical impact of the courses. Since the link between training and actual work practice often is only very weak, employee behavior seldom changes as a result of those training activities. In the long run, this approach may even lead to a situation in which training is viewed as a cost, rather than an investment for the future. When the organization has to cut down on expenses, the HRD department is usually one of the first where cuts are made.

This approach to training can be encountered in a decreasing number of organizations. Many organizations have moved on to what Barham & Rassam call 'the formalized approach'. This approach is characterized by the fact that the organization spends more time and money on HRD than organizations with a fragmented approach to HRD, and that the organization attempts to manage the whole HRD process in a systematic way. For instance, the training system is linked to the appraisal system to increase the probability that each employee receives the right training at the right time. Training needs are being assessed by looking at, and matching, both individual learning needs and organizational goals. Most of the training occurs off-the-job, but the establishment of close ties between job demands and skills acquired through training receives explicit attention, just as the stimulation of actual application of newly acquired knowledge and skills on the job (transfer of training).

Focused approach
Though the formalized approach is a step in the right direction compared to the fragmented approach, it still has many limitations. These become apparent when organizations became confronted with an increasing change of pace in their external environments (markets and technologies). This turbulence places high demands on an organization's capacity to learn and change. Companies in a turbulent environment experience the need for a more flexible approach to training and development, which is closely linked to the daily work of their employees. These organizations move towards a 'focused approach', where HRD policy is more closely linked to the organizational strategy, and HRD activities are closely linked to the actual demands of the daily work environment. HRD activities are delivered on a just-in-time basis and directly in the context of the job or task at hand. Much of the training takes place on the job, because it is recognized that the workplace provides a very rich learning environment. In the focused approach, HRD becomes a shared responsibility of line management, employees and HRD professionals.

8.4.2 Learning in the workplace

Partly due to the recognition that formal training comprises only a small part of all learning that occurs in an organization, the workplace is regarded more and more as an important place for learning. As a result, more training takes place on the job. Methods which alternate learning and working, such as Action Learning, also become increasingly popular. In the case of Action Learning, trainees work on a 'real life' problem they experience in the workplace. They receive support from a facilitator, who assists in the 'learning by doing' process. The facilitator also provides formal off-the-job training activities with respect to the content of the problem, and with regard to general subjects like problem solving and conflict management, whenever necessary.

Next to these formal learning activities, informal learning in the workplace receives more attention. Among other things, organizations try to stimulate this by:

- fostering a positive learning climate;
- working towards a result oriented leadership style in which the manager is primarily a coach (as opposed to a 'macho management style' where management takes the decisions and employees are not involved in the problem-solving process);
- appointing mentors to assist employees in their development.

8.4.3 Focus on performance (support)

Another important trend in the field of HRD is the focus on performance (Rummler & Brache, 1990). To some extent training makes way for performance improvement or performance support. The trainee is not taken away from the job, but receives assistance on a just-in-time, just-enough basis, *during* actual work activities. The work process is not interrupted for training activities. One result of this trend is the increased use of Electronic Performance Support Systems (EPSS) which provide support in the workplace, whenever the employee needs it. These systems combine the functions of (Winslow & Bramer, 1994):

- librarian (through the EPSS the employee has access to numerous data bases);
- consultant (for instant advice on the training program to follow);
- trainer (the employee can follow computer training on the job);
- on line help function on the computer system.

The type of support or training provided by an EPSS is, to a great degree, self-directed by the learner.

The focus on performance also leads to an increased attention for evaluation of HRD activities. Unlike the situation in the 1980s, when there was an enormous growth in training activities, companies in the 1990s try to minimize their training effort by training only when this is necessary to improve performance. This accent on effectiveness and the appreciation of results increases the need to evaluate training, in order to assess how much HRD activities have contributed to the performance of employees (Mulder, 1995a; Swanson, 1994).

8.4.4 Increasing use of information technology

The use of technology in computer applications that facilitate on-the-job and off-the-job learning, such as performance support systems and distance learning, has grown considerably in recent years. It is believed that the use of this technology will increase more in the future, and - in time - will change the *nature* of training. Until recently, information technology had been used mainly to provide training in a more cost-effective way, and not really to change the features of training methods significantly. This situation is now changing, the possibilities of technology are being used more and more as a basis for reforming training methods: to train and support learning in different ways. New technologies can help organizations to provide learning opportunities to employees in a flexible way with regard to time, content and place (for example in the form of EPSS systems). Employees have access to these kinds of learning opportunities at any time. Their learning needs can be met right away, they do not have to wait, as is the case with scheduled learning events (courses or workshops).

8.4.5 Towards new ways of organizing the HRD function

Developments in the field of HRD, such as outlined in the above, lead to changes in the way in which the HRD function is organized. Most noticeably, the following changes in the division of HRD tasks between line management, employees and HRD professionals may be observed:

- line management is increasingly expected to actively assess the learning needs of employees, and to act as a mentor or coach in the learning processes;
- employees have to manage their own learning more, to keep abreast of new developments in their work field. They are also more often requested to act as trainers for their colleagues, and thus share their own (expert) knowledge;
- the role of the HRD professional moves away from the role of trainer. Instead of a 'directive interventionist' (Barham & Rassam, 1989) the HRD professional acts more as a consultant to line management and as a facilitator of learning processes in which staff take an active role (Barham & Rassam, 1989; Laiken, 1993; Tjepkema & Wognum, 1995).

279

8.5 Effectiveness of HRD

As explained in sections 8.2.4 and 8.3.3, the effects of HRD can be evaluated at different levels, related to:
• learning achievements (knowledge and skills learned);
• workplace behavior (performance: application of the new knowledge and skills);
• organizational benefits (in terms of financial benefits or other organizational objectives).

Assessing HRD effectiveness should focus on these effects. A prerequisite for determining HRD effectiveness is that HRD goals are formulated in terms of the intended effects: the specific skills and knowledge to be obtained (the learning objectives) and the desired individual, group and/or organizational performance or organizational results. The appropriate level of effect evaluation depends on the level on which these goals are formulated.

The first level of evaluation does not provide many difficulties. Learning goals are usually formulated and most HRD activities, especially training, end with a brief examination to determine whether the learning goals have been achieved and the employee has indeed acquired the desired knowledge and skills.

Most companies are, however, more interested in the second level of evaluation, namely the effects of HRD on employee behaviour (individual and/or group performance) in the workplace (Mulder, 1995b). Organizations want to know whether employees actually apply the knowledge and skills during work. The methods used to determine the effects of HRD activities on employee performance, depend on the kind of activities carried out by the employee. In some instances, the effect of training is relatively easy to determine. In the case of a typewriting course, for example, the effect of the training can be determined by comparing the typing speed and the number of errors of the typist before and after the training. In most cases, however, it is far more difficult to compare ex ante and post training performance. The company will have to use indirect measures for the training effect, such as an decrease in the number of complaints by clients after the training. The problem with these indirect measures is that changes can never be completely attributed to the HRD activity. As an example, consider the case of a blanket salesman who attends a course to improve his communication skills in conversations with clients. After he returns from the course, he sells many more blankets than ever before, but it is also an extremely severe winter, one of the coldest in years. In order to establish the effect of the training, one would have to rule out the effect of the low temperature on the sales of blankets. As yet, there are few reliable research methods available to determine the effect of HRD activities, such as training, on employee performance, and relate these to the cost of training, but these are too difficult to apply and too laborious to be widely used in practice (for an overview see Witziers, 1995). Research in this field is continuing.

Next to the effects on employee performance, HRD managers and line managers are increasingly interested in the effect of HRD on the third level, that of the organization. This concerns questions whether the initial organizational problems are solved and/or the organizational targets are achieved (section 8.3.3.). It includes the question whether the eventual (financial) benefits of any HRD activity justify the investments, made to carry out these activities. It then concerns the establishment of any Return On Investment (ROI) of HRD investments. The results and financial benefits on the organizational level are very difficult to establish, because of the same attribution problem as indicated above. The number of intervening variables between the HRD activity and the eventual results and benefits for the organization is extremely large. There are some reliable methods for determining the organizational benefits of any HRD activity, but these are difficult to apply and are very time-consuming (e.g. Van Sandick & Schaap, 1993). Therefore, effect evaluation at this level is very rare. The determining of HRD effectiveness at this level is even more difficult, because of a more or less absence of strategic HRD policy-making to identify organizational needs and determine the specific goals of required HRD activities in the right terms (Wognum, 1994).

At this point, it should be mentioned that, though the importance of determining effectiveness of HRD activities is widely recognized, systematic evaluation of HRD efforts is certainly not a widespread activity in organizations. The lack of readily usable tools and techniques mentioned in the above, is one of the reasons. Another reason is the costs of evaluation activities. These are usually quite high for any thorough evaluation, because of the time-consuming nature of this kind of research. Another, more positive, reason why many organizations do not take the trouble to seriously evaluate HRD activities is that a change in performance sometimes readily is observable. If that is the case, organizations tend to be pragmatic: they see that HRD has had an effect and see no reason to try to determine the nature of this effect in greater detail (Mulder, 1995b).

8.6 Applying principles from corporate HRD in schools

An interesting question is whether the corporate HRD approach could also be applied within schools. In order to explore this issue, it is relevant to compare schools to similar organizations from business and industry. It is not very useful to compare HRD practices in schools to HRD practices within factories, for instance, because the type of work and the educational level of the employees are so different. The most meaningful comparisons can be drawn with companies that, like schools, can be characterized as professional bureaucracies (Mintzberg, 1979). The main characteristics of a professional bureaucracy are: a highly educated workforce (professionals) that has much control in fulfilling its daily tasks, and work that is not very predictable in nature, though the products or services offered are rather standard (not unique). Making these products, or delivering these services requires 'craftmanship' of the professional; this process cannot be standardized or automated. Some examples from business and industry include general hospitals, public accounting firms, IT-consultancy agencies (see also chapter 1).

Just as in many work organizations of the professional bureaucracy-type, HRD in schools is usually only a marginal organizational function. Further professional development, for instance to keep up with new developments, is mainly regarded as a responsibility of the professional himself. The organization usually only provides some resources (books, a training budget) and sometimes some advice on courses which teachers can best attend. Usually, the occupational group to which a professional belongs is very active in providing training for its members (Van der Krogt, 1990). In professional business and industry bureaucracies, however, this situation is now changing; professionals receive more guidance and support in their continuing education and development. Schools may benefit from these recent experiences with HRD in the corporate sector, in particular with regard to two aspects:

• Linking professional development to organizational objectives;
• Techniques for facilitating informal learning.

Linking professional development to school objectives

An essential feature of HRD in business and industry is the deliberate integration of training and development activities into the organization. Training and development should not be an isolated activity, but, should be linked to company policy on a strategic level. This is the first area in which schools might benefit from the corporate HRD tradition. Traditionally, professionals in a corporate setting as in schools, bear a great responsibility with regard to their own learning and development. This responsibility has not diminished, but the way in which the organization manages and supports professional learning is changing. Professional bureaucracies in business and industry are increasingly using training as a tool of management to reach organizational objectives, and don't want to leave the development of professionals in the hands of the individual or the occupational group as a whole (Tjepkema & Mulder, 1997). This is becoming more important for schools as well, as their autonomy is increasing. Because of decentralization and deregulation, it is becoming more important for schools to formulate their own organizational objectives and policies. Training and development of teaching staff can be an important tool in realizing these policies. In other words: for schools, too, it is becoming important to use training as a 'tool of management' (section 8.2.1). In such an approach, performance of the professional is the central issue. The main question is no longer which courses a professional wants to follow in a particular year, or which seminars the association of that particular occupation organizes. Instead, the main question is the desired improvement in performance of the professional, as viewed by himself and as necessary with regard to company policy.

Such an approach could also be used in schools (see Tjepkema & Mulder,1997). Suppose a school wants to implement new teaching methods in which the teacher's role is more that of a 'facilitator of learning' than that of a traditional teacher. In order to realize this role-shift, a particular teacher and his manager discuss the desired changes, and formulate performance objectives. In doing so, they consider both the individual wishes of the teacher and school policy with regard to the new teaching method. These objectives are as concrete as possible and reflect the mutual expectations with regard to the future behavior of the teacher. On the basis of these objectives, the teacher and his manager can then consider appropriate learning activities (see next section).

Facilitating learning from experience

The choosing of learning activities forms a second area in which schools might benefit from HRD in business and industry, specifically concerning the methods of training and development. Just as many employees in corporate settings, teachers have to acquire new skills, knowledge and insights on an on-going basis during their professional career. This comes as a consequence of the many changes within the field of education (new teaching methods, new organizational forms, etc.). Kwakman (1997) found that this professional development of teachers occurs mainly by means of four activities:

• Keeping up with new developments/insights;
• Applying and testing these new developments in their own classrooms;
• Reflecting on their own performance;
• Cooperation with others in developing policies and also in practice.

With respect to the first activity, keeping up with new developments, The Dutch Educational Inspection Board noted in its yearly Educational Report (1998) that it is ever more difficult for teachers to find time for this, due to factors such as work pressure and the increasing amount of developments teachers have to keep up with. Teachers do follow training seminars, but in practice, these do not always yield the desired results. One reason for this can be that because they are usually quite theoretical in nature, training seminars often provide teachers with too few tools to apply the new insights in the classroom. It therefore is worthwhile to consider ways in which teachers can be supported in learning in the workplace - within their own schools. In corporate settings, supporting this type of learning receives more attention nowadays (see section 8.4.2). This is especially true for professionals, whose jobs are usually characterized by a high degree of variety in tasks, autonomy (which provides room for experimentation) and the need to solve new problems, the workplace is an important source for new learning. Companies are increasingly seeking ways to improve the workplace as a learning environment and support professionals in learning from experience. For this group, the two main conditions for learning from experience are: time for reflection and the ability to consult with colleagues. Possible methods include: action learning projects, intervision networks and peer coaching. Of course, these methods in themselves are not enough to help teachers keep up with new developments. But they can complement activities such as attending a seminar or reading a book on a new teaching method, and can also help teachers to apply the new principles in their own practice (the second activity mentioned in the list above). Already, teachers can be seen increasingly using such methods that rely on learning from experience (Coenjaerts et al. 1997). But the initiative comes from the teachers themselves. It might be worthwhile for schools to explore in what ways they can help teachers to use such experiential learning methods (see section 8.2.1).

In order to give some idea of what this might mean for schools, we turn back to the example mentioned before: suppose the teacher and his manager have agreed on performance objectives. The next step would be selection of learning activities. In choosing these activities they not only consider learning objectives (in this case not only knowledge-oriented, but also skill-oriented), but also the experience and preferences (learning style) of the teacher. Of course, pragmatic arguments (such as budget and time constraints) also play a role. First, following a course on the subject and attending a seminar are decided upon as learning activities. But the choice is much broader; the teacher and manager also include more informal learning methods, namely: buying a book for self-study and visiting other schools in order to learn from them. The teacher also decides to start an intervision group with colleagues within the school, in which they jointly reflect on experiences and help each other to learn new skills. The school provides him with some time to do this, and promises support from the management secretary in setting up meetings and inviting participants (see Tjepkema & Mulder, 1997). Of course, these are just some examples; the possibilities are much broader.

Organization of this HRD approach
Suppose schools would start using this approach to HRD. An important issue is the role of

an HRD consultant. Most companies in business and industry use specialized (in-house or external) HRD consultants to support managers and professionals in selecting learning activities, and sometimes also in the process of formulating performance and learning objectives. Schools might also benefit from such specialized support and advice.

A second issue concerns the way in which agreements are formalized. In corporate settings, professional development plans, or learning contracts, are used ever more frequently to formalize agreements between management and professionals with regard to performance objectives and learning activities (Boak, 1998). After one year, these documents are used to assess (in a performance review) whether the professional and the organization have held up their end of the agreement, and new agreements are made.

In schools in which performance talks are not yet routine, teachers will have to get used to this way of working on professional development. It might even meet with some resistance, but the potential benefits are worthwhile. Because of the systematic way of working, management obtains a better grip on - in this example - the implementation of the planned educational improvement (the new teaching method), as well as the professionalization of teachers. At the same time, the teacher receives hands-on support with regard to his own development, by means of training activities and informal learning. Moreover, by not automatically linking 'professionalization' to courses, but regarding a broad spectrum of learning activities, it is to be expected that the great number of opportunities for learning in the workplace will be used more deliberately (Tjepkema & Mulder, 1997). Therefore, though it might be difficult to change current practices, it might be worthwhile for schools to consider a more systematic approach to their teachers' professional development, borrowing from experiences and principles used in business and industry.

8.7 Summary

Most companies provide formal schooling activities to their employees. We refer to these activities as corporate training and development or Human Resource Development (HRD). A comprehensive definition of HRD activities is the following:

HRD activities are:
- facilities that fit within the general company policy,
- which aim to realize specific learning processes in employees,
- which, in turn, are intended to - directly or indirectly - enhance current performance,
  as well as the development,
  of both employees and the organization as a whole.

The spontaneous, unplanned learning which occurs every day (informal learning) is not part of HRD. However, companies increasingly try to facilitate and stimulate this informal learning also, by creating so-called 'learning facilities'. These facilities can be considered to be HRD activities because, though it is not planned in space or time, learning is deliberately stimulated and the learning content is influenced.

Important to emphasize is that the goal of HRD is to bring about performance improvement of individuals and the organization. HRD activities are always undertaken with the objective to foster the attainment of organizational objectives. Because of this strategic focus, corporate HRD is called a '*tool of management*'. HRD may also function as a '*tool of personal development*'. In this viewpoint development of the individual (and not of the organization) is the overriding aim of HRD. Most organizations strive for a good mix between these two approaches.

The nature of HRD activities can differ considerably. A widely used classification of HRD activities distinguishes between:

* training: directly focused on the present job;
* education: focused on a future job;
* development: general growth, not focused on any specific job.

It is common to distinguish between *on-the-job* and *off-the-job* HRD. On-the-job HRD activities are offered in the actual workplace, whereas off-the-job HRD takes place outside the workplace, e.g. in a separate classroom within the company, or in a hotel.

The processes of planning and executing HRD activities in companies, as well as the people involved in it, is referred to as the corporate HRD function. This function consists of four activities:

* Analysis of training need
* Design and development of HRD activities
* Execution of planned activities
* Evaluation

There is no one best way to organize the HRD function. The optimal structure depends on the organizational context in which it is embedded. This organizational context consists of two levels:

* the *macro environment* surrounding the company for which the HRD function works (all forces which affect the company, such as demographic, social, economical, ecological, technological, political and cultural forces);
* the specific *company* for which the HRD function provides training and development activities. Company characteristics which exert strong influence on the HRD function, are the trade or industrial sector, technology, size, structure, culture, strategy of the organization and work force characteristics.

The structure of the HRD function varies enormously across companies. Important aspects of HRD structure are:

- the position of the HRD function within the organization, or in other words: where on the organizational chart is the HRD function located?
- the organization of the HRD function: who is involved in HRD, and how are tasks divided among the persons involved?

The technology of the HRD function encompasses all knowledge, skills and techniques used to 'transform' employees with inadequate or insufficient sets of qualifications into employees with the required skills, knowledge and attitudes for satisfactory job fulfilment by means of HRD activities. The HRD technology encompasses the expertise of the HRD staff, training materials, and the methods used to transform input into output.

It is the task of the HRD manager to manage - to a certain extent - all HRD activities, foster the integration of HRD into the organization, and secure the alignment of HRD activities with the company's problems, developments and main processes. Just like all other management activities, HRD management comprises four categories of tasks on four different management levels:

- strategical HRD management: policy-making processes with regard to HRD;
- tactical HRD management: creating favourable conditions for effective implementation of HRD activities;
- operational HRD management of the HRD core processes, e.g. management and control of specific HRD activities;
- institutional HRD management: creating conditions for strategical, tactical and operational management tasks

Of the many developments and challenges HRD professionals face, the following ones can be considered as being the most influential:

- the trend towards a focused approach to training and development;
- the importance of workplace learning;
- the focus on performance (support);
- the increasing use of information technology.

Though the importance of determining effectiveness of HRD activities is widely recognized, systematic evaluation of HRD efforts is certainly not a widespread activity in organizations.

PART III

Towards Integration

• CHAPTER 9 •

Linking School Management Theory to
School Effectiveness Research

R.J. Bosker & A.J. Visscher
University of Twente, The Netherlands

9.1 Introduction

In the previous chapters theory development on the management of educational organizations and research into the factors promoting school effectiveness were presented. This chapter links both approaches by first summarizing and synthesizing the outcomes of the chapters on the organizational features of educational institutions (section 9.2); then analyzing and reflecting upon the characteristics of school effectiveness (9.3.1); and finally discussing the problems of studying school effectiveness (9.3.2). Empirical evidence on the impact of the organizational features of schools on schools' effectiveness is then presented (section 9.3.3). Then an attempt to synthesize the organizational theories with the school effectiveness approach is made (9.4), while the chapter concludes that in future research school management and school effectiveness research should be better integrated (9.5).

9.2 A summary of school organizational characteristics

9.2.1 The general picture

In chapter 1 the school is characterized as an organization with a small strategic apex and technostructure, a thin middle line and a well-developed support staff. The largest part of the school organization is the operating core, where the work is only supervised and coordinated by higher school organizational levels, to a small extent. Few organizational activities are directed at the standardization and planning of teachers' work - which is complex and requires it coming under the professional control of the teachers themselves. Certain school staff work in more than one part of the organization (e.g. the strategic apex and middle line) whereby double role problems may occur.

Next to school organizational structure and processes (i.e. primary, control, or informal), the organizational culture of schools proves to differ and matter. School culture for instance plays a role in fundamental innovations when, among others, a change in values and norms is required.

Research reported in chapter 2 shows that according to school staff schools have to cope with various organizational problems. Communication and consultation at school level and within the management team can be problematical and school policy-making is limited. A teacher's workload is increased (more tasks and responsibilities), there is low job satisfaction and little time to maintain proper standards. Teachers also operate relatively autonomously: there is hardly any policy-making and evaluation regarding their daily work and little communication with colleagues and school managers. In general, teachers are not very motivated with regard to educational innovation. Implementing innovation is also a problem because of a school's limited decision-making capacity. Finally, communication within and between departments and committees, as well as the coordination of their activities, proved to be poor.

Certain structural constraints are assumed to limit managers' control over teachers (and thus students):

- the delegation of decision-making (for example to enable teachers to solve problems at a decentralized level), and allowing subordinates to exert influence in areas that officially fall under administrator responsibilities;
- teachers' individual autonomy;
- the professional demands of teachers may conflict with the routine, administrative demands of their jobs;
- the limited possibilities for career rewards.

Chapters 3-7 (chapter 2 is addressed in 9.3.1) address five essential theoretical issues on school organization: the structuring of the primary process, coordination and control, teacher motivation, school leadership, and the alignment of schools with their environment.

9.2.2 Organizational theoretical features of the primary process

Chapter 3 addresses the question concerning the features of the primary process and the operations technology used in this process by applying organizational theoretical concepts. Implications for the management of the teaching-learning process at school level are also presented.

The chapter describes the operations technology: the know-how, skills and methods for analyzing and transforming organizational input (in casu students) into output (trained and educated students). A distinction is made between three types of operations technology: long linked, mediating and intensive.

Although schools differ regarding the features of their primary process and the operations technology used, mediating technology - sorting students into 'production lines' that are considered to match their nature and abilities and then using the relevant standard approach for that particular 'production line' - is considered dominant in most schools. Schools certainly possess certain characteristics of the long linked technology (e.g. sequence of grades, subject matter, school types), however, this technology type is not present there in its pure form. There is no precise, unequivocal sequence of organizational activities that needs to be followed precisely to educate students to the desired level. Besides, the planned sequence in subject matter taught is not detailed for quite a number of subjects. Under given circumstances teachers deviate from the official transformational sequence - for instance, as a result of personal preference or the fact that students do not master specific subject matter (so that subject matter needs to be repeated or presented for the first time). Students within a group are also taught different contents and the technological sequence is not always the same for all students.

In intensive technology cooperation between teachers and counselors is extensive and is aimed at providing each student with the type of education appropriate to his/her needs. The selection, combination and sequence of instruction is among others determined by feedback from individual students. In most schools this type of technology is not observed.

The level of operations technological uncertainty depends on the variation in input, desired output and required work processes. However, in service organizations like schools aimed at changing human behavior, the vision of school staff on the extent to which input varies is decisive in creating acknowledged uncertainty in the teaching-learning process. In case input variation is to be perceived, variation in the technological process is also limited (craft or routine work). Perrow (1970) speaks of non-routine work and engineering in case the needs of the raw material for the teaching process (in this case students) are regarded to vary much. Perrow crosses the input-stability dimension with the 'known/unknown how to deal with exceptions' dimension, leading to a distinction between craft and routine work on the one hand (respectively unknown, known how to handle in case of a few exceptions), and non-routine work and engineering (respectively unknown, known how to handle in case of many exceptions) on the other.

The instructional strategies in cases of input and/or output exceptions are not known with certainty. In other words, teaching may be labeled as a craft (if few exceptions are assumed) or as non-routine work (many exceptions) requiring personal intuition and judgement. Nevertheless, teachers and schools have a repertoire of strategies from which they choose when they are confronted with variation. These may be called 'tried and true' and add stability to teacher behavior. The strategies are not always 'undoubtedly the best actions for the situation' but more like 'that's how we always do this and we are happy with it'.

Schools can make their input and teaching processes more certain by:

- selecting and sorting the input (students) into production lines (curricular tracks, homogeneous groups) and applying standard treatments ('pigeonholing');
- recruiting skilled professionals who know how to deal with uncertain teaching-learning processes and therefore reduce the need for managerial coordination.

Following Thompson (1967) the technology of schools is characterized by the extent and nature of interdependence between school staff. Just like in other organizations, schools have a certain degree of interdependence because of resources that need to be shared among staff. However, this type of interdependence does not imply interdependence between staff concerning the content of their work.

Sequential interdependence definitely exists in education, though not in its pure form. The input for organizational activities varies due to differences in the motivation and abilities of students. Interdependence among staff is probably strongest within subject departments.

Intensive technology is characterized as work being pushed forward and backward between staff, and students' reaction to the content and way of presentation determines the follow-up activity. Thus, interdependence between staff is strong. However, this type of interdependence proves to be rare in schools, the exception being remedial teaching practices.

The third operations technological dimension discussed, concerning the technology of schools is its complexity. This is considered complex with respect to the number of different tasks teachers have to fulfill when teaching (logical, strategical and institutional). Regarding role specialization, the technology of schools was labeled simple in chapter 3: mainly teaching staff and just a few managers and support staff. If a country's education system is seen as a system producing 'products' (in casu trained and educated students), the number of locations at which one or more production activities is executed is large. A student can for example start in kindergarten, and then proceed to primary, secondary and tertiary education. As a result, the need for coordination between all these activities and locations is enormous which makes the technology complex from this point of view.

As far as the relationship between technological features and organizational control is concerned, technological uncertainty in schools implies there is little room for formalization (written rules and procedures) and centralization (top-down control) of the primary process.

Where there is little technological interdependence, coordination is limited because of professional autonomy. However, maybe more interdependence combined with more coordination may enhance school effectiveness.

More technological complexity makes more role specialization desirable. In education, however, there is little differentiation in teaching roles probably because of the unpredictability of the primary process, the concomitant professional autonomy and the fact that student feedback is relevant for determining follow-up teacher actions.

9.2.3 Coordination and control

Chapter 4 outlines the extent to which coordination and control within schools can be explained by three well-known models on organizational coordination.

Coordination is characterized as the organizational 'glue' holding together organizational activities and directing them towards organizational goals so that school staff can adapt compatible behavior and contribute to achieving these goals. From the bureaucratic perspective on coordination, organizations have a set of clear, top-down, shared and guiding goals enabling them to achieve objective coordination by hierarchical control, prescriptive formal rules of behavior, evaluation and, where necessary, by modification. Although schools are generally not characterized by much specialization, formalization and standardization, they do possess certain bureaucracy features.

Government legislation on teaching (e.g. content and monitoring the achievement of national educational goals) influences what happens in schools. It is uncertain whether this has a negative impact on the quality of education. As a result of decentralization initiatives, there are fewer rules, less bureaucracy and more organic features in other areas than instruction and curriculum.

Although the existence of many official rules can lead to apathy among school staff and little enthusiasm for innovation, rules are not negative in every respect. They can for instance lead to more certainty and teacher satisfaction and reduce internal conflicts, since the government can function as the scapegoat of the problems.

Loosely coupled systems theory (Weick, 1976), institutional theory (Meyer & Rowan, 1983), and the concept of schools as organized anarchies and garbage can school decision-making (Cohen, March & Olson, 1972) relativize the rational bureaucratic view of coordination in schools. According to Weick, the image of the school as a bureaucracy is not applicable, since schools do not have:

- a set of rules influencing teacher behavior;
- feedback on organizational behavior and, where necessary, modification;
- evaluation of subordinate performance;
- agreement on organizational goals.

In the view of the critics of Weick's loosely coupled systems theory, he underestimates the influence of the external government in his theory and overestimates the importance and number of conflicts among school staff. According to Meyer & Rowan, coordination is achieved through ideologies and traditions ('the logic of confidence' and 'good faith'), whereas Cohen et al. stress that decision-making in schools is not very rational. In the opinion of the latter, staff contribute their own problems and goals towards school policy-making, and after a long discussion period decisions are taken that neither hurt anybody nor solve something.

The professional autonomy teachers have in their work is important to the professional bureaucratic perspective on organizational coordination (Mintzberg, 1979). In this organizational configuration teachers are not controlled so much by their managers but by their professional skills. Nevertheless, one may question the professionalism of teachers (how solid is their body of knowledge, for instance, in making instruction more suited to the needs of individual students?). According to critics of the professional bureaucracy perspective, school leaders have more power than they actually use, and can control teachers more than they usually do.

There proves to be some empirical evidence for each of the three different perspectives of school organizational coordination (bureaucracy, loosely coupled systems/institutional theory/garbage-can decision-making, professional bureaucracy). Each theory's validity depends on the individual school domain. Moreover, coordination differences exist between settings (e.g. countries, school types) and within settings (schools differ).

9.2.4 Teacher motivation and commitment

Teacher behavior in the classroom is especially influenced by pedagogical-didactical training and by their level of expertise in the subject being taught. In general teacher's professional existence is not easy at all. However, there appear to be vast differences between countries in the amount of teaching time per teacher per annum (e.g. almost twice as much in Switzerland as in Greece). Their workload is also influenced by non-teaching tasks: preparing lessons, correcting work, meetings, in-service training, parental visits, etcetera.

Teachers' salaries may be regarded as an indicator of the status of teaching and these differ considerably between countries (e.g. in Norway the average teacher salary is below the national average, whereas in Switzerland it is far above it).

The motivation of teaching staff concerns the extent to which they are willing to invest in reaching a certain goal. A distinction can be made between intrinsic motivation (the true pleasure in teaching) and extrinsic motivation (monetary or other rewards) of teaching staff.

The effort of staff towards the organization in terms of loyalty and agreeing certain objectives is called commitment. Various commitment theories (Kanter, 1968; Etzioni, 1975; Porter & Miles, 1974) stress different aspects: commitment as a personal characteristic, as an individual-organization relationship, or as an organizational feature. An interesting question is to what extent teachers are committed to their subjects, students and to their school.

A distinction is also made between primary and secondary demands on teachers. Primary factors have a direct effect on the teacher in the classroom and may result in negative emotions (e.g. lack of resources, increase in student violence). The declining status of the teaching profession, the increase in non-teaching tasks, and the limited career mobility are examples of secondary, more indirect factors that may diminish teacher motivation and commitment. Job satisfaction proves to be the most important factor for teachers, making effort.

Improving the commitment of teachers is constrained by:
• tension between professional loyalty (e.g. a widely-used teaching method for a certain subject) and bureaucratic loyalty (the demands made by the school);
• limited financial possibilities for rewarding good teachers.

Because of the high workload of teachers a plea is made for a more professional school organization providing teachers with better support, improved working conditions and more task differentiation (teachers specializing in what they do best) to increase teacher mobility. In general, human resources management should be strengthened in schools.

9.2.5 School leadership

What are the responsibilities and characteristics of school leaders, and is there a relationship between the situation they work in and their leadership style? Are there also substitutes for leadership and variants of educational leadership? These questions are answered in chapter 6 of this book.

Leadership can occur anywhere in the school, not just in the way the school leader behaves. It may be directed towards the content of education as well as towards school organizational strategy and results. 'Management' is of a somewhat different nature in that it concerns actions regarding the structure of the organization, the administration of technical matters, financial control and school buildings.

A school leader has various responsibilities:
• public (promoting the interests of the school externally);
• a pedagogical one (promoting school standards);
• an administrative one (managing school resources).

For these responsibilities school leaders have to collaborate with external authorities, teachers and other school staff.

According to leadership style theories, effective leaders are equally oriented towards school staff as towards the production tasks schools have to fulfil. The degree to which school leaders care for their staff and for the school's obligations determines their characteristics: an encouraging leader, or a routine leader; an authoritarian leader or a group leader.

Situational theories on the relationship between the specific working situation of leaders and their style of working claim that if one of the two is fixed the other should be adjusted, is redundant or supplementary.

In the case of substitutes for leadership, leadership itself is redundant. One can for instance think of substitutes for the person (e.g. professional staff who know how to operate), for tasks (e.g. routine tasks or motivating tasks resulting in desired actions), or for the organization (formalization of work, collaborative work units).

Educational leadership is not always the same everywhere, it can vary according to the level of intensity of school leaders' involvement in the educational domain: from formulating proposals, to planning activities, plus coordinating, supervising, evaluating, deciding.

9.2.6 Aligning the school organization with its environment

In chapter 7 the role and importance of the school environment is explained. Various types of school environments, and factors influencing school environmental uncertainty are also identified. Finally, strategies for aligning the school with its environment are described.

The school environment is changing in demographic, political, economic, social-cultural, technological, and vocational terms, which implies both threats and opportunities for schools.

A distinction is made between a school's internal environment (the school structure and staff), the task environment (environmental elements critical to the school's organizational functions e.g. parents, students, competitors, legislative bodies) and the macro-environment (forces influencing schools which are beyond their control: e.g. political, technological and economical).

The extent of environmental uncertainty depends on the resources schools can use, and on the environmental stability, complexity and structuredness.

Strategies for aligning the organization with its environment include:

- environment directed strategies: the environment playing a central role which implies that schools are not very active but adapt to their environment;
- management directed strategies: schools have an influence and redefine their specific

external environment to realize their own goals, e.g. via mergers, networking, cooptation;

- organization and environment directed strategies: an attempt is made to achieve a dynamic equilibrium between the organization and external stakeholders by the school interacting with the environment.

9.2.7 HRD in a corporate setting

Chapter 8 addresses human resource development (HRD) in corporations because knowledge and experience gained here can inspire HRD in schools.

First of all, the HRD concept and its objectives are explained. Then, the various positions and ways of organizing the HRD function are described and what could be the best organizational structure for the HRD function. Finally, the problem of measuring the impact of HRD is explored.

HRD is about planning and executing corporate training and development to enhance current performance of both employee and organization. In other words, HRD is a management tool and a tool of personal development.

HRD functions vary enormously with respect to their position within the organization and the way they are organized. There proves to be no best way of organizing the HRD function since the organizational context (the macro environment and the specific environment) is decisive for what organizational structure works best.

Although the importance of determining HRD effectiveness in terms of improved employee and company performance is recognized, systematic evaluation of the impact of HRD activities proves to be difficult (how certain can a change be attributed to HRD?) and rare.

9.2.8 An overall summary of the school organization chapters

The summaries of the theoretical chapters on school organization (9.2.1 to 9.2.6) reveal a picture of schools in which the autonomous activities of teachers in the operating core are dominant. The work of teachers is complex, fairly unpredictable - thereby difficult to formalize - and its planning, optimization, supervision and management by other school staff is restricted.

The professional isolation of teachers is related to certain school organizational problems. In schools there is insufficient:

- policy-making and evaluation concerning primary process activities;
- communication and consultation between school staff;
- organizational coordination and innovation.

In general, teachers' workload is high and their job satisfaction low.

Controlling teachers is constrained by the fact that the nature of teaching requires the delegation of decision-making to them, and by the limited financial possibilities for rewarding good teachers. Influencing the motivation and commitment of teachers requires a compromise between teachers' professional loyalty (loyalty towards the subject they teach) and their bureaucratic loyalty (towards the school). Moreover, schools must develop in the direction of modern labor organizations, with more possibilities for supporting teachers, task differentiation, and employee mobility - thus with more scope for managing their human resources. In this respect schools can take advantage from experience gained in business organizations with respect to improving personal development and job performance of employees.

At school level instruction in most schools is characterized by 'pigeonholing': determining a more or less standard 'production line' appropriate to the nature and abilities of students. The disruption of the planned teaching process and variation among students with respect to the course of their learning processes are too great to resemble a pure long-linked technology.

The uncertainty teachers have to deal with in regard to the instruction process depends to a certain extent on the perceived variation in input, output and concomitant throughput-variation. Depending on the extent of perceived variation they can follow a more routine or more non-routine and individualized teaching approach.

Although a teacher is dependent on colleagues concerning school resources and the sequence of instructional activities, compared to other organizations this dependence is relatively weak. However, this does not imply that more interdependence and coordination of teachers' activities would be undesirable.

Coordination of school activities can be achieved in various ways:

- government legislation on the 'what and how' of teaching (traditional bureaucratic coordination);
- 'the logic of confidence' and 'good faith' as far as teachers' performance is concerned;
- professional skills acquired during teacher training.

To what extent each of the above suggestions plays a role varies across countries (e.g. centralized or decentralized educational systems), school types, specific areas of coordination (e.g. instruction, finance) etcetera.

Different school contexts require different actions from school leaders. The latter vary in the extent to which they try to influence instruction, general school organizational policy, and the outcomes of schools. Some leaders direct their attentions namely to the functioning of their staff, others focus more on production processes. The existence of leadership substitutes (e.g. routine tasks, formalization and cooperation, professional skills) makes explicit leader actions redundant, to a certain extent.

School environments vary with respect to stability, complexity, structuredness and resources. Whereas schools used to be quite internally focused, nowadays a more active approach towards their environment has become more important since it poses both threats and opportunities. For example, in maintaining student enrollment levels, adapting the curriculum to changing demands, starting new school divisions and meeting the needs of various stakeholders (e.g. parents and employers). Schools can respond to this new situation in various ways: adapt, redefine the environment, or interact with it and try to find an equilibrium between the two.

9.3 Towards a link between educational management theory and school effectiveness research

First of all, the key features of the school effectiveness perspective are analyzed and discussed (9.3.1). Thereafter, some problems of studying school effectiveness are explained (9.3.2), while what is known about the impact of school organizational characteristics on the results of schools is explored in 9.3.3.

9.3.1 The characteristics of the school effectiveness perspective

Chapter 2 presents an overview of organizational-theoretical perspectives on school effectiveness and corresponding effectiveness criteria. The economic productivity view on effectiveness is favored (i.e. the quantity and quality of the primary process output). Other school effectiveness criteria such as adaptability to the environment, acquiring resources, staff satisfaction and motivation, consensus and continuity are considered to be means for the ultimate goal of productivity.

Next, an integrated school effectiveness model is presented, portraying the possible relationships between context-, input-, process-features and student achievement. An important distinction in Scheerens' model is the difference between school-level variables and classroom-level variables. The school organization is supposed to facilitate the process of instruction which in its turn facilitates student learning.

Cheng (1993) also addresses the question as to when a school is effective. He defines school effectiveness as "the extent to which a school can adapt to the internal and external constraints and achieve the multiple goals of its multiple constituencies in the long run" (Cheng, 1993, p. 17). His definition combines the following seven perspectives on school effectiveness:

- goal-model - achieving the stated goals;
- system-resource model - acquiring the necessary resources (e.g. student intake, financial and other resources);
- internal-process model - realizing a smooth and healthy schooling process;
- strategic-constituencies model - satisfying all strategic constituencies at least minimally;
- legitimacy model - surviving in a competitive environment by engaging in legitimate and/or marketing activities;
- organizational learning model - being capable of dealing with external and internal changes and barriers;
- ineffective model - a school is effective if it has no ineffective features.

According to Cheng, each of these models has its strengths and weaknesses and in different situations and time frames different models may be useful.

When these seven school effectiveness approaches are compared with the effectiveness criteria Scheerens mentions in chapter 2 there is a strong resemblance between the two. However, it also raises some interesting questions which put the regular school effectiveness approach into a clearer perspective.

Cheng's goal model is strongly related to the economic rationality model and the concomitant criterion of economic productivity. In the school effectiveness approach a school is supposed to be effective if it realizes its goals, particularly when evaluated by measuring the added value accomplished in the primary process.

An interesting question is the extent to which schools really have goals and, if they do, whether these comprise a clear, generally accepted and measurable set of goals. Moreover, to what extent do the activities in a school's primary process reflect a conscious attempt to achieve the school goals? In many countries the government defines core goals for each type of education. To what extent do teachers in various school grades work on these goals? The written goals (mission statements) of most schools are abstract statements that can neither serve as a guideline for teaching activities nor for evaluating a school's effectiveness.

Cheng points to the existence of multiple constituencies and goals. Between teachers of different secondary school subject departments and also perhaps within departments themselves the views on which goals to strive after (most) may vary considerably. It may even be that schools (partially) possess the features of Cheng's ineffectiveness model in which consensus on effectiveness criteria is lacking.

Other constituencies like parents, the school leader, the Ministry of Education, the public or industry also have a stake. To what extent their goals converge is unknown. It would be interesting to investigate which goals various members of school staff strive after and to what extent these goals are in line with the achievement tests used in school effectiveness research and with what parents, the Ministry, the general public and industry consider to be most valuable.

If the content of national examinations (e.g. in secondary education) and other national tests (e.g. in primary education) are considered to be an operationalization of the goals as defined by central bodies, these tests probably only partially cover the goals teachers work towards (especially via teaching activities in the upper grades). It is questionable how fair it is to judge schools on matters that may only partially reflect their goals and to neglect other goals they work on intensively. School effectiveness research focuses on the basic learning function of schooling. More specifically, it focuses on a restricted set of instrumental basic skills in mostly arithmetic and language. These basic skills concern the larger part of the curricular objectives in primary education, but only make up a small portion of what is taught in secondary education.

Neither normative educational objectives like citizenship, a democratic orientation and the like, nor higher-order instrumental skills subsumed under the concept of meta-cognition (e.g. learning to learn, problem solving, reflection on learning, independent learning, social learning) are included in what might be considered to be standard school effectiveness research studies. Not the study of general aptitude measures is the goal, rather to address the topic of meta-cognition within the context of specific subjects. In this respect, the school effectiveness approach may be labelled as narrow in focus. However, some examples exist of studies that have included affective measures in school effectiveness studies, such as student well-being in school, self-confidence, attitudes towards the subjects taught, motivation etcetera (see, for example, Knuver, 1993; Hill & Rowe, 1996; Grisay, 1997). The general pattern, however, is that schools do not matter much for these affective outcomes, in casu: schools hardly differ with respect to these variables. This may be the reason so little is published on this topic in scientific journals.

The second exception to this rule can be found in studies that include 'authentic' tests (e.g. Rowe & Hill, 1996). Hill and Rowe (1996), for instance, have used teacher ratings of student performance, which were based on considering various indicators (observations, test-scores, written materials, etcetera). Using such measures it appeared that schools differ widely. In line with this approach, school effectiveness studies that use results of examinations (that mostly go beyond simple knowledge reproduction) also have more curricular validity.

Next to the academic learning of students (their mastering of academic curricular objectives), the core tasks of schools are also considered to be selecting students according to their abilities and allocating them to further education and the labor market. However, since it is much more difficult to evaluate the last two tasks than the first, school performance with respect to selection and allocation is usually not evaluated in school effectiveness studies.

There are understandable reasons for the limited scope of school effectiveness studies. First of all, it is relatively easy to access data on student and school performance because they are collected for other purposes anyway. Besides, since these data are often available for all schools in a country, schools can be compared with respect to their performance on that basis. Lastly, the basic skills concern important outcomes especially in primary education.

However, the fact that something is important and easy measurable does not imply that no attention needs to be paid to the other important outcomes mentioned. An important area for example may be the lasting effects of primary schools on secondary schools (see for instance Goldstein & Sammons, 1997), or the functioning of students in further education and on the labor market when studying quality differences between secondary schools.

What else does a comparison between Cheng's definition of school effectiveness and the traditional productivity-oriented definition reveal? In addition to the goal model, Cheng presents other models that are strongly related to Scheerens' effectiveness criteria: the system-resource model (Scheerens' resources criterion), the legitimacy model (continuity), and the organizational learning model (partly the criterion of adaptability). Scheerens' staff satisfaction/motivation and consensus criteria most probably belong to the internal process model that stresses the value of healthy and smooth-running school processes. This model also includes such aspects of school organizational life as leadership, communication, participation and coordination as well as features of the primary process as teaching methods used and classroom management.

Cheng also refers to another aspect of the organizational learning model whereby schools can improve their performance through using school processes such as internal process monitoring, program evaluation and developmental planning. This part of the organizational learning model is in line with Scheerens' school level factor 'evaluative potential'.

All effectiveness criteria that are not directly related to productivity are regarded by Scheerens as preconditions for the productivity goal. In our view they therefore deserve to be included in studies of school effectiveness; the assumed relationships should be studied empirically. Are schools that are more capable of adapting to relevant environmental changes, are more successful in acquiring resources, have more continuity and staff consensus, and better motivated staff, indeed better producers of the primary output?

In his integrated model Scheerens has included those factors he considers most promising for influencing the primary process and the output of schools. A comparison of the integrated model with the contents of this book shows that the model contains aspects of school organizational features that are considered to determine school functioning in school organizational science literature. Of the topics treated in this book, the following are virtually missing: school organizational structuring of the primary process, various modes of coordination and control, the extent of teacher motivation and commitment, ways of aligning the school with its environment and strategies for human resource management within schools. It seems worthwhile to include these organizational aspects of school functioning in school effectiveness research more, and to determine their relationship with the primary process and the outcomes of schooling. Is there, for example, a difference between effective and non-effective schools in how they structure the instruction process across grades, and how they coordinate and control school processes, align with the environment and manage their human resources?

Quinn (1988) also distinguishes between a number of perspectives on organizations. Like Scheerens and Cheng, he mentions the rational goal model in which productivity, organizational results and profits are central. In the human relations model the cooperation, involvement and morale of staff are key elements whereas innovation, growth and the acquisition of resources characterize the open systems model. Quinn's last model concerns the internal process model, which is characterized by the measurement and control of the internal process and by continuity.

According to Quinn, one of these models is always dominant in any given situation, depending on the development phase the organization is in and the features of its environment (stable-dynamic; simple-complex). It is important to note that in Quinn's view multiple perspectives on organizational effectiveness criteria can co-exist. In other words, in contrast with what is often assumed, he claims that there is no contradiction between the four models.

Reflecting on the nature of the Quinn models leads to the following observations. In the goal model, 'profit' is one of the core concepts whereas in school effectiveness research school productivity is typically defined as the average value added by schools. One may conclude that what is actually being followed in this type of research is a truncated economic approach since the value schools add to their organizational input is computed without paying attention to the production costs involved, including physical (e.g. buildings, teaching material) and human resources (e.g. labor time, staff burn-out). Are effective schools, for instance, also rich and attractive work environments for staff, or is teacher burn-out in those institutions above average? The economic perspective would be purer in school effectiveness studies if these were able to clarify the costs of being effective. This economic line of research on the functioning of schools is known as the quest for the education productivity function (e.g. Hanushek, 1994; Monk, 1992; Wenglinsky, 1997). Probably the combination of the economic and the school effectiveness research traditions can be fruitful in studying schools in education systems that have private next to public education, or in which educational investments are related to the amount of local taxes collected (such as in the United States of America). Resources in that case are equally available to schools, and it would be interesting to find out how these are used in terms of optimizing school and classroom process features.

In the open systems model, organizational growth and innovation are considered important for organizational survival in a competitive environment. Like corporations, schools may become less vulnerable and more viable by increasing their size, and by realizing economies of scale. This is likely to be especially true for schools with opportunities for entrepreneurial activities that can benefit from undertaking new activities.

If the rational model is chosen as the most important model, an interesting question is which organizational arrangement in terms of the human relations model, the internal process model and the open systems model, is best suited to accomplishing high productivity. Put differently, what combination of elements creates the best mix? Moreover, what are the (undesired) side effects of this best mix?

Quinn's statement that the four different perspectives can co-exist raises the question why school effectiveness is not looked at more comprehensively by considering that schools are effective to the extent that they are:

- productive (also taking into account production costs) with respect to basic and higher order skills and normative qualifications;
- sound from a human relations point of view;
- innovative and adapt to their environment?

If a choice has to be made between the Quinn models and traditional effectiveness criteria, the productivity perspective should receive priority. However, it is certainly not the only thing that matters and that needs to be studied in research on schools. The explanatory power of the other models is rarely considered in school effectiveness research. At the same time little research in educational management relates organizational arrangements to school effects in terms of added value. Current educational management theory presented in the foregoing chapters can serve as a good starting point for integrating both approaches and gaining more insight into how school organizational features influence what happens in classrooms, and the outcomes schools produce.

The conclusion of this section may be that the school effectiveness productivity approach is important but narrow. The instruments used only partly reflect the goals of school staff and other stakeholders. A better coverage of the goals schools pursue, and are expected to pursue, is desirable. In addition to the productivity criterion, other criteria considered to be means for accomplishing productivity need to be given greater attention. This will increase our insight into how organizational aspects of schools influence their primary process and results. It also will provide the basis for a more comprehensive concept of school effectiveness, for instance, by including production costs, job satisfaction and adaptation as evaluation criteria. Given the priority of the productivity criterion one can view these as subordinate criteria for which, however, optimalization should be sought under the constraint of maintaining and enhancing productivity. Another point concerns the causal ordering of the various criteria. The ordering suggested in chapter 2 of this book ('resources' as exogenous, 'adaptability' and 'teacher commitment' as intermediate, and 'productivity' as the criterion with of course a reciprocal relation with teacher commitment) should be put to an empirical test. The mix of school organizational conditions that enhance focal instruction and learning processes also requires further study.

9.3.2 Persisting problems in school effectiveness research

Having described the main characteristics of the school effectiveness approach, certain problems of studying school effectiveness are discussed.

First, we need to address the question of defining a school effect. Since the main subject of study of this book concerns the school as an organization, the question of which school organizational arrangements are more effective than others is crucial. If the ultimate criterion lies in student achievement, then the true effect of an organizational arrangement lies in increased student achievement. By the latter is meant, what progress have students made in achievement, and have students in school organizational setting A achieved more than students in organizational setting B? Operationally, learning gains can be assessed by students taking a pre-test at school entrance and a post-test at certification. However, that is not very practical since, for example, if achievement in the mastery of Greek is studied, virtually no student has any mastery of that language at school entrance. Therefore, it has been tried to isolate powerful predictors of student learning, like students' socioeconomic status, aptitude, perseverance, motivation, mastery of the native language etcetera. On the basis of these variables measured 'at say' the age of 12, students' mastery of the Greek language, at say, the age of 16 is predicted. Thus, we are interested in the following function:

achievement = f (IQ, SES, previous achievement, motivation)

For any given student his actual achievement level is determined and his expected achievement level derived from the function. To give a simple example: if two students from two different schools have the same achievement level, however, the first student has a below average IQ and the second an average IQ, then the first student achieves above expectation, whereas the second student performs below expectation. To put it somewhat differently: the first is an 'overachieving', the second an 'underachieving' student. Now, suppose two schools are studied, one having many overachieving and the second many underachieving students. The inference can be made that the first school is more effective than the second. Why is it then necessary to take the extent of overachievement and not simply achievement as a dependent variable? This is the case because some schools attract the more privileged and/or brighter students while others attract the more underprivileged and/or less bright students. We want to correct for these 'input' differences while assessing 'output' differences. Generally, this is called the 'value-added' approach, by which we literally mean: the gain in achievement caused by the school (output minus input). However, in practice this concept is used to indicate the extent of overachievement "caused" by the school.

If schools A and B are exactly alike, except for one organizational variable (i.e. team consensus), and school A is more effective than school B in that it has a higher overachievement, there is a case for arguing that team consensus is related to school effectiveness. Of course this inference can only be made if the sample of schools is large enough (more than two schools). The problem is that very little school effectiveness research is carried out in accordance with the described value added approach.

A second feature of school effectiveness models is that they are based on empirical research. This normally is considered their strength, however it can also be considered to be a serious drawback, since usually the criterion variable is not a fail/pass variable (let alone that cost considerations are mostly out of scope), but a continuous variable (the extent of value added to student achievement) on which no standard has been defined. In this approach the underlying hypothesis might be phrased as: "If school leaders demonstrate more educational leadership student achievement levels will rise". However, what if all school leaders actually demonstrate a sufficient level of educational leadership, and the effect of this variable on student achievement levels shows a pattern that might be described as a diminishing rate of return? By the latter is meant that achievement levels will hardly rise at the upper ends of the educational leadership scale. If this pattern occurs for most school organizational variables, then there is less need to be concerned with failures to reject null hypotheses (there is no relation) in empirical research. Most of the suggestions for school improvement (i.e. aimed at raising achievement levels) derived from organizational theory may then hardly be verifiable, although they are true at face value. It may be this dilemma that is faced when trying to combine educational management theories with the school effectiveness paradigm. Let us therefore closely examine the diminishing rate of return pattern (see Figure 9.1).

Figure 9.1 describes the relationship between the two variables as follows: an increase in leadership at the lower levels of this scale leads to an increase in (value added to) student achievement. However, at the upper end of the leadership scale hardly any achievement gain is made (something like 10% of the gain that would be observed at the lower parts of the scales).

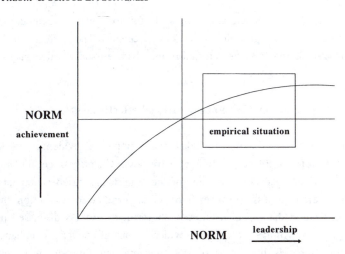

Figure 9.1: *A hypothetical relationship between educational leadership and student achievement*

The theory is expressed by the curvilinear line. The empirical situation is also described in Figure 9.1. All students achieve at the upper end of the imaginary achievement distribution and all school leaders behave at the upper end of the imaginary distribution for educational leadership as well. Stated differently, in the empirical situation we are in an area where, for both variables at the upper tail of the distribution, theory predicts only a very small effect. Moreover, although some students achieve below the standard, no school leader behaves in such a way that from a normative viewpoint this educational leadership would be evaluated as insufficient. The situation described is known in research methodology as 'restriction of range' which is caused by the fact that observational studies instead of experimental studies are carried out. The implication is that the variation encountered in educational practice is the basis, instead of the manipulation of variables in experimental settings. The aforementioned phenomenon was indeed observed in a study on the quality of instruction (cf. Lam, 1996) where 95% of the teachers had a more than sufficient level of classroom management and instructional skills. One therefore may wish to look at standards for particular organizational variables of interest, such as the differences that occur between below standard and theoretically very good organizational arrangements.

Another important problem in establishing the relations of interest empirically is that the link between school organizational variables and the value added to student achievement is rather loose since this link runs via the teacher. However, the quality of instruction depends on many other characteristics as well: for example on available text books, teacher training, student grouping practices etcetera. The effect of the school organizational variable that may be detected in the observed added value may then be very weak.

9.3.3 Empirical evidence on school organizational effectiveness

Chapters three to seven do not include much empirical evidence on how school organizational features influence school effectiveness. Chapter three (dealing with the primary process of schools) contains most of the empirically based statements on factors related to school effectiveness. However, most of these relate to instruction characteristics instead of organization theoretical features of the primary process discussed in chapter 3. The reason for the limited empirical evidence on effectiveness enhancing school organizational features is that most of the concepts and theories dealt with in these chapters have not been studied empirically from the school effectiveness perspective - that is by including value-added based student achievement measures and determining whether effective schools have organizational characteristics in line with the contents of those chapters.

In general, the chapters on school organization contain valuable information on the role, importance and alternative ways of:

- organizing the primary process at school level;
- school organizational coordination;
- school leadership;
- promoting teacher commitment;
- adapting the school to the environment.

There is a need for studies that among others clarify whether:

- primary process arrangements at school level make a difference to primary process output;
- increasing school organizational coordination improves school effectiveness;
- higher levels of teacher motivation and commitment influence higher levels of student achievement;
- different types of school leadership have different impacts on the output of schools;
- specific strategies for adapting to the school environment are preferable because of their impact on school effects.

Although this knowledge is lacking, some empirical evidence on school effectiveness enhancing variables is available. This was summarized by Witziers & Bosker (in Scheerens & Bosker, 1997), who carried out a statistical meta-analysis on studies that reported effects for one or more of six school-level factors (see Table 9.1).

Table 9.1   *Results of a meta-analysis on presumed effectiveness enhancing school organizational factors (effect sizes are correlations)*

School organizational factor	Effect size
Achievement pressure for basic subjects	0.14
Educational leadership	0.05
Monitoring/Evaluation	0.15
Cooperation/Consensus	0.03
Parental involvement	0.13
Orderly climate	0.11

The factors in Table 9.1 are very similar to the school-level factors included in the Scheerens model (Chapter 2, figure 2.3). However, there are certain differences. One of the presumed effectiveness enhancing school-level factors in Scheerens' model - the quality of school curricula in terms of content covered and formal structure - has not been included in the meta-analysis, whereas parental involvement has been included, although it is not considered a school-level factor but an input variable in the Scheerens model.

The six factors mentioned all have a significant but modest relationship with student achievement. Nevertheless, for four variables (achievement pressure, monitoring/evaluation, parental involvement, and orderly climate) effects are found that are more than trivial. Two variables, however, that are expected to relate to student achievement in the Scheerens model show hardly any effect: educational leadership, and consensus and cooperation. The situation is even more complex: in the meta-analyses a distinction was made between various kinds of situations that characterize the studies included in the meta-analysis. Achievement pressure for basic subjects only appears to have a non-trivial effect in studies conducted in the United States. Moreover, the effect of an orderly climate appears to be very small, also in sophisticatedly designed studies using value added measures of student achievement. The educational leadership effect is also only positive in primary schools studies conducted outside the Netherlands. Thus, only the monitoring and evaluation effect is consistently high. Given the meager empirical evidence for the school-level factors Scheerens distinguishes, must one conclude that organization and management in schools is not important at all? This position is rejected for a number of reasons, which relate to the complexity of the phenomenon under study and the research methodology applied when studying school organization and management.

The first problem concerns coordination. In education, this is already achieved externally to a high degree, namely through teacher training and national examination standards. Nevertheless, achievement pressure, which can also be seen as an indicator of internal school coordination by standardization of outputs, still has a strong effect on attainment. Since there is more than one way to achieve coordination, this might also explain why consensus and cooperation (indicators of coordination by mutual adjustment) and, educational leadership (an indicator of coordination by direct supervision) have such weak effects. Why coordinate in these ways what is already being coordinated in other ways? Instead, it might be argued that since coordination is largely achieved by teacher training, a loose coordination mechanism (pressure for achievement) combined with a control mechanism (monitoring and evaluation) might be sufficient.

Related to this problem is another problem that might explain the small effects of educational leadership on student achievement. In addition to objections that can be made to the way educational leadership is often measured, namely by reports written by the principals themselves instead of by their teachers, the concept of leadership can often be characterized as being naive. Although theory stresses the fact that leadership may be exercised by several school staff and in various ways (see Chapter 6), it is usually only operationalized as a principal trait. Another conceptual problem relates to the conceptualization of focal relationships. Usually, direct relationships between school organizational variables and student performance are studied. The underlying implicit causal model being that school organization features are related to the way teachers function and that teachers affect student learning. It may be more fruitful to research empirically this causal chain that is later referred to as the indirect effects model.

A final problem with management theories is that many of them are based on the contingency perspective (Lawrence & Lorsh, 1969). This perspective is formulated by Mintzberg (1979) in his well-known extended configuration hypothesis: an organization is effective if its organizational parameters are internally consistent and fit the contingency factors as well. However, it is almost impossible to falsify this theory for various reasons:

1. Contingency theory is a theory on organizations in general, and not very specific on one particular organization (e.g. schools). This may explain why schools should be structured and managed in a different way than corporations, but it hardly tells us anything on how to improve the structure of educational organizations (it mainly points to aspects that may lead to ineffectiveness);

2. Since there are many organizational parameters and contingency factors to consider, it is not feasible to describe empirically a situation that should be effective because one or more organizational parameters or contingency factors that may be seen as causing the observed ineffectiveness are always missing in a study;

3. The theory may not so much be about observed direct relations, but about the future performance of school organizations that are structured and managed ideally. The central proposition of contingency theory is that "there is no one best way to organize". It is claimed that the best way depends on situational characteristics. This issue is mentioned again in the final section of this chapter when we look into 'total design'.

At this point contingency theory is simplified, and it is contended that its central elements comprise an interactive or a synergetic model. These relate to two of six models Bosker & Scheerens (in Scheerens & Bosker, 1997) originally formulated to distinguish various approaches to studying school organizational effects (for a further discussion and illustrations see Scheerens & Bosker, 1997).

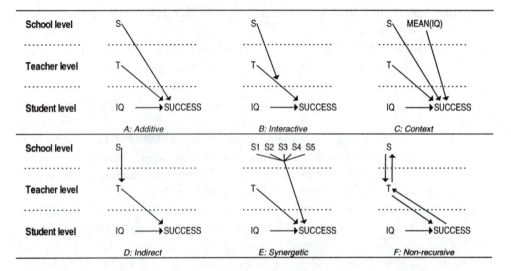

Figure 9.2:   *Alternative causal models of educational effectiveness (source: Scheerens & Bosker, 1997)*

The first model, the direct effect model, is rather simple, since it assumes that optimal organizational structures and management practices effect student learning over and above the effects of instruction and classroom management.

The second model, the interactive model, refines this idea since it states that some kind of consistency between teaching and the organizational structure of schools is necessary. For example, although it is known how important coordination is, it is impossible to say how it should be done always and under what circumstances. Organizations differ and it also depends on what aspect is being looked at when determining the most effective structure.

Some forms of consistency between school organization and teaching practices should be present, otherwise good instruction will not effect on student learning.

The third model can be seen as an alternative hypothesis: it presumes there may be automatic mechanisms that result in students in schools with an high socioeconomic intake making more progress because of peer group norms, mutual support, etcetera. The flipside of this is that organizational structure is not crucial in itself (unless the school makes a complete mess of it).

The fourth model states that the organization and management of schools affect teacher behavior and thus indirectly student learning.

The fifth model, the synergetic model, is basically in accordance with the previous model, though it is more complex since it requires internal consistency between the various organizational design parameters in order to effect student learning.

The final model (the reciprocal or non-recursive school effects model) is the most complicated one because it states that teachers adapt to organizational settings, and principals react to teacher behavior. This results in a two-way causation (schools influence teachers and teachers influence schools), whereby student learning may only be affected directly by what teachers do or do not do.

The fourth and sixth model require a different approach to studying educational effectiveness:

- Instead of demonstrating links between organizational variables and the value added to student achievement, first of all the link between these school organization variables and the behavior of teachers (which is supposed to be the intermediating link between organizational features and school effects) may be sorted out;

- In keeping with this it might as well be sorted out what the effects of organizational conditions are on the supportive, conditional effectiveness criteria (such as adaptability, teacher commitment, and safe guarding resources), since this may say something about indirect effects. In the latter case it may be worthwhile considering why some schools have increasing numbers of students enrolling, whereas the student intake decreases at others.

Next to the six models, a seventh may be formulated: the compensatory model of school effects. In this model an inadequate structuring of the school or poor school management may be compensated by extra teacher efforts. The latter implies that other effectiveness criteria may also be looked at since, if such compensation mechanisms exist, the organization is obviously not managed/structured efficiently (at what price are its students' achievement levels still maintained and when is teacher burn out caused?).

The models are presented here to stress the importance of a careful conceptualization of the relationship between school organizational features and student achievement. As the models show, this relationship may be far more complex than what might be called the null-model of direct effects. The models also point us to the importance of formulating different school organizational research questions, and the application of a different research methodology, on which will be elaborated more in section 9.5. First it is attempted to synthesize the organizational theories with the school effectiveness research tradition.

9.4 A synthesis

In an attempt to synthesize the various contributions to this book the school organizational perspective has to be reconciled with the school effectiveness approach. To do this, a distinction needs to be made between the daily, routine functioning of schools, and the periods in which changes have to be realized.

When looking at the integral school effectiveness model presented in the second chapter, the following school-level factors prove to be effectiveness enhancing:

• achievement oriented policy
• educational leadership
• consensus and cooperative planning among teachers
• quality of school curricula
• orderly atmosphere
• evaluation possibilities

All of these factors are supposed to be directly related to student achievement, which is not surprising since the first school effectiveness studies started the other way around. Instead of predicting student achievement from organizational variables, outlier schools (i.e. schools that did extremely well or extremely poor in terms of their average student achievement) were selected, and thereafter differences in the organization of positive and negative outlier schools were analyzed. In the next phase of school effectiveness research these school organizational factors were tested on their presumed predictive power with respect to (the value added to) student achievement. As has been shown already, some of these factors only appear to have a very modest relationship with student achievement.

If we turn to the organizational chapters of the book, in which the features of school organizations are analyzed, these school characteristics do not match the list of school effectiveness factors very well. On the other hand, empirical evidence that the organizational factors are potentially effectiveness enhancing is rather meager.

The difference between the list of school effectiveness enhancing factors and the features prominent in school organizational literature may be explained by a difference in focus. In the school effectiveness tradition the focus is on student achievement, whereas in school organizational literature the focus is on the smooth running of a school as an organization. Lee, Bryk and Smith (1993) propose to reconcile the two approaches by defining two separate sets of outcomes: teacher outcomes (satisfaction & efficacy and commitment & effort) and student outcomes (engagement and achievement) without linking these. Thus the underlying value position is that both types of outcomes are valuable and interesting in themselves, a position which has also been taken in previous sections of this book. In terms of this approach a school then is effective to the degree that it maximizes both student achievement and engagement as well as teacher satisfaction and commitment.

A different attempt to reconcile or even to synthesize both approaches is to argue that the school effectiveness perspective is valuable when keeping a school on the right track (i.e. optimizing the output of the primary process in a stable environment, every now and then making small adaptations to stay on course), whereas the school organization perspective is valuable when major curricular or organizational changes are needed. The adaptations necessary in a rather stable environment (e.g. because of changes in the curricular, student population, funding, etc.), however, also presuppose that the organization is functioning well with respect to leadership, alignment with the environment, staff qualifications, commitment, coordination etcetera.

We will briefly discuss four different situations:
1. effective schools in a stable environment
2. ineffective schools in a stable environment
3. effective schools in a dynamic environment
4. ineffective schools in a dynamic environment

In the first situation the school is operating in a rather stable environment and adds much value to student achievement. The organizational factors are primarily supportive. Leadership, coordination and control, and human resource development are shaped to support the primary process of schooling, thus reassuring the commitment of teachers and satisfying the needs of stakeholders (i.e. parents, students, employers, society at large). In this case the primary intention of the school organization is to buffer the primary processes of instruction and learning against external disturbances. Leadership and coordination function to bring about small changes within the organization, if necessary, supported by human resources development activities in order to maintain and improve the functioning of the teaching staff.

In the second situation the environment is (rather) stable, but the school is ineffective. In this case it does not help to try to bring about change in the school effectiveness model factors (achievement oriented policy, etc.) without first looking carefully into the organizational features of the school. Changing the effectiveness enhancing factors will at best lead to short-term improvements instead of lasting effects. The school as a whole might even 'collapse' under these efforts to increase its effectiveness, if not supported by molding school organizational conditions (e.g. the HRD-function, coordination mechanisms, etc.) properly.

In the third case the school is effective, but it has to cope with strong environmental turbulence (e.g. large scale curricular and organization innovations, or a sharp decline in student enrollment). Since this involves change, key organizational factors become vitally important. Without leadership, coordinated effort, commitment, a carefully chosen and implemented human resource development strategy, change processes are doomed to failure. Tight coupling is needed instead of loose in order to bring the school safely through the transition period.

In the last instance, the school is ineffective and operates in a turbulent environment that demands change. What has been claimed for the second situation (an ineffective school in a stable environment) holds a fortiori for this variant. In this case structural change (dismissal of certain teachers, coordinators or even the principal; a restructuring of the organization as a whole) is needed if improvements aimed at the productivity of the school are to be successful.

It is important to note that in all instances the educational effectiveness model points to effectiveness enhancing factors, implying that these are central to increasing the value a school can add to student achievement. The main proposition that emerges from the preceding paragraphs (yet to be proven empirically; for a first attempt see Bosker, 1990, and Bosker & Van der Velden, 1989a and b) is that, ceteris paribus, the set of organizational factors and school effectiveness enhancing factors together comprise the necessary (yet not sufficient, since in the end it depends on the quality of the primary processes) conditions for lasting educational excellence within schools. We will return to this in the final section, when discussing the idea of 'total design'.

9.5 Implications for future research

In this book various authors have looked at different ways of structuring and managing schools and the consequences of these on the way these institutions function. It appeared hard to demonstrate the link between school organizational characteristics and the output of schools in terms of the gain in student achievement. Although it has been shown that it is not easy to ground educational management theories empirically, this should not hinder us from doing this. What should be done in future research to increase our insight into the mechanisms that determine what happens in schools and what influences school effects? To answer this question issues that should have a high priority are indicated:

1. alternative (organizational) effectiveness criteria;
2. means-to-ends relationships;
3. applying the economic production approach to studies on school organizational effectiveness;
4. taking into account the fact that students are socialized in a variety of groups and institutions in the course of their life;
5. focusing more on educational leadership, coordination, teacher commitment, aligning the school to its environment, and the organizational structuring of the primary process;
6. improving schools by using an integrated organizational design approach.

While we have discussed the various approaches to school (organizational) effectiveness, we must conclude that, although the productivity viewpoint deserves priority over other criteria, alternative effectiveness criteria have their own legitimacy. As far as we are concerned this is obvious for educational objectives that are often not taken into account in school effectiveness research, like citizenship, employability, social skills, meta-cognitive skills, etcetera. Studying in how far schools succeed in attaining these goals is difficult, if only for the reason that it requires a study on how students function in further education, on the labor market, in society and in their private lives. This makes such a research endeavour however all the more challenging, and its results the more interesting. If, for example, such results are not in line with current research regarding school effectiveness with respect to student achievement in the basic subjects, this may lead to a re-evaluation of the school curriculum itself, or at least to a re-evaluation of how differences in standards between schools really matter (and what we mean by 'standards').

It has been said that with such effectiveness criteria as well-being, motivation, attitudes and beliefs of students, schools hardly differ, and that this may be why so little is published in this area. But we might recall again our plea to consider a standards framework: schools may not differ in this respect, but can it be acceptable that, say, 20 percent of students feel bored at school? Should we not persist in discovering organizational settings in which students are better stimulated?

The latter also applies to teachers' labor conditions, from which alternative effectiveness criteria are derived which are referred to as the healthiness of educational organizations. Schools also are labor organizations, and in this respect it is obvious to ask how they manage their human resources. Under what organizational conditions do teachers enjoy their work, how do schools succeed in continuously developing teachers' knowledge and competencies, and how do they secure the commitment of their teachers?

The last set of alternative effectiveness criteria that deserves further attention concerns the "open systems" point of view, by which is meant that schools continuously have to adapt to their environment to survive as an organization. This adaptation has to do with changing national standards, changes in the curriculum, but also with innovations regarding the organization of schooling (e.g. to encourage group or project work, self-regulated learning). This requires an organization to be able to as and when needed innovate, but also to encourage the teachers to implement innovation. This line of research has a longstanding tradition (cf. Fullan, 1991), but what would provide a new element would be to search for an association between school organizational structures and innovative behavior.

Another more urgent point on the research agenda should be the way schools safeguard the intake of sufficient numbers of students, or even how they manage to increase these numbers. Is it simply because other local schools lack sufficient quality, or is it because a school communicates well with its stakeholders (i.e. parents who are faced with a choice of schools)? Or, more importantly, what has enrollment got to do with the quality of the functioning of a school, especially the features of its primary process, and/or with its productivity? This issue deserves careful research, especially taking into account the way the school is portrayed in published "league tables". This latter point is added to explore the reverse relationship as well: not only do schools 'manipulate' their environment, a process that was referred to as strategic aligning, the environment actively may affect the functioning of the school as well. League tables, for instance, may be seen as a source consulted by parents in choosing a school for their child. If league tables are (proxy) indicators of the quality of the schools' organization and its primary process, then schools may be forced to adjust and to improve the latter if their position in the table is poor. Or conversely: if its position in the table is good this may be a force stimulating conservatism and reducing innovative behavior.

The latter leads to the second point necessary for providing more insight into the organizational functioning of schools. If the alternative effectiveness criteria are subordinate to the ultimate criterion of productivity, may it not be that these former have a means-to-end relationship with the output-related criterion? Do smooth-running organizations with proper resources indeed have a higher productivity, i.e. add more value to what students already know and are capable of when entering a school? If alternative organizational effectiveness criteria are only alternative because they are means and not ends in themselves, we might need to re-evaluate their status if they prove to enhance productivity. This question may be sorted out first before going into more detailed research on such 'loose' links as educational leadership and increased student achievement. This may be considered even less important than opening the black box, which leads us to propose a progressive research agenda which might include the following questions (as an example we take educational leadership). What is the relationship between educational leadership and the organizational health of a school and the way it adapts to its environment? What is the relationship between educational leadership and the quality of the primary process (i.e. teaching)? Is there a relationship between educational leadership and the influence schools have on student achievement levels?

It may be worthwhile to combine the economic approach to school productivity with the educational approach to effectiveness. This may be a quite straightforward connection: instead of looking into standard effectiveness criteria derived from student achievement, we might look into the returns of schooling (i.e. drop-out rates, percentage of students who gained formal qualifications etcetera; see Bosker, 1990 or Bosker & Hofman, 1994). Another simple link would be to find an expression of the relationship between organizational variables and the value added to student achievement which combines the well-known concept of effect size with monetary inputs, e.g. by dividing the non-standardized regression coefficient (that is the expression of such a relationship) by the increase in monetary inputs associated with attaining a change of one scalepoint in the organizational variable of interest (Cohn & Geske, 1990). A further specification may be to estimate the relationship between growth in enrollment figures (which implies growth in resources) and various (alternative) effectiveness criteria.

School effectiveness research usually simplifies what is actually taking place in education. By using the value-added concept it is suggested that schools influence their intake from the time students enter to when they leave. The truth is slightly different. There has been no study - as far as we know - that really assessed the impact of a school from start to finish on its students. The reason is that students change schools, drop-out, repeat grades, etcetera. Future school effectiveness research has to take this into account as well as the fact that they are also educated in other socializing groups (family, homework classes, etc.). Moreover, such a future study should take into account the fact that there may also be long-term effects of previous learning experiences in schools. Goldstein and Sammons (1996), for example, discovered that in England, primary school effects even showed up at the age of sixteen, i.e. the minimum secondary school leaving age.

This book focuses on such central school organizational concepts as educational leadership, coordination, teacher commitment, the structuring of the primary process and the link between school and environment. For each of these topics a number of questions remain unresolved. For school leaders, for instance, we need to elaborate more on the ideal balance between educational and administrative leadership. For teacher commitment we need to further our understanding of the nature of its relationship to increasing student achievement. Do highly committed teachers induce more learning gains, or is it the situation in reverse? Numerous examples of remaining research questions have already been mentioned regarding coordination and aligning the school to its environment. A

320

pressing question concerning the primary process is whether schools that create more interdependence, also increase their coordination efforts, and their general productivity in the long run.

Finally, the interactive, synergetic view on school organizations deserves further attention. It is far too simplistic to assume that if we want to improve early reading literacy for instance, educational leadership or another factor is the key to success. Instead, one needs to restructure the primary process, for example, by introducing Reading Recovery (a scheme in which pupils-at-risk have one-to-one reading tuition half an hour each day, for six consecutive weeks). As Slavin (1996) showed, the preconditions to make effects sustainable include the reorganization of classroom teaching. Thereafter, organizational conditions beyond classroom level come into the picture. These include, as Crévola & Hill (1997) state a changed set of beliefs and understandings of the team, cooperation, leadership and support for teachers dealing with the reading problems, and intervision. Without such organizational conditions the approach itself may never be lasting. However, without a focused restructuring of the primary process itself there may not be any effect at all. This approach concerns a combination of what has been called an interactive and a synergetic model of educational effectiveness. For school organizational research the challenge is to demonstrate empirically that without sufficient school organizational support even a rigorous redesigning of the primary process may fail to be sustainable. It might well be that monocausal theories serve as a source of inspiration for design activities. However, in the end it is the 'total design' (and not the sum of the partial theories) that 'does the trick'.

9.6 Summary

This chapter began by summarizing the main issues of the preceding chapters on organizing educational institutions (9.2.8). The characteristics of the traditional school effectiveness perspective were then analyzed and discussed, and a plea made to expand that approach with theoretical elements on organization. Next, some crucial problems of researching school effectiveness were explained (9.3.2). This was followed by empirical evidence on the relationship between school organizational features and the output of schools and explained by clarifying the nature of the phenomenon under study and the research methodology used (9.3.3). In 9.4 the school organization and the school effectiveness perspective are synthesized. The chapter ends by defining a research agenda to increase our insight into the mechanisms that determine what happens in schools and their effects. Proposals for future research include:

* paying attention to alternative effectiveness criteria;

- starting research that increases our insight into the way schools are organized;
- connecting the link between the economic productivity approach of schools and educational effectiveness;
- a more precise study of the impact of schooling on students;
- using concepts in educational effectiveness research that are based in (school) organizational theory;
- testing the interactive, synergetic model of school effectiveness.

This book stresses the importance of studying school organizational variables. It concludes that one has to be extremely precise for every organizational feature in determining which ones are likely to affect student performance directly or indirectly, and how this influence takes place. Next to this a design approach to school organizations is advocated, in which the primary process is designed in function of the focal learning processes of interest, thereafter the organization of the school is designed so that optimal enhancing preconditions are provided.

• REFERENCES •

Achilles, C.M., & Lintz, M.N. (1986). *Evaluation of an "effective schools" intervention.* Paper presented at the Annual Meeting of the American Education Research Association, San Francisco.

Addison, R.M., & Haig, C. (1994). The HRD Manager. In W.R. Tracey, *Human Resources Management & Development Handbook* (second edition). New York: AMACOM.

Adkinson, J.A. (1981). Women in school administration: A review of the research. *Review of Educational Research, 51,* 311-343.

American Society for training and development (1994). Trends that will influence workplace learning and performance in the next five years. *Training and Development, 48,* 29-32.

Ashton, P.T., & Webb, R.B. (1986). *Making a difference: teachers' sense of efficacy and student achievement.* London: Longman.

Astuto, T., & Clark, D. (1985). Strength of organizational coupling in the instructional effective school. *Urban Education, 19,* 331-355.

Averch, H.A. et al. (1974). *How effective is schooling?: a critical review of research.* A Rand educational policy study. Englewood Cliffs: Educational Technology Publications.

Ax, J. (1985). *Planningsgedrag van leraren, een empirisch onderzoek naar de onderwijsplanning door leraren in het voortgezet onderwijs* [Planning behavior of teachers, an empirical study on instructional planning by teachers in secondary education]. Lisse: Swets & Zeitlinger.

Bacharach, S. (1990). *Educational reform: making sense of it all.* Boston: Allyn & Bacon.

Bagley, C., Woods, P., & Glatter, R. (1996). Scanning the market. School strategies for discovering parental perspectives. *Educational Management & Administration, 24,* 125-138.

Ball, S.J., & Lacey, C. (1980). Subject disciplines as the opportunity for group action. In P. Woods (Ed.), *Teacher strategies* (pp. 143-161). London: Croom Helm.

Barham, K., & Rassam, C. (1989). *Shaping the corporate future: leading executives share their vision and strategies.* London: Unwin Hyman.

Barnard, Ch.I. (1952). *Organisation and management.* Cambridge, Mass.: Harvard University Press.

Barr, R., & Dreeben, R. (1988). *How schools work.* Chicago: University of Chicago Press.

Becker, H. (1953). The teacher in an authority system. *Journal of Educational Sociology, 26,* 128-141.

Bennis, W. (1982). Leadership transforms vision into action. *Industry Week,* May, p. 55.

Bennis, W.G., Benne, K.D., & Chin, R. (1969). *The planning of change*. London: Holt Rinehart & Winston.

Benveniste, G. (1987). *The design of school accountability systems*. Paper presented at the Washington conference on educational indicators.

Bergenhenegouwen, G.J., Mooijman, E.A.M., & Tillema, H.H. (1992). *Strategisch opleiden in organisaties* [Strategic HRD in organizations.]. Deventer: Kluwer Bedrijfswetenschappen.

Bidwell, C.E. (1965). The school as formal organization. In J. March (Ed.), *Handbook of organizations* (pp. 973-1002). Chicago: Rand McNally.

Blake, R.B., & Mouton, J.S. (1964). *The managerial grid*. Houston: Gulf Publishing.

Blake, R.B., Mouton, J.S., & Williams, M.S. (1981). *The academic administrator grid*. San Francisco: Jossey-Bass Publishers.

Blakely, G.L., Martinec, C.L., & Lane, M.L. (1994). Management development programs: the effects of management level and corporate strategy. *Human Resource Development Quarterly, 5*, 5-19.

Boak, G. (1998). *A complete guide to learning contracts*. Aldershot: Gower.

Boerman, P. (1998). *Decentrale besluitvorming en organisatie-effectiviteit*. [Decentralized decision-making and organizational effectiveness]. Amsterdam: SCO-Kohnstamm Institute & University of Amsterdam.

Bolman, L., & Deal, T.E. (1994). Looking for leadership: Another search party's report. *Educational Administration Quarterly, 30,* 77-96.

Bolman, L., & Heller, R. (1995). Research on school leadership. State of the art. In: S. Bacharach, Br. Mundell (Eds.), *Images of schools. Structures and roles in organizational behavior* (pp. 315-358). Thousand Oaks: Corwin Press Inc.

Bomers, G.B.J. (1990). De lerende organisatie: de enige zekerheid voor organisaties is permanente verandering [The learning organization: the only certainty for organizations is permanent change]. *Harvard Holland Review, 22,* 21-31.

Boorsma, P.B., & Nijzink, J.P. (1984). *Doelmatigheidsprikkels en hoger onderwijsbeleid* [Dimensions of school quality]. Enschede: Technische Hogeschool Twente.

Bosker, R.J. (1990). *Extra kansen dankzij de school?* [Extra chances thanks to the school?] (Ph.D. thesis). Nijmegen: ITS/OoMO.

Bosker, R.J., & Hofman, W.H.A. (1994). School effects on drop out: a multi-level logistic approach to assessing school-level correlates of drop out of ethnic minorities. *Tijdschrift voor Onderwijsresearch, 19,* 50-64.

Bosker, R.J., & Velden R.K.W. van der (1989a). School effects on educational perspectives. In B. Bakker, J. Dronkers & W. Meijnen (Eds.), *Educational opportunities in the welfare state. Longitudinal research in educational and occupational attainment in the Netherlands* (pp.131-150). Nijmegen: OoMO-reeks.

324

Bosker, R.J., & Velden, R.K.W. van der (1989b). The effects of schools on the educational career of disadvantaged pupils. In B.P.M. Creemers, T. Peters & D. Reynolds (Eds.), *School effectiveness and school improvement* (pp. 141-155). Lisse: Swets & Zeitlinger.

Bosker, R.J., & Witziers, B. (1996). *Schoolleiders en schooleffectiviteit: een meta-analyse van onderzoek naar de relatie tussen schoolleiderschap en leerprestaties.* [School leaders and school effectiveness: a meta-analysis of research on the relationship between school leadership and student achievement]. Enschede: University of Twente.

Bossert, S. (1979). *Tasks and social relationships in classrooms.* Cambridge, England: Cambridge University Press.

Bossert, S.T., Dwyer, D.C., Rowan, B., & Lee, G.V. (1982). The instructional management role of the principal. *Educational Administration Quarterly, 18,* 34-64.

Boyd, W.L., & Crowson, R.L. (1981). The changing concept and practice of public school administration. In D.C. Berliner (Ed.), *Review of Research in Education, 9,* (311-373). Washington D.C.: AERA.

Brandsma, H.P.,& Knuver, A.W.M. (1988). Oranisatorische verschillen tussen basisscholen en hun effect op leerlingprestaties [Organizational differences between primary schools and their effects on achievement]. *Tijdschrift voor Onderwijsresearch, 13,* 201-12.

Brekelmans, M., & Wubbels, Th. (1994). Veranderingen in het interpersoonlijke gedrag van docenten gedurende hun beroepsloopbaan [Changes in interpersonal behavior of teachers during their professional career]. *Pedagogische Studiën, 7,* 242-255.

Breton, A., & Wintrobe, R. (1982). *The logic of bureaucratic conduct.* Cambridge: Cambridge University Press.

Brookover, W.B., Beady, C., & Flood, P. et al. (1979). *School social systems and student achievement - schools can make a difference.* New York: Praeger Publishers.

Brophy, J.E. (1983). Classroom organisation and management. *The Elementary School Journal, 82,* 266-285.

Brophy, J. & Good, Th.L. (1986). Teacher behavior and student achievement. In: M.C. Wittrock (Ed.), *Handbook of Research on Teaching* (pp. 328-375). New York: McMillan Inc.

Burns, T., & Stalker, G.M. (1961). *The management of innovation.* London: Tavistock.

Cameron, K.S., & Whetten, D.A. (Eds.) (1983). *Organizational Effectiveness. A comparison of multiple models.* New York: Academic Press.

Carnevale, A.P., Gainer, L.J., & Villet, J. (1990). *Training in America. The organization and strategic role of training.* San Francisco: Jossey-Bass Publishers.

Chaleff, I. (1995). *The courageous follower.* San Francisco: Berrett-Koehler Publications.

Cheng, Y.C. (1993). *The pursuit of school effectiveness*. Hong Kong: The Chinese University of Hong Kong.

Chubb, J.E., & Moe, T.M. (1990). *Politics, markets and American schools*. Washington D.C.: Brookings Institution.

Clune, J., & Witte, J.F. (1990). *Choice and control in American education: Vol. 1. The theory of choice and control in education*. New York: Falmer Press.

Coenjaerts, D., Stevens, J., & van Horebeek, G. (1997). Leerprofijt halen uit beroepspraktijk [Using work practices as a source for learning]. *Thema, 4*, 40-45.

Cohen, P.S., March, J.G., & Olson, J.P. (1972). A garbage can model of organizational choice. *Administrative Science Quarterly, 17*, 1-25.

Cohn, E., & Geske, T.G. (1990). *The economics of education*. Oxford: Pergamon Press.

Coleman, J.S. et al. (1966). *Equality of educational opportunity*. Washington D.C.: U.S. Government Printing Office.

Coleman, P., & Collinge, J. (1991). In the web: Internal and external influences affecting school improvement. *School Effectiveness and School Improvement, 2*, 262-285.

Coleman, J.S., & Hoffer, T. (1987). *Public and private high schools. The impact of communities*. New York: Basic Books Inc.

Coleman, P., & Laroque, L. (1990). *Struggling to be good enough. Administrative practices & school district ethos*. London/NewYork: The Falmer Press.

Collins, A., & Stevens, A. (1982). Goals and strategies of inquiry teachers. In R. Glaser (Ed.), *Advances in Instructional Psychology, Vol. II*. Hillsdale, N.J.: Lawrence Erlbaum Associates.

Commissie Toekomst Leraarschap (1993). *Een beroep met perspectief; De toekomst van het leraarschap*. [A profession with perspective; The future of the teaching profession]. Leiderdorp: Graficon.

Conley, S., & Levinson, R. (1993). Teacher work redesign and job satisfaction. *Educational Administration Quarterly, 29, 4*, 453-478.

Coonen, H. (1987). *De opleiding van leraren basisonderwijs: een studie van ontwikkelingen in de theorie en praktijk van het opleidingsonderwijs* [Training primary schools teachers: a study on developments in the theory and practice of training]. Leiden: Rijksuniversiteit Leiden.

Corcoran, Th.B. (1985). Effective secondary schools. In A.M.J. Kyle (Ed.), *Reaching for excellence: an effective schools sourcebook*. Washington, DC: US Government Printing Office.

Corwin, R.G., & Borman, K.M. (1988). School as a workplace: structural constraints on administration. In J. Boyan (Ed.), *Handbook of Research on Educational Administration* (pp. 209-237). New York: Longman.

Cotton, K. (1995). *Effective schooling practices: a research synthesis. 1995 Update.* School Improvement Research Studies. Northwest Regional Educational Laboratory.

Creemers, B.P.M. (1994). *The Effective Classroom.* London: Cassell.

Creemers, B.P.M. (1994). Effective instruction as a basis for effective education in schools. *Tijdschift voor Onderwijsresearch, 19,* 3-16.

Creemers, B.P.M. (1996). The school effectiveness knowledge base. In D. Reynolds, R. Bollen, B. Creemers, D. Hopkins, L. Stoll & N. Lagerweij, *Making good schools.* London: Routledge.

Creemers, B.P.M., Reezigt, G., Van der Werf, G., & Hoeben, W. (1997). *Developments in educational effectiveness theory and research in the Netherlands.* Unpublished paper. Groningen: Groningen Institute for Educational Research.

Crévola, C.A., & Hill, P.W. (1997). *The early literacy research project: Success for all in Victoria, Australia.* Paper presented at the Annual Conference of the American Education Research Association, Chicago, March 1997.

Crisci, P. (1991). *Using the current paradigms in teacher training to prepare principals and mentor teachers to appraise classroom instruction.* Kent: Center for School Personnel Relations.

Crooks, T.J. (1988). The impact of classroom evaluation practices on students. *Review of Educational Research, 58,* 438-481.

Cuban, L. (1984). Transforming the frog into a prince: effective schools, policy and practice at the district level. *Harvard Educational Review, 54,* 129-151.

Cuban, L. (1988). *The managerial imperative and the practice of leadership in schools.* Albany: State University of New York Pres.

Cyert, R., & March, J. (1963). *A behavioral theory of the firm.* Englewood Cliffs, New Jersey: Prentice-Hall.

Daft, R.L. (1992). *Organization theory and design.* St. Paul: West Publishing Company.

Dalin, P. (1988). Reconceptualising the school improvement process: charting a paradigm shift. In D. Reynolds & B.P.M. Creemers (Eds.), *School effectiveness and improvement: proceedings of the First International Congress* (pp. 30-46). Groningen/Cardiff: RION/University of Wales College of Cardiff.

de Caluwé, L.I.A., & Petri, M.W. (1985). De school als vuilnisvat organisatie [The school as a garbage can organization]. In B.P.M. Creemers & H.G.I. Giesbers (Eds.), *Handboek Schoolorganisatie en Onderwijsmanagement* (pp. 1520-1 - 1520-13). Alphen a/d Rijn: Samson.

de Leeuw, A.C.J. (1974). *Systeemleer en Organisatiekunde* [Control theory and organizational science]. Leiden: Stenfert Kroese.

de Leeuw, A.C.J. (1982). *Organisaties: management, analyse, ontwerp en verandering.* [Organizations: management, analysis, design and change]. Assen: Van Gorcum.

Dekker, J.M., & Wognum, A.A.M. (1994). Vorming van opleidingsbeleid afgestemd op ondernemingsbeleid: methoden uit de praktijk van vijf arbeidsorganisaties [An analysis of HRD policy-making tuned to the strategy of the company: a framework and five cases]. *Gedrag en Organisatie, 7,* 284-300.

Douglas Willms, J. (1992). *Monitoring school performance.* Washington D.C.: Falmer Press.

Doyle, W. (1985). Effective secondary classroom practices. In M.J. Kyle (Ed.), *Reaching for excellence. An effective schools sourcebook.* Washington: U.S. Government Printing Office.

Dutch Educational Inspection [Inspectie van het Onderwijs] (1998). *Onderwijsverslag 1997* [Educational report 1997]. Utrecht: Inspectie van het Onderwijs.

Edmonds, R. (1979). Effective schools for the urban poor. *Educational Leadership, 35,* 15-24.

Emery, F.E., & Trist, E.L. (1969). The causal texture of organizational environment. In F.E. Emery (Ed.), *Systems thinking: selected readings* (pp. 241-257). Harmondsworth: Penguin.

Esteve, J. (1989). Teacher burnout and teacher stress. In M. Cole & S. Walker (Eds.), *Teaching and Stress.* Philadelphia: Open University Press.

Etzioni, A. (1964). *Modern organizations.* Englewood Cliffs, NJ: Prentice-Hall.

Etzioni, A. (1975). *Comparative analysis of complex organizations.* New York: Free Press.

Faerman, S.R., & Quinn, R.E. (1985). Effectiveness: the perspective from organization theory. *The Review of Higher Education, 9,* 83-100.

Fidler, B. (1996). *Strategic planning for school improvement.* London: Pitman Publishing.

Fiedler, F.E. (1967). *A theory of leader effectiveness.* New York: Mc Graw Hill.

Firestone, W.A., & Herriott, R.E. (1982a). Prescriptions for effective elementary schools don't fit secondary schools. *Educational Administration Quarterly, 18,* 39-59.

Firestone, W.A., & Herriott, R.E. (1982b). Two images of schools as organizations. *Educational Administration Quarterly, 18,* 35-59.

Floden, R., Porter, A., Alford, L., Freeman, D., Irwin, S., Schmidt, W., & Schwille, J. (1988). Instructional leadership at the district level: a closer look at autonomy and control. *Educational Administration Quarterly, 24,* 96-124.

Ford, J.K., & Noe, R.A. (1987). Self-assessed training needs: the effects of attitudes toward training, managerial level, and function. *Personnel Psychology, 40,* 39-54.

Ford, J.K., Major, D.A., Seaton, F.W.H., & Krifcher Felber, H. (1993). Effects of organizational, training system, and individual characteristics on training director scanning practices. *Human Resource Development Quarterly, 4,* 333-351.

Fraser, B.J., Walberg, H.J., Welch, W.W., & Hattie, J.A. (1987). Syntheses of educational productivity research. Special Issue of the *International Journal of Educational Research, 11.*

Freeston, K.R. (1987). Leader substitutes in educational organizations. *Educational administration quarterly, 23,* 45-59.

Friebel, A.J.J.M. (1994). *Planning van onderwijs en het gebruik van planningsdocumenten: doet het ertoe?* [Instructional planning and the use of planning documents]. Oldenzaal: Dinkeldruk.

Friedkin, N.E., & Necochea, J. (1988). School system size and performance: a contingency perspective. *Educational Evaluation and Policy Analysis, 10,* 237-249.

Frissen, P., & van der Putten, M. (1990). *Opleiden en cultuur* [Training, development and culture]. In J.W.M. Kessels, & C.A. Smit (Red.), Opleiden en cultuur (pp. 1-21) Deventer: Kluwer Bedrijfswetenschappen.

Fullan, M. (1991). *The new meaning of educational change.* London: Cassell.

Galbraith, J. (1973). *Designing complex organizations.* Reading: Addison-Wesley.

Geurts, J. (1989). *Van Niemandsland naar beroepenstruktuur. Een studie over de aansluiting tussen onderwijs en arbeid op het niveau van aankomend vakmanschap* [From no man's land to vocational structure. A study on the transition from education to work at the level of prospective craftsmanship]. Nijmegen: ITS.

Giesbers, J.H.G.I., & Marx, E.C.H. (1986). Autonome versus centrale regelgeving: een verkenning [Autonomous versus central rules: an exploration]. *Pedagogisch Tijdschrift, 11,* 305-313.

Gilley, J.W., & Eggland, S.A. (1989). *Principles of human resource development.* Reading: Addison-Wesley.

Gillijns (1991). *Leerlingvolgsystemen* [Student monitoring systems]. Tilburg: Zwijssen.

Glaser, R., & Chi, M.T. (1988). Overview. In M.T. Chi et al.(Eds.), *The nature of expertise* (pp. xv-xxviii). Hillsdale, NJ: Lawrence Erlbaum.

Glasman, N.S., & J. Biniaminov (1981). Input-output analysis of schools. *Review of Educational Research, 51,* 509-539.

Goldring, E.B. (1995a). Striking a balance. Boundary spanning and environmental management in schools. In S.B. Bacharach, & B. Mundell, *Images of schools. Structures and roles in organizational behavior* (pp. 283-314). Thousands Oaks: Corwin Press, Inc.

Goldring, E.B. (1995b). School restructuring: responding to external environments. In R.T. Ogawa (Ed.), *Advances in research and theories of school management and educational policy* (pp. 43-67). Greenwich/Connecticut: Jai Press Inc.

Goldstein, H. & Sammons, P. (1997). The influence of secondary and junior schools on sixteen year examination performance: a cross-classified multilevel analysis. *School Effectiveness and Improvement, 8*(2), p. 219-230.

Gooren, W.A.J. (1989). Kwetsbare en weerbare scholen en het welbevinden van de leraar [Vulnerable and able-bodied schools and teacher satisfaction]. In J. Scheerens, & J.C. Verhoeven (Eds.), *Schoolorganisatie, beleid en onderwijskwaliteit.* Lisse: Swets & Zeitlinger.

Gouldner, A.W. (1955). *Patterns of Industrial Bureaucracy.* London: Routledge and Kegan Paul.

Green, T.F. (1971). *The Activities of Teaching.* New York: McGraw-Hill.

Grisay, A. (1997). *Évolution des acquis cognitifs et socio-affectifs des élèves au cours des années de collège.* Paris: Ministère de l'Éducation Nationale.

Guthrie, J.W. (1990). The evolution of educational management: eroding myths and emerging models. In B. Mitchell, & L.L. Cunningham (Eds.), *Educational leadership and changing contexts of families, communities, and schools.* Chicago: NSSE.

Hage, J. (1980). *Theories of organization: form, processes and transformation.* New York: Wiley.

Hall, G., Rutherford, W.L., Hord, Sh., & Huling, L.L. (1984). Effects of three principal styles on school improvement, *Educational Leadership, 22-29.*

Hallinger, Ph. (1992). The evolving role of American principals: from managerial to instructional to transformational leaders. *Journal of Educational Administration, 30,* 35-48.

Hallinger, Ph., & Heck, R.H. (1996). Reassessing the principals's role in school effectiveness: a review of empirical research. *Educational Administration Quarterly, 32,* 5-44.

Hallinger, Ph., & Heck, R.H. (1998). Exploring the principal's contributions tot school effectiveness: 1980 - 1995. *School Effectiveness and School Improvement, 9,* 157-191.

Hallinger, Ph., Leithwood, K., & Murphy, J. (Eds) (1993). *Cognitive perspectives on educational leadership.* New York: Teachers College Press.

Hallinger, Ph., & Murphy, J. (1985). Assessing the instructional management behavior of principals. *The Elementary School Journal, 86,* 217-247.

Halpin, A.W., & Winer, B.J. (1957). A factorial study of the leader behavior descriptions. In R.M. Stogdill, & A.E. Coons (Eds.), *Leadership behavior: its description and measurement.* Columbus: Ohio State University.

Hamrick, D., & Brandon, G. (1988). Executive values. *The executive effect: concepts and methods for studying top executives* (pp. 3-34). London: JAI Press.

Handy, C.B. (1976). *Understanding organizations.* Penguin: Harmondsworth.

Hanson, E.M. (1979). *Educational administration and organizational behavior.* Boston: Allyn & Bacon.

Hanson, E.M. (1981). *Educational administration and organizational behavior.* Boston: Allyn & Bacon.

Hanushek, E.A. (1979). Conceptual and empirical issues in the estimation of educational production functions. *Journal of Human Resources, 14,* 351-388.

Hanushek, E.A. (1986). The economics of schooling: production and efficiency in public schools. *Journal of Economic Literature, 24,* 1141-1177.

Hanushek, E.A. (1994). *Making schools work: improving performance and controlling costs.* Washington, D.C.: Brookings Institution.

Hargreaves, D.H. (1995). School culture, school effectiveness and school improvement. *School Effectiveness and School Improvement, 6,* 23-46.

Hauser, R.M., Sewell, W.H., & Alwin, D.F. (1976). High School effects on achievement. In W.H. Sewell, R.M. Hauser, & D.L. Featherman (Eds.), *Schooling and achievement in American Society.* New York: Academic Press.

Hermans, H.L.C., Backx, H.A.M., & Pors, W.E. (1993). *Hoofdlijnen onderwijsrecht* [Key elements of educational law]. Alphen a/d Rijn: Samsom H.D. Tjeen Willink.

Herzberg, F. (1966). *Work and the Nature of Man.* Pittsburgh, Pa.: World.

Hill, T. (1994). Primary head teachers: their job satisfaction and future career aspirations. *Educational Research, 36,* 223-235.

Hill, P. (1995). *School effectiveness and improvement: present realities and future possibilities* (Inaugural lecture). Melbourne: Faculty of Education.

Hill, P.W., & Rowe, K.J. (1996). Multilevel modelling in school effectiveness research. *School Effectiveness and School Improvement, 7,* 1-34.

Hodge, B.J., & Hankin, M.D. (1988). Scanning the external environment. In T.D. Connors (ed.), *The non-profit organization handbook* (pp. 6.3-6.23). New York.

Hofman, R.H. (1992). *Schoolbesturen en de kwaliteit van het onderwijs* [School boards and the quality of education]. Groningen: RION.

Hofman, R. (1995). Contextual influences on school effectiveness: The role of school boards. *School effectiveness and School Improvement, 6,* 308-331.

Hopes, C. (Ed.) (1986). *The school leader and school improvement. Case studies from ten OECD countries.* OECD/CERI/ISIP International School Improvement Project, Technical report nr. 2. Leuven: Acco.

Hopkins, D. (1987). *Doing school based review.* Leuven, Belgium: ACCO.

Hopkins, D., Ainscow, M., & West, M. (1994). *School improvement in an era of change.* New York: Cassell.

Hopkins, D., & Leask, M. (1989). Performance Indicators and School Development. *School Organization, 9,* 3-20.

House, R.J. (1971). A path-goal theory of leader effectiveness, *Administrative Science Quarterly, 16,* 321-338.

House, R.J., & Baetz, M.L. (1979). Leadership: some empirical generalizations and research directions. In B.M. Staw (Ed.), *Research in organizational behavior.* Greenwich: JAI Press.

Hoy, W.K., & Miskel, C.G. (1982). *Educational administration: theory, research, and practice.* New York: Random House.

Hoy, W.K., & Ferguson, J. (1985). A theoretical framework and exploration of organizational effectiveness of schools. *Educational Administration Quarterly, 21,* 117-34.

Hrebiniak, L., & Joyce, W. (1985). Organizational adaptation: strategic choice and environmental determinism. *Administrative Science Quarterly, 30,* 336-349.

Huberman, A.M. (1983). Répertoires, recettes et vie de classe: Comment les enseignants utilisent l'information. *Education et Recherche, 5,* 157-177.

Huberman, M. (1993). *The lives of teachers.* New York: Teachers College Press.

Huberman, M., & Grounauer, M. (1993). Teachers' motivations and satisfactions. In M. Huberman, *The lives of teachers.* New York: Teachers College Press.

Hylkema, W.F.S. (1990). *Docenten en hun vaksecties* [Teachers and their departments]. Nijmegen: Katholieke Universiteit Nijmegen.

Idenburg, Ph.J. (1975). *Theorie van het onderwijsbeleid* [The theory of educational policy]. Groningen: Wolters-Noordhoff.

Imants, J. (1996). *Leiding geven aan basisscholen* [Leading primary schools]. Leiden: DSWO Press.

Ingersoll, R.H. (1993). Loosely coupled organizations revisited. *Research in the sociology of organizations, 11,* 81-112.

Ingersoll, R.M. (1994). Organizational control in secondary schools. *Harvard Educational Review, 64,* 150-172.

James, E. (1991). Public policies toward private education. *International Journal of Educational Research, 15,* 353-498.

Jencks, C. et al. (1972). *Inequality.* New York: Basic Books.

Jencks, C. et al. (1979). *Who gets ahead? The determinants of economic success in America.* New York: Basic Books.

Joyce, B., & Showers, B. (1988). *Student achievement through staff development.* New York: Longman.

Kanter, R.M. (1968). Commitment and social organization: A study of commitment mechanisms in Utopian communities. *American Sociological Review, 33,* 499-517.

Katz, D., & Kahn, R.L. (1978). *The social psychology of organizations*. New York: John Wiley & Sons.

Kerr, St., & Jermier, J. (1978). Substitutes for Leadership: their meaning and measurement, *Organizational Behavior and Human Performance, 22*, 375-403.

Kessels, J.W.M., & Smit, C. (1989). *Opleidingskunde: een bedrijfsgerichte benadering van leerprocessen* [Educational Science: a company-oriented approach to learning processes]. Deventer: Kluwer.

Keuning, D., & Eppink, D.J. (1993). *Management en organisatie. Theorie en toepassing.* [Management and organization. Theory and application] Leiden/Antwerpen: Stenfert Kroese.

Kickert, W.J.M. (1979). *Organization of decision-making: a system-theoretical approach.* Amsterdam: North-Holland Publishing Company.

Kieser, A., & Kubicek, H. (1977). *Organization.* Berlin: De Gruyter Lehrbuch.

Kirkpatrick, D.L. (1987). Evaluation. In R.L.Craig (Ed.), *Training and Development Handbook. Guide for Human Resource Development.* New York: McGraw-Hill.

Kmerz, J.T., & Willower, D.J. (1982). Elementary school prinicpals' work behavior. *Educational Administration Quarterly, 18*, 62-78.

Knuver, J.W.M. (1993). *De relatie tussen school- en klaskenmerken en het affectief functioneren van leerlingen.* [The relationship between school and class characteristics and student functioning].(Ph.D-thesis). Groningen: Rion.

Kogan, M. (1986). *Educational accountability: an analytic overview.* London: Hutchinson Educational.

Kotler, P., & Fox, K.F.A. (1985). *Strategic Marketing for Educational Institutions.* Englewood Cliffs: Prentice Hall Inc.

Krüger, M.L. (1994). *Sekseverschillen in schoolleiderschap* [Gender differences in school leadership]. Alphen aan den Rijn: Samson H.D. Tjeenk Willink.

Krüger, M.L. (1996). Sekse van de schooldirecteur in relatie tot de gerichtheid op het primaire proces [Principal's gender interrelationship with the directedness to the primary process]. *Pedagogische Studiën, 73*, 25-41.

Kruijd, D. (1991). Opleiden op de werkplek: een terreinverkenning [Training in the workplace: an exploration]. *Capita Selecta Opleiders in Organisaties*, aflevering 6. Deventer: Kluwer.

Kulik, C.L.C., & Kulik, J.A. (1982). Effects of ability grouping on secondary school students: a meta-analysis of research findings. *American Educational Research Journal, 19*, 415-428.

Kwakman, K. (1992). *Intentioneel en informeel leren in arbeidsorganisaties* [Intentional and informal learning in work organizations]. Doctoraalscriptie. Nijmegen: Katholieke Universiteit Nijmegen.

Kwakman, C.H.E. (1997). *Professional learning on the job: a qualitative study for one profession.* Paper presented at the Academy of Human Resource Development conference, March, Atlanta.

Kyle, M.J. (Ed.) (1985). *Reaching for excellence. An effective schools sourcebook.* Washington D.C.: U.S. Government Printing Office.

Laiken, M. (1993). From trainer to consultant in 5 (not so easy!) steps. *Performance and Instruction, 32,* 32-36.

Lam, J.F. (1996). *Tijd en kwaliteit in het basisonderwijs* [Time and quality in primary education]. (Ph.D.-thesis). Enschede: Universiteit Twente.

Lammers, C.J. (1983). *Organisaties vergelijkenderwijs. Ontwikkeling en relevantie van het sociologisch denken over organisaties* [Organisations compared. Development and relevance of sociological thinking on organizations]. Utrecht/Antwerpen: Het Spectrum.

Lawrence, P.R. & Lorsch, J.W. (1969). *Organization and environment; managing differentiation and integration.* Homewood: Irwin.

Lee, V.E., Bryk, A.S., & Smith, J.B. (1993). The organization of effective secondary schools. In L. Darling-Hammond (Ed.), *Review of Research in Education* (pp. 171-268). Washington: AERA.

Leithwood, K.A., Begley, P.T., & Cousins, J.B. (1990). The nature, causes and consequences of principals' practice: an agenda for future research. *Journal of Educational Administration, 28,* 5-31.

Leithwood, K.A., & Montgomery, D.J. (1982). The role of the elementary school principal in program improvement. *Review of Educational Research, 52,* 309-339.

Leithwood, K.A., & Montgomery, D. (1986). *Improving principal effectiveness: the principal profile.* Toronto: OISE Press.

Leithwood, K.A., & Stager, M. (1986). *Differences in problem solving processes used by moderately and highly effective principals.* AERA paper, San Francisco annual meeting.

Leithwood, K.A., & Steinbach, R. (1991). Indicators of transformational leadership in the everyday problem solving of school administrators, *Journal of Personnel Evaluation in Education, 4,* 221-244.

Leithwood, K.A. & Steinbach, R. (1995). *Expert problem solving: evidence from school and district leaders.* Albany, NY: SUNY Press.

Leithwood, K.A., Steinbach, R., & Raun, T. (1993). Superintendent's group problem solving processes, *Educational Administration Quarterly, 29,* 364-391.

Leithwood, K., Tomlinson, D., & Genge, M. (1996). Transformational school leadership. In K. Leithwood, J. Chapman, D. Corson, Ph. Hallinger, & A. Hart (Eds.), *International Handbook of Educational Leadership* (pp. 785-840). Dordrecht: Kluwer Academic Publishers.

Leune, J.M.G. (1985). Onderwijsbeleid als object van sociologisch onderzoek [Educational policy as an object of sociological research]. In J.L. Peschar, & A.A. Wesselingh (Eds.), *Onderwijssociologie, een inleiding* (pp. 511-536). Groningen: Wolters-Noordhoff.

Levin, B. (1993). School response to a changing environment. *Journal of Educational Administration, 31*, 4-21.

Levin, H.H. (1988). Cost-effectiveness and educational policy. *Educational Evaluation and Policy Analysis, 10*, 51-69.

Levine, D.U., & Lezotte, L.W. (1990). *Unusually effective schools: a review and analysis of research and practice.* Madison, WI: National Center for Effective Schools Research and development.

Lezotte, L.W., Edmonds, R., & Ratner, G. (1974). *A final report: remedy for school failure to equitably deliver school basic skills.* Michigan State University.

Lieberman, A., Saxl, E.R., & Miles, M.B. (1988). Teacher Leadership: ideology and practice. In A. Lieberman (Ed.), *Building a professional culture in schools* (pp. 148-167). New York: Teacher College Press.

Liket, T., van Marwijk-Kooij, L., & Bruggen, J. van (1985). Autonomy and central control with regard to three educational and three organizational aspects of schools. In T. Liket, L. van Marwijk-Kooij, & J. van Bruggen, *Report of the conference on autonomy and central legislation in education.* Noordwijkerhout: European Forum for Educational Administration.

Likert, R. (1961). *New patterns of management.* New York: McGraw Hill.

Little, J.W. (1982). Norms of collegiality and experimentation: workplace conditions of school succes. *American Educational Research Journal, 19*, 325-340.

Little, J.W. (1988). Assessing the prospects for teacher leadership. In A. Lieberman (Ed.), *Building a professional culture in schools* (pp. 78-108). New York: Teacher College Press.

Lockheed, M.E. (1988). *The measurement of educational efficiency and effectiveness.* New Orleans: AERA paper.

London, M. (1989). *Managing the training enterprise. High-quality, cost-effective employee training in organizations.* San Francisco/Oxford: Jossey-Bass Publishers.

Lortie, D.C. (1969). The balance of control and autonomy in elementary school teaching. In A. Etzioni (Ed.), *The semi professions and their organization.* New York: Free Press.

Lortie, D. (1975). *School teacher: A sociological study*. Chicago: University of Chicago Press.

Lortie, D.C. (1977). The balance of control and autonomy in elementary school teaching. In D.A. Erickson (Ed.), *Educational organization and administration*. Berkeley: McCutchan Publ.

Luyten, J.W., & Snijders, T. (1996). Teacher effects and school effects. *Educational Research and Evaluation, 2*, 1-24.

March, J.G., & Simon, H.A. (1958). *Organizations*. New York: Wiley.

Marx, E.C.H. (1986). Schoolorganisatorische aspecten van waardengerichtheid in het onderwijs bij uiteenlopende schoolculturen [School organizational aspects of value directedness in education in the case of various school cultures]. In B.P.M. Creemers, J. Giesbers, C.A. van Vilsteren, & C. van der Perre (Eds.), *Handboek Schoolorganisatie en Onderwijsmanagement*. Alphen aan den Rijn: Samsom.

Marx, E.C.H. (1987). Vermogen van scholen tot het voeren van bestuurlijk beleid [The capacity of schools to develop administrative policy]. In L. Genemans (Ed.), *Autonomie van scholen en deregulering* (pp. 7-27). Nijmegen: Instituut voor Toegepaste Sociale Wetenschapen.

Maslow, A.H. (1970). *Motivations and Personality*. New York: Harper & Row.

Maslowski, R. (1997). School cultuur: kenmerken en veranderingsmogelijkheden [School culture: features and possibilities for change]. *Handboek Schoolorganisatie en Onderwijsmanagement* (pp. 1400-1 - 1400-25). Alphen aan den Rijn: Samsom.

May, L.S. (1987). Applying quality management concepts and techniques to training evaluation. In L.S. May, C.A. Moore, & S.J. Zammit (Eds.), *Evaluating business and industry training* (pp. 125-139). Boston/Dordrecht/Lancaster: Kluwer Academic Publishers.

McCormack-Larkin, M. (1985). Ingredients of a successful school effectiveness project. *Educational Leadership*, March, 31-37.

McLagan (1983). *The competency model for the training and development field*. Washington: ASTD.

McPherson, R.B., Crowson, R., & Pitner, N.J. (1986). *Managing Uncertainty: administrative theory and practice in education*. Columbus: C.E. Merril Publishing Company.

Meindl, J.R., Ehrlich, S.B., & Dukerich, J.M. (1985). The romance of leadership, *Administrative Science Quarterly, 30*, 78- 102.

Merton, R.K. (1952). *Reader in Bureaucracy*. Glencoe: The Free Press.

Meskin, J.D. (1979). Women as principals: their performance as educational administrators. In D. Erickson, & T.L. Teller, *The principal in metropolitan schools*. Berkeley: McCutchan.

Meyer, J.W., & Rowan, B. (1983a). Innovation and knowledge use in American public education. In W.R. Scott, & J.W. Meyer (Eds.), *Organizational environments* (pp. 233-260). Beverly Hills, Ca.: Sage.

Meyer, J.W., & Rowan, B. (1983b). Institutionalized organizations: formal structure as myth and ceremony. In W.R. Scott, & J.W. Meyer (Eds.), *Organizational environments* (pp. 71-98). Beverly Hills: Sage.

Meyer, J.W., & Rowan, B. (1983c). The structure of educational organizations. In J. Baldridge, & T. Deal (Eds.), *The dynamics of organizational change in education* (pp. 60-89). California: Berkeley.

Miles, R.E., & Snow, C.C. (1978). *Organizational strategy, structure, and process.* Tokyo: McGraw-Hill Kogakusha Ltd.

Miller, S.K., Cohen, S.R., & Sayre, K.A. (1985). Significant achievement games using the effective schools model. *Educational Leadership*, March, 28-43.

Ministerie van Onderwijs en wetenschappen (1994). *Vitaal leraarschap* [The future of the teaching profession]. Den Haag: SDU

Mintzberg, H. (1979). *The structuring of organizations.* Englewoord Cliffs: Prentice Hall.

Mintzberg, H. (1979). *Structure in Fives: designing effective organization.* Englewood Cliffs: Prentice-Hall.

Mintzberg, H. (1981). Organization design: fashion or fit? *Harvard Business Review*, January/February, 103-116.

Mintzberg, H. (1983). *Power in and around organizations.* Englewood Cliffs: Prentice Hall.

Mintzberg, H. (1989). *Mintzberg on management.* New York: Free Press.

Miskal, C.G. (1982). Motivation in Educational Organizations, *Educational Administration Quarterly, 18*, 65-88.

Monk, D.H. (1992). Education Productivity Research: An update and assessment of its role in education finance reform. *Education Evaluation and Policy Analysis, 14*, 307-332.

Morgan, G. (1986). *Images of Organizations.* Beverly Hills: Sage.

Morine-Dershimer, G. (1978). How teachers "see" their pupils. *Educational Research Quarterly, 3*, 43-52.

Mortimore, P., Sammons, P., Stoll, L., Lewis, D., & Ecob, R. (1988). *School matters: the junior years.* Somerset: Open Books.

Mosteller, F., & Moynihan, D.D. (Eds.) (1972). *On equality of educational opportunity.* New York: Random House.

Mowday, R.T., Porter, L.W., & Steers, R.M. (1982). Employee-Organization Linkages. *The psychology of commitment, absenteeism, and turnover.* New York: Academic Press.

337

Mulder, M. (1995a). Branche en bedrijfsopleidingen: structuur, omvang en ontwikkelingen. [HRD on the sector and corporate level: structure, size and developments] In M. Mulder, & S. de Grave (Eds.), *Ontwikkelingen in branche en bedrijfsopleidingen* [Developments in HRD on the sector and corporate level]. Utrecht: Lemma.

Mulder, M. (1995b). Evaluatie, kosten en effectiviteit van opleidingen. [Evaluation, costs and effectiveness of training]. In M. Mulder, & S. de Grave (Eds.), *Ontwikkelingen in branche en bedrijfsopleidingen* [Developments in HRD on the sector and corporate level]. Utrecht: Lemma.

Mulder, M., Akkermans, J.S., & Bentvelsen, N. (1989). *Bedrijfsopleidingen in Nederland* [Corporate training & development in The Netherlands]. Den Haag: Instituut voor Onderzoek van het Onderwijs.

Murphy, J. (1988). Methodological, measurement, and conceptual problems in the study of instructional leadership. *Educational Evaluation and Policy Analysis, 10,* 117-139.

Murphy, J. (1990). *The educational reform movement of the 1980s: perspectives and cases.* Berkeley, CA: McCutchan.

Murphy, J. (1991). *Restructuring schools: capturing and assessing the phenomena.* New York: Teachers College Press.

Murphy, J., & Seashore Louis, K. (1994). *Reshaping the principalship: insights from transformational reform efforts.* Thousand Oakes, CA: Corwin Press.

Muschewske, R.C. (1994). Invited reaction: level and strategy should and do make a difference! *Human Resource Development Quarterly, 5,* 21-25.

Nadler, L., & Nadler, Z. (1989). *Developing Human Resources.* San Francisco: Jossey-Bass Publishers.

Nadler, L., & Wiggs, G.D. (1986). *Managing Human Resource Development.* San Francisco: Jossey-Bass Publishers.

National Commission on Excellence in Education (1983). *A nation at risk. The imperative for educational reform.* Washington DC: Government Printing Office.

Neave, G. (1992). *The teaching nation; prospects for teachers in the European community.* Exeter: BPCC Wheatons Ltd.

Niederberger, J.M. (1984). *Organizationssoziologie der Schule.* Stuttgart: F. Enke.

Niskanen, W.A. (1971). *Bureaucracy and representative government.* Chicago: Aldine-Atherton.

Nonaka, I., & Takeuchi, H. (1995). *The knowledge creating company: how Japanese companies create the dynamics of innovation.* New York, Oxford: University Press.

Oakes, J. (1987). *Conceptual and measurement issues in the construction of school quality indicators.* Paper presented at the AERA-annual meeting, Washington D.C.

OECD (1990). *The teacher today. Tasks, Conditions, Policies.* Paris: OECD.

OECD (1993). *Education at a Glance 2.* Paris: OECD.

OECD (1995). *Education at a Glance 3.* Paris: OECD.

OECD (1996a). *Education at a Glance. OECD Indicators.* Paris: OECD.

OECD (1996b). *Education at a Glance. Analysis.* Paris: OECD.

Ogawa, R., & Bossert, St. (1995). Leadership as an organizational quality. *Educational Administration Quarterly, 31,* 224-243.

Ouchi, W.G. (1977). The relationship between organizational structure and organizational control. *Administrative Science Quarterly, 22,* 95-113.

Pelgrum, W.J., & Plomp, Tj. (1991). *The use of computers in education worldwide: results from the IEA Computers in Education survey in 19 educational systems.* Oxford: Pergamon Press.

Perrow, C.H. (1970). *Complex Organizations: A Sociological Review.* Belmont, Calif.: Wadsworth.

Perrow, C.H. (1970). *Organizational analysis: a sociological view.* London: Tavistock.

Perrow, C.H. (1970). *Organizational structure: extensions and replications. The Aston II programme.* Lexington: Saxon House/Lexington Books.

Peters T.J., & Waterman, R.H. (1982). *In search of excellence.* New York: Harper & Row.

Pfeffer, J., & Salancik, G.R. (1978). *The external control of organizations: a resource dependence perspective.* New York: Harper & Row.

Pijl, S.J. (1988). *Het gebruik van diagnostische informatie* [The use of diagnostic information]. Unpublished doctoral dissertation, University of Groningen, Groningen.

Pitner, N.J. (1986). Substitutes for principal leader behavior: an exploratory study. *Educational Administration Quarterly, 22,* 23-42.

Popper (1959). *The logic of scientific discovery.* London: Hutchinson & Co.

Porter, A.C., & Brophy, J.E. (1988). Synthesis of research on good teaching: insights from the work of the Institute of Research on Teaching. *Educational Leadership, 48,* 74-52.

Porter, L.W., & Miles, R.E. (1974). Motivation and Management. In J.W. McGuire (Ed.), *Contemporary Management: Issues and Viewpoints.* New Yersey: Prentice Hall.

Pounder, D.G., Ogawa, R., & Ann Adams, E. (1995). Leadership as an organization-wide phenomenon: its impact on school performance. *Educational Administration Quarterly, 31,* 564-588.

Prick, L.G.M. (1983). *Het beroep van leraar.* [The teaching profession]. Amsterdam: VU Boekhandel/Uitgeverij.

Prick, L.G.M. (1990). Personeelsbeleid in het onderwijs. de bittere noodzaak van een nieuwe aanpak [Human Resource Management in education: the need for a new approach]. *MESO focus* 6 Culemborg: Educaboek.

Pröpper, I.M.A.M. (1993). *Inleiding in de organisatietheorie*. [Introduction into organizational theory.] 's-Gravenhage: VUGA.

Pugh, D.S., & Hickson, D.J. (1976). *Organizational structure: extensions and replications. The Aston II programme*. Lexington: Saxon House/Lexington Books.

Pugh, D.S., & Hinings, C.R. (1977). *Organizational structure in its context. The Aston I programme*. Lexington: Saxon House/Lexington Books.

Purkey, S.C., & Smith, M.S. (1983). Effective schools: a review. *The Elementary School Journal, 83*, 427-542.

Quinn, R.E. (1988). *Beyond rational management: mastering the paradoxes and competing demands of high performance*. San Francisco: Jossey-Bass.

Ralph, J.H., & Fennessey, J. (1983). Science or reform: some questions about the effective schools model. *Phi Delta Kappan*, 689-695.

Reyes, P. (Ed.) (1990). *Teachers and their workplace. Commitment, performance and productivity*. London: Sage Publications.

Reynolds, D., Sammons, P., Stoll, L., & Barber, M. (1995). School effectiveness and school improvement in the United Kingdom. In B.P.M. Creemers, & N.Osinga (Eds.), *Country Reports* (pp. 17-24). Leeuwarden: GCO.

Rhebergen, B., & Wognum, A.A.M. (1996). Supporting the career development of older employees: an HRD point of view. In E.F. Holton III (Ed.), *Conference/Proceedings Academy of Human Resource Development*, February 29 - March 3, 1996, Minneapolis, USA.

Riehl, C., Pallas, G., & Natriello, G. (1992) More responsive high schools student information and problem-solving. Paper presented at the Annual Meeting of the American Educational Research Association, San Francisco.

Rijkers, A.A.M. (1991). *Praktijkboek voor opleiders: de kern van de zaak*. [Practitioner's book for trainers: the heart of the matter]. Schoonhoven: Academic Service.

Robinson, G.G., & Robinson, J.C. (1989). *Training for impact; how to link training to business needs and measure the results*. San Francisco: Jossey-Bass Publishers.

Rosenholtz, S.J. (1985). Effective schools: Interpreting the evidence. *American Journal of Education, 93*, 352-388.

Rosenholtz, S.J. (1987). Education reform stratgies. Will they increase teacher commitment? *American Journal of Education, 95*, 534-562.

Rosenholtz, S.J. (1989). *Teachers workplace: The social organization of schools*. New York: Longman.

Rosenthal R., & Jacobson, L. (1968). *Pygmalion in the classroom. New York:* Holt, Rinehart & Winston.

Rossi, P.H., & Freeman, H.E. (1993). *Evaluation: a systematic approach*. London: Sage Publications.

Rothwell, W.J., & Kazanas, H.C. (1989). *Strategic Human Resource Development.* Englewood Cliffs: Prentice Hall.

Rowan, B. (1995). The organizational design of schools. In S.B. Bacharach, & B. Mundell (Eds.), *Structures and roles in organizational behavior* (pp. 11-42). Greenwich: JAI Press.

Rowan, B., Raudenbush, S., & Cheong, Y.F. (1993). Teaching as a nonroutine task: implications for the management of schools. *Educational Administration Quarterly, 29,* 479-500.

Rowe, K.J., & Hill, P.W. (1996). Assessing, recording and reporting student's educational progress: the case for 'subject profiles'. *Assessment in Education, 3,* 309-351.

Rowe, K.J., Hill, P.W., & Holmes-Smith, P. (1994). *The Victorian Quality Schools Project: A report on the first stage of a longitudinal study of school and teacher effectiveness.* Paper presented at the International Congress for School Effectiveness and Improvement, The World Congress Centre, Melbourne, Australia, January 3-6, 1994.

Rummler, G.R., & Brache, A.P. (1990). *Improving performance: how to manage the white space on the organization chart.* San Francisco: Jossey-Bass Publishers.

Rutter, M., Maughan, B., Mortimore, P., Ouston, J., & Smith, A. (1979). *Fifteen thousand hours: secondary schools and their effects on children.* Cambridge, Mass: Harvard University Press.

Sammons, P., Hillman, J., & Mortimore, P. (1995). *Key characteristics of effective schools: A review of school effectiveness research.* London: Ofsted.

Satter, J. (1981). De school als georganiseerde anarchie [The school as an organized anarchy]. *Meso, 1,* 23-24.

Schachter, H.L. (1989). *Frederick Taylor and the public administration: a reevaluation.* Albany, N.Y.: University of New York Press.

Scheerens, J. (1989a). *Wat maakt scholen effectief? Samenvatting en analyse van onderzoeksresultaten* [What makes schools effective? Summary and analysis of research findings]. Den Haag: Stichting voor Onderzoek van het Onderwijs.

Scheerens, J. (1989b). Process-indicators of school functioning: a selection based on the research literature on school effectiveness. Paper presented at the OECD-seminar in Semmering, Austria, September 1989.

Scheerens, J. (1989c). Waarom privatisering in het onderwijs? [Why privatize in education?]. In J. Scheerens (Ed.), *Privatisering in het onderwijs* (pp. 1-14). Enschede: Faculteit der Toegepaste Onderwijskunde.

Scheerens, J. (1992). *Effective Schooling, Research, Theory and Practice.* London: Cassell.

Scheerens, J. (1993a). Foundational and fundamental studies on educational effectiveness, issues for a research agenda. *School Effectiveness and School Improvement, 4.*

Scheerens, J. (1993b). The School-level Context of Instructional Effectiveness: A Comparison Between School Effectiveness and Restructuring Models. *Tijdschrift voor Onderwijsresearch.*

Scheerens, J. (1995). The selection and definition of international indicators on teachers. In J. Scheerens (Ed.), *Measuring Educational Quality Conditions.* Paris: OECD.

Scheerens, J., & Bosker, R.J. (1997). *The foundations of educational effectiveness.* Oxford: Elsevier Science Ltd.

Scheerens, J., & Creemers, B.P.M. (Eds.) (1989). Developments in school effectiveness research. Special issue of the *International Journal of Educational Research, 13.*

Scheerens, J., Vermeulen, C.J.A.J., & Pelgrum, W.J. (1989). Generalizability of instructional and school effectiveness indicators across nations. *International Journal of Educational Research, 13,* 789-799.

Scheerens, J., & van Vilsteren, C.A. (1988). De school als organisatie. [The school as an organization]. In B. Creemers, J. Giesbers, C. van Vilsteren, & C. van der Perre (Eds.), *Onderwijskundig Lexicon II.* Alphen aan den Rijn: Samsom, F 1100-1 - F 1100-29.

Schein, E.H. (1985). *Organizational culture and leadership.* Washington/London: Jossey Bass.

Schuit, H. (1994). *Organisatieproblemen in het voortgezet onderwijs* [Organizational problems in secondary education]. Nijmegen: Katholieke Universiteit Nijmegen.

Selden, R.W. (1990). Developing educational indicators: a state-national-perspective. In N. Bottani, & I. Delfau, Indicators of the quality of educational systems: an international perspective. Special issue of the *International Journal of Educational Research, 14.*

Selznick, Ph. (1984). *Leadership in Administration. A sociological interpretation.* Berkely: University of California Press.

Senge, P.M. (1990). *The fifth discipline, the art and practice of the learning organization.* New York: Doubledag Currency.

Sergiovanni, T.J. (1984). Leadership and excellence in schooling, *Educational Leadership, 41,* p. 6.

Sergiovanni, T.J. (1987). Teacher motivation and commitment: requirements for effective schooling. In T.J. Sergiovanni, *The principalship. A reflective practice perspective* (pp. 235-257). Boston: Allyn and Bacon, inc.

Sergiovanni, T.J. (1990). Advances in leadership theory and practice. In P.W. Thurston, & L.S. Lotto (Eds.), *Advances in Educational Administration, Vol. 1 (Part A): perspectives on educational reform* (pp. 1-35). Thousand Oaks: Corwin Press.

Sergiovanni, T.J., & Corbally, J.E. (Eds.) (1986). *Leadership and organizational culture: new perspectives on administrative theory and practice.* Urbana, Ill.: University of Illinois Press.

Shakeshaft, C. (1987). *Women in educational administration.* Beverly Hills: Sage Publishers.

Shavelson, R.J., & Stern, P. (1981). Research on teachers' pedagogical thoughts, judgements, decisions, and behaviour. *Review of Educational Research, 51,* 455-498.

Silver, H. (1994). *Good schools, effective schools: judgement and their histories.* London: Cassell.

Simon, H. (1957). *Administrative behavior.* New York: McMillan.

Siskin, L.S. (1994). *Realms of knowledge: academic departments in secondary schools.* London: Falmer Press.

Slavin, R.E. (1996). *Success for all.* Lisse: Swets & Zeitlinger.

Smets, P. (1981). *Schoolorganisatie, problemen van een theorie over schoolorganisaties in het voortgezet onderwijs.* [School organization, problems of a theory on school organizations in secondary education]. Nijmegen: ITS.

Smets, P. (1985). De school als organisatie [The school as an organization]. In J.L. Peschar,& A.A. Wesselingh (Eds.), *Onderwijssociologie, een inleiding* (pp. 251-278). Groningen: Wolters-Noordhoff.

Snellen, I.TH.M. (1981). *Gezondheidszorg en management: Beleidsvragen in de gezondheidszorg.* [Health Care and management: questions of policy in health services]. Alphen aan den Rijn: Samsom.

Sredl, H.J., & Rothwell, W.J. (1987). *The ASTD Reference Guide to Professional Training Roles & Competencies* Vol.1. Amherst/Massachusetts.: HRD Press Inc.

Stager, M., & Leithwood, K.A. (1989). Cognitive flexibility and inflexibility in principals' problem solving, *The Alberta Journal of Educational Research, 35,* 217-236.

Stinchcombe, A.L. (1990). *Information and organizations.* Berkeley/Los Angeles/Oxford: University of California Press.

Stoel, W. (1994). *De taakinhoud, de taakomvang en de taakbelasting van schoolleiders in het basisonderwijs* [Task content, task size and task load of school leaders in primary education]. Enschede: University of Twente.

Stogdill, R. (1948). Personal factors associated with leadership: a survey of the literature. *Journal of Psychology, 25,* 35-71.

Streumer, J.N., & van der Klink, M.R. (1996). HRD in de toekomst. [HRD in the future]. *Onderwijsonderzoek in Nederland en Vlaanderen 1996.* Tilburg: Proceedings van de Onderwijs Research Dagen 1996.

Stringfield, S., & Herman, R. (1995). Assessment of the state of school effectiveness research in the United States of America. In B.P.M. Creemers, & N.Osinga (Eds.), *Country Reports* (pp. 18-27). Leeuwarden: GCO.

Swanson, R.A. (1994). *Analysis for improving performance: tools for diagnosing organizations and documenting workplace expertise.* San Francisco: Berret-Koehler.

Taeuber, R.C. (Ed.) (1987). Education data system redesign. Special issue of the *International Journal of Educational Research, 11,* 391-511.

Taylor, F.W. (1915). *Principles of scientific management,* New York: Harper.

Teddlie, C. (1994). The study of context in school effects research: history, methods, results, and theoretical implications. In D. Reynolds, B.P.M. Creemers, P.S. Nesselrodt, E.C. Schaffer, S. Stringfield, & C. Teddlie (Eds.), *Advances in School Effectiveness Research and Practice.* Oxford: Pergamon.

Teddlie, C., Stringfield, S., & Wimpelberg, R. (1987). *Contextual differences in effective schooling in Louisiana.* AERA-paper. Washington.

Thijssen, J.G.L. (1988). *Bedrijfsopleidingen als werkterrein* [Corporate training as work field]. Den Haag: VUGA/ROI.

Thijssen, J.G.L. (1996). *Leren, leeftijd en loopbaanperspectief: opleidingsdeelname door oudere personeelsleden als component van Human Resource Development.* [Learning, age and career prospect: training participation of older employees as a component of Human Resource Development]. Deventer: Kluwer.

Thompson, J.D. (1967). *Organizations in Action.* New York: McGraw Hill.

Thorndike, R.L. (1973). *Reading comprehension education in fifteen countries.* Stockholm: Alonqvist & Wiksell.

Tjepkema, S., & Mulder, M. (1997). Deskundigheidsbevordering in het bedrijfsleven [The organisation of professionalisation processes in a corporate context]. In: *Thema, 4,* 40-45.

Tjepkema, S., & Wognum, A.A.M. (1995). *Van opleider naar adviseur? Taakgebieden van opleidingsfunctionarissen in leergerichte organisaties.* [From trainer to consultant? Roles and tasks of HRD professionals in learning-oriented organizations.] Enschede: Universiteit Twente.

Torrington, D., & Weightman, J. (1989). *The reality of school management.* Oxford: Blackwell Education.

Tyler, R. (1950). *Basic principles of curriculum and instruction.* Chicago: University of Chicago Press.

Tyler, W. (1988). *School organisation: a sociological perspective.* London: Croom Helm.

Unesco (1976). *Towards a system of educational indicators.* Division of Educational Policy and Planning, Paris.

van Amelsvoort, H.W.C.H., & Scheerens, J. (1996). International comparative indicators on teachers. *International Journal of Educational Research, 25,* 267-277.

van Amelsvoort, H.W.C.H., & Witziers, B. (1995). Deregulering en de marktpositie van scholen [Deregulation and the market position of schools]. *Tijdschrift voor Onderwijsresearch, 20,* 19-36.

van Dam, N.H.M., & Marcus, J.A. (1995). *Een praktijkgerichte benadering van organisatie & management* [A practice-based approach to organization and management.]. Houten: Stenfert Kroese.

van de Ven, A.H., & Drazin, R. (1985). The concept of fit in contingency theory. *Research in Organizational Behavior.* Greenwich/London: Jai Press Inc, 333-365.

van der Krogt, F.J. (1990). De leerfunctie in verschillende organisaties: hoe verschillende soorten bedrijven het leren van hun medewerkers organiseren [The learning function in different organisations: how different types of companies organize the learning of their employees]. *Opleiding & Ontwikkeling, 11,* 17-24.

van der Krogt, F.J., & Oosting, J. (1988). *Relaties tussen scholen en hun omgeving: een onderzoek naar de externe contacten en het arbeidsmarktbeleid van MBO-scholen.* [Relationships between schools and their environments: a study on external contacts and the labor market policy of schools for senior secondary vocational education]. Enschede: University of Twente.

van der Krogt, F.J., & Plomp, C.M. (1987). Vier modellen voor de organisatie van opleidingsafdelingen [Four models for the organization of HRD departments]. *Capita Selecta opleiders in organisaties, 8.* Deventer: Kluwer Bedrijfswetenschappen.

van der Krogt, T.P.W.M. (1985). Het besturen van professionals [Managing professionals]. *Besturen in verandering, 16,* 1-16.

van der Werf, M.P.C. (1988). *Het schoolwerkplan in het basisonderwijs; ontwikkeling, implementatie en opbrengst* [The school work plan in primary education; development, implementation and outcomes]. Amsterdam: Swets & Zeitlinger.

van Dongen, D., Hamers, P., Dijk, I. van, Gooren, W., Kommers, H., & Jansen, X. (1989). *Organisatie- en managementproblemen van scholen.* [Organizational and management problems of schools]. Tilburg: Instituut voor sociaal-wetenschappelijk onderzoek van de Katholieke Universiteit Brabant.

van Ginkel, A.J.H. (1985). *Demotivatie bij leraren. Een onderzoek naar burnout- en demotivatie verschijnselen bij leraren in het algemeen voortgezet onderwijs* [Demotivation of teachers in general secondary educaton]. Rotterdam: Erasmus Universiteit.

van Hoewijk, R. (1989). Cultuur in schoolorganisatie [Culture in school organization]. In B.P.M. Creemers, J. Giesbers, C. van Vilsteren, & C. van der Perre (Eds.), *Handboek Schoolorganisatie en Onderwijsmanagement* (pp. 2130-1 - 2130-29). Alphen aan den Rijn: Samsom.

van Hoof, J.J. (1986). *Aansluiting tussen onderwijs en arbeidsmarkt: recente ontwikkelingen en uitgangspunten voor beleid* [Transition from education to work: recent developments and policy starting-points]. 's-Gravenhage: OSA.

van Hulst, W.G.H., & Willems, J.G.L.M. (1992). *Externe organisatie. Een kennismaking met het ondernemingsgedrag in markt-economische stelsels* [An introduction to enterprising behaviour in market economic systems.]. Leiden/Antwerpen: Stenfert Kroese.

van Sandick, A.S., & Schaap, A.M. (1993) *Rendement van een bedrijfsopleiding.* [ROI of a corporate training programme]. Zaandam: Albert Heijn Opleidingen.

van Velzen, W.G., Miles, M.B., Ekholm, M., Hamayer, U., & Robin, D. (1984). *Making school improvement work: a conceptual guide to practice.* Leuven: ACCO.

van Vilsteren, C.A. (1984). De school als professioneel-bureaucratische organisatie [The school as a professional bureaucratic organization]. In B.P.M. Creemers, & H.G.I. Giesbers (Eds.), *Handboek schoolorganisatie en onderwijsmanagement* (pp. 1510-1 - 1510-27). Alphen a/d Rijn: Samsom.

van Vilsteren, C.A., & Visscher, A.J. (1987). Schoolwerkplanning: mogelijk in schoolorganisaties? [School work planning: possible in schools?]. In B.P.M. Creemers, & H.G.I. Giesbers (Eds.), *Handboek schoolorganisatie en onderwijsmanagement* (pp. 6120-1 - 6120-24). Deventer: Samsom.

van Vilsteren, C.A., & Witziers, B. (1990). Vaksecties en schoolleiding: twee ontwikkelingparameters van schoolorganisaties [Subject departments and school leadership: two developmental parameters of schools]. In J. Imants, & W. Weijzen (Eds.), *Organisatie van Onderwijsinstellingen* (pp. 61-70). Amsterdam/Lisse: Swets & Zeitlinger.

van Wieringen, A.M.L. (1989). *Bestuur en management van onderwijsinstellingen* [Adminstration and management of educational institutions]. Groningen: Wolters-Noordhoff.

Vereniging Nederlandse Gemeenten (1996). *Onderwijsbeleid op lokaal niveau* [Educational policies at the local level]. Den Haag: VNG.

Versloot, A.M. (1984). Rationeel handelen in onzekere situaties; de contingentietheorie van J.D. Thompson [Acting rational in uncertain situations]. In B.P.M. Creemers, & H.G.I. Giesbers (Eds.), *Handboek schoolorganisatie en onderwijsmanagement* (pp. 1430-1 - 1430-27). Deventer: Samsom.

Versloot, A.M. (1990). *Ouders en vrijheid van onderwijs: schoolkeuze in de provincie Utrecht* [Parents and the freedom to provide education: school choice in the province Utrecht]. Utrecht: University of Utrecht.

Visscher, A.J. (1992). *Design and evaluation of a computer-assisted management information system for secondary school (Ph.D. thesis)*. Enschede: University of Twente.

Visscher, A.J. (1996). The implications of how school staff handle information for the usage of school information systems. *International Journal of Educational Research, 25,* 323-334.

Visscher, A.J., & Spuck, D.W. (1991). Computer-assisted school administration and management: the state of the art in seven nations. *Journal of Research on Computing in Education, 24,* 146-168.

Voogt, J.C. (1989). *Scholen doorgelicht: een studie over schooldiagnose* [A study on school diagnosis]. De Lier: Academisch Boeken Centrum.

Vroom, V.H. (1964). *Work and Motivation.* New York: Wiley.

Vroom, V., & Yetton, Ph. (1973). *Leadership and decision-making.* Pittsburgh: University of Pittsburgh.

Walberg, H.J. (1984). Improving the productivity of American Schools. *Educational Leadership, 41,* 19-27.

Waller, A. (1932). *The sociology of teaching.* New York: Wiley.

Wansink, H. (1992). *Een school om voor te kiezen, naar een actuele onderwijspolitiek* [A school to choose for, towards an up-to-date educational policy]. Amsterdam: Bert Bakker.

Weber, G. (1971). Inner-city children can be taught to read: four successful schools. Washington D.C.: Council for Basic Education.

Weick, K.E. (1976). Educational organizations as loosely coupled systems. *Administrative Science Quarterly, 21,* 1-19.

Weick, K.E. (1982). Administering Education in loosely coupled schools. *Phi Delta Kappan, 63,* 673-676.

Weick, K.E. (1984). Management of organizational change among loosely coupled elements. In P. Goodman (Ed.), *Change in organizations* (pp. 2-24). San Francisco: Jossey-Bass.

Weldy, R. (1979). *Principals: what they do and who they are.* Reston: NASSP.

Wenglinsky, H. (1997). *When money matters.* Princetown: Ets.

Wexley K.N., & Latham, G.P. (1991). *Developing and Training Human Resources in organizations* (2nd ed.). New York: Harper Collins Publishers.

Windham, D.M. (1988). Effectiveness indicators in the economic analysis of educational activities. Special issue of the *International Journal of Educational Research, 12.*

Winslow, C.D., & Bramer, W.L. (1994). *Future work: putting knowledge to work in the knowledge economy.* New York: The Free Press.

Wise, A. (1977). Why educational policies often fail: the hyperrationalization hypothesis. *Curriculum Studies, 9,* 43-57.

Wise, A., Darling-Hammond, L., McLaughlin, M., & Bernstein, H. (1985). Teacher evaluation: a study of effective practices. *Elementary School Journal, 86,* 61-121.

Witziers, B. (1992). *Coördinatie binnen scholen voor voortgezet onderwijs* [Coordination within secondary schools]. Enschede: University of Twente.

Witziers, B. (1995) Kosteneffectiviteitsanalyse [Cost and effectiveness analysis] In P. Schramade (Ed.), *Handboek voor Effectief Opleiden* (pp. 1.01 - 1.23). Den Haag: Delwel .

Witziers, B., & de Groot, I.N. (1993). *Concurrentie tussen scholen. Een onderzoek naar de marketingmiddelen die scholen inzetten om hun concurrentiepositie te verbeteren en de wettelijke context waarbinnen scholen concurreren.* [Competition between schools. How schools try to improve their market position within the Dutch legislative framework.]. Enschede: University of Twente.

Wognum, A.A.M. (1994). Assessing HRD effectiveness from a strategic point of view. *Tijdschrift voor Onderwijswetenschappen, 24,* 77-89.

Wognum, A.A.M. (1995). HRD Policy Making in Companies: An interpretation of the differences. In E.F. Holton III (Ed.), *Conference Proceedings Academy of Human Resource Development,* March 2-5, 1995 St.Louis, USA.

Woods, P.A., Bagley, C., & R. Glatter (1998). *School Choice and Competition: Markets in the Public Interest?* London/New York: Routledge.

Woodward, J. (1965). *Industrial organization: theory and practice.* London: Oxford University Press.

Yekovich, F.R. (1993). A theoretical view of the development of expertise in credit administration. In P. Hallinger et.al., *Cognitive perspectives on educational leadership* (pp. 146-166). New York: Teachers College Press.

• SUBJECT INDEX •

CONTEXTS OF LEARNING
Classrooms, Schools and Society